# *ABOUT THE AUTHOR*

Reb Moshe Steinerman grew up as a religious Jew on the hillsides of Maryland. During his teenage years, Reb Moshe developed his talent for photography, while connecting to nature and speaking to Hashem. He later found his path through Breslav *Chassidus*, while maintaining closeness to the *Litvish* style of learning. He studied in the Baltimore yeshiva, Ner Yisrael; then married and moved to Lakewood, New Jersey. After settling down, he began to write *Kavanos Halev*, with the blessing of Rav Malkiel Kotler *shlita*, Rosh Yeshiva of Beis Midrash Gevoha.

After establishing one of the first Jewish outreach websites, ilovetorah.com in 1996, Reb Moshe's teachings became popular among the full spectrum of Jews, from the unaffiliated to ultra-Orthodox. His teachings, including hundreds of stories of *tzaddikim*, gained popularity due to the ideal of drawing Jews together. Reb Moshe made *aliyah* to Tzfat in 2003 and has been doing his Jewish outreach with the English-speaking Jewish community through his Jewish videos and audio *shiurim*.

In 2012, Reb Moshe, with his wife and children, moved to Jerusalem. Some of his other books are *Kavanos Halev (Meditations of the Heart)*, *Tikkun Shechinah*, *Tovim Meoros (Glimpse of Light)*, *Chassidus, Kabbalah & Meditation*, *Prayers of the Heart*, *Yom LeYom (Day by Day)*, *Pesukei Torah (Passages of Torah)*, *Pathways of the Righteous*, *A Journey into Holiness*, *Newly Born Jew* and *The True Intentions of the Baal Shem Tov*. Thousands have read the advice contained in these books, with life-changing results.

*In Memory of my father Shlomo Zavel ben Yaakov ZT"L
And all the great souls of our people*

*I grew up in a house filled with the Torah learning of my father, who studied most of the day. Although there were no Jews in this remote part of Maryland, my father was a man of chesed to all people and was known for his brilliance in Torah scholarship.*

*In Memory of My grandparents Yaakov ben Zavel, Toba Esther bas Gedalaya Aharon Hakohein, Yehudah ben Ike, Isabbela Bas Israel*

*My great-grandmother Nechama bas Sara Rivka, My Uncle Shmuel Yosef ben Gedalya Aharon Hakohein*

*My father-in-law Menachem ben Reuven*

*Reb Chaim ben Reuven & Ahavah bas Reuven*

מְסִילַת

הַשַׁ"ס

*Mesilas HaShas*

# The Path to Finishing Talmud

Written by
Reb Moshe Steinerman

Edited by Rochel Steinerman

ilovetorah Jewish Outreach Network

ilovetorah Jewish Publishing
First Published 2019
ISBN: 13: 978-1-947706-10-1
Copyright: ilovetorah Jewish Publishing

moshe@ilovetorah.com

Editor: Rochel Steinerman

Artwork by Boris Shapiro.

*I want to say a special thank you to the Nikolsberg Rebbe and the Biala Rebbe for their encouragement and blessings. Most of all, I offer thanks to my wife, Rochel, for her faithful support.*

*Dedicated to my wife Rochel and to my children Shlomo Nachman, Yaakov Yosef, Gedalya Aharon Tzvi, Esther Rivka, Yeshiya Michel, Dovid Shmuel, Eliyahu Yisrael may it bring forth the light of your neshamos.*

# *Dear Reader,*

Ilovetorah Jewish Outreach is a non-profit and books and *Torah* classes are available at low costs. Therefore, we appreciate your donation to help Reb Moshe Steinerman and ilovetorah.com to continue their work on behalf of the Jewish people. We also ask that you pass on these books to others once you are finished with them.

Thank you,
Reb Moshe Steinerman
www.ilovetorah.com

# RABBINIC APPROVALS / HASKAMAHS

בס"ד

**RABBI DOVID B. KAPLAN**
RABBI OF WEST NEW YORK
5308 PALISADE AVENUE • WEST NEW YORK, NJ 07093
201-867-6859 • WESTNEWYORKSHUL@GMAIL.COM

דוד ברוך הלוי קאפלאן
רב ואב"ד דק"ק
וועסט ניו יארק

י' שבט ה'תשע"ז / February 6, 2017

Dear Friends,

Shalom and Blessings!

For approximately twenty years I have followed the works of Rabbi Moshe Steinerman, Shlit"a, a pioneer in the use of social media to encourage people and bring them closer to G-d.

Over the years Rabbi Steinerman has produced, and made public at no charge, hundreds of videos sharing his Torah wisdom, his holy stories, and his touching songs. Rabbi Steinerman has written a number of books, all promoting true Jewish Torah spirituality. Rabbi Steinerman's works have touched many thousands of Jews, and even spirituality-seeking non-Jews, from all walks of life and at all points of the globe.

Rabbi Steinerman is a tomim (pure-hearted one) in the most flattering sense of the word.

I give my full approbation and recommendation to all of Rabbi Steinerman's works.

I wish Rabbi Steinerman much success in all his endeavors.

May G-d bless Rabbi Moshe Steinerman, his wife, Rebbetzin Rochel Steinerman, and their beautiful children; and may G-d grant them health, success, and nachas!

With blessings,

Rabbi Dovid B. Kaplan

9

הובא לפני גליונות בעניני קירוב רחוקים לקרב אחינו בני ישראל אל
אביהם שבשמים, כידוע מהבעש"ט זיע"א שאמר "אימתי קאתי מר
לכשיפוצו מעינותיך חוצה" ואפריון נמטי"ה להאי גברא יקירא מיקירי
צפת עיה"ק תובב"א כמע"כ מוהר"ר משה שטיינרמן שליט"א אשר כבר
עוסק רבות בשנים לקרב רחוקים לתורה וליהדות, וכעת מוציא לאור
ספר בשם "מסילת הש"ס" וראיתי דברים נחמדים מאוד וניכר מתוך
הדברים שהרב בעל המחבר - אהבת השי"ת ואהבת התורה וישראל
בלבבו, ובטחוני כי הספר יביא תועלת גדולה לכל עם ישראל.

ויה"ר שיזכה לבוא לגומרה ברוב פאר והדר ונזכה לגאולתן של ישראל
בב"א.

בכבוד רב:
אהרן פנחס חיים אליעזר
בלאאו"ר בלולה'ה אביאלא

Rabbi M. Lebovits
Grand Rabbi of
Nikolsburg
53 Decatur Avenue
Spring Valley, N.Y. 10977

יוסף יחיאל מיכל
לעבאוויטש
ניקלשבורג
מאנסי - ספרינג וואלי, נ. י.

בעזהשי"ת

כשורותי אלו באתי להעיד על מעשה אותן, מופלא מופלג כהפלגת חכמים ונבונים,
ירא וחרד לדבר ה', ומשתוקק לקרב לבות ישראל לאביהם שבשמים,
ה"ה הרב משה שטיינערמאן שליט"א בעיה"ק צפת תובב"א

שעלה בידו להעלות על הספר דברים נפלאים שאסף מספרים הקדושים, בענין אהבה
אחוה שלום וריעות, לראות מעלות חברינו ולא חסרונם, ועי"ז להיות נמנעים מדברי
ריבות ומחלוקת, ולתקן עון שנאת חנם אשר בשביל זה נחרב בית מקדשינו
ותפארתינו, וכמשאהו"ל (רש"י, ובזקרא רבה ט"ו ט) על ויהן שם ישראל, שניתנה תורה באופן
שחנו שם כאיש אחד בלב אחד.

וניכר בספר כי עמל ויגע הרבה להוציא מתח"י דבר נאה ומתוקן, ע"כ אף ידי תכון
עמו להוציאו לאור עולם. ויהי רצון שהפץ ה' בידו יצליח, ויברך ה' חילו ופועל ידו
תרצה, שיברך על המוגמר להגדיל תורה ולהאדירה ולהפיצו בקרב ישראל, עד ביאת
גוא"צ בב"א.

א"ד הכותב לכבוד התורה ומרביציה.
י"ט חשון תשס"ו

[signature]

Rabbi Abraham Y. S. Friedman
161 Maple Avenue #C Spring Valley NY 10977
Tel: 845-425-5043 Fax: 845-425-8045

בעזהשי"ת

ישפות השם החיים והשלו', לכבוד ידידי מאז ומקדם מיקירי קרתא
דירושלים יראה שלם, זוכה ומזכה אחרים, להיות דבוק באלקינו, ה"ה
הר"ר משה שטיינרמאן שליט"א.

שמחתי מאוד לשמוע ממך, מאתר רחוק וקירוב הלבבות, בעסק
תורתך הקדושה ועבודתך בלי לאות, וכה יעזור ה' להלאה ביתר שאת
ויתר עז. והנה שלחת את הספר שלקטת בעניני דביקות בה', לקרב
לבבות בני ישראל לאבינו שבשמים בשפת אנגלית, אבל דא עקא
השפה לא ידענו, ע"כ לא זכיתי לקרותו, ע"כ א"א לי ליתן הסכמה פרטי
על ספרך, ובכלל קיבלתי על עצמי שלא ליתן הסכמות, ובפרט כשאין
לי פנאי לקרות הספר מתחלתו עד סופו, אבל בכלליות זכרתי לך חסד
נעוריך, היאך הי' המתיקות שלך בעבדות השם פה בעירינו, ובנועם
המדות, וחזקה על חבר שאינו מוציא מתחת ידו דבר שאינו מתוקן,
ובפרט שכל מגמתך להרבות כבוד שמים, שבודאי סייעתא דשמיא
ילוך כל ימיך לראות רב נחת מיגיע"ח ומפרי ידיך, שתתקבל הספר
בסבר פנים יפות אצל אחינו בני ישראל שמדברים בשפת האנגלית
שיתקרבו לאבינו שבשמים ולהדבק בו באמת כאות נפשך, ולהרבות
פעלים לתורה לעבודה ועבודה וקדושה בדביקות עם מדות טובות, בנייחותא
נייחא בעליונים ונייחא בתחתונים עד ביאת גואל צדק בב"א.

כי"ד ידידך השמח בהצלחתך ובעבודתך
אברהם יחזקאל שרגא פרידמאן
אשכנז קאמא

# TABLE OF CONTENTS

ABOUT THE AUTHOR ..................................................... 3

............................................................................. 6

Dear Reader, ............................................................. 7

RABBINIC APPROVALS / HASKAMAHS ............................ 9

TABLE OF CONTENTS ................................................. 15

OVERVIEW .............................................................. 18

INTRODUCTION ....................................................... 21

Derech Eretz ........................................................... 24

Physical Health ....................................................... 33
    Healthy Eating Habits ............................................. 35
    Torah as Medicine .................................................. 38
    The Role of the Doctor ............................................ 39
    Joy ..................................................................... 42
    Faith in Healing .................................................... 45

Working and Learning ............................................. 47
    Materialism .......................................................... 54
    Work with Emunah ................................................ 56
    The Torah will Sustain Me ....................................... 57
    The Journey Continues ........................................... 61
    Work of the Sages ................................................. 68
    To Conclude ......................................................... 70

Ratzon Hashem ...................................................... 72
    Wisdom ............................................................... 76
    Repentance .......................................................... 78
    Sleep .................................................................. 79
    Knowing what to Do ............................................... 80
    Supporting a Torah Scholar ...................................... 81
    Wearing Tefillin .................................................... 82
    Guard Your Ears .................................................... 84
    A Good Listener .................................................... 85

Weighing Ones Words.................................................88
Stoicism...................................................................92
A Woman's Derech................................................96

**Torah Lishmah**.....................................................**100**
Set Times for Learning Torah ........................107
Arrogance vs Lishmah ......................................108
D'vekus in Learning ...........................................111
Torah by Heart ...................................................114

**Building yourself up** ...........................................**119**

**Teaching our Children**.......................................**131**

**Teaching the Masses** .........................................**137**
Yeshivas Chachmei Lublin and Daf Yomi ...............142

**Study Tanach** ......................................................**147**

**Study Mishnah**....................................................**151**
Other Works........................................................156

**The Benefits of Ein Yaakov**..............................**157**

**Founding of the Talmuds** ..................................**160**

**Talmud Yerushalmi**...........................................**169**

**The Great Talmud**..............................................**174**

**Talmud For Halacha** ..........................................**184**

**Types of Seder**....................................................**191**

**Chazarah (Review)** .............................................**201**
How to Remember............................................203
Total Dedication to learning ..........................206

**The Chavrusa of your Dreams**.........................**211**

**Kollel's and Yeshivah Curriculum**...................**214**

**A Gift of Tears** ....................................................**223**

**Feeling the Realness of the Talmud**...............**231**

**Ahavas Yisrael** ...................................................**235**
Neglecting One's Partner ...............................243

**Mussar Seder** .....................................................**246**

Introduction to the Talmud.............................................253

Learning Mesechtos Charts .............................................264

A Timeline of the Transmission of Torah .......................265

Talmud Chapters and Blats Guide ..................................267

*הדרן*.............................................................................278

Glossary........................................................................280

# OVERVIEW

With the help of Hashem, I undertook to write this important work. If someone truly loves *Torah*, they must feel a calling inside to share the *Torah* with others. What greater thing to share than the path to completing the *Talmud*?

Many have attempted to complete the entire *Talmud* only to fail. Some have exerted an enormous amount of time and energy, yet in the wrong ways. The truth is, everyone, no matter what skill level or learning ability, is capable of completing this important work.

Unlike other books, this book, *The Path to Finishing Talmud*, is a guide for the simple folk to complete all of the fundamental *Torah* works. It also aims to inspire and refocus the *Torah* scholar in their learning so they can complete the *Talmud* easily and often. In order to become a true *talmud chacham*, there are many factors besides just book knowledge. Therefore, I have written this guide to include information that is lifechanging and inspiring to help you grow in your *Torah* learning.

"Make books your companions. Let your bookshelves be your gardens. Bask in their beauty, gather their fruit, pluck their roses, take their spices and myrrh. And when your soul be weary, change from garden to garden, and from prospect to prospect." (*Ibn Tibbon*)

There are many great Jewish books but there is nothing similar to the *Talmud*. So vast with knowledge and beauty, the *Talmud* is not just a *Torah* work but rather a guide to all of the *Torah*. Inside the *Talmud* are secrets to great wisdom and abundance. With great *zechus* and joy, this work is now available to everyone in many languages and easily accessible. However, few complete the entire vast work, and many find the doors still locked to its beauty. In this book, we will take a step back and reenter the world of *Torah* learning from its roots, the *Tanach* and the *Mishnah*. We will give you the keys not only to complete your path towards finishing the *Talmud*, but we will fill in all the fundamental tools you are missing in order to be a competent *Torah* scholar.

In the words of the great master of Jewish literature, Rabbi Moshe Chayim Luzzatto, "When I wrote my book, *Mesilas Yeshorim*, I did not write it to teach people information that they had not known previously. Rather, my intention was to remind them of knowledge they already possessed. Nonetheless, to the same degree that this knowledge is well-known and its truth self-evident, to that degree people forget about these matters and are not consciously aware of them in their daily lives." (*Mesilas Yeshorim*, Intro)

# *INTRODUCTION*

Most Jews will sadly never complete the entire *Talmud* in their lifetime. I wish to change that scenario by opening up the gems of the *Talmud* to every person seeking wisdom. Our sages said, "All the parts of the *Torah* are needed by each other; what one-part locks away, another part unlocks." (*Bamidbar Rabbah* 19:28) Rabbi Malkiel Kotler remarks on this, "It follows that one cannot truly know any part of the *Torah* without knowing all of it." It is the study of the *Talmud* that connects all the parts of the *Torah* into one.

Rav Tanchum bar Chanilai teaches, "Leolam, forevermore, one should divide shenotav, his years, one third *mikra* (*Tanach*), one third *Mishnah* and one third *Talmud.*" (*Avodah Zara* 19b) This is because a person does not know how long one will live. The *Talmud* explains that the term shenotav refers not to years, but to "days". Tosafos explains that we should spend two days each week learning *Tanach*, *Mishna* and *Talmud* respectively. Tosafos then explains a more literal understanding of the *Talmud*. That we should divide each day's learning into three equal parts of *Tanach*, *Mishnah* and *Talmud*. That way, each day before our last, we will have studied a full circle of *Torah*.

However, Rabbeinu Tam gives a whole new practical meaning to Rav Tanchum's teaching. Basing himself on Rav Yochanan's teaching (*Sanhedrin* 24a) that "Bavel" can be read as a play on the word balul, a mixture, combining *Tanach*, *Mishnah* and *Talmud* study, Rabbeinu Tam argued that one fulfills the obligation to learn *Tanach*, *Mishnah* and *Talmud* by (exclusively) learning *Talmud Bavli*.

Therefore, every *Torah* scholar should study the *Talmud* daily in order to fill their soul with the proper balance of light. When we study *Torah* with balance, fulfilling our souls' daily needs, this reflects on our life. I often meet many Jews that seem to be off-balance in their nature and have a more troubled life. All this could be corrected through the daily study of *Talmud*.

Rabbi Meir Shapiro, *rosh hayeshivah* of Chachmei Lublin, had some of the greatest Talmudical minds attend his great *yeshivah* during the pre-holocaust era. He understood the importance of daily Talmudic study and saw how important daf yomi, a page a day of *Talmud* would be as a tremendously necessary unifying factor among the Jewish people. He said that if you look at a page of the *Talmud*, you see the words of the greatest Jewish minds covering the entire spectrum of Jewish life and history. Without his vision, the *Talmud* would remain out of the grasp of the simple folk and today would be studied only among the elite.

Throughout the years, his emphasis on studying a page of *Talmud* a day has inspired thousands of people to complete the entire *Shas*. People who work full time jobs or who have little prior *Torah* knowledge, can pick up a translated *Talmud* and study in a *daf yomi* class or on their own.

Rabbi Meir Shapiro's legacy of spreading the *Talmud* is legendary and continues to spread worldwide. However, he is not personally here to guide us in our study. Could you imagine his reaction to the widespread *Talmud* study of our generation thanks to his innovative idea? Imagine him standing on the podium of Madison Square Garden during the seven-year celebration of *Siyum HaShas*. Since its inception, *daf yomi* has become the norm and standard for *Talmud* study in *shuls, yeshivos* and *kollel's* around the world. While *daf yomi* might be the basis for our *Talmud* study, I don't think Rabbi Shapiro meant it for the average scholar as their only daily *Talmud* ritual. It was simply meant as a foundation for daily study. Granted, most people certainly do need *daf yomi* in their life, for without it, would they make sure to otherwise study all three foundational forms of daily study during their busy schedule?

It is motivating knowing that others around the globe are also studying the same material as you; that you can turn to another Jew in synagogue and simply discuss similar *Torah* topics, but for the scholar who wants to become a great *Talmud Chacham, daf yomi* seems to fall right in the middle of the mix of his daily study. Therefore, it should not be his lone study of *Talmud*.

This manual has been written in order to encourage people to take upon themselves to finish the entire *Shas*. Whether it's through *daf yomi* or through the faster study methods that I will encourage. The main thing is to complete the *Talmud* and have this wonderful wisdom as the basis of your life. The *Talmud* suggests that a person is not a complete man until he completes the entire *Talmud*. It says in the Psalms, "Who shall utter the mighty acts of Hashem, [who] can declare all of His praise?" (*Tehillim* 106:2) The Talmud in *Horayos* (13b) explains that we understand this to mean: For whom is it fitting to utter the mighty acts of Hashem? Only one who can declare ALL His praise. "Praise" is a sobriquet for "words of Torah." Therefore, to be complete in Torah, one must master all the tractates, be competent in all of *Shas*. We will go through various aspects of learning and hopefully help you to find the right path towards completing this important work.

Every scholar will have his own opinion on which ways are best to study. There is plenty of room for everyone's theory. The main thing is to study *lishmah* and come close to Hashem.

For me, I can't simply complete *Shas* over and over again without sharing my methods with others. The way to enjoy anything in life is to share it and perform it with others. I, a simple and regular person, without profound knowledge and plenty of learning obstacles, managed to complete both *Talmud Bavli* and *Talmud Yerushalmi* numerous times, therefore, so can you. For the next few rounds of *Shas*, I'd like to enjoy my study knowing I have helped others to complete *Shas* as well. However, as you will learn from this book, there are plenty of fundamental steps one needs to take first in order to prepare themselves for this great undertaking. Should you allow yourself to be humble and openminded, this book will ensure and create a wonderous path towards true *avodas Hashem lishmah*.

Let's conclude with the holy words that the Lubliner Rav always concluded his letters. "By the one who writes with a heart full of longing for the love of *Torah*, for the opportunity to witness the uplifting of the *Torah's* honor and its scholars." May this work bear fruit and help to inspire many new scholars.

# Derech Eretz

It might surprise you that we will start out the first chapter of this book on the topic of *derech eretz* and we will complete this work with a chapter on *mussar*. Let me explain to you why: "If there is no *derech eretz*, there is no *Torah*." (*Mishnah Avos* 3:7) Rabbi Yisrael Salanter once said, "You can finish *Shas* many times but if you don't learn *mussar* and improve on your *midos*, you will not have grown."

The Kotzker Rebbe once asked a young man who had come to see him, what he had learned. The man responded that he had learned and completed the entire *Talmud*.

To this the *rebbe* reacted with, "And what did the *Talmud* teach you?"

Similarly, another young man was asked if he knew how to learn, to which he responded affirmatively.

In that case, said the *rebbe*, you surely know that *Torah* means, "to teach." If so, tell me, what did *Torah* teach you? (...*And Nothing but the Truth*, p. 90)

Rabbi Samson Raphael Hirsch explains, "*Derech eretz* includes everything that results from the fact that man's existence, mission and social life is conducted on earth, using earthly means and conditions. Therefore, this term especially describes ways of earning a livelihood and maintaining social order. It also includes the customs and considerations of etiquette – which the social order generates – as well as everything concerning humanistic and civic education. (*R.S.R. Hirsch, Siddur, Avos* 2:2)

Rabbi Yishma'el, son of Rabbi Nachmani, said, "*Derech eretz* preceded the Torah by twenty-six generations, as it is written: 'To guard the way to the Tree of Life' (*Genesis 3:24*) – 'the way' refers to *derech eretz*, followed by 'the Tree of Life', which is the Torah." (*Vayikra Rabba 9:3*) This seems to imply that in order to be successful in *Torah*, you must balance your growth in *derech eretz* and *midos*.

Bar Kappara expounded: "What is a small verse upon which all the fundamentals of *Torah* depend? It is in this: 'In all your ways you must know Him, and He will straighten your paths.'" (*Proverbs* 3:6) The Rambam explains this verse to mean that all of one's activities must be performed for the sake of Heaven. Thus, when one eats, sleeps, transacts business, or engages in any other mundane act, they must not merely intend his physical benefit, but must act in the knowledge that through the performance of this action they will be better able to serve their Creator. (*Hilchos De'os* 3:2, 3)

You might wonder, if *talmud Torah* is *keneged kulam*, Torah study is equal to all the commandments, why should we be bothered with the rest of the commandments? What could be better than a person locking themselves in the *bais midrash* and learning *Torah* with no other activities?

The simple answer is, this is not the *ratzon* Hashem, the will of Hashem. *Talmud Torah* is *keneged kulam* because *Torah* study leads to the performance of all the *mitzvos*. If Hashem only wanted scholars to seclude themselves with the *Torah*, He would have only given us this one commandment alone.

I've met many scholars that did just that, locked themselves in the *bais midrash* and they missed the point of learning. Meanwhile, their family barely had food, clothing and the basic necessities to survive. They think that there is learning *lishmah,* but their learning is just selfish and full of pride. The *Torah* has to be brought into the home. The children should see their father learning in the house in order to inspire them. The wife shouldn't feel as if all household and financial burdens fall only upon her shoulders. If you are going to be a great scholar, you will certainly need to budget your time wisely so that you can put in the proper hours to increase your wisdom in *Torah*. You would be surprised at how many hours you waist that could be utilized for more *Torah* study, or at the very least, as quality time spent with your family. It might be great that you're learning hours a day in *kollel*, but how do you spend your time traveling to and from *kollel?* Why aren't you learning every moment, even while waiting on line for an appointment?

It is very important not to lose awareness of your family and surroundings. There is nothing more special than giving your love of *Torah* over to your family and children. It is they who will carry your legacy.

A man once came to the Kotzker Rebbe, requesting his blessing and prayer that his children might grow up with a desire to study *Torah* diligently. The rebbe answered him: "If this is your true desire, you should occupy yourself with the study of *Torah*. Then your children will grow up to copy your ways. But if you don't busy yourself with *Torah*, and desire it only for your children, in this too your children will copy your ways. They themselves will not study, but they will want their own children to do so."

"Actually," added the Kotzker, "this concept is mentioned explicitly in the *Torah*. In *Devarim* (4:19), it says: 'Only take heed and guard your soul exceedingly, so that you do not forget the facts that your own eyes have seen, and that they do not depart from your heart all the days of your life; and make them known to your children's children.'

"If you forget the words of the *Torah* and do not occupy yourself with them; then they will do as you do, and only mention the *Torah* to their children." (...*And Nothing but the Truth*, p. 128)

The *Torah* is best appreciated when in sync with good *midos* and *derech eretz*, sharing it with the world and others around you. I am sure that your years will be extended should you give up hours a day of your study in order to do kindness or to teach *Torah* to others.

In *Parshas Vayera*, Rav Shlomo Breuer has a beautiful thought on this concept of, "taking for me *teruma*." Whenever we 'give,' whether we do *chesed* with our bodies or we do *chesed* with our means, every giving is actually a 'taking.' Whenever a person does a *chesed*, he is really doing more for himself than for the person to whom he is giving.

The *Gemarah* learns, even if there is a powerful decree set against someone, *Torah* and *chesed* can annul it. Abaya and Rava were descendants of *b'nei* Eli. Rava lived forty years and Abaya who was more involved in *chesed*, lived for sixty years. (*Rosh HaShanah* 18)

When Rav Yaakov Kamenetzky was already elderly, he would give up hours of his time to help *Klal Yisrael*. He would say, "It's an investment. If others depend on me, Hashem will give me more years to help them." *Bli ayan hara*, Rav Yaakov is still living, well into his 90's and is still learning and serving the Jewish people.

The Chofetz Chaim explains that people may neglect to do *chesed* out of ignorance. They simply don't know the *halachos* or the many details of when this *midah* applies. In addition, people may be unaware of the power of *chesed* and how strongly it can affect a person's judgment in the next world. In *parshas Noach*, Rashi notes that just as a person leaves his children as a physical remembrance, a person's charitable deeds are his spiritual legacy. Rav Moshe Feinstein writes that we learn from this that just as a person loves his children, he should love and desire to do virtuous deeds.

Rabbi Simchah Zisel Ziv describes *derech eretz*, involvement with the needs of society, as the bottom rungs of the *Torah* ladder, leading from earth to heaven. He emphasizes that one cannot hope to ascend this ladder without first climbing the lower rungs by being involved with the needs of

26

society. (*Lishmor es Derek 'Etz HaChaiyim'* in *'Or RaShaZ, Genesis* p.51)

We can learn a lesson in *derech eretz* from the great teacher of Israel, Moshe Rabbenu. Moshe went and returned to Yisro, his father-in-law, and said to him, "Let me now go back to my brethren who are in Egypt and see if they are still alive." And Yisro said to Moshe, "Go in peace." (*Shemos* 4:18)

Rabbi Eliyahu Safran explains, "Rashi notes that when Moshe was commanded to return to Egypt to fulfill his destiny to lead the people from bondage, he first approached his father-in-law, and asked his permission. Astonishing! That the Creator of all should command Moses to deliver *B'nai Yisrael* from their bondage and before doing so Moses asked permission from Yisro?

"Of course, Moses understood Hashem's command, and the profound urgency of the directive, but he also knew that he could hardly fulfill Hashem's command if he failed at Hashem's desire for him to be a *mensch*. Of course, Hashem wants us to heed His commands. By the same token though, He does not want us to be arrogant, rude and abusive."

How could Moshe have possibly heeded Hashem's command to go and save his enslaved brethren and not first bid farewell to Yisro? According to R' Nosson Tzvi Finkel, the Alter of Slabodka, "If he would not have expressed his appreciation and recognition to his father-in-law for all he has done for him, Hashem would not have wanted him for the leader of His nation." A leader who knows not how to express *hakaras hatov* cannot possibly assume the mantle of leadership of *Klal Yisrael*.

What does the term *derech eretz* mean? Literally translated, it means "the way of the land". Being conscious of the environment, people around you, having social etiquette/good manners, ethical character/sensitivity to others, earning a living, contribution to society and an intimate family life.

Sometimes we can get so hooked into *Torah* study that we forget to practice our learning in practical life situations. However, that is why there are so many Talmudic and *halachic* teachings that deal with issues between a man and his colleague, in order to place *deretz eretz* forefront in our minds. Children often learn for their first *mesechtos*, the *Bava* tractates of *gemarah* instead of *Brachos* which is first in the proper sequence. *Rosh chedarim* often do this in order to sink into the young minds that part of *Torah* which deals with treating one's fellow with dignity.

There are two small tractates in the *Babylonian Talmud* (part of what is known as "the smaller tractates"), which are both entitled: *Derech Eretz*. The first is: *Derech Eretz Rabba*, the large one, and the second *Derech Eretz Zuta*, the small one. These are two independent *mesechtos*, with the former dealing with many rules of social conduct told through stories of the private lives of many of our sages. These *mesechtos* should not be overlooked and as soon as you complete the main *Talmud*, you should complete them thereafter. Don't leave any part of the *Torah* unturned but rather pursue every last part so that in your lifetime you will have completed all the important works.

There are many examples throughout *mesechtos Derech Eretz* which deal with correct etiquette. One such example can be found in *mesechtos Derech Eretz Rabba* (Chapter 7) regarding two people who are sitting at the table. It is only proper that the younger of the two should not begin eating until the older one has done so. This is a common courtesy. A second example of correct social etiquette is brought in the *Midrash Bamidbar Rabba* (14, 21) regarding the opening verse of the book of *Vayikra*, which states, "And Hashem called out to Moshe and spoke to him." The *Midrash* questions why it is that Hashem needed to call out to Moshe before speaking to him. It answers that the *Torah* is teaching us *derech eretz*, namely that one should not start speaking to anyone until you first call out to them. This means a person should not startle somebody else by speaking to them before they have acknowledged their presence and called out to them to engage in a conversation. There are many such examples of the term *derech eretz* which all clearly come to teach us the appropriate protocols, social etiquette and good manners when it comes to interacting with others.

Having a refined ethical character and being sensitive to others is of utter importance if one is to represent the *Torah*. Since a *Torah* scholar represents the *Torah*, he must act with a higher standard than others. We learn this also from Rav Yochanan. The *Talmud* says that Rav Yochanan would make sure not to walk more than four *amos* without study… he didn't have to do this, but he felt that because he was a *Torah* scholar, he had to be extra stringent, especially in public. As he viewed this as a desecration of Hashem's name in public. (*Yoma* 86a) We too should emulate him and conduct ourselves with a higher standard of *derech eretz*. Through this *kiddush* Hashem, we encourage others to observe the commandments and to fear Hashem.

There are many sources, especially in *mesechtos Derech Eretz Zuta*, which highlight the many ethical teachings of our sages with respect to character refinement, personal morality and sensitivity in dealing with others. These focus on dealing with other people in a gentle, patient and empathetic way, a readiness to forgive and desire to make peace among people. A further clear example of this is quoted in *Vayikra Rabba* (9:3) where the story is told of Rabbi Yanai, who encountered a particular man who declared the following to the sage: "Never in my life have I, after hearing negative reports about someone else, ever repeated this to the person, nor have I ever seen two people arguing without proactively making peace between them."

Rabbi Yanai then said, "...you possess great *derech eretz*." These sources highlight the ethical focus in life in dealing with others in a compassionate, gentle and kind way. Rabbi Yanai identified this display of sensitivity to others and especially in avoiding disputes and creating peace and harmony between people as a clear display of *derech eretz*.

The Alter Rebbe shared his house with his oldest married son, Rabbi Dov Ber (who later succeeded him as the Mitteler Rebbe). Rabbi Dov Ber was known for his unusual power of concentration. Once, when Rabbi Dov Ber was engrossed in learning, his baby, sleeping in its cradle nearby, fell out and began to cry. The infant's father did not hear the baby's cries. But the infant's grandfather, the Alter Rebbe, also engrossed in his studies in his room on the upper floor at the time, most certainly did. He interrupted his studies, went downstairs, picked the baby up, soothed it and returned it in its cradle. Through all this Rabbi Dov Ber remained quite oblivious.

Subsequently, the Alter Rebbe admonished his son: "No matter how engrossed one may be in the loftiest occupation, one must never remain insensitive to the cry of a child."

In order to exemplify the *Torah*, we must study it in such a way that it is not just a tool for wisdom but one which changes our character.

"Always be diligent with regard to your *Torah* study such that you try to apply what you learn. When you get up from studying, see if there is something in what you learned that you can apply and do." (Ramban's letter to his son, in *Reshis Chochmah, Sh'ar haAhavah*, chap. 6, #74)

According to the Sfas Emes, the *Torah* and *derech eretz* are connected on a deep and fundamental level. The quality of one's *Torah* learning directly corresponds to the amount of energy and effort one dedicates to bettering society and *derech eretz*.

The *Talmud* in *Sota* says, "It begins and ends with acts of kindness." The Lubavitch Rebbe explains, "The Jew must know that he was created in order to turn the world into the sort of world which G-d wants it to be, first and foremost through deeds of kindness."

What do the sages say about the passage, "And you shall love the L-rd your G-d?" (*Devarim* 6:5) "The name of Heaven shall become beloved through you; [this obligates a Jew to] study Scripture and *Mishnah*, serve scholars, conduct his business dealings honestly and converse with his fellow-beings in a calm manner. What do people say about such a person? 'More power to his father who taught him *Torah*, more power to his teacher who taught him *Torah*, woe to those who did not learn *Torah*.'" (*Yoma* 86a)

I think it can be common for a scholar to have anger problems. His anger is different though, he wants to return to his study and *avodas* Hashem and others don't understand this. He feels that situations and people are interfering with his Devine connection. However, anger is still anger. We learn from Hillel that there is no place for this in a *Torah* scholar. (*Shabbos* 31a)

Yaakov Avinu strongly admonishes his children Shimon and Levi, "Accursed is their rage for it is intense, and their wrath for it is harsh..." (*Bereshis* 49:7)

Shlomo Hamelech warns "Anger resides in the bosom of fools." (*Koheles* 7:9) The *Midrash* criticizes Moshe for becoming angry: Rabbi Eliezer states, "In three instances Moshe came to be angry and thus came to err. Upon being angry at Elazar and Itamar the sons of Aharon; after being angry with the commanding soldiers who returned from battle with Midian; and upon being angry at the Children of Israel when they demanded water." (*Sifri, Matos*)

Rav Chaim Vital taught, "Before we ever get to the point of performing *mitzvos*, there is a need to develop our basic character. The traits that comprise our character determine the way in which we fulfill the *mitzvos*. We must spend our energy in perfecting these aspects of ourselves - once these are properly developed, we can perform the *mitzvos* with relative ease." (*Sha'arei Kedusha*, part 1, gate 2)

When the *Midrash* in *Shemos Rabbah* (35:2) instructs us that a person should refrain from using wood from a fruit-bearing tree to build his house and calls that rule a lesson in *derech eretz*, its primary concern seems to be ecological and economic. Or when the late Talmudic tractate *Derech Eretz Rabbah* advises us neither to rejoice among people who are weeping nor weep among people who are rejoicing, it is apparently teaching us to be sensitive to the feelings of others and to care for our own reputations as well. "Happy is the man whose deeds are greater than his learning." (*Tanna de'Bei Eliyahu Rabbah* 17)

And Rava said: "Jerusalem was destroyed only because there were no more faithful people there, as it is stated: 'Roam about the streets of Jerusalem and see, and search its plazas, if you can find a person, who acts justly, who seeks integrity, that I should forgive it.'" (*Jeremiah* 5:1) (*Shabbos* 119b) It is the act of kindness that will rebuild the holy Temple.

Due to what reason was the First Temple destroyed? It was

demolished due to the fact that there were three negative matters that existed during the First Temple: Idol worship, forbidden sexual relations, and bloodshed... However, considering that the people during the Second Temple period were engaged in *Torah* study, observance of *mitzvos*, and acts of kindness, and that they did not perform the sinful acts that were performed in the First Temple, why was the Second Temple destroyed? It was destroyed due to the fact that there was wanton hatred during that period. This comes to teach you that the sin of wanton hatred is equivalent to the three severe transgressions: Idol worship, forbidden sexual relations and bloodshed. (*Yoma* 9b)

Rabbi Yochanan said: What is the meaning of that which is written: "Happy is the man who fears always, but he who hardens his heart shall fall into mischief?" (*Proverbs* 28:14) Jerusalem was destroyed on account of Kamtza and bar Kamtza... The *Gemarah* explains: The *Talmud* (*Gitten* 56) reports of a man who wanted to throw a party for all his friends, so he drew up a guest list and instructed his servant to send out the invitations. One of the men on the guest list was named "Kamtza," but the servant made a mistake and invited "Bar Kamtza" instead. This was a terrible mistake because Bar Kamtza was actually a sworn enemy of the host!

When Bar Kamtza obtained his invitation, he was very grateful to think that the host had finally made amends. But when Bar Kamtza showed up at the party, the host took one glance at him and told his servant to immediately eject Bar Kamtza from the premises.

When asked to leave, Bar Kamtza said: "I understand the mistake. Since it's embarrassing for me to leave the party, I'll gladly pay the cost of my meal if you'll allow me to remain." The host would hear nothing of this and insisted his demand to have Bar Kamtza removed.

Bar Kamtza appealed again: "I'd even be willing to pay half the cost of the entire party, if only I'd be allowed to stay."

Once more, the request was denied. Once again, the distraught Bar Kamtza pleaded: "I'll pay for the entire party! Just please don't embarrass me in this way!"

The host holding onto his grudge, however, stuck to his guns and threw Bar Kamtza out. The rabbis who had observed this exchange did not protest, and Bar Kamtza took this to mean that they approved of the host's behavior.

Bar Kamtza was so hurt and upset, that he went straight to the Roman authorities and gave slanderous reports of disloyal behavior among the Jews. This fueled the Romans' anger, and they proceeded to attack and destroy the Holy Temple.

In our generation, there are plenty of instances of bullying and embarrassing others, however, our main problem is a lack of kindness. We ignore those who are not in our immediate circle. People are depressed, lonely, lacking basic needs and we just ignore them.

The *Bais HaMikdash* will be rebuilt because of acts of kindness and peace among fellow Jews. Since that is the case, every *yeshivah* student, *kollel* guy, family, and Jew should constantly be involved in acts of kindness. We must reiterate the importance of *derech eretz* coinciding along with one's *Torah* devotions.

# *Physical Health*

Part of *derech eretz* is to take care of oneself. Your family relies on you not just for your *Torah* study and to provide for them but to be there for them by living a long and healthy life.

Taking care of our physical needs is even considered an act of kindness. We see this from some *tzaddikim* who when going to bathe and to eat, applied to themselves the verse, "He who treats himself [fairly] is a man of kindness."

It is fairly common for scholars to forget to eat healthy, sleep well and exercise. I think it's because they don't know enough *Torah's* on this concept. They think that exercise was only spoken about by the Rambam. It isn't understood by them that this too is a *mitzvah* and requirement. As it says, "Take care of yourself and guard your soul diligently." (*Devarim* 4:9)

Not having the ease of public transportation as we do today, the scholars of old were used to walking from place to place. Though their diet might be limited due to a lack of funds, they didn't obsess over processed foods and sugar. They ate what they needed and no more. Today scholars can be inactive with long days behind the *shtender*, taking transportation instead of a brisk walk to *shul* as was common decades ago. Therefore, good health and hygiene can sometimes be forgotten about.

Rav Sheshes engaged in moving beams and other heavy items, declaring that work is laudable because of the exercise it affords. Rashi is quoted as saying that Rav Sheshes did this for health reasons, especially during the winter, in order to perspire. (*Gitten* 67b)

I think it would be wise that *yeshivos* and rabbis encourage exercise along with *Torah* learning. Today when you have mp3 players, there is no reason why a scholar can't exercise while still immersed in learning *Torah*.

A scholar might reason that he doesn't have time to worry about physical exercise and that the *Torah* will take care of him in all ways. However, if he were healthy, he could learn far more *Torah* and make even better use of his time.

The Rambam emphasizes, "Exercise is the most important priority in maintaining good health and keeping up our resistance to the majority of illnesses. Through exercise it is even possible to neutralize the damage caused by many unhealthy habits." (*Hanhagos HaBrius* 1:3) "Even if you eat healthy foods and take proper care of your health in other respects, if you sit back comfortably and skip exercising, you will suffer from constant aches and pains and your strength will decrease." (*Hilchos De'os* 4:15)

Rabbi Yaakov Emden told, "All the natural scientists agree that lack of exercise is the cause of most of man's ailments." So, if you don't want to be *bittle Torah*, take care of yourself. The *Talmud* and *Shulchan Aruch* also rebukes a person who treats the learning of hygiene contemptuously. Another words, in all ways, take diligent care of your mind and body.

Rabbi Dov Ber, the Mezritcher Magid said, "A small hole in the body – a big hole in the soul."

The Rambam teaches, "Bodily health and well-being are part of the path to Hashem. This is since it is virtually impossible to know or understand anything of the Creator if one is sick. One must therefore avoid anything that may harm the body and cultivate healthful habits." (*Hilchos De'os* 4:1)

We cannot ignore the importance of preventative health care. It's all too easy for someone to wait till they are sick and weak to then address their issues. In our generation when health issues caused by a lack of self-awareness and self-care are so predominate in our societies, the rabbis must once again call to the masses to take better care of themselves.

Heart attacks, cancers, obesity, diabetes and other illnesses may be prevented beforehand through good diet and exercise. Our schools and *yeshivos* serve junk food to students. Parents turn a blind eye on their children's diets often allowing them to overdose on sugars and processed foods. Rarely do you hear a *shiur* from a *rav* pleading for you to take better care of yourself. If someone is conscious of their health too much, they appear to others as a freak and that something is wrong with them, when it is quite the contrary. However, with all matters in life, don't be obsessive! I knew people personally who took unbelievable care of themselves, obsessing over vitamins, herbs, yoga and meditation, even though they lived a long life, they were very surprised to find themselves with a heart attack and other health complications. Therefore, take diligent care of yourself as this is a *mitzvah*, but there is no need to become a slave to the physical body.

Rabbi Moshe Chaim Luzzatto wrote, "Man's use of the world for his own needs should be circumscribed by the limits imposed by Hashem's Will and shouldn't include anything forbidden by Hashem. It should be motivated by the need to best maintain his health and preserve his life, and not merely to satisfy his physical desires and superfluous cravings. One's motivation in maintaining his body should furthermore be only so that the soul should be able to use it in the service of its Creator without being hampered by the body's weakness and incapability. When man makes use of the world in this way, this in itself becomes an act of perfection. Through it one can attain the same virtue as in keeping the other commandments. Indeed, one of the commandments requires that we keep our bodies fit so that we can serve Hashem." (*Derech Hashem* I: 4:7; cf. *Shulchan Aruch, Aruch Chaim* #231 & *Choshen Mishpat* #427:8)

## *Healthy Eating Habits*

Through a proper diet and care for his health, man can live for a long time. (*Shaar HaShamayim* 156)

The Talmudic dictum that "more people are killed by the cooking pot than suffer from starvation" (*Shabbat* 33a), proves that the rabbis of the Talmud were fully aware of the dangers of bad eating habits.

In the words of the *Kitzur Shulchan Aruch* (32:7): "Every person should consult with medical experts to choose the foods best suited to his or her particular constitution, place and time."

All of us are diverse, we have different DNA and sensitivities. I think more people should run to a dietitian than to the doctor. If they would just eat the right foods for their particular body's requirements, so much hardship would be avoided. Not all dietitians are good though, you have to research and find the best. Also, you should study the Rambam's health advice, as much of it is still practical today. Educate yourself so that your aware of the benefits and drawbacks of eating each type of food.

"One should have in mind that he eats and drinks solely to maintain his body and its organs in health and vigor. He should not partake of everything which the palate craves, like a dog, but should choose foods that are wholesome to the body, whether these be sweet or bitter; and should avoid eating things that are injurious to the body." (*Hilchos Da'os* 3:2)

Regard thy table as the table before the L-rd; chew well and hurry not. (*Zohar* IV, 246a)

Besides encouraging eating in moderation, Rebbe Nachman also put great emphasis on how we eat. "Be careful not to gulp your food down hurriedly," he said. "Eat at a moderate pace, calmly and with the same table manners you would show if an important guest were present. You should always eat in this manner, even while eating alone." (*Tzaddik* #515)

The *Gemarah* in *Brachos* (57b) has some very good advice for health especially when it comes to eating and drinking. However, the rabbis have advised not to recommend specific healing techniques from the *Talmud* due to our bodily changes over hundreds of years. Why, because if someone were to use these remedies and they didn't work, they would then assume that all the *Talmud* is false. Therefore, be wise and use the advice that makes sense to you. Even though we can't advise someone to heal themselves from the Talmud's health instruction, this doesn't mean that the remedies stated don't work. I get offended as a lover of the *Talmud*, when people simply disrespect any of the holy words. The *Torah's* wisdom is endless, and one would be a fool to disregard it.

Here are a few examples of very relevant advice from the *Talmud*:

"Food is better for the man up to the age of forty; after forty, drink is better." (*Shabbos* 152a)

"Most people die from overeating than from undernourishment." (*Shabbos* 33a)

"Too much sitting may cause hemorrhoids; too much standing hurts the heart; too much walking hurts the eyes; so, divide your time between the three." (*Kesubos* 111a)

This is great advice from the *Talmud* and most certainly still applies today. Therefore, please don't cast off any of the holy words as totally irrelevant. Just understand that they have their place in history and one should use the advice wisely.

Bread is the staff of life. This fact is mentioned in each of the three sections of Scripture: *Torah, Nevi'im* and *Kesuvim*. In *Bereshis* (18:5) we find that Avraham told the three travelers who appeared to him, "I will fetch a morsel of bread that you may sustain yourselves." In *Shoftim* (19:5) it is written: "Sustain your heart with a morsel of bread." In *Tehillim* (104:15) we are taught: "Bread sustains the heart of man." (*Bereshis Rabbah* 48:11)

The Talmud says, "Sixty runners may run but will not overtake a man that takes bread in the morning. Rabbah bar Mari explains: For it is written, 'They shall not hunger nor thirst, neither shall the heat nor sun smite them.' (*Isaiah* 49:10) Rav suggests another source to him: You derive it from that text, but I derive it from an earlier place, 'And ye shall serve the L-rd your G-d.' (*Shemos* 23:25) This [as has been explained] refers to the reading of *Shema* and the *tefillah*, as the verse continues, 'And he will bless thy bread and thy water.' This refers to the bread dipped in salt and to the pitcher of water. We therefore conclude, 'I will take [*machalah*, i.e.] sickness away from the midst of thee.'

"It was [also] taught: *machalah* means the gall bladder; and why is it called *machalah*? Because eighty-three various kinds of illnesses may result from it [as the numerical value of *machalah* amounts exactly to this]; but

36

they all are neutralized by partaking in the morning of bread dipped in salt followed by a pitcher of water." (*Bava Kamma* 29b)

The Rambam says, "Since, by keeping the body in health and vigor, one walks in the ways of Hashem – it being impossible during sickness to have any understanding or knowledge of the Creator – it is man's duty to avoid whatever is injurious to the body and cultivate habits conducive to health and vigor. These are as follows: One should not take food except when one is hungry; nor drink unless one is thirsty. One should not neglect the calls of nature for a single moment but respond to them immediately." (*Hilchos Da'os* 4:1)

The Rambam talks about eating more than one's body requires. He says, "Over-eating is like a deadly poison to any constitution and is the principal cause of all diseases. Most maladies that afflict mankind result from unhealthy food or are due to the patient filling his stomach with an excess of food that may even have been wholesome. Thus, Shlomo, in his wisdom, said, 'He who keeps mouth and tongue, keeps his soul from troubles.' (*Proverbs* 21:23) – which can be applied to the individual who guards his mouth from unhealthy food and over-eating." (*Rambam, Da'os* 5:15)

So, what is the right amount to eat? The Rambam explains, "Food should not be taken to repletion; during a meal, about one-third less should be eaten than the quantity that would give a feeling of satiety, and only a little water should be drunk – and that mixed with wine." (*Hilchos Da'os* 4:2)

"In all your ways know Him." (*Proverbs* 3:6) The Rambam expounds: This verse refers to one who eats, drinks and nourishes his being in order to be healthy and strong for the purpose of serving Hashem. He has the same reward as one who fasts. How do we know this? From the verse: "A waste for you, all of whom get up early!" For there are *talmidei chachamim* who chase sleep from their eyes and study much *Torah* and there are *talmidei chachamim* who sleep abundantly in order to have strength to acquire a zealous heart for the purpose of studying *Torah*; and the actual fact is that he can learn in an hour that which the other, tired one, pains himself two hours to digest! And certainly, both of them receive the same exact reward. Therefore, the verse says, "A waist for you" since for naught you are afflicting yourself to rise early and to stay up late Friday nights. All of you who shun sleep-this is for nothing, as it is written: "For Hashem gives sleep to his cherished friend." This means: One who sleeps abundantly for the purpose of strengthening his mind in *Torah*, to him Hashem will give a portion of *Torah* wisdom exactly like the portion of one who shuns sleep from his eyes and afflicts himself! Why? Because everything, all of a person's actions and thoughts are weighed in Heaven according to one's sincere and heartfelt intentions. (*Taz Even Ha'Ezer* 25)

# Torah as Medicine

"The *Torah* is an emollient for every wound." (*Devarim Rabbah* 8)

Rabbi Yaakov Abuchatzeira taught, "There is no healing like that provided by the *Torah*." (*Sha'arei Aruchah* 64)

The *Torah* teaches us in *Shemos* (15:26), "And He said, If you hearken to the voice of the L-rd, your G-d, and you do what is proper in His eyes, and you listen closely to His commandments and observe all His statutes, all the sicknesses that I have visited upon Egypt I will not visit upon you, for I, the L-rd, heal you."

Rashi explains, I will not visit upon you: And if I do bring [sickness upon you], it is as if it has not been brought, "for I, the L-rd, heal you." This is its *Medrashic* interpretation (see *Sanhedrin* 101a, *Mechilta*). According to its simple meaning, [we explain:] "for I, the L-rd, am your Physician," and [I] teach you the *Torah* and the *mitzvos* in order that you be saved from them [illnesses], like this physician who says to a person, "Do not eat things that will cause you to relapse into the grip of illness." This [warning] refers to listening closely to the commandments, and so [Scripture] says: "It shall be healing for your navel." (*Proverbs* 3:8) — [from *Mechilta*] (Rashi on *Shemos* 15:26)

Do you want to avoid getting an earache, or indeed any other pain, in the first place? Then turn your ear to the *Torah* and you'll inherit life, as it is written, "Incline your ear and come to Me, hear and your soul shall live." (*Yeshiyahu* 55:3) For as Rabbi Levi said, "Man is made up of two hundred and forty-eight limbs, and all of them receive vitality from the ear." (*Devarim Rabbah* 10:1)

The spiritual connotations of the various body parts can be found in *Kabbalah* and *Chassidus*, which are founded on the principle that man was created in the image of Hashem. As Job said, "From my flesh I see G-d." (*Iyuv* 19:26) The various parts of the human body correspond to various aspects of the higher spiritual worlds, and the *Kabbalah* is filled with references to the spiritual significance of various parts of the body.

Rabbi Yehoshua ben Levi told, "Someone with a headache should busy himself with *Torah*, as it is said, 'For they shall be a diadem of grace for your head' (*Proverbs* 1:9). Someone with a sore throat should busy himself with *Torah*, as it is said, 'and chains about your neck.' (ibid.)

Someone with stomach pains should busy himself with *Torah*, as it is said, 'it shall be health to your navel' (ibid. 3:8). Someone with aching bones should busy himself with *Torah*, as it is said, 'and marrow to your bones' (ibid.). And if his whole body is aching, he should busy himself with *Torah*, as it is said (ibid. 4:22), 'and health to all his flesh.'" (*Eruvin* 54a).

"Rabbi Yehudah the son of Rabbi Chiya said, Come and see the difference between Hashem and human beings. When a human being prescribes a medicine, it may be good for one person but harmful to another. Not so the Holy One, blessed be He. The *Torah* He gave to the Jewish people is an elixir of life for the whole body, as it is said (*Proverbs* 4:22), 'and health to all his flesh.'" (ibid.)

## *The Role of the Doctor*

The Ramban teaches: "When the Jewish People are in a state of spiritual perfection, their physical bodies are not governed by nature at all. This pertains to the nation as a whole and to each individual Jew. 'For Hashem will bless their bread and their water and remove illness from their midst' (*Shemos* 23:25). They will have no need for doctors, nor will they have to follow medical procedures, even as precautionary measures, 'for I, G-d, am your healer.'" (*Shemos* 15:26) (Ramban on *Vayikra* 26:11).

Rebbe Nachman was known to dislike most doctors. He advised only to visit them under extreme circumstances. However, there was one which he made an exception, on behalf of his precious *rebbetzin* who was ill at the time. His name was Doctor Guardia - Rabbi Aharon ben Shimon Rofey. If you hear this story, you will understand why this doctor was special and extraordinary.

Once a poverty-stricken woman came running to Dr. Guardia. She pounded on his door, crying "Doctor! Help! Have pity! You must save my husband! He's the father of eight children! We're totally impoverished! He already struggles to provide for us, and now he's stretched out on his bed like a stone. Have pity on our children! Do what you can, Doctor!" After hearing the woman out, Dr. Guardia casually went back into his house.

"It's urgent!" cried the desperate woman. "It's only a matter of moments! Help!"

"Yes," responded Dr. Guardia, patiently brushing his coat, "I'm on my way." He picked up his hat and started cleaning it with a brush. More and more distraught, the woman cried out: "Is your heart made of stone? You have the power to save his life - how can you carry on like this?" Unaffected by her pleads, Dr. Guardia carried on brushing his hat. Finally, in disgust, the woman cried, "Enough! It's impossible to trust this doctor. Only You, Master of the World, You alone can help!" As she turned to depart, Doctor Guardia soared out of the house and went running on ahead to her house. By the time she arrived, the doctor was already giving her husband medicine, and in due course he recovered.

Afterwards the man's wife questioned Doctor Guardia why he had taken so long to leave his house. "Don't you understand?" he responded. "It's not the doctor who heals, but the angel who goes with him. When you unthinkingly said that only the doctor can help, I knew very well that no angel would be willing to accompany me, because the angels do not attach themselves to those who forget their Creator. I therefore had to do everything I could to get you to understand that only Hashem can help. When you finally began trusting only in Hashem, I was able to come to your house and attend to your husband" (*The Magid of Mezritch*, by R.Y. Klapholtz).

The Rambam tells: "One day a person may notice a change in his digestion or feel a mild headache or a slight pain in some other part of his body, and so on. When this occurs, don't be in a hurry to take medications for these kinds of minor problems. Nature will take care of them without any necessity for medicines. Follow your normal health regime. If you try treating these minor ailments, either you will do the wrong thing and cause harm or, if you do the right thing, while you may succeed in restoring the normal balance, you have also taught your body to become lazy, and it will no longer function properly without outside assistance." (*Hanhagos HaBri'us* 4:3)

I think many of us have lost confidence on our bodies ability to care for itself. If you look at a simple cut on the skin, within a day or two it starts to heal itself, scabbing in order to protect itself. Even our emotional health, we have become lazy with and we rely on medicines to curb our anxieties and sadness, when in fact, most of us can control our emotions more than we realize. It's just that we have forgotten how.

Many rabbis were against visiting doctors and taking medicines haphazardly. Some of which were, Rabbi Pinchas Shapiro of Koretz (1726-91), Rabbi Barukh of Medzeboz (1757-1810) and Rabbi Yaakov Yitzchak Horovitz, the Chozeh (Seer) of Lublin (1745-1815) – and Rebbe Nachman. In more recent times, Rabbi Yisrael Meir Kagan of Radin, the Chafetz Chaim (1839-1933), is also said to have avoided doctors. His son writes: "My mother told me that when I was young, they virtually never consulted doctors. If one of us was sick, my father's advice was to distribute bread to the poor, while he would go up to the attic and pray."

40

*(Letters of the Chafetz Chaim Part III, p. 12)*

It seems quite clear that most illnesses are a message from Hashem, that you have to make some sort of action here below in order to invoke healing. Going to the doctor alone isn't enough. There has to be an effort of *emunah*, an increase in *mitzvos* and only then to seeking medicinal answers.

There was a certain sick person whom a great and famous Jewish doctor had given up all hope of curing. The man was incapable of speaking. The Baal Shem Tov was visiting his town and was asked to come to see if he could help.

The Baal Shem Tov told them to prepare the invalid a meat soup and said that as soon as he ate it, he would begin to speak. As instructed, they gave him the soup and he recovered. Amazed, the doctor said to the Baal Shem Tov, "How did you cure him? I know that his blood vessels were irreparably damaged."

The Baal Shem Tov explained, "Your approach to his sickness was physical while mine was spiritual. A person has two hundred and forty-eight limbs and three hundred and sixty-five veins and arteries corresponding to the two hundred and forty-eight positive precepts of the *Torah* and its three hundred and sixty-five prohibitions. When someone fails to carry out a positive *mitzvah* the corresponding limb is damaged, and when he contravenes a prohibition the corresponding blood vessel is damaged. If he contravenes many prohibitions, then many blood vessels become damaged. The blood no longer flows properly, and the person is in danger. So, I spoke to his soul and persuaded her to repent, and she undertook to do so. This way all his limbs and blood vessels were repaired, and I could heal him'" (*Shevachey HaBaal Shem Tov* #125).

The other day, my son injured his foot and I went in to get him an x-ray. As I pulled out the ticket to wait online, the number 248 popped up. I turned to my son and said, "Do you know what this means? It means that all your limbs and bones are intact."

He responded, "Does that mean we can go home and not do the x-ray?"

I smiled and said, "I know everything will be fine now, but we still have to do things in the way of the world." Sure enough, even though it clearly appeared broken, everything was fine.

The Lubavitcher Rebbe taught: "We know that our *Torah*, the *Torah* of life, teaches us in the verse 'and he will surely heal' (*Shemos* 21:19) that the doctor has been given sanction to heal. Thereby, it automatically follows that it is necessary to follow the instructions of a competent

41

doctor. Yet at the same time, one must clearly know that Hashem is the Healer of all flesh and the Worker of wonders. A 'particular man and a particular drug' are merely His agents and means. It follows that first and foremost one must work to improve and strengthen one's spiritual health. Thereby, he strengthens his attachment to Hashem, and then `you are all alive this day' (*Devarim* 4:4) with actual physical vitality and in all one's limbs." (*Refuah Shelemah* p.23)

The Lubavitcher Rebbe also wrote encouraging words to a doctor: "When patients consult you about their physical problems, I trust that, like many G-d-fearing doctors, you too take the opportunity to inspire and encourage them to work to heal their souls as well. Everyone in this orphaned generation needs this, since 'no one on earth is so righteous that he does only good and does not sin' (*Koheles* 7:20). Moreover, we see clearly that an improvement in a person's spiritual health also brings an improvement in his or her physical health - quite literally..." (*Refuah Shelemah* p. 21)

Harav Elazar M. Shach explains, "A *tzaddik*, righteous person, is not perfect. It is possible for a *tzaddik* to err. To err is human; to ignore one's error is unforgiveable and indicates that he is witless."

The Lubavitcher Rebbe wrote to one ill person as follows: "Regarding your quotation from the Rambam that the Holy One, blessed be He, does not perform miracles going beyond the bounds of nature for a single individual, the fact is that we have seen with our own eyes miracles beyond nature performed for individuals. We have particularly seen this in the last few years, and especially in the case of medical problems in the interior of the body. Time and time again, the doctors have been wrong in their diagnoses even after all the tests" (*Refuah Shelemah* pp.35-6).

Even though Rebbe Nachman was not a huge fan of doctors, he said, "Sometimes when people don't want to suffer a little, they end up suffering a lot!" (*Siach Sarfey Kodesh* 1-6) It is far preferable to have a medical problem treated punctually in its initial stages than to allow it to develop into what may turn out to be catastrophic proportions. Therefore, if you know you have a severe problem, don't delay and take care of yourself but only go to the very best of doctors.

# Joy

Rebbe Nachman taught, "All the illness that afflicts people comes only because of a lack of joy... And joy is the great healer." (*Likutey Moharan* II, 24) Thereby, "It's a great *mitzvah* to be happy always!" (ibid.)

"When one's limbs are heavy with depression, this in turn weighs down on the vital spirit animating one's heart, which becomes even weaker. The heartbeat becomes weaker, and then the limbs become even heavier. Following suit, the heartbeat becomes weaker. And so, the cycle continues, until the person's soul goes out of him, G-d forbid" (*Likutey Moharan* I, 56:9).

Giving an answer as to how we can break out of this vicious cycle, Rebbe Nachman continues:

"Through a deep, heaving sigh one can bring new life to one's spirit, restoring the heartbeat to health and saving oneself from depression. And then the pulse returns to normal in all the limbs..." (ibid.)

The very sigh of sorrow and yearning to return to Hashem and feel better is itself the first step to redemption. For in the words of the Baal Shem Tov: "When a person recognizes the wounds of his heart and the sickness of his soul, this knowledge itself is his salvation, and this is what heals him. This is unlike when a person lacks all such awareness and does not realize that he is spiritually sick. Then there is no remedy for his mortal malady" (*Keter Shem Tov* #25).

Being satisfied with little and one's lot, helps a great deal towards attaining joy. All too often we overlook the simple breath of life and the blessing to serve Hashem as the greatest joy. Rebbe Nachman tells us a parable to better understand this.

Once there was a simpleton who learned how to make shoes, but because he was simple, it took him a long time before he grasped it. Even though he was not completely proficient in his craft, he still married and made a living from his work. Being simple, however, and not too proficient in his work, his living was very scanty. He barely even had time to eat since, not being fully proficient, he had to work constantly. As he worked busily, driving the awl through the leather, inserting the thick thread and drawing it through in the way shoemakers do, he would take a bite of bread.

He always remained happy. He was simply full of joy all the time. He possessed every kind of food, drink and clothing. He would ask to his wife: "My wife! Give me to eat!" She would give him a slice of bread and he would eat it. Afterwards he would say: "Give me beans and gravy." She would cut him another piece of bread and he would eat it, praising the food. "This gravy is so beautiful! It is so good!"

He would request her to give him meat and other good foods. For every kind of food that he asked, she would give him a piece of bread. He would take the most exquisite delight in it, highly praising the food. "So tasty! So good!" he would say as if he was actually eating that very food.

And the truth is that when he ate the bread, he truly did taste each kind of food that he wanted, all because of his great simplicity and joy.

Similarly, he would request to his wife: "Give me liquor!" She would give him water, and he would praise it highly. "What beautiful liquor this is! Give me honey mead!" Once again, she would give him water, and he would praise the mead. "Give me wine!" She would give him water, and he would enjoy it and praise it as if he was actually drinking the drink he had requested.

As far as their cloths were concerned, he and his wife possessed one single thick sheepskin coat which they had to share. When he needed to wear an overcoat to go to the market, he would request, "My wife, give me the overcoat!" and she would give it to him. When he needed to wear a fine fur coat to make a social visit, he would ask, "My wife, give me the fur coat!" She would give him the sheepskin and he would take immense pleasure in it, praising it lavishly: "What a beautiful fur coat this is!"

When he required a caftan to go to the synagogue, he would tell his wife, "Give me the caftan!" She would give him the sheepskin and he would praise it saying, "What a fine, beautiful caftan this is!" Likewise, when he needed to wear a silk coat, she would give him the sheepskin. He would praise it and take the highest delight in it: "What a lovely, beautiful silk coat!" He was simply filled with joy and delight at all times.

Upon finishing making a shoe, it would all too often turn out triangular as he was not fully proficient in his craft. However, he would take the shoe in his hand and praise it greatly. He would take immense delight in it, saying: "My wife, how beautiful and wonderful this shoe is. How sweet this shoe is. This shoe is pure honey and sugar!"

"If so," she would question, "why do the other shoemakers take three gold coins for a pair of shoes while you only receive one and a half?"

"What do I care?" he would remark. "That is their work, and this is my work! Besides, why do we need to speak about other people? Let us embrace how much clear profit I made on this shoe. He then calculated the numbers. The leather costs such and such; the glue, the thread, the filling cost such and such. In the end I made a profit of ten groschen! Why should I mind when I make such a wonderful profit?" He was simply filled with joy and delight at all times. (*Rebbe Nachman's Stories*, pp.168-173)

Rabbi Chaim of Volozhin said, "Joy is included among the 48 tools for acquiring *Torah*. This is because you will accomplish more in one hour of *Torah* study when you are in a joyous state than from many hours of studying when you are sad or depressed." (*Ruach Chaim*, ch. 4, 6:6)

# Faith in Healing

"If you will listen carefully to the voice of Hashem your G-d and do what is right in His eyes, and give ear to His commandments and keep all His statutes, I will put none of the diseases upon you that I have put on the Egyptians, for I am Hashem your Healer" (*Shemos* 15:26).

Rebbe Nachman noticed the collapse of faith as the essential sickness of the age and indeed the cause of some of the most pernicious physical diseases afflicting our societies. "The main thing is faith!" he cried out. "Every person must search within himself and strengthen himself in faith. For there are people suffering from the most terrible afflictions, and the only reason they are sick is because of the collapse of faith. The *Torah* says, 'G-d will send you wondrous plagues, great and faithful plagues and great and faithful 'sicknesses' (*Devarim* 28:59). The plagues and sicknesses are called 'faithful' because they come on account of a lack of faith" (*Likutey Moharan* II, 5:1).

"When a person fails to focus on the ultimate purpose - the תכלית (*tachlis*) - what is the point of their life? The soul constantly yearns to do the will of their Maker. When the soul sees that this person is not carrying out His Will, it becomes filled with yearning to return to its Source and prepares to leave the body. Because of this, the person becomes sick and the power of the soul is weakened, owing to the fact that it is trying to withdraw from the body since they are not carrying out the soul's desire. The soul's only wish is that they should carry out Hashem's Will.

"The reason a person's health returns through taking medicines is that their soul notices that they are able to control themselves and to act contrary to their physical desires and habits. Perhaps they are accustomed to eating bread and other foods, but now they curb their desires and submits to a medical regime, taking bitter medicines for the sake of their health. The soul sees that they have the power to control their impulses in order to achieve a certain goal, and the soul therefore returns to them in the hope that they will curb their desires for the sake of the true purpose - which is to carry out the will of the Creator." (*Likutey Moharan* I, 268)

Rabbi Noson explains, "The intention of *Birkas HaMazon*, the Grace after Meals, is to bless the food as it passes through the digestive system in order to channel nutrients and energy to the limbs of the body and bring satisfaction. This is why the Grace comprises the verse, 'You open Your hands and satisfy the desire of every living being.' (*Psalms* 145:16) That is, we gratefully request that Hashem should satisfy the desire of every living being by channeling to each one the energy and strength it needs by means of the 'word of G-d'. For through the 'word of G-d,' all the various kinds of energies each individual requires can be channeled through any kind of food and drink" (*Likutey Halakhos, Birkas HaRei'ach* 2:3).

It is written, "Peace! Peace to the one who is far off and the one who is close, says Hashem... and I will heal him." (*Yeshiyahu* 57:19) Sometimes the distance is really the idea of drawing near. We think that Hashem doesn't want us near to Him and that is why we are sick and weak when it is the contrary.

"The Holy One, blessed be He, yearns for the prayers of the righteous. Therefore, He restrains (detains and causes delay) the salvation of the *tzaddikim*; and advances the salvation of the wicked." (*Bereshis Rabbah* 68:5; *Pesikta Zutrasi* 29:18)

# *Working and Learning*

Rabban Gamliel, the son of Rabbi Yehudah Hanasi said, "It is good to study *Torah* and work (*derech eretz*), for between the two, you will not come to sin." (*Pirkei Avos* 2:2) Why is this? Because, "Idleness leads to immorality." (*Y. Kesubos* 5:5) "One who earns a livelihood from his labor is very fortunate. He is saved from many sins." (*Midrash Gadol Ugedolah* 14)

However, earning a living without a balance of *Torah* in your life, will lead you to toil for naught and eventually fall into sin. Thereby, everyone who is versed in the Scriptures and in the *Mishnah* and earns a livelihood will not sin readily. (*Kiddushin* 40b) *Torah* along with earning a living is the proper path for most individuals as it says in the *Talmud*, "One who earns his livelihood from the toil of his hands is greater than one who fears Hashem." (*Bereshis* 8a)

*Derech eretz* really is about having balance. "Without flour (sustenance) no learning; without learning, no flour (sustenance)." (*Avos* 3:17) Too many people wait to the last moment to seek a balance between working and learning. In the end, they only suffer from this when it's too late and they have already run out of funds completely. How many bills have to pile up before a person realizes that there is something wrong with their service of Hashem?

Even though I showed you the proper way is to work and study both, I am a greater fan of full-time learning. That is, when done correctly for the right individual. Many people shun both pathways when each individual must weigh what is best for his soul and family.

The *Gemarah* relates the story of Ilfa and Rabbi Yochanan. Ilfa and Rabbi Yochanan suffered from abject poverty while they immersed themselves in *Torah* learning. Their situation became so difficult that they decided to leave the *beis midrash* and go to work in fulfillment of the verse, "There will be no destitute among you." (*Devarim* 15:4) When they were on their way to find work, Rabbi Yochanan overheard two *malachei ha'shares* conversing with each other. The *malachim* said that these two people deserved to be killed for leaving the life of eternity (*Torah* study) and involving themselves in the temporary life of pursuing a material livelihood. The *malachim* added that the only reason they did not kill Ilfa and Rabbi Yochanan is because the fate of one of them would soon take a propitious turn. Rabbi Yochanan heard this conversation and decided to

47

continue learning *Torah* in poverty and not to go to work. Rabbi Yochanan figured since he was the one who heard it, it would be him who would prosper soon. Ilfa, who did not hear the words of the *malachim*, went off to work.

By the time Ilfa returned from his business endeavors, Rabbi Yochanan had been inaugurated as the *rosh hayeshivah*, a position of great prestige and wealth (Rashi). The people of the town said to Ilfa upon his return, "Had you stayed and learned *Torah* [like Rebbi Yochanan], you would have become the *rosh hayeshivah*!"

When Ilfa heard this, he ascended the mast of a ship and suspended himself in the crow's nest at the top. He proclaimed, "If anyone can ask me a question which I cannot answer about the source in the *Mishnah* of any statement of Rabbi Chiya and Rabbi Oshiya in the *beraisa*, I will jump down from here and drown myself!" (*Tannis* 21)

Rav Refoel Dovid gave a beautiful explanation for this *Gemarah* (as cited in *Ha'Meir, Parshas Vayechi* 5742). Rav Refoel Dovid explained that when Ilfa returned from his business endeavors, he felt that he was being criticized for not having attained the heights in *Torah* which he could have attained. He felt that this criticism was unjust. He maintained that his choice to follow the path of "*Torah im derech eretz*," learning *Torah* while working for a livelihood, was justified. He wanted to prove to his detractors that his *Torah* learning had not suffered at all as a result of his involvement in pursuing a livelihood. (as Rashi writes, "[Ilfa said:] Even though I became involved in commerce, I did not forget any of my learning.")

Ilfa was a merchant who, like the people of Zevulun, traveled by ship to faraway places to trade his wares. (This might be why he was called Ilfa; the word "*Ilfa*" in *Aramaic* means "ship.") By climbing to the top of the mast of the ship, Ilfa demonstrated that although he had reached the pinnacle of success in his business, his involvement in business had not interfered with his *Torah* learning.

He declared that he was prepared to answer any question in *Torah* that would be posed to him, and if he would be unable to answer it he would "jump down" from the top of the ship -- that is, he would leave his immensely successful business and wealth, abandoning his *derech* of learning and working together -- and "drown himself" completely in the sea of *Torah*, as Rabbi Yochanan had done. If his *Torah* learning had suffered as a result of his involvement in business, he was willing to jump down from the world of business success and immerse himself in the sea of *Torah*.

According to this explanation, Ilfa felt no regret for the path he had chosen. He considered himself to have chosen the correct way in the service of Hashem, just as Rabbi Yochanan felt that he had chosen the correct way in the service of Hashem.

A lot of parents feeling the pressure to set up their children in *parnasa*, might push them to get a degree in a profession they don't enjoy, just because it's profitable. In our generation, we see plenty of people with degrees who are out of work. We see an endless amount of people working in professions and jobs that they don't enjoy. Work instead of a blessing feels like a daily torcher.

Don't feel trapped by this as there is hope. Don't allow someone to convince you that you have to keep this particular job or attend years of university study if that isn't, your desire. Rather, you should do what is best for you and what makes you happy. Allow Hashem to send His blessing down upon you.

Rabbi Meir says, "One should always teach his son a clean and easy profession and pray to Him to whom wealth and property belong. For a profession does not contain [the potential for] poverty and wealth, for poverty is not because one's profession nor is wealth due to the profession, but all depends on merit." (*Mishnah Kiddushin* 82a)

Rabbi Shimon ben Elazar says, "Have you ever seen a wild beast or a bird with a profession? Yet they are sustained without trouble. Now, were they not created only to serve me, while I was created to serve my Master, surely then I should make a living without trouble! But my evil acts have done me in and withheld my livelihood." (*Mishnah Kiddushin* 82a)

The *Gemarah* (*Kiddushin* 82a) teaches further: "Rabbi Nehorai said, 'I set aside all trades that exist and I teach my son only *Torah*, for all trades serve a person in his youth but forsake him in his old age, while *Torah* study stands by a person in his old age and his youth.'"

Rabbi Aryeh Leib Burstein (*rabbi* in Grodno, Poland and London, England; died 1925) explains: "Work is harder for the elderly than for the young, while *Torah* study becomes easier and easier as time goes on. This proves that *Torah* study is a person's natural activity while work is not. Why? Because the essence of man is his intelligence, not his body. Thus, said Rabbi Nehorai, 'I would rather teach my son *Torah*, for that is what comes naturally to a person;' therefore, it must be what he was meant to do." (*Derashos Ha'maggid Mi'Horodna*)

I always tell my children, "You were brought into this world to learn *Torah*." That *Torah* has to come first in your mind and everything else should be secondary. Always learn a little *Torah* and then afterwards have your fun. I explain to them that work is good for you too, it keeps your mind busy and it's never good to be idle with your time.

I think some people (and sadly children,) don't believe they were meant to be a scholar and learn *Torah*. This prospective comes because in *yeshivah* it is always the smartest student that stands out as being the best and the worthiest to learn, but this isn't secular wisdom here, this is the holy *Torah*. The *Torah* is meant for everyone on their own level of understanding. The greatest scholar could be the simple Jew that struggles to learn simple *p'shat,* yet he tries with all his might. His *Gan-Eden* could easily surpass the wisest man. If only the *yeshivos* would appreciate all the children the same, making them feel worthy of the *Torah* even for their smallest of accomplishments. Unfortunately, nobody seems to give these students the confidence in *Torah* to succeed.

I would love to do a test and take all those who work full-time and those who study full-time and have them flip rolls for a month. I'd like to see who would uncover more of the *Torah's* secrets. There are so many people I see pouring their entire life over business that truly belong in full-time *yeshivah*. If only they took their business and organizational skills over to the study of *Torah*, I know they would excel and be leaders in our generation. Then others, I see in *kollel* struggling with *parnasa*, unorganized in their learning; I'd like to give them a job for a few years to help them learn time-management and the benefits of working hard. Then when they would later return to their studies full-time, they would be a completely different person, excelling to their true potential in *Torah*. Just like work needs to be done with organization, so too one's study of *Torah*. Sometimes working a job can teach this idea to a scholar while the *yeshivah* system has failed too.

We all have a lot to learn when it comes to *derech eretz* and the study of *Torah*. Much of this can be learned from the example set by our holy sages of old. It is good to read many books of *mussar*. *Derech eretz* also means that if you are declaring yourself a type of scholar who studies full-time, then don't waste time. Keep a tight schedule and value every minute. Appreciate this precious gift you have been given to be blessed to study the holy *Torah*.

The Rogatchover knew all of *Talmud Bavli* and *Yerushalmi*, by heart. At his fingertips, he could recall the entire Rambam, *Shulchan Aruch*, and countless other *seforim*. Still he would constantly review *Shas*, making a *siyum* in honor of completing the entire *Talmud* regularly, every five months. One time, he requested that his family prepare a *seudas siyum* just a few weeks after a previous one had been held, on schedule. They questioned the *rav*, "Did you actually finish *Shas* again in such a brief period?"

The Path to Finishing Shas

"Not exactly," he clarified. "This *siyum* is for a special *seder* that I maintain during unscheduled waiting periods. You know, people tell me to be ready for a *bris* at eight a.m., but they don't pick me up until eight-fifteen. Or they invite me to attend a wedding at six-thirty, and it does not start until seven. I have a special *seder* during those waiting periods, and I've just completed *Shas* in accordance with that *seder*." The *rav* indeed loved learning *Torah* and hence he had indeed completed *Shas* 101 times during his lifetime. (My Book, *A Journey into Holiness*, p. 184)

It is said of Rabbi Dovid Lifshitz that his command for *Torah* was really beyond the comprehension of his students. No matter where in *Shas* one spoke to him, he could discuss the *sugya* in depth, quoting the language of the *Gemarah* perfectly. He had full command of the *shitos* of the *Rishonim* and *Gedolei Acharonim*. All this ability comes from learning *Torah* diligently and being organized.

Ulla gives us an effective way of weighing if we should continue our studies. If we see that we are overwhelmed, forgetting our studies and constantly with anxiety, it is time to work more. However, if your *Torah* study is completely *lishmah*, then the anxieties will dissipate.

Ulla taught: "Thoughts (i.e. anxiety) regarding one's livelihood cause him to forget even words of *Torah*, as it is stated: 'He abolishes the thoughts of the clever, and their hands will not accomplish *tushiyah*.' Ulla's dictum is qualified: Rabbah said: But if they're engaged in the study of *Torah* for its own sake [such anxiety] will not cause them to forget their learning. As it is stated: Many are the thoughts in the heart of man, but the counsel of Hashem, only it will endure. (*Proverbs* 19:21) This is to say: Counsel (i.e. *Torah*) that has within it the word of Hashem (i.e. that is studied for its own sake) will endure forever." (*Sanhedrin* 26b)

I think it's extremely important for most young men to learn vocational skills along with their *yeshivah* study so they have the ability to support their families later in life when they can no longer afford to study. It is the *yeshivas* that should arrange *kosher* programs for them and not make them feel inadequate for wanting to have a fuller education. I'm not *chas-v-shalom* saying that they should have a full secular education but that some basic vocational skills should be learned. What do you expect the *bachur* to do once he is married if he has no idea how to use his hands? Do you expect him to collect charity and make a *chillul* Hashem that he hasn't any idea how to care for his basic needs?

Many students grow up thinking that working is bad. That you are on a lower level if you hold a job instead of being in *yeshivah*. I love the idea of encouraging people to study *Torah* but let's also welcome some

51

reality.

The Tur and *Shulchan Aruch*, citing a *Mishnah*, state: "Then [after his *Torah* studies] he goes about his business, for; 'All *Torah* that is not combined with work will end in failure and cause sin.'" (*SA Orach Chayim* 156, citing *M Avos* 2:2)

How many married men fall into sin because they feel a pressure to study full-time when their minds are incapable? We have to arrange *Torah* study and education programs that fit the individual student in their growth. Not every *yeshivah bachur* fits the general mold and we need to be open to each individual's needs and guide them accordingly. However, I have seen many great minds taken out of the *Torah* environment in order to study in college because of their parent's "worry", for their future. Today in the work force we see that street skills can be just as important as a strong education in obtaining a job... so therefore, part of the vocational education alongside of *yeshivah* study could be general business courses for young men to understand sales, marketing and basic skill sets.

As far as going to the army here in Israel, I don't think any person, religious or not, should be forced into something that they may not feel fits their goals and personality. An army is as weak as its weakest link... why would you want someone to be there who doesn't desire this lifestyle? Instead, make the army a place where people will have more opportunities. If you want religious people to join, then you must cater to their goals and lifestyle... with the highest standards in modesty, *kosherus*... giving them *shabbatons*, *shiurim* and the best *Torah* education and speakers. Obviously, the secular people pushing such agendas don't need a bunch of *yeshivah bachurim* in the army but only wish to disturb the *charedi* lifestyle that they are opposed to. An army motivated by political ideals that may jeopardize the life of their soldiers is totally against *halacha*. How many times because of political reasons has the enemy of Israel been given priority over the safety of Israeli soldiers and civilians? I don't wish to speak more on this subject but no matter your opinion, we need to respect one another.

Rabbi Elchanan Wasserman writes, "If he engages in secular studies to learn an occupation and gain a livelihood, there is no prohibition, for the learning of a trade is a *mitzvah*... But if one sees that his son yearns for *Torah*, and is gifted enough to become a *Torah* leader, in regard to such a son, R. Nehorai said: 'I will neglect every occupation in the world and teach my son only *Torah*,' although R. Nehorai did not dispute the obligation to teach one's son a trade.

"But if one's profession does not require this study and he only wants to amuse himself with it, this might be forbidden because it wastes

52

time that should be devoted to *Torah* study... Aside from this, perhaps he should not study them regularly, lest they become as important to him as the *Torah*... For indeed, all science is necessary to maintain the world, but it is not the goal, only the means thereto... and one who makes secular studies his steady occupation seems to indicate that they are an end in themselves, which is contrary to the *Torah*." (*Kovetz Shi'urim* II 47)

How many people have we seen lost in secular knowledge and hobbies? It is good and heathy to have outside interests, it's just that they have to be secondary to one's love of *Torah*. When you embark on completing *Shas*, you will see that nothing else really interests you but *Torah*. Still, it is a must that you are still able to function as a normal member of society.

Most scholars should be able to pay their own bills and have enough *sechel* to get a job before their funds are depleted and they are in huge dept. Unfortunately, too many scholars and even *rabbanim* are scarce for the basic necessities of their families. Their deficit can be so deep that we as a nation are responsible to rescue them. I'm sure you know of a few scholars that do everything *lishmah*. Do you ever ask them if they need anything? Because you really should!

Rabbi Yaakov Emden declared:

"Even the angels who descended from on high conformed to the customs of the places they visited. Therefore, while you are still among men, do not attempt to be an angel, to survive without paying attention to your body; rather, eat and drink that which benefits you (for your good, for your benefit and for your true advantage) and face ever upwards, sow and build, buy and sell, do whatever you have the opportunity for, and follow the way of the world in everything." (*Migdal 'Oz, Bais HaMidos, Aliyah Derech Eretz* 8)

The Maharal writes: "Just as one should reject absolutely that which is improper according to the *Torah*, so too is it improper to reject that which is not rejected by the *Torah*. The fool thinks that by adding such restrictions he strengthens the *Torah*, but, in fact, this is... only vitiation of the *Torah*." (Maharal, *Be-eir HaGolah* II *s.v. amnam ma'aseh ov.*)

My point in bringing this up is that people reach a point of being so devoted to their studies that they lose sight of basic *derech eretz*. This can be to such an extent that their health suffers, which then has a significant impact on their ability to study *Torah*. The *Talmud* suggests, don't wait until the last minute to take care of your financial and other needs because if you do, you will end up having to leave *Torah* completely till you get back on your feet. (See *Brachos* 35b, Rashi; see *Avos* 2:2)

The Meiri explains, "It is better to devote a small part of the year almost exclusively to one's livelihood and thereby be free to study *Torah* undisturbed the rest of the year than to spread the workload over the entire year and thus be burdened constantly with the concerns of livelihood." (ibid. Meiri) This means, when opportunity strikes, take it and then put away funds so that you can learn for the rest of the year.

So, my friends, exercise, eat a healthy diet, don't sit behind your *Gemarah* while everything is collapsing for your family. Learn *Torah* with a strong mind and heart, with confidence, *shalom bayis* and with balance.

"Being dependent upon others is not only embarrassing but leads to self-esteem problems. A person should rather accept employment at work that is strange to him, rather than be dependent on people." (*Bava Basra* 110a) Remember, your studying Torah should be a *kiddush* Hashem to everyone around you.

## Materialism

The Chofetz Chaim said, "When someone tells me he is making a living, 'but it wouldn't hurt if things were a little better,' I ask, 'How do you know it wouldn't?'"

Most people that I find who run after money, making work their primary goal, seem to be unhappy in life. "He who has one hundred desires two hundred." (*Koheles Rabbasi* 1:34)

Rabbi Eliyahu Dessler stated, "The feeling of ownership of material possessions is based on an illusion. In reality a person does not have a direct connection with whatever is outside him. Only what you have acquired spiritually is truly yours. Hence, your main focus in life should be on acquiring positive inner traits. A person who seeks only to increase his external possessions is lacking internal possessions, which are what really counts." (*Michtav M'Eliyahu* vol. 3, p. 291)

When you have your own business, once you secure a client, you don't take the rest of the day off, rather, you simply move on to the next one. Work seems unending even though it doesn't have to be that way. The Chofetz Chaim remarked, "People say, 'time is money,' but I say, 'money is time,' for every luxury cost so many precious hours of one's life."

But people don't view it this way. They think they have to save up money for not only a rainy day but their children's and then grandchildren's rainy days. No wonder they are not happy, they are constantly thinking about rainy days when most days are filled with sunshine.

I was once complaining to Rabbi Mann, of Tzfat, about how I

54

couldn't go out on my *kiruv* video adventures because of so many rainy winter days. The Rav turned to me and said, "go mark off the calendar and you will see that there are very few days that it actually rains."

This is what happens to us. We have a few bad days which we drag out in our minds to be longer than they need to be. We do this every day, one sad thing that happens to us, we suffer from it the entire day when it only has to last a moment and then we could move on.

We feel we have to succeed in our materialistic desires, or we get downtrodden. "Those who chase happiness through the pursuit of materialistic pleasures, are actually running away from contentment." (*Divrei Chassidim*)

Man enters this world with closed hands, as if to say, "The world is mine." He leaves with open hands, as if to say, "I take nothing with me." (*Koheles Rabbasi* 1:34)

We can learn an important lesson from Rabbi Eliezer ben Charsom as to focus on what is important and not to get caught too much in business. "Rabbi Eliezer inherited from his father a thousand ships and a thousand towns, but he never went to see them for he did not want to waste a second from *Torah* study." (*Yoma* 35b) It's not that Rabbi Eliezer waisted away the blessing, it was that he hired people to maintain his businesses. Beyond that, why should he waist his precious mind and energy pursuing things of this world. He never visited any of these towns or ships, rather he would take a flask of flower on his shoulder and go from *bais midrash* to *bais midrash* to study *Torah*. The Maharsha explains, Rabbi Eliezer took the flour on his shoulders to fulfill the words of the sages, "If there is no flour, there is no *Torah*." Therefore, even if you have all your needs to study *Torah* full-time, it might be wise even symbolically to do a little something as a *tikkun* for Adam HaRishon. (Since we were punished for his sin by having to work). This way, you can make sure that you are never completely idle with your time, have a part-time job that is unpressured. However, blessed be He who watches his time and is blessed to use every moment for *Torah* and *chesed*.

Through the study of the *Torah*, materialistic desires dwindle. Rabbi Yaakov Abuchatzeira taught, "*Torah* study makes him happy, and even if there were no punishment for those who neglect its study, he would not quit it because of his great love of Hashem. All the money in the world is as unimportant to him as a piece of broken pottery compared to the study of the *Torah*. (*Alef Binah* 28)

In Israel, we don't have as many materialistic competitions with our friends and neighbors as in other parts of the world. A scholar who lives simply is more praiseworthy for living humbly. In fact, when I purchase a materialistic need that my neighbor may not have, I might even feel embarrassed by it. I also feel as if I now have more responsibility thereby, which I have to guard and worry about. Israel seems to naturally teach this important lesson, "less is more."

# Work with Emunah

"Being that man's sustenance is set in Heaven and is as miraculous as the splitting of the Red Sea why did Hashem burden him with the yoke of working (*hishtadlus*) to make a living? The answer is, man is commanded to sweat for his daily bread only as a test to see whether he will see through the veil of natural law (*teva*) and perceive Divine *hashgacha*. Thus, the typical man is placed in a position which he is asked to realize that the true source of his sustenance is Heaven, even though it may seem that his level of financial success is attributable to the work he puts into it." (*Michtav M'Eliyahu* I)

I think this point is not made often enough by the *rabbis*. Often the idea of *emunah* is brushed upon but it doesn't go deeper. We are told to have more *emunah* and trust in Hashem and everything will be okay, but along with *emunah* must come other aspects. Your *emunah* can't grow if you don't also work to increase other *midos* like fear of Heaven, love of Hashem and purity.

Frequently the *rabbis* of Yavneh would say "I am a creature and my fellow-human being is a creature: my work is in the village and his labor in the field; I awaken early to do my work and he to his. As he does not deem his occupation superior to mine, so I do not consider my occupation superior to his. You might say that I accomplish a lot, and he accomplishes a little, but we are taught: 'It matters not whether a lot or a little, if only one directs his heart to Heaven.'" (*Berachos* 17a)

Often you will see people laboring profusely at their job until it exhausts them. They have convinced themselves that it is truly their labor that is the only factor in their success. Meanwhile, years go by and their family suffers from a lack of attention. They know that Hashem has to bless their work in order that they are successful but this *emunah* is only on the surface. Slowly the *Torah* and family has become secondary to their work.

The real test of Adam HaRishon is connecting one's labor to the hand of Hashem. Rabbi Tzvi Elimelech of Dinov said, "Pray every day for your livelihood... so that you will have faith that all your food and other needs come to you from Divine providence and not ultimately from the work you do." (*Hanhagos Adam*, #30)

"Nor bread to the wise." (*Koheles* 9:11)

A young man, who considered himself brilliant and an example of perfection, came to the Kotzker complaining that he was having difficulty earning a living.

"Do you know the meaning of this verse in *Koheles*?" asked the Rebbe.

"It simply means that Hashem says to those who think so highly of themselves: If you think you're so smart, go find a livelihood yourself." (*…And Nothing but the Truth*, p. 66)

Rabbi Avraham of Slonim has some great advice on how to train oneself to appreciate Hashem's providence. "Whenever you see and recognize the workings of Hashem's providence in your life, stop and give praise and thanks to Him, blessed be He, who has bestowed on you, as a gift, this precious vision." (*Toras Avos*, p. 154)

## *The Torah will Sustain Me*

Rabbi Yehudah said in the name of Shmuel: "What is the meaning of, 'And make men as the fish of the sea?' It is to tell you that just as fish die as soon as they ascend to the land, so do men who leave their source of life, which is the *Torah* and its commandments." (*Avodah Zarah* 3b)

"הלחם אשר נתן י-ה-ו-ה לכם לאכלה": "The bread that Hashem has given you to eat." (*Shemos* 16:15) This verse contains 22 letters of the "*Aleph Bais*" (the letters of which the *Torah* is composed of). This is a sign that if a man immerses himself in the *Torah*, he will have a livelihood without toil, just like the Israelites in the desert.

Rabbi Yaakov Abuchatzeira taught, "One must know that all income comes from Hashem, and that the extra toil that people invest in their livelihoods is for nothing." (*Petuchei Chotem – Beshalach*)

The *Talmud* says, "Him who undergoes privations of the sake of *Torah* study in this world, Hashem will satisfy in the World to Come." (*Sanhedrin* 100a)

There comes a certain point in a scholar's life where they simply cannot live without constant *Torah* study. They are willing to live below the standard of living and do whatever it takes to simply stay engrossed inside a *sefer* all day. When the scholar's wife shares this same holy energy, miracles are wrought in heaven so that the future or current *talmud chacham* can study. This doesn't mean that they don't have any hardships, it's just that there is nothing that physically can stand in the way of *Torah* study. Rabbi Yaakov Abuchatzeira taught, "The merit of one who learns *Torah* through difficulties is greater than that of one who learns it through comfort." (*Alef Binah* 97)

It is important that this is felt from both sides, both husband and wife, so that there will be blessing in his learning. If he pushes full-time study before she is ready, she will be depressed and there won't be the same blessing in the learning. You can't simply sit behind your *sefer* while someone else is suffering, even if it's just emotional suffering and things are really fine. Remember *derech eretz* has to be part of your learning, so if one's wife can't handle her husband learning, he will have to find a way to satisfy both worlds. He should not be angry, as this too is G-d's Will. There are many *tikkunim* that have to also be rectified with truthful business dealings and healthy relationships with others. Rabbi Yaakov Abuchatzeira taught, "One who grasps the trait of truthfulness is as if he fulfills the entire *Torah*." (*Ginzei Hamelech – Tikkun Hateshuvah*)

Rav Chiya used to pray, "Let the *Torah* be our steady occupation." (*Berachos* 16b) I personally believe that if someone earnestly craves *Torah* every moment, Hashem will look down upon him and take care of his material needs. There are some people who simply can't live without full-time *Torah* study. What is he supposed to do? For him, he literally feels ill spiritually and even physically if he doesn't study. He should daven with tears and beg Hashem to be blessed to study. Also, he should visit many *tzaddikim* and get *brachos* from them in order to be blessed to study *Torah*. May the Talmudic expression be upon him, צַדִּיק גּוֹזֵר וְהקב"ה מְקַיֵּם, The *tzaddik* (righteous person) decrees, and G-d fulfills." (*Mo'ed Katan* 16b)

The verse in *Proverbs* states, "If a man has a worry in his heart, he should bend it over and a good matter shall gladden it." (*Proverbs* 12:25) The Vilna Gaon explains that "good" refers to *Torah*, for anyone who accepts upon himself the yoke of *Torah* will have the burden of worry removed from himself, as it states in *Avos of Rabbi Natan*, "Anyone who places the words of the *Torah* on his heart shall have the fears of sword, hunger, and the like nullified from himself." It is quoted in the name of Hagaon Harav Nachum of Chernobyl that, "all worries are forbidden besides for worrying about worrying." Meaning if your worrying too often, this isn't healthy so stop worrying much and just live!

Rebbe Nachman and many other *tzaddikim* point out that the word *Gemarah* is an acronym for Gavriel, Michael, Rephael and Uriel, since learning *Gemarah* affords a very great protection from any troubles and especially spiritual hardship.

I, and many others, have felt this craving for *Torah*. For me, though, I spent years in *kiruv* and in study, there finally was a point of no return where I could no longer imagine myself not learning full-time. So, what did I do? I went to all my *rabbis* for their blessing in order to study. Each one insisted that I work half-day and study half-day, which is more of the *Chassidic* mindset. I told them that I agree with them completely but at this point, it's impossible for me not to devote myself completely to my studies, so I asked for their blessing and left. One by one, the *rabbis* surprisingly suggested I still work half-day. However, in my heart, I felt it was time to learn every moment and I just wanted a holy *tzaddik* to stand behind me completely. Finally, I came upon one of my *rabbis* who was a *masmid* and he told me, "go ahead but if you see that you have too much anxiety from this, then stop and work part-time." If I would have approached more *yeshivish rabbanim* instead, probably they would have agreed earlier for me to study full-time if my family approved. However, the *Chassidish* mindset in our generation is that one can serve Hashem through all things and it's important to have some steady work.

Honestly, at no point did I think I would leave my family to suffer from my actions. I made sure they were a part of the study and that I brought this positive energy into the home. Rabbi Mann, of Tzfat once told me, "Make sure to study *Torah* in the house in order to elevate your home and family." So many guys are always in the *shuls* while the wife spreads the *Torah* inside the home. Remember, the *Shechinah* also resides in the home. Even though there are less distractions in the *bais midrash*, it's good for one's family to physically see the father studying. Often, I have met scholars who don't even have a set time to study with their own children. They rely upon the schools to teach basic *halachos* when surprisingly, today they seem to forget to teach our children the most basic *halachos*. The *cheder* systems weren't created to obliviate the personal *Torah* connection between father and child. It was only there to enhance it and to allow those who didn't have a father to not to be without a *Torah* education. Someone in Lakewood once expressed to Rav Schenuer Kotler about how if he stays in *kollel* his children will be deprived of many things they would otherwise have. Rav Schenuer responded, "providing them with a father who is a *talmud chacham* is more important than any of those things. And you should think hard before depriving them of that."

As I grew up, my father Shlomo Zavel ben Yaakov zt"l, had a special plan for me. He wanted me to study *Torah* more than anything but as a teenager, I still enjoyed playing sports, hiking and the usual things that *frum* teenagers get into. In order to mold me into a *ben Torah*, every morning when I arose for school, my father purposely awoke beforehand and was studying *Torah*. Many times, he was listening to Rav Avigdor Miller on tape. I grew up with his Rav Miller's *shiurim*, maybe I heard thousands of hours of his *shiurim*. When I would return from school in the afternoon, my father was learning *Tanach* or *Mishniyos*. He would actually repeat each passage three or four times as he learned each *pasuk*. Until the late evening hours, he was always in his studies making sure I saw him learning at all times. Even though it might have taken years to impact me, slowly, it trained my mind that this is the path for the righteous. If work came his way, he did this too. However, he did find himself jobless most of my life, but it was a blessing in disguise as he turned himself into a sweet *talmud chacham*. Kind acts were also his forte. If anyone, Jew or non-Jew needed a favor, he was there making a *kiddush* Hashem.

After seeing me excel in photography, having art-shows at multiple galleries, on his deathbed, my father turned to me and said, "I taught you a *parnasa* as the *Torah* requires and you are a good photographer already and it's enough. You don't have to keep getting better and better, it's now time for you to learn *Torah*. *Torah* comes first." I was actually upset at the time as I loved my photography adventures and my father's blessings were known to always be fulfilled. This was one of our last conversations but surely, after completing my large, one-man gallery show, I threw in the towel. I just couldn't do it anymore, his blessing came true and it was enough business like he had said, I didn't have to become a famous photographer anymore. Work is there just to earn your needs and help you to spend most of your time in *Torah*. So, I studied *Torah* and everything else became secondary. The Lubavitch Rebbe says that if you have a talent, you should use it to serve Hashem. This talent is still secondary to learning *Torah* and if you do utilize your talent, find a way to help people with it. Using my artistic skillset, I created the ilovetorah *kiruv* network creating *Torah* videos in his memory and till this day, twenty some odd years later, I continue to honor my father's wishes with *Torah* study being the primary concern.

I am happy to serve Hashem in all ways. So, if someone contacts me for a *soferus* job to buy *tefillin* or *mezuzos*, I try to complete the order. If a blessing arrives, why not pursue it quickly and then return to your study. Work helps a person not to be idle with their time and to appreciate the time they do have to study.

The *Mishnah* teaches, "Be daring as a leopard, light as an eagle, quick as a deer and strong as a lion to do the Will of your Father in Heaven." (*Pirkei Avos* 5:23)

The holy way of the holy Rabbi Dovid of Amshinov was to always walk quickly as if almost running... for he was always either running to do a *mitzvah* or running away from a transgression. (*Siah Sarfei Kodesh*, II, p. 121, #467)

The *Midrash* states, "All of the deeds of the righteous are done quickly." (*Bamidbar Rabbah* 10:7) Rabbi Luzzatto teaches, "The man whose soul yearns to perform the Will of his Creator will not be lazy in the performance of His *mitzvos*. His movements will be as the quick movements of a fire, and he will not rest or be still until the deed has been completed." (*Mesilas Yesharim* ch.6)

## *The Journey Continues*

Let me tell you a bit more on how I arrived at this point. People used to have a lot more pride in their work. Therefore, they felt some satisfaction in what they did, even if it wasn't the most pleasurable job. Today, it's fairly common that most people dislike what they do and thereby perform their work half-heartedly. It has become no more than an act to bring in an income.

Work should actually be fulfilling. A person should have a job in a field that they enjoy. One can't be expected to work well if they don't enjoy what they are doing. If you're ever going to start a business or find a new job, it is better to be paid less and do what you enjoy then to suffer in a field that brings you no satisfaction.

Throughout my teen years, we had to take aptitude tests in school to determine what area of work would suit us best. I never needed to take these tests because even at a young age, I knew what I enjoyed and what I wanted to do. When I was fourteen years old, I took a course in journalism and writing. I told my friends that I am going to write books one day and sure enough, here we are.

Years ago, I had a profitable business which I then sold because it didn't give me any enjoyment. The idea of enjoying what you do, probably seems foreign to many people. You just work because you have too. Life is so precious that it's a shame to waist it away in a bad job that doesn't make you feel fulfilled. Often people write me for a blessing as they just lost their job, or they tell me that their job is in jeopardy. I confirm that I will pray for them but inside I feel so happy, thinking, Hashem probably has a wonderful new job in store for them. I have seen it happen often. This is usually a blessing in disguise.

It is important to make your work secondary and your *Torah* life primary. This doesn't necessarily mean that your day has to have a lot more hours of *Torah* study than work, even though that would be quite beneficial. It means that your primary focus in life is *Torah* and that work is there just to fulfil your family's basic needs or to support others. However, there is no reason why your work can't be fulfilling or that it should drain the life out of you. I pray you find the right work and co-workers to share your time with. That you see Hashem in all matters and that you serve Him, wholeheartedly. *Amen.*

Each person must have a set time both day and night when they will study *Torah*. Many people that who work full-time believe that they don't have more than twenty minutes a day to study. I remember saying something like this once, when my work took over my life. This thought is mere foolishness and it shows that *Torah* is not your primary focus. Somehow, you're just not comfortable learning in your current environment and situation. If you can't study for 1-2 hours a day, then you need to refocus your lifestyle, maybe even change jobs or relocate to a less expensive neighborhood, as there is always time for *Torah*. After-all, you were primarily created for this purpose.

I found that when I was working eighty hours a week on my own business as an entrepreneur, monitoring thousands of clients, it became increasingly difficult to study. There are both good and unhealthy habits that come along with owning your own business. Some people dream their entire life about owning their own business and when the dream comes to fruition, they realize that entrepreneurship is a twenty-four-hour job. You might be doing what you enjoy but it can take over your entire existence.

When you own your own business, you are constantly thinking about its upkeep and there is always more work that you can do. This isn't the Will of G-d, to work endlessly. Therefore, set hours and learn how to separate your work from family and study. Hashem wants us to have balance in our life. Working for another person, while doing what you enjoy, does have its benefits because at the end of the day you can leave it behind you and every day have quality time without concerns. Even with the worst job, the day still ends, and you can put its troubles behind you. When you work for yourself, it seems like the day never really ends. It will take a lot of self-discipline and training to separate work from home. Certainly, it can be done but it takes a lot of will power and self-discipline.

This is what makes *Shabbos* observance so special. When *Shabbos* comes, everything has to stop. Even if you don't have great discipline, as a religious Jew, you simply can't work on *Shabbos*, no matter what and this saves the entrepreneur from going mad. I honestly don't know how a nonobservant Jew survives without keeping *Shabbos*.

A person who works all week long, can accomplish in one day what others in *yeshivah* struggle to attain all week. That same energy you used to work and provide for your family can now be channeled into complete devotion to Hashem. When you appreciate your time, a lot more can happen with it.

If you were to add up all the vacation times and breaks that *yeshivah* students take and give 100% effort to your *Shabbos* alone, even though you work full-time, you could accomplish nearly the same as them in learning. Just think about it. If you were to study *Torah* 12 hours every *Shabbos* and just 2 hours each weekday, that's 24 hours of *Torah* study. Now just think if you make *Torah* your main focus during the week and studied 4 hours a day, plus *Shabbos*. That totals 36 hours of *Torah* study each week, equivalent to full-time *Torah* study. This is while maintaining a full-time job. Since you're not taking *bain hazmanim* off from *Torah* study and learning all *Shabbos*, you have now exceeded expectations, especially since you have trained yourself to be disciplined in your time. Since every moment is precious, you will work hard during the hours you devote towards learning. Therefore, you can become a *masmid* even if have no choice but to work a full day.

Let's be serious here. Not to hurt anyone's feelings, but many people in *yeshivah* slack off quite a bit. If you were to attack your *Torah* study with true devotion, not wasting anytime since your time is so precious, your study of 36 hours would outshine most anyone.

It might surprise you, but I am a huge fan of people working for a living. I think it gives them discipline. You can't know how to study *Torah* full-time if you don't learn basic work habits that only a job can teach you. There are rare individuals that become *masmidim* in *Torah*, who never worked but it's not usual to see. Most people in *kollel* never give 100 percent, not because they don't want too, it's because they don't know how too. Working a job before enrolling in *kollel* would be quite beneficial to many. Of course, this is just my opinion, and you're entitled to your own. One thing is for sure, we all have to stop making excuses, organize our time better and learn more *Torah*. Not only this, we have to make our *Torah* study more enjoyable and learn at our true level, not the level we pretend to be on.

For years I studied *Torah* most of the day, but it wasn't until after I owned a business and learned how to manage my time, that my *Torah* study really took off. Learning *Torah* always felt unpressured and was something relaxing to do. After doing business, I approached my study in the same way as my business; I set daily goals and had a winning attitude. I accomplished more when I worked and studied half-day than when I was previously learning *Torah* full-time, without work and discipline.

It is a very *Chassidish* prospective to both work and learn half-day as we mentioned previously. In the more *yeshivish* world, full-time *Torah* study is preferred. Speaking with a father of many married boys, he told me that all his sons are *baruch* Hashem, religious. Most are learning full-time in *kollel* but the one that works every day is the best *Torah* scholar of them all. He has completed the most *sefarim* and can run circles around his brothers in *Torah* wisdom.

If you start to utilize your free time better, making *Shabbos* a day for total self-sacrifice in *Torah* study, allotting a couple hours each day for *Torah*, no matter what, then you will start to appreciate the value of learning. Your *Torah* study will be so strong that G-d Himself will desire to hear more of it. Slowly you will have to work less and less in order to make a living. One day, you will not have to work at all because G-d will provide everything so that He can enjoy such a person's study. With the help of Hashem because you built up good habits, Hashem will help you to find a way to learn *Torah* 8-12 hours a day because He enjoys the *Torah* study of those who learn *lishmah*.

I don't know if a regular guy who never worked in his life will ever truly appreciate how blessed he is to be able to sit and study *Torah*. Young students who are in *yeshivah gedola* have it made; they can study free from all worries. Most of us will have to build ourselves to such a place through complete self-sacrifice in the ways I mentioned. However, those who toil for it, your *Torah* study will be far higher than those who are given the time to study freely, having all their needs fulfilled on a fully set table, never having really worked.

I know I have touched upon my own experiences quite a lot here, but I think Hashem wanted me to experience both sides of the coin in order to share my experiences. I originally worked as a freelancing web designer with off and on jobs, all the while studying *Torah* most of the day. Then I opened affiliate companies that prospered well, continuing to study *Torah* as well. Not enjoying working for others, I opened my own financial trading business that did prosper.

Suddenly I found myself working eighty hours a week and it was taking over my life as I mentioned earlier. Every time I tried to find good workers to take more off my shoulders, there was a constant flow of new work. My team of 15 offshore Indian telemarketers could not handle more than a simple customer support question. Any technical question, I had to respond to immediately. So, we opened an office in the USA as well as the Indian office in order to help. This office had workers round the clock, 24 hours a day, except for *Shabbos*. I had to take my work with me everywhere on a portable laptop, checking email and answering support tickets constantly.

It seemed more difficult than I realized to clone my business skills off to others. The goal of most successful businessmen is to make clones of themselves so that they can then expand their business into other fields. You're CEO is supposed to be a mirror image of you and handle all business as if it was you. In today's generation, when people want easy work without effort, this was nearly impossible to accomplish. Rather, there was just one of me and an endless amount of business to handle.

The Karlin-Stalin Rebbe once visited Tzfat and wanted me to take him around Friday in my car and to spend *Shabbos* with him in Jerusalem. Immersed in my workload, I explained that I had no choice but to be working Friday afternoon. It wasn't even by choice, the business required me, and nobody could replace that. If I wasn't around, the workload would be double or triple when I returned. It simply wasn't possible. The Rebbe was very disappointed and he attempted to explain to me what I already knew, this couldn't continue. I have since committed *bli neder*, never to put myself in that position again. Thankfully, in the years to come, as soon as midday arrived, I was so happy to move on to the *Shabbos* mindset and put my work on the shelf.

At some point, I just put my foot down and started making set times each day for study, even when the business was booming. However, my *Torah* learning suffered still, my study didn't seem as pure as I would have liked it to be because I would still think about the business during my studies. So, I made a commitment to study *Torah* on *Shabbos* full-time and this started to bring life back into me. There were days that I even skipped sleeping on *Shabbos*, just to secure the *Torah* study that my soul demanded. On the first day of *Succos*, I studied 18 hours, so desperately I wanted to make up for the *Torah* time lost from my time working that week. You have to understand, after six days of constant clients and maintaining computer servers, the financial money flow, multiple business websites and the like, I was bursting for the tranquility of a *blat* of *Gemarah*! Slowly, I started increasing my time learning *Torah* during the weekdays. Soon, I realized that I would rather not have money than to own a business that consumes me and most of my time. I sold the business, just in order to save myself. My partner who

65

was also in the same boat, was so happy when I told him I had found a buyer. Even though he wasn't religious, he knew that both of our priorities had changed and that neither of us loved money enough to sacrifice peace of mind and family.

A few months after the business was sold, the new owner called me and asked me if I could to come work for them. My value in the business was irreplaceable. I stuck to my ego and they agreed upon my requested salary with commissions, which was the same as I had made when I owned the business. I agreed upon one final condition. I would only work thirty hours a week and that at 4:00 PM every day, I would close my work to study *Torah* the rest of the day. They happily agreed.

This was like a dream come true. To perform the same workload but to be completely organized with my mind and heart. Sure enough, the next thing I knew it, I was studying *Torah* stronger than ever before, surpassing the times when I was studying so called, "full-time" in the *kollel yeshivah* environment, years prior. *Shabbos* didn't change, I still put in those huge hours of study, yet now I could work full-time and still put in 40-60 hours of *Torah* study each week. It was amazing, and I soon completed the entire *Talmud*.

I don't know if I ever could have accomplished this had I not worked in business previously. I had learned time-management and knew how to complete any task or goal that needed to be finished. After a year or so, maybe because Hashem desired me to study *Torah*, the business moved in a different direction and I found myself studying *Torah* full-time. However, this time around it was different. My approach to *Torah* learning was fierce; I appreciated every minute of it and how blessed I was.

So, when someone tells me that they don't have time to study, I snicker. I managed my own company with a dozen employees and stilled studied. Maybe not at first but I figured it out. There is always time available to learn *Torah*; The question is whether you know how to manage your time and if you want it bad enough.

If you see that your *Torah* is secondary, you have to question if you should continue what you're doing because at the end of your life, *Torah* is the only thing that your taking with you. All the money your accumulating from your job, where does it really go? Do you feel you need to live more materialistically and own more possessions thereby? Do you still hold onto what is truly important in life? Spending time with your family and performing the Will of G-d. Hillel condemns the poor (who plead poverty as an excuse for not studying *Torah*). (*Yoma* 35b) Some of the greatest scholars studied *Torah* barely having a tenth of what we complain about today. We need to straighten out our priorities.

Rabbi Yochanan explains that only people like R. Shimon bar Yochai and his companions are excused from interrupting their *Torah* study for prayers, since, "Their *Torah* was their steady occupation; but people such as we, do have to interrupt their studies for prayer." (*Shabbos* 11a)

I hope you reach the level of Rabbi Shimon one day but until then, you have to build yourself up slowly. The sages have warned people not to completely overlook working. There is a time and place for full-time study. Make sure you are really there and if not, fix yourself or find work.

The Rosh comments: "Every scholar whose *Torah* study is his steady occupation… makes his *Torah* fixed and his work transitory, thinks about *Torah* constantly and does not forgo it for unimportant things, only for earning his livelihood, which is his duty – for 'combining *Torah* study with *derech eretz* is beautiful and any Torah not associated with work will fail and lead to transgression'"… (*Responsa Rosh*, 15:8, as quoted by *Tur Yoreh De'ah* 243)

The Rambam, cited by the Tur and Rema, writes: "Anyone who intends to occupy himself with *Torah*, not to do work, and to subsist on charity, has profaned G-d's name, disgraced the *Torah*, extinguished the light of the law, brought evil upon himself, and taken his life from the world; for it is forbidden to benefit personally from the *Torah* in this world." (*MT Talmud Torah* 3:10; *SA Yoreh De'ah* 246:21) He also notes this in his commentary on the *Mishnah*, "And [the Talmudic sages] did not permit themselves to seek money from others, for they saw that it would be perceived as a profanation of G-d's name. The masses would deem *Torah* study just another occupation, and it would thus become contemptible in their eyes. Whoever took money would, therefore, be guilty of 'treating the word of G-d contemptuously.'" (Rambam on *Avos* 4:5)

I have friends who are learning full-time who complain to me about how much financial debt they are in. Their wife flips between working full-time and being a mother. The children are sometimes even neglected. Slowly their *shalom bayis* is faltering and nothing is changing. I suggest different vocational jobs they can do to fix this. However, having lived a sheltered lifestyle in *yeshivah* for years and years, they seem no longer capable of taking care of their problems. Their learning didn't teach them *derech eretz* and it's hard to teach it now. The real solution should have come during the early years of *yeshivah*, encouraging or maybe even offering some vocational training in *yeshivah*.

Mesilas HaShas - **מסילת הש"ס**

*Bachurim* are brought up many times with an unrealistic mindset that they will simply live off a *kollel* salary and support their family. They also have unrealistic ideals as too what a *frum* marriage is all about. A reality check was in order years ago, but it's never too late. Either they will learn this on their own or their struggles will teach them it the hard way, *chas-v-shalom*.

R. Menachem Mendel Kargau writes: "If a person chooses the effortless way of providing for himself and his household [by not working], his *Torah* will have no permanence... (*Responsa Giduley Taharah* 7)

Eliyahu of blessed memory used to say: "Heaven and earth testify that to a scholar who studies the *Torah* for the sake of Hashem, and who supports himself, the verse applies: "When you eat of the labor of your hands, happy will you be, and it shall be well with you." (*Seder Eliyahu Zutta* 15:197)

Another bad habit is living off of credit. The greatest thing I ever did for myself and my family was to completely desist using credit cards. It is a pit that a person can never climb out of. The only solution is to completely, one hundred percent STOP and never use one again. Whenever I tell someone this, they respond, "What about building my credit?" These same people and some of them are *rabbis,* live completely off credit and preach about having more *emunah.* Well I have a reality check for you, using credit isn't *emunah.* It is a bad habit and it can destroy your life. You have to reprogram yourself. *Chazal* teach us that the heart craves only what the mind sees. Don't window shop unnecessarily. Only buy what you can afford at the time and the items you truly require. Don't make payments on the items you buy but have patience and purchase them in the right time. If you don't have money, it's a sign from Hashem to make some change and to increase your prayers.

## *Work of the Sages*

A craftsman fulfills the *mitzvah* of loving one's fellow if he has in mind that he is making his product for the benefit of the person who will use it, and not merely as a source of income. (*Imrei Daas*, pp. 49-50)

"And Chanoch walked with Hashem." (*Bereshis* 5:24)

The *Midrash* relates that Chanoch was a shoemaker whose mind was absorbed with elevated thoughts as he stitched shoes. Rabbi Yisrael Salanter clarified that those elevated thoughts were not of a mystical nature. Rather, Chanoch took scrupulous care that each stich be perfect so as not to fraud his customers. Moreover, he tried to make each shoe as comfortable as possible in order to give his customers pleasure. His foremost motivation was to help others rather than merely to sell shoes for a living. (*Michtav M'Eliyahu*, vol. 1, pp. 34-35)

Sloppy workmanship constitutes cheating the customer. The *Torah* requires you to produce as perfect a product as you are able. Moreover, no matter how mundane one's vocation may be, it can be elevated by keeping in mind that one is helping others (ibid.)

The *tzaddikim* even though they might have had a profession, they viewed it as a way to do kindness to others and to the world. They worked diligently and understood that every action in the world can be used to draw nearer to Hashem.

"Whether he is standing in his shop or in the marketplace, every businessman should have a book in his pocket – such as a *Chumash*, *Tanya*, *Mishnayos* or *Tehillim* – so that whenever he has a free moment he can read a verse of *Chumash*, or a few lines of *Tanya*, or a *Mishnah*, or a passage of *Tehillim*." (*Likkutei Dibburim*, p. 158)

I think a lot of *tzaddikim* enjoyed being small business owners, that way, they could take breaks between clients and work in order to study more. "When Rabbi Shimon of Zloshin and Rabbi Meir of Zhorik were at work, in the free moments between sales, they both stood at their booths reciting *Psalms*." (*Sneh Boar b'Kotzk*, p. 247)

"Rabbi Moshe Leib was known throughout the city for his piety... He would sit in his store studying *Torah*." (*Ha-Gaon ha-Kadosh Baal Yismach Moshe, p. 353*)

Here are some examples of jobs held by the *tzaddikim*:

Aba Chilkiah hired himself out for the purpose of hoeing fields. (*Tannis* 32a)

Rabbi Abbin was a carpenter by trade. (*Shabbos* 23b)

Rabbi Ada was a surveyor of land. (*Bava Metzia* 107b)

Rabbi Papa manufactured '*sheichar*' (mixed wine; beer of dates or barely, or a concoction of both). (*Pesachim* 113b)

Aba Umna was a bleeder by trade. (Bloodletting for medical purposes.) (*Tannis* 21a)

Rabbi Oshiya mended (sewed) Shoes. (*Pesachim* 113b)

Chanan was a tailor (cloth-mender). (*Avodah Zara* 39a)

Bar Amorai was a fisherman who searched for coral-wood and pearls. (*Rosh HaShanah* 23a)

Daniel was a tailor (cloth-mender). (*Vayikra Rabbah* 32)

Hillel the elder chopped wood for sale. (*Yoma* 35a)

Rabbi Chanina mended (sewed) shoes. (*Pesachim* 113b)

Rabbi Chisda manufactured '*sheichar*' (mixed wine; beer of dates or barely, or a concoction of both). (*Pesachim* 113b)

Shammai was a builder (mason). (*Shabbos* 31a)

Shimon Ha'Pakuli was a cotton dealer. (*Megillah* 17b)

Shimon twisted threads into yarn for the purpose of weaving. (*D'mai* 4:1)

Rabbi Sheishes carried beams. (*Gittin* 67b)

Rabbi Yehudah was a tailor (cloth-mender). (*Bava Basra* 164b)

Rabbi Yehudah was a baker of bread. (*Bava Basra* 132b)

Rabbi Yehoshua was a blacksmith. (*Berachos* 28a)

Rabbi Yochanan HaSandler was a shoemaker. (*Avos* 4)

Rabbi Yochanan was an engraver. (*Pesachim* 3a)

Rabbi Yose manufactured nets for hunting and fishing. (*Y. Berachos* 4)

Yose b. Chalafta dressed (worked-out) hides. (*Shabbos* 49b)

Rabbi Yosef worked the millstone at the mill. (*Gittin* 67b)

Rabbi Yitzchok was a blacksmith. (*Chullin* 100a)

Levi manufactured nets for hunting and fishing. (*Yoma* 85a)

Rabbi Meir was a scribe (copyist, clerk). (*Eruvin* 13a)

Rabbi Nechunia dug pits for hire. (*Shekalim* 5)

Rabbi Akiva carried bundles. (*Avos de R' Noson* 6)

Aba bar Zemina was a tailor (cloth mender). (*Y. Sanhedrin* 3)

Aba Hoshea of Turya was a washer (of cloths and other fabrics). (*Y. Bava Kamma* 10)

## To Conclude

There is nothing more beautiful than the study of *Torah*. The fulfilment of learning *Torah* heaps wonderous benefits in this world and the next. Make sure that your lifestyle is one of self-growth and *derech eretz*. Don't ignore the world if the world needs you.

If your family requires your assistance more, you will get this time back from Hashem in other ways. We are here to serve Hashem and do His Will. His Will is not for every man to remain in the *bais midrash* even though that should be the ultimate goal of every man as it says, "There is no wealth greater than the wealth of *Torah*." (*Alef Binah* 67)

Don't hide from your problems behind your *Gemarah*. Rather elevate your life according to the holy sages and follow their ways with a true understanding of your own level. There is nothing selfish about the

70

*Torah. Torah* study was created in order to teach a man how to be holy and be kind to others. Make your *Torah* about *derech eretz* and it will reap far more benefits then closing yourself in your own world. The idea of *tikkun*, which is one of the main accomplishments of *Torah* study, requires a scholar to see outside his *daled amos*.

Rabbi Meir Yechiel of Ostrovtze lead his community of *baalei batim* emphasizing study *Torah* in their daily schedule. The love of the *Torah* was felt by everyone in the town. This was so much so that even among the wealthiest businessmen, owners of vast riches, were always in attendance in the *beis midrash*. There they sat each day, from four until ten in the morning, only interrupting their study for prayers. Business was limited from ten in the morning until four in the afternoon, and they prospered greatly in both learning and work. As soon as four in the afternoon arrived, they concluded their business activities without exception. You would have thought that they would return home at this time but instead they headed directly to the *bais midrash* to learn once again. There they sat until ten at night. Then finally they would return to their homes. It wasn't just this town alone that acted with such fear of Heaven and devotion to learning. Before the war, it was common in many towns to treat *Torah* study with such profound respect and to make work only secondary to *Torah*.

In the days of Yermiyahu people were complaining they didn't have time to study *Torah* as they were too busy with a livelihood. So, Yermiyahu instructed them to go into the *ahron* and he showed them the *mana* that Aharon Hakohein was told to hide there... Then he said, "see this mana, that should remind you that *parnasa* only comes from Hashem."

71

# Ratzon Hashem

How do we ascertain what is the *Ratzon* Hashem, the Will of G-d. In other words, how do we know what G-d wants us to do? Obviously, we have both the written and oral *Torah* to guide us as our basis. We also have the 613 commandments to direct us as well as the rabbinic laws. However, even with all of this, we still struggle daily trying to figure out how to best serve G-d.

Performing the *mitzvos l'shem Shamayim*, for the sake of Heaven is vital, but how to you come to the lofty place of *l'shem Shamayim*? Is the goal of serving Hashem, total and complete self-sacrifice?

It may appear that the only people doing the complete *Ratzon* Hashem are the sages of the generation. The rest of us seem to just fill up space, baring little potential for excellence. This bares, the question, what is the capability of the *benoni*, the average Jew?

Most of us do not have as our personal goal the idea of becoming a *tzaddik* or *talmud chacham*. We don't remotely believe that this is within our spiritual reach. Why though? Who has taught us that we lack the potential of stardom?

This book seeks to remove all the obstacles that keep us from reaching our true potential. We do not look at those with disabilities as having less ability than others. In fact, we seek to remove the pre-conceived notions that people with physical or emotional problems have less potential when in fact, they are born with more loftier souls.

We seek to reset one's perspective in *avodas* Hashem, making the true goal of service to be the performance of the *mitzvos l'shem Shamayim*. It says in the *Talmud*, "There is one who acquires his place in *ohlom habah* only through years of spiritual striving or suffering and there is another who acquires his *ohlom habah* in an instance." (*Avodah Zara* 17a) If this is the case, then our entire Jewish education has been distorted. We have put too much emphasis on what makes a person considered in our society as a "holy and devout person", being only those that fit into the regular mold of *tzaddikim*. Yet, we overlook the holiness of complete simplicity in the service of Hashem, and how this too could reach the same platform of success or even higher than the preconceived notion of what a *tzaddik* is.

The *ba'al teshuvah* builds his own life from the inside-out and writes his own script. His experience of life is much deeper and his commitment to Torah much more real. (*Likutei Sichos* volume 9, end of pg. 63) As the *Talmud* says, "A *ba'al teshuvah* can reach even a higher level than someone *frum* from birth. Thus they 'sit in a place that the perfect *tzaddikim* cannot reach'". (*Brachos* 34b) "The *ba'al teshuvah*, having experienced distance, is now driven towards the divine with a force the perfectly righteous could never attain." (*Zohar* 129b)

If you look at any king or man of high stature. Surprisingly, around him are the simpler folk. He is not interested in those that also think they have arrived at this place due to their stature or great wisdom. He simply wants his closest followers to be completely devoted and reliable; People who would immediately perform his will at any given time.

Even though the sages are appointed leaders from Heaven to guide us in life, we too are made from the same matter. As they have been created with the four elements, fire, water, air and earth, so too were we. We are all synonymous with the limbs of Adam Harishon, the first man. If one limb is faulty, the entire body suffers. There really isn't one person who is greater than another because we are all one entity. The Jewish people are in no way similar to other nations. If one Jew sins, we all feel it, we are all affected. Should a person perform *mitzvos* and study *Torah*, that too effects every single Jew in the world.

People look at the sages as lofty, unreachable *rabbis* that are beyond their scope. That they are far above the regular status of society. What they don't realize is the inherent humanness of the sages. How every pain and suffering we experience in our life, they had to go through the same thing in some way in order to arrive at the solid foundation of *avodas* Hashem that you see them with today.

There are very few *rabbis* that don't suffer themselves from physical or emotional disorders. In fact, it is these so-called obstacles that enabled them to persevere to the highest platform. Do you think it is normal for a human being to sit and study in a room for fourteen hours a day like many of the great rabbis? Many of them had Asperger's, ADD, OCD, diabetes and other illnesses. They overcame their own personal disabilities because they didn't conform to societies predetermined ideas that illness is debilitating. So instead, they took the good points out of their disorder and used it to exemplify the *mitzvos*. May the sages be healthy, live long and be protected from all harm, *amen*.

Do you think it's normal much of what we do as orthodox Jews? To the outside world, we all appear "ill". How much more so the great sages who exemplify the *mitzvos!* Not all *mitzvos* can be explained, that is part of their beauty. If the *mitzvos* were all logical, then free choice and faith would be missing. If you were to take any *Torah* scholar and have them evaluated by a psychiatrist, the results would be absurd. This is because a righteous person breathes differently. There have been doctors over the years that took the pulse of some *tzaddikim* and didn't understand how they were even alive. Emotionally, physically, a *Torah* scholar is a freak of nature, quite frankly.

R' Motele of Hornosteipel once acquired a hiccough that persisted for many days. Despite all efforts at using various home remedies to suppress it, it remained because he also suffered from heart disease, there was concern that his heart might not handle the additional stress. Accompanied by his *gabbai*, they went to consult a neurologist in Kiev. The neurologist stated that the only way to halt the hiccough was by delivering a shock to the spinal cord. This was accomplished by heating an iron poker to glowing and running it down the spinal column. Since the time of modern medicine had not yet arrived, they agreed to the awful treatment. R' Motele said, "Nu," and proceeded to remove his shirt.

The doctor ran the red-hot poker down his spine, but there seemed to be no reaction from R' Motele. He turned up the heat on the poker. When R' Motele did not utter a sound, nor flinch even a muscle, the doctor was perplexed. He once again reheated the poker and did a second application, this time applying a lot more pressure. When there was again no feedback, the doctor threw down the poker and shouted, "I can't believe this. He is some kind of angel rather than a human being. Why, a short while back I had a burly Cossack here for this treatment, and I no sooner removed the poker from the fire than he jumped out the window. Here I have scaled him twice and he does not even react at all!"

R' Motele did not quite understand the Russian doctor's words so he requested his *gabbai* to translate the doctor's comment. The *gabbai* simply stated, "He said that the *rebbe* is an angel," and went on to tell about the Cossack who jumped out the window before he was even touched.

R' Motele smiled and explained, "Sometimes a person comes to me with his *tzaros*, and I desperately want to help him, but there is nothing I can do. If I don't jump out the window from my anguish at that point, I certainly don't have to now." (My Book, *A Journey into Holiness* p. 169)

I once had to bring someone to an appointment to see a non-Jewish psychiatrist for their social security evaluation. I advised the person to just tell the doctor everything you do as an orthodox Jew. Not needing to exaggerate a single thing, the doctor wrote up his evaluation that the person was completely insane and needing the social security benefits.

I'm not against diagnosing people with illnesses, I think it's good to understand yourself and get help in how to deal with your challenges. Unfortunately, many people shy away from really trying to know and understand themselves. However, misdiagnosis is ramped and over medication is commonplace. Half the world is addicted to some drug or something. All of this is simply because people don't understand the *Ratzon* Hashem.

People don't have enough self-confidence. They don't know how to use their personal challenge, whether its physical or emotional to their advantage. That is what separates the sages from us. It isn't their great wisdom or so called born "superhero abilities". It is their ability to focus on their strengths and utilize them. Strengths which to others are disabilities.

Whatever is the most difficult thing for you to overcome in life, inside this, there lies your strength. If you unlock this, you open the treasured gates into your soul's holiness. Your true potential is revealed, and you too become a sage. You too acquire *Ohlom Habah* in a so-called "instant". This is the *Ratzon* Hashem. To find and perfect your own personal soul, which in turn completes all the other Jewish souls attached to you. However, I must warn you, when you try to perfect yourself, there will be trails and obstacles that you will face. You must persevere through them as if someone sent you on an important mission.

In order for us to help you, you must leave all negativity behind you. Maybe in the past, people told you that you couldn't succeed in anything your set out to do. This is no longer the case. We will reach into the crevasses of your heart and surge through those internal and external blockades that distance you from your true potential. The disabilities that once haunted you will now become your strengths. The sages whom you fear because they are so remote from your level are no longer unreachable. All the important *Torah* works which were only available to the greatest sages will soon belong to you. The *Tanach*, *Mishnah*, and the entire *Talmud* will soon be within your grasp.

The places where you seem to fail the most in life; business, friendships, marriage, parenthood, *Torah* study, prayer will soon be easily available to you like never before. As you connect yourself to the *Ratzon* Hashem, the Will of G-d, everything becomes within your reach. You're no longer on the scale of mankind and society, your potential reaches beyond such limitations. It doesn't matter if people judge you, love you, hate you, as long as you love yourself and give life your very best effort.

# Wisdom

Rabbi Yaakov Abuchatzeira taught, "From the very nature of the *Torah* and its holiness, even if one studies it without a teacher, it teaches itself, as it is written, 'The testimony of Hashem is trustworthy; it enlightens the simple.' (*Tehillim* 19:8) Even if a person is simple and ignorant, if he studies the *Torah*, it will teach him knowledge and wisdom. It will lead him on the proper path and proper behavior. This is one clarification of the verse, 'I have become educated from all my teachers.' (*Tehillim* 119:99), with 'my teachers' understood as the books one studies from, since by looking into books and studying each word carefully, reviewing them and analyzing them, one can learn one thing from another. Likewise, the meaning of 'for Your testimonies are a conversation to me' (ibid.) can be taken as meaning 'The Torah itself in all of its glory, appears to me, speaks to me and teaches me.' It is 'Your testimonies' themselves that speak to me and teach me." (*Alef Binah* 112)

The Kotzker Rebbe said, "A wise man is preferred over a prophet, for wisdom, too, is prophecy." Maybe years ago, wisdom was relative to how many books you completed and how much exposure you had to different societies. The wise were few and usually very wealthy, raised above societies norms. Today, things are different. There are wealthy people who never went to secondary school and who failed completely in the system of learning.

This proves that wisdom is very much connected to a person's *da'as* (understanding). You can be the wisest person in the world but if you don't know how to apply it properly, it does nothing for you. That is when *da'as* takes the lead. *Da'as* enables you to apply what you learned and use it.

In today's society, *da'as* is found in all types of places. The wise are obsolete, they have very little to do with society, as their wisdom has encouraged them to separate from others. The entire world has gone crazy, why would the wise want any part of it?

However, the *Torah* forces the wise to interact with society. It isn't enough for a sage to close his study door and come close to Hashem alone. If he does this, he is not a true sage, connected in his soul root to Moshe Rabbeinu. It says that in each generation, the sages are compared to and have a spark of Moshe. You cannot be blessed with this spark if you enclose it. Even a candle needs a little bit of air to continue its flame. The goal of every *tzaddik* is to light more flames and fill the world with light.

That is a true *tzaddik*.

As we have said before, the purpose of this book is to unlock the *tzaddik* and potential within each person. So therefore, the wisdom that you have learned, always meditate on how to apply it to your daily life. Robotic study of the *Torah* does little compared to study with the purpose of performance. Maybe in the non-Jewish world, knowledge is power but in the *Torah* world, performance of the *mitzvos* is power.

Rabbi Yisrael Salanter once said, "A person could complete the entire *Talmud* many times, but it doesn't mean his *midos* will improve." To improve your character traits, you have to work very hard on self-reflection, *hisbodidus* (meditation) and have the will to change for the better. *Torah* study is certainly a major part of this equation, but it isn't everything. You could be so involved in your study that you lash out with anger at your family or to anyone that interrupts you. You're a work in progress, don't ever think you're a finish product. The biggest mistake of the wise is thinking they have plateaued over everybody else. The goal of the wise should be to realize that they know absolutely nothing.

Rabbi Yaakov Abuchatzeira taught, "Through the *Talmud*, the *Torah* is elucidated clearly and thoroughly. This is since all of the laws of the *Torah* are explained in it properly and all of the *Mishnayos* and *braisos* are resolved. It might be that this is alluded to in the verse, 'And He established testimony among Yaakov and He placed *Torah* among *Yisrael*' (*Tehillim* 78:5), for '*eidus*', 'testimony', has the same *gematria* value as '*Talmud*' and through the *Talmud* the *Torah* is clarified and fixed for *Yisrael*. This is true given that without the *Talmud*, the *Torah* has no fixed existence. That is what is meant by 'and He established testimony among Yaakov' is He established the *Talmud* among Yaakov that 'He placed the *Torah* among Yisrael,' since it was through the *Talmud* that the *Torah* was established in Israel, with its sources and in all its authenticity.

"And this is what is meant by the verse, 'The testimony of Hashem is trustworthy; it enlightens the simple' (*Tehillim* 19:8). For through the testimonies, which is the *Talmud*, wisdom was given to the simple, for without the *Talmud*, everyone is a simpleton.

"It could also be that this is what was meant by our sages when they said, 'If you have acquired wisdom what are you missing, if you are missing wisdom what have you acquired?' (*Vayikra Rabbah* 1:5) Consequently, what is meant is, '[If you have acquired *Talmud*,] you have no lack in *Torah*,' but 'if you are missing wisdom' which is *Talmud*, 'what [*Torah*] have you acquired?' You cannot have acquired anything, for even if you know all of *Chumash* and *Mishnah*, the main thing is the *Talmud*."

(*Alef Binah* 11)

# Repentance

"All holidays mention that a *chatos* sin offering is brought but on *Shavuos* there is no mention of sin with this offering. This is because when a person excepts the *Torah* anew, deciding to dedicate their life to the study of *Torah*, the *Torah* itself brings atonement." (*Y. Rosh HaShanah* 20b)

A person could be an expert in knowing the *Torah's* wisdom when it comes to repentance while having little clue how to actually apply it. The Kotzker Rebbe says that a person could decide that they want to repent but they could still be heading in the wrong direction. He gives a *mashal* of a person who is sailing on a boat and he turns around completely, yet the boat is still heading the same direction. The same is true with half-hearted repentance he explains. Even though you say and accept that you want to change your path, you still continue on the same wrong path. This truly isn't repentance. Rather, it is like the repentance of a fool. He tricks himself into thinking he is doing something which he is not.

So, to truly repent, you have to physically change the direction that you're going. If the boat won't turn around, then get off of it and change boats. You might have to change your entire life around, just to properly repent. This requires a true commitment.

What is the *Ratzon* Hashem when it pertains to repentance? I think that even gradual change doesn't go unnoticed by Hashem. However, for some, only a major charge will do anything. Otherwise, they are like the person who continues to sail in the wrong direction. He just turns himself around, pretending to change, yet the boat still continues in the same direction as before.

There are people with forms of mental illness that make it more difficult to change their unhealthy habits. These people are not excused from sin, but it makes sense that its more difficult for them to repent. For them, what might be an easy repentance for another, becomes a huge mountain for them to overcome. Did Satan not know this when he convinced them into sinning in the first place? Of course, he did, so why roll over and allow him to have control over you?

So, what do you do when it feels almost impossible to change? Well, you might need counseling or a friend to lend you an ear. Maybe you need a big *tzaddik* to help you find your way out. It might take a tremendous amount of reciting the *Tehillim* and praying over and over. But still, you must understand that G-d would never have given you a test that you can't overcome. Call to Him and He will answer. If it doesn't work, pray profusely to Him and beg for His assistance. It might feel that your trapped but you're not, inside the problem bares the solution, if only you could look closer into the details of the issue.

"A man should know that it is his sins that have darkened the light of his soul so that the light of *Torah* and of wisdom do not illuminate it. As it is written, 'Your sins have made a screen of separation between you and your G-d.' (*Yeshiyahu* 59:2) So, you must repent in order to break the screen of the surrounding shells. The proof of this is what is said in the *tikkunim* [*Kabbalah*], that when a person is studying *halacha*, and he has questions and difficulties in understanding, he can remedy this by giving some *tzedaka* or performing some *mitzvah*, and immediately the truth will be revealed to him. Because the difficulties in comprehension are shells which darken the light of his intellect, and when he repents and gives *tzedaka* he breaks the shells." (*Totzaos Chaim*, p. 32)

Before prayer and *Torah* study, after having meditated on *teshuvah*, arouse your heart to fear of Hashem based on your love for Him because without such fear and love, the prayer or *Torah* will not ascend to Heaven. [It will not attain to a high and effective spiritual level]. The arousal should be done by means of meditating on Hashem's greatness and exaltedness [to increase your fear and awe], and on all the overflowing goodness that He bestows on us [in order to arouse the love in your heart] ... You should also continually pause during your *Torah* learning to meditate upon this. (Rabbi Tzvi Elimelech of Dinov, *Hanhagos Adam*, #10)

## Sleep

Years ago, a person's bedroom and bed were a safe haven for them. It was a place where problems were left behind, and one would calmly read a book to relax. In today's generation, our bedrooms are filled with technology. We wonder why we have insomnia, going from doctor to doctor. Some of us try sleep medication and others consume herbs. Instead of removing the technology from our bedrooms, we add more technology in order to enable us to sleep. We have to make our bedrooms a safe haven again! We have to love reading an enjoyable book, even when it's not *Shabbos*!

So, what does Hashem want from us by requiring us to sleep? If you think about it, when we eat, we are serving Hashem through reciting *brachos* and consuming food in order to have energy to serve Hashem. When we work or learn *Torah*, we are also doing the Will of Hashem. But when it comes to sleeping, we look at it as something physically necessary and that it has no real spiritual benefit. However, the contrary is true.

Through a proper sleep, we replenish our minds that they can be clear to serve Hashem. Having a refreshing sleep, we can serve Hashem with more joy and clarity. Should we not sleep well, we are sluggish, more prone to wasting time and our *Torah* study will not be as fulfilling.

When you retire at night, think to yourself, this too is a *mitzvah*? Then, those hours that you're lying-in bed transform into a *mitzvah* for Hashem. It really is one of the easiest *mitzvos* you can accomplish. Can you imagine a person going to a king of flesh and blood in order to serve him and the king commands you to take a nap?

If only you would approach your bedtime like you would performing other commandments, reciting the *Kriyas Shema* with your full concentration. Making self-reflection of your day before closing your eyes, removing all sins by a short confession to Hashem. Leaving a wash basin next to your bed, so that your *neshamah* is comforted knowing that you will wash away the *tuma* of sleep immediately upon arising. So, the question remains, do you appreciate the greatness of sleep and its benefits?

The reality is that many people have had insomnia for so many years that just heading to bed, subconsciously brings anxiety. We worry sometimes that we don't have enough hours to sleep, since we went to bed late and have to get up early. But the truth is, if we rest peacefully, even a few hours can be plenty. We have to remove the anxiety that surrounds our sleep and take away all the unhealthy habits. We don't even give ourselves a chance when it comes to making our sleep time something holy. Even those who have illnesses that effect their sleep, must admit that they could improve on their sleep habits through natural means and self-discipline if they put in the effort.

## *Knowing what to Do*

"I received it from my masters that when they wanted to do something and were in doubt whether to do it or not, they would take a *Chumash* or *Tanach*, open it and look at the first verse on the page to see at what it hinted." (*Keter Ha-Yehudi*, p. 7, n.1)

The Baal Shem Tov said, "When you learn *Torah*, and later in the day you have to make a decision about some action and you do not know if you should do it or not, you can understand what course to take from the power of the *Torah* that you learned earlier - but this is on condition that you are always in *d'vekus* with Hashem, blessed be He. Then He will arrange that you will always know what to do from what you studied that day. But if you just walk with Hashem sporadically, then He, too, will do so with you." (*Tzavas HaRivash, Sefer Baal Shem Tov al ha-Torah*, vol. 2, p.20)

A businesswoman once sought the advice of Rabbi Elchanan Wasserman as to whether or not he should enter a particular business venture. After the question was asked to him, Rabbi Wasserman opened a *Gemarah* and studied from it for a few minutes while his petitioner waited patiently. At last Rabbi Wasserman closed the *Gemarah*, gave his advice and the man left. Rabbi Wasserman perceived that a *talmud* who had been standing in the room looked somewhat baffled. The *bachur* did not understand the connection between the man's commercial business and the subject matter which Rabbi Wasserman had studied. Rabbi Wasserman explained, "The words of the *Gemarah* illuminate one's mind and force him to think straight. After I studied a little, Hashem helped me to give the man sound advice."

What is also important to understand is that once a person has studied, his mind is given new clarity as to what to do. I once had to make a major life decision so I went to the Hornostyple Rebbe of Beitar Illit, he told me, "How can you make a decision if you haven't yet *davened Marriv*?" So, certainly a person, the second they get confused, should find their way to a *bais midrash*, a *siddur* or a *sefer*.

## Supporting a Torah Scholar

Not everyone is cut out for full-time study, however, I believe today, anyone can accomplish this challenging task should they so desire. There are many modern technologies to help a person to study and be entertained thereby if so needed. For those who find that working and doing kindness is their personal path, let them support a devoted scholar so he can study. This was the path of Zevulun.

Rav Bun asked, "Seeing that the twelve tribes were arranged below in the same order as above (in *Shamayim*), why is Zevulun everywhere placed before Issachar in the blessings, although Issachar devoted himself to the *Torah*, which should always come first? The reason is that Zevulun took out of his own mouth and gave to Issachar. From this we learn that he who supports a student of the *Torah* is blessed from above and below, and not only so, but he is privileged to eat of two tables, a privilege granted to no other man. He is granted wealth in this world, and he is granted a portion in the next world. Hence it says of Zevulun, that 'he shall dwell at the haven of the sea,' that is to say, in this world, 'and shall be for a haven of ships', in the future world." (*Zohar* 242a)

## Wearing Tefillin

From the *Gemarah* in *Menachos* it certainly appears that the *Amoraim* wore their *tefillin* all day long. The *Gemarah* asks (36a), "Until when, may one wear his *tefillin*?" The first *Tanna* answers, "until the sun [finishes] setting," R' Yaakov states, "he may leave the *tefillin* on until pedestrians have vanished from the market", and the sages state, "until the time of sleeping." Furthermore, the Rambam states explicitly (*Hilchos Tefillin* 4:25), that the *kedusha* of *tefillin* is so great, that as long as one wears them on the head and arm, his personality will remain humble and G-d fearing. Therefore, one should make every effort to wear them all day long, for that is indeed the proper *mitzvah*. The Rambam then adds, that it is told about Rav, the disciple of Rabbeinu HaKadosh that all his life no-one saw him walking four *amos* without *Torah*, without *tzitzis*, or without *tefillin*. The Rambam then concludes, although it is meritorious to wear *tefillin* all day there is a special *mitzvah* to wear them during *tefillah*.

Rav Joseph B. Soloveitchik explains, "*Tefillin* is the only *mitzvah* of the *Torah* that even the non-Jewish world will look upon us with awe and respect, as the *Torah* states, 'Then all the people of the earth will see that the Name of HaShem is proclaimed upon you and they will revere you' (*Devarim* 28:10). So, although it is not our *minhag* to wear the *tefillin* all day, nevertheless, the concept of doing so is certainly a meritorious one."

"He who engages in *Torah* while wrapped in *tallis* and *tefillin* will attain spiritual elevation [literally: to a *nefesh*, *ruach* and *neshamah*, the three soul levels]." (*Sha'ar ha-Kedusha*, chap. 6, #58)

I don't know why it seems strange for a scholar to sit in *yeshivah* and study with his *tefillin* on. I once asked a friend in *kollel* why he didn't do so, and his only reason was that he felt people would look at him strangely. Obviously, there are basic *halachos* one should keep while wearing *tefillin*, like refraining from talking idle words but these things you should already be careful of while studying *Torah*. (Though the actual *halacha* says that most people in our times are incapable in keep themselves clean for an extended period of time, see the *Shulchan Aruch*, Orach Chayim, 37:2). Still, *chazal* teaches us that "Every minute you wear *tefillin*, you fulfill all the commandments of the Torah." Therefore, one should certainly make more effort in this should they be capable.

Rav Eliyashuv was asked if there is an *inyan* to wear *tallis* and *tefillin* all day. He answered that a *tallis* isn't necessary, since one wears a *tallis katan*, and regarding *tefillin,* a person needs a *guf naki* (clean body & mind). He was then asked if one knows with certainty that he will have a *guf naki* is it then an *inyan* to do it. He answered "*Halevei*" that one can do such a thing and if one can do such a thing then a *bracha* should be upon him. (*Sefer Vayishma Moshe* 2, *Tefillin*)

The *Sefer HaChinuch* (no. 421) states that "*guf naki*" does not refer to someone who has no sins or impurity, implying that someone else had suggested that it did. The author explicitly condemns those who are strict on the holiness of this *mitzvah* and thereby deprive the masses of the *mitzvah*. Rather, "*guf naki*" refers to the ability to refrain from passing gas and thinking improper thoughts while wearing the *tefillin.*

Since most scholars can control their thoughts for the most part and keep their stomach in check, the only demanding thing would be to not forget that you're wearing *tefillin,* but if you're learning *Torah* or praying then that isn't a problem. This to me sounds like something people of today are more capable of doing then given credit for. Maybe this is why Rav Yochanan, Rabbi Yochanan ben Zakai, Rabbi Yehoshua ben Karcha (as quoted in the *Gemarah*) and others thought it necessary never to walk four *amos* in public without wearing *tefillin.* They thought this was the only way to teach *klal Yisrael* how important and special the *mitzvah* of *tefillin* is.

For hundreds of years, *tefillin* has been a *mitzvah* that was treated with laxity. The *Gemarah* specifically condemns those who never wear *tefillin.* (*Rosh Hashanah* 13a) Tosafos writes that one should not be surprised that at that time people were lax in *tefillin,* since they were in the times of the *Talmud* also. (*Shabbos* 49a sv. ke-Elisha) The Beis Yosef (*Even Ha-Ezer* 65) quotes the *Kol Bo,* who suggests that in some communities, ashes are not placed on a groom's forehead because the community members do not wear *tefillin.*

So, why is such an easy *mitzvah* so difficult to perform? It is because its reward is truly beyond measure. "One who is meticulous concerning the *mitzvah* of *tefillin* and treats *tefillin* appropriately according to its holiness, merits a long life in this world and a portion in the world to come… One who is meticulous regarding the *mitzvah* of *tefillin* will not face the fire of *Gehenam* and will have his iniquities forgiven." (*Kitzur Shulchan Aruch, siman* 10, laws of the *mitzvah* of *tefillin,* seif 1)

The Gaon of Vilna related that a person who can keep his body clean should wear *tefillin* all day long. The Gra said that if he had the strength he would go out in the markets and streets to make people do so, but the great *rabbis* did not follow his example. (תורגם ע"י)

"You should learn *Torah* every day, at least something, while you still have *tefillin* on [that is, after the Morning Prayers]." (*Derech Chayim*, 4-31)

A young *rabbi* wearing his *tefillin*, once came to Rav Chaim Pinchas Scheinberg with his friend. His friend asked the *rav*, "What does the *rav* think about wearing *tefillin* all day?"

The *rav* responded, "You shouldn't wear it." The *rabbi* pointed to the *rav's* own *tefillin* he was wearing at the time and said, "What is that?" with a smile.

"Because if you do," continued Rav Scheinberg, "people will think you're a sociopath." People will think you're not normal, that there is something wrong with you, you're anti-social, that you think you're better than everyone else. The *rabbi* responded, "I understand what you're saying but let's say, I don't care what people say or think of me."

"That's fine," continued the *rav*. "I am just letting you know that you might suffer from this."

I remember meeting Rav Chaim Pinchas Scheinberg many times, I can't remember even once that he wasn't wearing his *tefillin*. Also, he was always happy. Come to think of it, I've rarely seen someone wearing *tefillin* where they don't have a happy shine on their face or a great light of *kedusha* upon them. It is just sad that we live in a world of *frum Yidden* that would actually be judgmental of another person performing a holy *mitzvah* with perseverance.

## Guard Your Ears

I don't think you need me to discuss the importance of not listening to *lashon hara*. Let's assume that you are already careful with this as a future or current scholar. Therefore, let us move on and discuss the importance of protecting your ears from hearing that which is not holy.

Rabbi Uri of Strelisk said, "You should guard your ears more so than all your other senses, even though what you hear is not completely in your control and sometimes, something which damages your soul, *chas-v-shalom*, will penetrate into your ear." (*Imrei Kodesh ha-Shalem*, p. 15, #40)

"When you merit to bend your ears to truthfully hear all the speech in the world, you will perceive that everything is crying out to you and giving you hints to return to Him, blessed be He. This is because all the things and words in this world have the glory of Hashem which cries out. When you accustom yourself to hear, in everything spoken, just the inside, the [inner] voice of Hashem within it, the light of your soul will shine on you with the light of understanding, with an awesome and wonderful illumination." (*Tikkun Krias Shema al ha-Milah mai ha-Arizal*, Bratzlav, p. 81)

"There is no speech from which you cannot hear the voice of instruction in how to serve Hashem. This is even so in words spoken in the marketplace when one person speaks to another about buying and selling… Perhaps this was a hint of King David, in the Psalm where he declares, 'I will hear what Hashem says,' that is, even from the words spoken in the marketplace." (*DhTvhY*, III p. 77, *Tochachas Mussar* #1, from *Or ha-Meir*)

The holy *rabbi*, the Rebbe Reb Elimelech of Lizensk, and his holy brother, Reb Zushya [of Hanipol], were wandering for a number of years "in exile," sharing the fate of the Divine Presence, which is in exile, so as to heal the spiritual breach in the world.

One time, they arrived in a certain village, and though the head of the village wasn't in his house, his wife took them in as guests. When her husband returned home in the middle of the night, he lit a candle on the table as he worked to mend a rip in his fur coat.

The two brothers who were in bed, yet still awake, overheard his wife calling to him saying, "Hurry up and fix the coat while the candle is still burning." One brother said to the other, "Did you hear what the lady of the house is saying to her husband?"

This is a great teaching, to fix yourself quickly and repent while your soul is still within you. (*Siah Sarfei Kodesh*, II, p. 80, #260)

Once you begin to take control over what goes in your ear, you will start to really appreciate all the good messages that Hashem sends you through others.

## A Good Listener

The Chofetz Chayim writes that although it is usually commendable to speak as little as possible, it is a moral obligation to boost the spirits of someone who is dejected, by conversing with him at length. Helping a person overcome his worries and sadness is very important." (*Chovas Hashmirah, maalos hasmirah*, no. 11)

A person who frequently came to speak with Rabbi Dov Baiish Wiedenfeld, the Rabbi of Tshabin, enjoyed telling the *rabbi* their *Torah* thoughts. Even though this person was very longwinded and what they said did not have much substance, Rabbi Wiedenfeld would patiently listen to them. Someone once asked the Rabbi of Tshabin why he wasted so much precious time on the man. Rabbi Widenfeld smilingly replied, "Isn't this *chesed*?" (*Rabosainu* p. 237)

"You should receive every person with warmth, and bear his yoke, and treat him with gentleness, as if he were your king. It is part of human kindness to listen to him talk, even if he overdoes it; but at the very same time you should not forget the Creator, blessed be He, at all." (*Zos Zichron*, p.3)

Here is a relevant story about the great teacher of *mussar*, Rabbi Yisrael Salanter:

Once our master, teacher and *rabbi* had a conversation with one of his relatives about worldly things and he was speaking with him in a jovial way. One of his students, who was a G-d fearing person, heard the drift of this conversation and it appeared to him that the *rabbi* was talking needlessly. So, afterwards he spoke with him about the subject of avoiding idle conversation and dared to ask him about the discussion with that man.

Our teacher, in his humility, did not take resentment at the question, but responded to him, unfolding that this person was very depressed, and it was very much an act of kindness to try to cheer him up and remove his anxiety and sadness. "And," said Rabbi Salanter, "with what could I bring him some joy – by talking with him about fear of G-d and *mussar*? No, the only way was to talk with him in a pleasant and amusing manner about things of this world."

From this story we can judge how carefully our *rabbi* weighed all his words in the scale of the fear of Hashem. (*Or Yisrael*, p. 112)

"Then the L-rd, G-d formed man from the dust of the ground and breathed into his nostrils the breath of life; and the man became a living soul." (*Bereshis* 2:7)

Onkelos identifies the words "a living soul" (*nefesh chaya*) as a soul which can speak. Man, then, is elevated above all animals for Hashem has imparted him the ability to talk. However, this unique faculty elevates man only when he uses it for worthy purposes. Someone who misuses his speech by speaking against others is considered lower than a beast. A beast cannot destroy through speech, whereas man can slay with his tongue. (*Chofetz Chayim in Shmiras Halashon* 1:3)

Sometimes overlooked, is speaking in a low tone. This is a very important habit to create, as through it, a person becomes more relaxed and G-d fearing.

Rabbi Chayim of Volozhin said, "If a person is unable to admonish others in a pleasant tone of voice, he is exempt from the obligation to deliver reproof." (*Keser Rosh*, no. 143; *Minchas Shmuel*, p.34) That would mean that screaming in the streets at people who are not following the laws of *Shabbos* isn't the correct method. Pushing people to change and follow *halacha* might also not work, a person has to use tact.

Rabbi Rafael of Bershad would teach, "Be careful even about the tone of your voice. For example, if you have to tell a person in your family not to do something, you should not speak in an angry or strict tone, but softly and gently. He would also remind us about what is written in the Rambam's letter, that all your speech with your fellow man should be spoken gently." (*Midrash Pinchas*, p. 40, #32)

"It is a beneficial spiritual practice to 'go upward' [to raise each thing to its spiritual root Above] when conversing with others. When the people you are with are conversing about something connected with some kind of love for example, you should turn your mind to love of Hashem, and contemplate of how you should love only Him, blessed be He; or when the conversation is about wealth, you should think here too that is the same when the discussion is about anything relating beauty, splendor, or glory. So too, when the talk is about worldly fears, think that you should fear only Hashem. The same goes with all other things. You should attend to what is before you, and as a result you will never cease from Hashem – consciousness, even when you are conversing with other people." (*Darkei Tzedek*, p. 3, #15)

The Baal Shem Tov said, "Sometimes when I am sitting among people who are conversing idly, I first attach myself in *d'vekus* with Hashem, blessed be He, and then I bind all their words with greater attachment [to their spiritual roots]." (*Likkutim Yekarim*, p. 5a)

Rabbi Shlomo never engaged in any idle conversation; even from his youth he was careful about this. He would guard himself against hearing idle talk, and even more so, profane speech, *chas v'shalom*.

While he was young, he was living with a tailor, and he would not return to the house until all were asleep. One time, during the bitter frigid winter, it happened that they closed the *beis midrash* early for some reason, and [not being able to stay there to study and pray] he was forced to return home.

Upon approaching the shared house, however, he heard the tailor, as usual, still at work with his young helpers. Also, as usual, which is why he normally stayed late in the *beis midrash*, they were talking about indecent and unclean things. As a result, Rabbi Shlomo refused to enter. Instead, he stayed outside walking this way and that, for it was very cold outside. He became so cold that he almost died. He found himself just laying down on the earth from weakness. However, despite this, he would still not go in, for he was determined that he would not hear idle conversation. While he lay there almost lifeless, a miracle occurred, and the one candle they had inside went out. Having no choice, the workers were forced to finish for the night and retire early to sleep. Seeing this, he finally went inside. "From then on," the holy Rabbi Shlomo said, "my ears developed the ability to hear what people are whispering even at far distances." (*Eser* Ataros, p. 21, #3) (*Pathways of the Righteous* p. 88)

Rabbi Shmelke of Nikolsburg told, "A *tzaddik* needs to refine his limbs and train them so that even with his eyes fully open he will not notice evil, and with his ears he will hear no evil talk." (*Ha-Hozeh mi-Lublin*, p. 20)

About the Chozeh of Lublin, Rabbi Shmelke said of him that in those two years [learning by Rabbi Shmelke], he attained all his spiritual levels. Because it was there, that he taught himself that his vision and his speech should be dedicated to the service of Hashem alone. As we know from future stories of him, his spiritual vision was profound. (*Niflaos ha-Rebbe*, p. 50, #102, #104; p. 51, #106; p. 71, #185) (my book, *Pathways of the Righteous* p. 84)

## *Weighing Ones Words*

As much as possible, avoid idle conversation. This was one of the ten pious customs of Rav [a famous *rabbi* of the *Talmud*], who during all of his life never talked idly. (Rabbi Moshe Cordevero, in the list of his *hanhagos*, #23, *Reshis Chachmah*, Walman edition p.50)

There is nothing so beneficial for purifying the soul as keeping a reign over your mouth and eschewing idle conversation. Not only is this the case, but it aids significantly in having *kavanah* in prayer, as alien thoughts do not intrude and distract you.

Rabbi Yaakov Abuchatzeira taught, "One who wishes to sanctify himself must refrain from speaking idle chatter." (*Ma'aglei Tzedek* 86)

He also said, "A person must never permit a lie to leave his lips, even about trivial matters, for there is nothing more disreputable than a lie. One who learns Hashem's pure *Torah*, the *Torah* of truth, should be particularly careful not to allow any false matter to leave his mouth, for how can one whose occupation is pure truth utter lies – such a one builds on the one hand and destroys on the other." (*Alef Binah* 59)

There is a tale of a *chassid* who, after his death, appeared to his wife in a dream, and seeing the hair of his head and beard all aglow like a torch, in his glory, she questioned him, "By what did you merit all this?" He responded that it was because he spoke as little as possible of things other than *Torah* and fear of Hashem – for the Holy One, blessed be He, is sure to care for those who exert themselves to avoid profane talk. (*Kav ha-Yashar*, chap. 12)

Rabbi Yaakov Hagiz writes, "Watch over your mouth and your speech, for this is an important fence in the service of Hashem. Therefore, be very careful not to speak unnecessarily." (*Zichro l'Vnair Yisrael* #1, in YHvT, p. 38)

The *pasuk* in *Koheles* states (9:17), "Words of the wise are heard pleasantly." Rashi explains this to mean that his words are accepted by the people who hear them. When you begin to guard your words carefully, you will see that people will respect your opinion more.

"Never allow anything be uttered by you unless you know that it is the Will of Hashem that you say it." (*Derech Chayim*, 2-17)

Many people take upon themselves many fasts in order to purify their body and souls, ignoring the consequences to their health in doing so. The thing is, if a person would watch their speech more carefully instead, they would do far less *avairos* that they would feel they need to fast for. We learn in the *Kabbalah* that a person's mouth is symbolic with the *Shechinah*. If one's lips are on guard and holy, the *Shechinah* rests with that person.

"It is healthier not to fast by abstaining from food – for when you fast from talking it will not hurt your body or your soul, as it will not weaken you [causing you to lessen your Divine service]." (*Rosh ha-Givah* quoted in *Or Yesharim*, p. 90)

"Never allow anything unclean or ugly cross your lips, not even the word for excrement." (*Derech Chayim* 5-16)

"Attaching your speech to Hashem is very important. This is the way of the sages. That everything you do, every action or thought, you connect it to Hashem-consciousness.

"When you want to maintain your G-d-consciousness while talking with others, see to it that everything you verbalize is directed to Hashem. Also, you can think that all the words you speak are coming to you from Hashem who gives you the power of speech and as a result you will not forget Hashem when you converse." (*Darkei Tzedek*, p. 4, #16)

The Tchebiner Rav was asked, what is the correct *derech halimud*? He replied, "My father (Rav Weidenfeld) never demanded of me that I learn *Torah* eighteen hours a day. But what he did demand was that while I learn, that I should totally forget about everything else in the world. Only if a person learns in such a fashion, can he expect to become a *Gadol b'Torah*."

"The essence of the perfection of the *tzaddikim* is that they constantly have their minds on Hashem and attach to Him without any separation whatsoever, *chas-v-shalom*. Even when they express something about their worldly needs, they direct and form their speech so that they will not be separated from Hashem, *chas-v-shalom*. Their words are chosen to carry two meanings, to arouse some fear of Hashem, *d'vekus* or unification. So too, with what he hears from someone speaking to him, he also understands his words as if they were holy words... You make certain to teach yourself to be able to talk in your ordinary speech in a way that you are not separated from your *d'vekus*." (from *Divrei Moshe*; found in *Lev Sameah ha-Chadash*, p. 73, *Derech Emunah u'Maasah Rav*, p. 31)

The Baal Shem Tov advised that, "When speaking to your friend, and just talking about this and that, at the same moment you should be doing unifications [meditations that unite the upper and lower worlds]. The Maharsha, in his interpretation [on *Rosh HaShanah* 3b] said that when Nechemiah was conversing with the King Artahshasta, he was with the same words really praying to Hashem, blessed be He." (*Sefer Baal Shem Tov al ha-Torah*, vol. 1, p. 253)

Here is a story to explain to you the great merit in watching over your speech. After the passing of Reb Yehuda ben Shoshan in the upper Galil, he appeared in a dream to his *talmid*, Reb Lapidos. During the dream, his face shone like the sun, like a blazing torch. The *talmid* questioned what he had done to merit such *kedusha*, and he explained that throughout his lifetime he had not spoken unnecessarily. A person's speech is similar to that of the *malachim* and one should use it for *kedusha*." (*Raishis Chochmah*, gate of love 86) (Excerpt from my book, *A Journey Into Holiness*, P. 86)

Our holy master, the Holy Jew of Pshischa, sent a message with some *chassidim*, that they should come to him. So, they traveled to Pshischa, and upon arriving near the city at dusk, they came across their *rebbe*, the Holy Jew. The *rebbe* had gone out for a walk in the countryside with some disciples. When the *chassidim* noticed their master, they jumped out of the carriage, and ran to him to receive the greeting of peace. However, when the Holy Jew greeted them, he remarked, "Young men, why don't I see any of your words?" [With his spiritual insight, he did not see that these *chassidim* had any hold in the World of Speech.]

The *chassidim* answered simply, "Why should we speak unnecessarily? Isn't it better instead just to speak words in learning *Torah* and praying?"

Seeing a greater potential for them, his holy master responded, "If that's the situation, prepare a pipe for yourselves, and get enough tobacco for the whole night; come to me after the evening prayers, and I'll teach you how to speak." As spoken, the *rebbe* and *chassidim* sat together the entire night, while the *rebbe* taught them how to speak. After this, they began to talk again. (*Ohel Elimelech*, p. 72, #172) (From my book, *Pathways of the Righteous* p. 84)

"Whenever you mention someone, anyone in conversation, make it a habit to bless him, with a good eye and a good heart." (*Derech Chayim*, 7-8)

"Be careful never to speak against the Jewish people; never say that a certain Jewish custom is no good, or any other bad thing, *chas-v-shalom*. But rather accustom your tongue always to speak good about the people Israel, and in their defense." (ibid. 7-43)

"You should refrain from speaking derogatorily of any man, and even of any creature or animal." (Rabbi Moshe Cordovero, his *hanhagos*, #7, in *Reishis Chachmah*)

"Never speak derogatorily of any creature of Hashem, not even a cow or a wild animal or birds." (*Derech Chayim*, 7-44)

The Baal Shem Tov taught, "When you talk, do not think that you are the one speaking – because it is the Divine life-energy within you, Hashem, blessed me He, speaking in you. [Through this recognition], you lift up the act of speech to its Source. Also, equanimity is included in this reflection; for just as everything you speak is from Him, blessed be He, so is everything that your fellow man speaks from Him." (*Tzavaas HaRivash*, p. 21)

Rabbi Yaakov Abuchatzeira taught, "'How do I love Your *Torah*.' explained the Psalmist. By this, he also means, how do I show my love for Your *Torah*? The Psalmist answers, 'I love it so much that I limit all my other discussions, even regarding things which I require for my health and welfare. I only mention them with the greatest brevity, since I have no desire for any talk other than that involving Your *Torah*. I shall not dwell on mundane matters, even those regarding my own needs, for I am always concerned lest I stretch a mundane subject and thereby forget the holy ones. This is why I always minimize discussing other topics even for my personal needs. Instead, I endeavor to be preoccupied with *Torah*, and speak about it all day long.'" (*Ma'agalei Tzedek* 40)

"The main building-up of the *Shechinah* depends on our speech in the form of prayers and *Torah* study. That is, providing that they are done whole-heartedly. In this regard, the verse writes, 'For [the *Torah*] is not an empty thing for you,' (*Devarim* 32:47) which our Sages have explained to mean 'If it is empty, it is because of you.' (*Yerushalmi Peah* 1:5) In other words, the *Torah* cautions people not to doubt that the *Shechinah* can be built up on high through speech, for the verse, 'It is not an empty thing' also means 'Speech is not empty' ['*davar*' means both 'thing' and 'speech'].

Speech surely precipitates deeds and establishes on high. Therefore, 'if you say it is empty, it seems empty because of you,' who did not sanctify yourself sufficient to be able to grasp the enormous impact speech has in creating actions and edifices on high." (*Ginzei Hamelech - Likutei Shoshanim*)

## Stoicism

Once Rabbi Zalman of Volzhin was traveling with his brother Rav Chayim and they were mistreated by an innkeeper. The short-tempered innkeeper yelled insults at the two brothers and refused to allow them to stay at the inn. As they were parting the inn, Rav Chayim noticed that his brother was crying.

"Why are you crying?" questioned Rav Chayim. "I didn't take what he said to heart, and you shouldn't either."

"I'm not crying because of his insults," responded Rav Zalman. "But when he shouted, I felt a bit of pain. I am crying now because I didn't reach the level of being oblivious to insults." (*Toldos Odom*)

It is very important to serve Hashem without worrying what people think or regardless of the outcome, should it work out in the way you want or not, is irrelevant. All that matters, is that you did your best and that you served your Maker.

The two pillars of stoicism consist of the dichotomy of control, that some things are up to us, other things are not up to us. Some things are in our power to change by being motivated, having desire and doing, yet all we can do is try, the total outcome is still entirely up to Hashem. Therefore, we should be more worried about our intention and our efforts which are totally under our control.

Excerpt from my book, *Chassidus Kabbalah and Meditation:*

When an initiate wanted to learn *Kabbalah*, the first thing the society asked him was, "are you stoic?" Rabbi Abner related, "A sage once came to one of the meditators and asked to be accepted into their society. The meditator replied, 'My son, blessed are you to Hashem. Your intentions are good. But tell me, have you attained stoicism or not?'

"The sage said, 'Master, explain your words.'

"The meditator said, 'If one man is praising you and another is insulting you, are the two not equal in your eyes?'

"He replied, 'No my master. I have pleasure from those who praise me, and pain from those who degrade me. But I do not take revenge or bear a grudge.'

"The other said, 'Go in peace my son. You have not attained
92

stoicism. You have not reached a level where your soul does not feel the praise of one who honors you, nor the degradation of one who insults you. You are not prepared for your thoughts to bind on high, that you should come and meditate (*hisboded*). Go and increase the humbleness of your heart; learn to treat everything equally until you become stoic. Only then will you be able to meditate.'" (*Shaarey Kedushah*, 4th part)

"This is the generation of those who seek Him, the seekers of Your Presence." (*Tehillim* 24: 3-6)

Even though we must adhere to these warnings and take them to heart, Dovid Hamelech reminds us that we are seekers. Explorers who will stop at nothing to attain our goal of coming close to Hashem. To do this, we must exemplify the characteristic of being *bitul*, nullification. There are a few ways to achieve *bitul,* and only when all of them come together, do you become a complete person. It is not enough to think of yourself as nothing compared to Hashem. You must also think yourself lower than every Jew in the world. There must be no difference between insults and praise, sweet foods or bitter.

Rabbi Isaac of Acco writes in the name of Rabbi Moshe, a disciple of Rabbi Joseph Gikatalia:

"If a person's heart compels him to rectify his traits, perfecting his personality and deeds, he should pursue humility to the ultimate degree. He should, 'be insulted but not insult, hear himself scorned but not respond.' The Divine Presence will then immediately rest upon him, and he will not have to learn from any mortal being, for the spirit of Hashem will teach him." (*Reishis Chachmah*, *Anavah*, 3, 119d)

We found this in the books of the Kabbalists who were worthy of the way of truth:

One of the great rectifications for one who wishes to know Hashem is that he should be among those who are, "insulted but do not insult." This should be true even with people of whom he is not afraid and before whom he has no shame, such as his wife and children. Even if members of his household insult him, he should not answer, except to correct their ways. Inwardly, he should feel no anger, but his heart should always be joyful, while, attached to Hashem.

"My angelic master taught me this: Do not worry about anything in the world, other than that which will influence your worship of Hashem. With regard to all worldly things, everything should be the same as its opposite.

This is the mystery of the words of the sage, who asked an initiate who wished to involve himself in *yichudim* (unifications), 'Have you attained stoicism?' If a person does not see that good in the physical world is exactly the same as evil, it is impossible for him to unify all things." (Rabbi Yosef Caro, *Maggid Mesharim, BeShalach* p.57a)

Pride, even the slightest thought of it, is a very grave matter. Any ulterior motive derives from pride. Every thought is a complete structure. With pride, therefore, one causes a serious blemish above and "repels the feet of the *Shechinah*," as is written, "Everyone who is proud in heart is an abomination to Hashem." (*Proverbs* 16:5; *Tzava'as Harivash* 92, end excerpt)

The wrong way to look at something is to assume that success is based on the desired outcome. Having serenity in life is knowing you always do your best, it is not about reaching perfection, you're happy no matter the outcome, this way you never have anxiety when things don't work out. The main thing is that you are a higher step then you were yesterday because you have tried and given your best. I was once explaining to a friend that I have very low expectations of others, especially friends, that way I am never disappointed. This idea caught him by surprise. He said, that sounds like a very dreary way to live. I think it's the perfect way to live. Give and expect nothing in return, that is true happiness. A happy life is a life well balanced. Never going to emotional extremes, moderation, courage and integrity, calm under pressure and with total *emunah* that Hashem is in control of the final outcome.

When we suffer, it's not really from the events in our life. You see people who live far worse lives than you, or who are in far more pain, yet they process this uncomfortable situation without judgement. They accept the *Ratzon* Hashem in a simple way.

In order to have self-discipline, you need to find your purpose. For a Jew, this is easy. Our purpose is to simply do the Will of Hashem. The stoic thinks, what do I have to complain about if I am doing what I was created for. A Jew also realizes, for what do I have to become proud for, for wisdom is from Hashem.

Self-discipline is about finding compelling reasons to do something, then committing to see that task or activity through to the very end. It is the ability to set yourself to take action; To do what you need to do. This is regardless of your physical or mental state, whether you feel like it or not. Your success will be dependent on committing to every single step and action that will lead to your desired goal, the *Ratzon* Hashem. Setting milestones will help, setting many short goals that lead to the final goal. This training is what is necessary to become a pure *talmud chacham*.

Be careful of succumbing to being overwhelmed. If your overwhelmed, you will procrastinate, becoming stagnant and you will forgo your self-discipline. Therefore, pace yourself and be consistent. Failure is part of reaching your goals and with consistency, it's okay to fail because the next day, you will just improve and continue towards your goal.

A stoic person, in order to train themselves, will take small steps of being uncomfortable and looking the other way. For instance, if they feel it's difficult to give lots of charity, they will pursue this, pushing themselves all the more to give charity many times over. To eat something which they don't like in order to show themselves that it really doesn't matter.

Don't allow yourself to be bothered by petty things, not whining or complaining. Don't fall into self-pity but act to fix that which needs fixing. You don't see ants, spiders, and bees complaining. They were created for a purpose and stick to that purpose, doing their best and knowing that Hashem will provide for them.

"There are those who have no *emunah* in the Holy One, blessed be He, and have no desire to meditate on His ways: they likewise labor day and night for food, in fear that they may be short of bread – all because they are not of the faithful." (*Zohar* III, 63a)

By putting off what we desire now, we will receive far better in the future. Most *mitzvos* have delayed reactions and benefits, yet we must do them knowing that we are reaping benefits for the future.

You will always have naysayers, people criticizing you when you are doing the Will of Hashem. Use this to strengthen your resolve instead of letting anyone or anything get to you or to stand in your way. People are afraid of progress as they are unable to set goals for themselves. Keep away from this negative energy. Being upset from someone who you don't know or really respect, is foolish. It's like being upset about the weather, it's a waste of your energy and time. Instead, seek honest feedback from those that you respect. Socialize with people you admire, with good character traits in order to model your lifestyle around them. Emulate even those who are from the past, holy Sages that can be your role model. Use their experience to your advantage to help you to find your own personal path.

Self-examination is also important. Scrutinize yourself and understand your weak points. Then with self-honesty, you can begin to fix your faults. The more self-aware you are about yourself, the more you will be able to fix your characteristics. Don't just recognize your faults but understand them. Forgiving yourself prevents you from continuing to put things off. Think about all the good that you have done and be grateful for all the wonderful things that Hashem did for you today.

Another helpful tool in serving Hashem is meditation. To learn more about this, see my book, *Chassidus Kabbalah and Meditation*.

## A Woman's Derech

"Women are exempt from the *mitzvah* of *talmud Torah*." (*Shulchan Oruch, Yoreh Deah* 246:6, *Hilchos Talmud Torah* 1:14). However, they must understand the areas of the Written and Oral *Torah* that pertain to practical observance. Therefore, they are required to study in order to fulfill their obligations properly, but not to study as a *mitzvah* in itself. (See *Beis HaLevi*, Vol. 1)

Women should familiarize themselves with practical *halacha* since it is them that usually runs the household with the children. Therefore, they need to know the ins and outs of practical *halacha* that applies to them and their family.

Not limiting herself to just *halacha*, she should branch out into the learning of *Tanach*. This is recommended by the Chafetz Chayim and others. It is said that the Chasam Sofer would study the *aggadic* sections of the *Talmud* with his daughters.

This is what is practical for most woman. Of course, there are always exceptions but it's important to understand the logic behind these *halachos*. It is not that she can't comprehend the material, obviously there are plenty of brilliant women. Rebbetzin Miriam, the Maharshal's grandmother, led a *yeshivah* for many years. She lectured to advanced students from behind a curtain. (*Responsa of the Maharshal*, No 3)

Rabbi Meir's wife, B'ruriah, taught her students 300 passages of Jewish law in a single day. Tractate *Chullin* (109b) quotes a *halachic* query posed by Yalta, Rav Nachman's wife.

"New *halachic* insights are cited in the name of the Drishah's mother, Rebbetzin Baylah. After prayers, she wasted no time, but went directly to her studies, the weekly portion with Rashi and the classical commentaries... She was as accomplished as any man in *Torah* discussions... Her lips would occasionally utter new insights into Midrashic interpretations of the sages... She was especially well-versed in laws pertaining to women, particularly the laws of *niddah*. Her erudition approached that of the recognized *halachic* authorities of the day." (See Into. to Drishah's commentary on the *Tur, Yoreh Deah*)

My main point in bringing this up is in order to encourage men to give more respect to women. I think a lot of *shalom bayis* problems could be avoided if men were taught the proper way, that women should not be looked upon as objects but rather that they have similar greatness. It is just that the *Torah* channels this light in the direction that is best for their soul roots and the entire family.

"A woman who sacrifices material desires and uncomplainingly runs the home herself so that her husband and children can devote themselves fully to *Torah* study is considered an equal partner in their *mitzvah* of *talmud Torah*. Her spiritual reward is equivalent to that which accrues to her husband and children for their studies." (*Remah, Yoreh Deah* 246:6; *Shulchan Aruch HaRav, Hilchos Talmud Torah* 14)

Can you imagine if all the *kollel* wives were to setup hidden cameras outside the *kollel* doors? What would they say to all the *bittle Torah* and long breaks the husbands take, while they labor tirelessly in the home or work? Then on the way traveling to and from *yeshivah*, why isn't he learning *Torah* every minute with a *sefer* or mp3 player? Either he is a scholar and a *masmid* or he is not. I think many guys don't realize how they are perfectly capable of turning themselves into a *masmid* should they desire to. If you are someone learning in *kollel*, how can you not strive for this? A *masmid* doesn't have to be only part of the elite, anyone can attain this level.

The Chazon Ish once reprimanded a young *Torah* scholar, "Your spouse has entered into a partnership with you similar to that of Zevulun and Yissachar. If you waste your time from your studies, you are in breach of contract!" (Intro. *Chanukah V'Megillah, HaGoan Rav Turtzin*)

"Rabbi Eliezer said that he who teaches his daughter *Torah* is considered to have taught her *tiflus*." (*Mishnah Sota* 3:4)

According to Rav Y.Z. Ciechanowicz, it is not only permitted but even mandatory to teach women the laws which pertain to them; furthermore, concerning the laws which do not pertain to women, the censure pronounced by Rabbi Eliezer only applies to one who urges them to study, but not if they come of their own accord to learn. However, this is without delving into the conjectures and argumentations, only the final, straightforward decision. (*Toras Yerucham* 1)

The Ma'ayan Ganim speculates that the censure may refer only to teaching women at a tender age, when their intellect is not firmly established. Later on, however, if they aspire to it, "let them ascend the mountain of Hashem." (As quoted in *Torah Temimah* on *Devarim* 11, no. 48)

The Rambam agrees with Rabbi Eliezer yet has his own input. He agrees that women earn reward if they learn; however, this reward is similar to one who fulfills a *mitzvah* voluntarily. He adds that the censure applies only to the Oral *Torah*, but not to the Written *Torah*; and while a father should not teach even the Written *Torah* to his daughter, it is not like teaching her levity if he does. (*Talmud Torah* 1:13)

"If they learn on their own, we can see that they are exceptional; this is what the Rambam meant by saying that they do have a reward if they learn properly." (*Perishah* on *SA Yoreh Deah* 246, note 15)

The Rambam better explains a practical reason why women don't study the *Mishnah* and *Talmud*. He notes that since women are not generally free to dedicate themselves to long-term, intense *Torah* study, their knowledge will be superficial. Without a thorough and sophisticated understanding of *Torah*, which can only be developed through years of intensive, time-consuming study, the *Torah* might, *chas-v-shalom*, appear trivial and irrelevant to them. According to this interpretation, *tiflus* is related to the root *tafel*, which appears in the verse, "Can that which is tasteless (*tafel*) be eaten without salt." (*Iyov* 6:6) (*Hilchos Talmud Torah* 1:13)

Another interpretation of Rabbi Eliezer's statement can be found in the *Torah Temimah* which bases its understanding along with another *pasuk*. The *Talmud* says, "Hashem has placed greater understanding in women than in men." (*Niddah* 45b) The implication here is that women might rely on their intuitive understanding before acquiring a firm foundation in *Torah* logic and thereby distort the intention of the law. *Chazal* address this danger by saying, "Without knowledge, there is no understanding." (*Avos* 3:17)

Because women's intuition is so great that they might rely upon it. This might be beneficial in cases of giving advice but when it comes to *halacha*, some points are not logical. The *Talmud* says, "איתתך גוצא גחין ותלחוש לה, If your wife is short, bend down and whisper to her." (*Baba Metzia* 59a) As every married man learns, his wife generally has wise words to share and she is worth listening to, even if it means humbling himself. "Her ways are ways of pleasantness, and all her paths are peace." (*Proverbs* 3:18)

The author of the responsa Rav Pe'alim relates that his grandmother was won't to learn eighteen chapters of *Mishnayos* every morning before dawn. (*Ben Ish Chay, Rav Pe'alim I, Sod Yesharim* 9) On the other hand, though, the contemporary sage, Rabbi Moshe Feinstein writes, "One who teaches his daughter *Mishnayos* 'is as if he taught her levity.'" (*Igros Moshe, Yoreh Deah* III, 87)

Based on these findings, it is very obvious that just as men should focus on foundational *Torah* study first before they embark on in depth *Talmud*, so too, women should work on studying *Tanach* and *halacha*. They should happily complete these works which will bring them to further fear of G-d. It is in no way demeaning and after they have fulfilled these requirements, let them add the *aggadic* study of the *Talmud* such as *Ayin Yaakov* to their library of knowledge. Let them master these works as their beauty is unrecognized, and they are in no way limiting. The wisdom of the *Torah* is endless.

The *Talmud* in *Chullin* (104b, see also *Megillah* 15a, *Avos* 6:6) says that if you tell over a *d'var Torah* in the name of the person who said it, it brings redemption to the world. But then it goes on to give an example of this and uses the story of how Esther gave over a *Torah vort* in the name of Mordechai. Now out of all the stories, why did the *Talmud* choose Esther for this example? Because, how much more so should women be careful about this. If they say over a *halacha* or *Torah vort*, they have a better chance at making a mistake, since they don't always hear things firsthand. So, that is why the *Talmud* chose this story, to remind women to be extra careful to always quote their sources... Of course, men too!

Rabbi Mordechai Menachem Reich taught, "*eizer kenegdo*" (a helpmate opposite him) and "*Shas*" each have the *gematria* value of 360, which indicates that a women's greatest help to her husband is aiding him in his conquest of *Shas*.

# *Torah Lishmah*

Rabbi Meir said: "Whoever occupies himself with the study of *Torah* for its own sake merits many things; and not only that, but the entire world is worthwhile because of him. He is called Friend, beloved of G-d, one who loves the Omnipresent G-d and who loves mankind; he brings joy to the Omnipresent G-d and joy to mankind. It [the *Torah*] clothes him with humility and reverence, and prepares him to be righteous, pious, upright and faithful; and it puts him far from sin and brings him near to virtue. People enjoy from him the benefit of counsel and sound wisdom, understanding and strength – as it is stated [of *Torah*]:

"'Mine are counsel and sound wisdom; I am understanding, might is mine.' (*Proverbs* 8:14)

"And it gives him sovereignty and dominion, and penetrating judgment. To him are revealed mysteries of *Torah*; and he becomes an ever-flowing fountain that never fails and as a river that never runs dry, which constantly gains in vigor. He becomes modest, patient and forgiving of insults; and it makes him great and exalted above all creations." (*Avos* chapter 6)

Rabbi Yaakov Abuchatzeira taught, "The perfect man is one who serves Hashem in fear, love and immense joy, with no thought of reward in his heart, neither in this world nor the world to come." (*Ma'aglei Tzedek* 107)

"One should occupy himself with *Torah* and the commandments even *shelo lishmah*, for through *shelo lishmah* he will come to *lishmah*." (*Pesachim* 50b)

If you want to define what is *Torah lishmah*, some great sages have clarified this. It isn't just sitting behind your *Gemarah* thinking that you're fixing the world by *Torah* study alone. The world around you can't just simply fall apart while you are immersed in your studies. That would be learning in order to have knowledge but actual *lishmah* requires practice.

It is written, "For the fundamental aim of occupying oneself with *Torah* is to bring it to fruition... The object of studying *Torah lishmah* is undoubtedly to know it in order to practice its commandments." (*Reishis Chachmah*, Intro)

100

Rabbi Yaakov Abuchatzeira taught, "It is known that one who studies *Torah* and practices it gives strength to the forces of holiness, while a person who studies and does not practice as he should, strengthens the other force, *chas-v-shalom*, and brings it in instead of holiness. The verse defines this metaphorically as "a maidservant who inherits [the place of] her mistress." (*Proverbs* 30:23) The result is that one brings in profanity instead of holiness and impurity instead of purity. About this we learn, "When you teach *Torah* which you learn and practice for its own sake, you thereby make a distinction between the holy and the profane, and between the pure and the impure, so that the latter should not come in place of holiness. Also, when you learn and practice, your lessons to *B'nei Yisrael* are effective and they fulfill them and do whatever they hear from you." (*Petuchei Chotem – Shemini*)

It says in *Midrash Shemuel*, "One learns *lishmah* if he learns in order to practice." (*Midrash Shemuel*, on *Avos* 2:5)

Rabbi Yaakov Emden said, "This is *Torah lishmah*: in order to fulfill it." (*Lechem Shamayim* on last chapter of *M Avos*, beginning)

The Chafetz Chaim said, "As is written in the holy books, the essence of *Torah* study *lishmah* is knowing the *halacha* [i.e. practice] clearly in every field of the *Talmud*." (*Likutey Halachos*, first intro)

Rabbi Moshe Alshich, "The object is not study but deed; that is, exposition is nothing unless it leads to deed." (*Alshich* on *Avos* 1:17)

The Gaon of Vilna instructed, "For the goal and primary purpose of occupying oneself with *Torah* is to find the smooth, straight path of serving Hashem." (Harra on *Proverbs* 23:26)

Rabbi Chaim of Volozhin said, "This is the entire fruition of learning *Talmud*: to extract from its practical rules of law." (Intro to Hagra's glosses on *SA Aruch Chaim*) And elsewhere: "Don't think study is the object – deed is." (*Rusach Chayim*, Avos 1:17)

Let's break down the various ways of serving Hashem *lishmah*:

To study *Torah* merely because it was a command may be the simplest understanding of "*Torah lishmah*". This is indicated by the *Gemarah Sotah* 22b and Rashi and Tosefos' commentary there. See Maharsha to *Nedarim* (62) where he states that the highest form of learning is that which is done "to fulfill the *mitzvah*, out of love for the one who gave the command".

Learning for the purpose of knowing how to observe the mitzvos appears to have a lot of support. One can bring support for this idea from the *Gemarah Berachos* (17a), which states that the purpose of wisdom is תשובה ומעשים טובים, repentance and virtuous deeds, and the Maharsha

101

there assumes that this is referring to *Torah* wisdom as its being learned לשמה.

Studying *Torah* for the sake of better knowing or loving G-d is unquestionably a good thing. This appears to be the definition of the Meiri to *Pesachim* (50b) who indicates that the only *'lishmah'* is for the sake of the love of Hashem.

*Nefesh Hachayim* (4:3) says that studying for the love of learning, to increase one's knowledge and to discover the intellectual depth of the *Torah* is the highest goal of learning "*lishmah*". He bases this on a Rosh (to *Nedarim* 62a), and this is also clearly stated by the *Ohr Hachayim* to *Bamidbar* (24:6). This may not contradict the opinion of the Rambam, who besides for stating that learning should be done out of love of Hashem, one should also do/study "what's true simply because it's true". Additionally, the son of the Rambam writes in a *teshuvah* (no. 82) that those who learn *Torah lishmah* are those who do so "to find the truth".

The Alter Rebbe in *Hilchos Talmud Torah* (4:3) defines *lishmah* as learning *leshem Shamayim* - for the sake of Heaven. In other words, to do what Hashem wants, and not to receive a reward in this world or the next, or because of fear of punishment in this world or the next. Certainly not to be a "*gadol*" or any other such intention to use the *Torah*, or to win arguments, etc.

I study *Mishnah*... I think I know something. *Talmud*... I think I know even more... Then, I study *Kabbalah* and realize I know nothing and have to start all over again from the *Chumash*. This is when you can see the wise words of King Solomon come to fruition. That the ultimate goal of knowledge is to realize that we know nothing at all. This is a good indication that your study is *Torah lishmah*... if your ego grows as you study... it's not truthful... if you are more embarrassed by your lack of knowledge even though you have attained more... then you know the study is pure.

Rav Matisyahu Solomon said in the eleventh *Siyum HaShas*, "It's not sufficient just to learn *daf yomi* or to try to just understand a *blat* of *Gemarah*, we have to be *maminim* in every word and *blat* of the *Gemarah* and we have to be *maminim* in the words of *chazal*... We have to remember and understand, to demand of ourselves *emunah*... *Shas* is not just strictly the study of ancient texts. *Shas*... is *emunah* based knowledge, it is a challenge both to the intellect and our faith." *Shas,* we have *emunah* that every word is *Torah min hashamayim*; *Shas* is our *Torah shebal peh* without which the *Torah shebechsav* has no meaning. *Shas* is the foundation of our faith."

The Chasam Sofer said, "He who learns *Torah* to know it is very meritorious, but he will not succeed in his learning as well as he would if his purpose were to learn in order to teach… The ultimate goal, however, is to fulfill the commandments of Hashem and refrain from that which is forbidden. Therefore, we should approach *Torah* study with the intention of understanding the practice of its commandments, for that is the basic goal." (*Derashos Chasam Sofer*, pp. 409-410)

I think we can link this idea to that of *derech eretz*. While people of the world around you are suffering from not knowing Hashem, how can you study *Torah* only inside your four *amos*? Not everyone was designed with the best social skills, to go out and spread *Torah* but there is always some way to do so.

I believe that every true *Torah* scholar should write a book and compose *chiddushai Torah* if he is able to do so properly. He thereby creates a legacy for his family and children. I wish my father had left me more than just a notebook of *Torah* thoughts. If only I could remember all of his *Torah* from my youth, but I was too young to appreciate them. All I can do is remember his purity and *derech eretz* but his *chiddushei Torah*, many are lost for now.

I've encouraged so many *rabbis, chavrusos* to not just study the *Torah* but to actually write *Torah* books themselves. It is so healthy for the mind to write down thoughts and to express itself outwardly, just like its healthy for an artist to draw or a musician to compose a new song. The *Torah* was created to be shared. Don't lock it up behind the *bais midrash* walls but release it to others. The *Talmud* says, "A person acquires the *Torah* through learning, sharing it and living it." Therefore, you have to perform all three actions… Then if you really, really want to receive the *Torah* like Moshe Rabbienu, you have to pray that your mind should be open and that you be worthy of receiving it as a gift. The Chofetz Chayim states, "Whenever a person suffers in any way for the honor of Hashem, he is lifted to a higher station in the World to Come."

The *Gemarah* says, "The entire forty days that Moshe stood upon *Har Sinai*, he would learn *Torah* and then forget it…" He *mamash* suffered to attain the *Torah*. Then on the 40th day, Hashem gave it to him as a present. (*Nedarim* 38a, also see, *Y. Horayos* 3:5, with P'nei Moshe)

The *Gemarah* says, "One who reviews a subject forty times, is guaranteed it will be rooted in his memory as if it were placed in his pocket." If you take the word בלבו, in his heart, it comes to the *gematria* of 40. Also, the word, לי, mine, with proper review the Torah becomes a true part of your heart.

The *Gemarah* states that one of the three good gifts that Hashem gave to *Yisrael* only comes through suffering. Which gift is that? *Torah*.

The word for gift in Hebrew is מַתָּנָה. Every morning in *birchas HaTorah* we say, "Blessed are You, Hashem... Who selected us from all the nations וְנָתַן, and gave, to us His *Torah*..."

What's the connection between the words מַתָּנָה, gift, and נָתַן, gave?

They both contain the root word of תֵּן which means to give. Hashem is telling us, "I gave you the *Torah* as a gift. However, don't think it will come easily to you." As *Avos* says, "Prepare yourself to learn *Torah* because it is not an inheritance for you." Rabbeinu Yonah says, "You will never master the *Torah's* wisdom until you make the effort to acquire it. *Torah* is not an inheritance that is passed down from father to son.

Rabbi Yaakov Abuchatzeira taught, "It would have seemed natural since Moshe Rabbienu received all the *Torah* both written and oral on *Har Sinai*, for him to have written down everything completely. However, Hashem wanted to give all the descendants of *B'nei Yisrael* the merit to reveal by themselves those aspects of *Torah* which each of their *neshamos*, their souls, individually received at *Mount Sinai*. Therefore, the oral *Torah* was not written down. Nevertheless, it was all given to Moshe Rabbeinu at Mount Sinai." (*Petuchei Chotem, Tetzaveh*)

Rabbi Yaakov Abuchatzeira also said, "One who desires to offer *chiddushim* in *Torah* must base them on valid precedents of the finest provenance. As the *Zohar Hakodesh* says, '*Hakadosh Baruch Hu* builds new worlds in heaven and on earth from the true *chiddushim* of Israel.' This is derived from the verses, 'And I have set My words in your mouth and I have covered you with the shade of My hand, to establish heaven and to found the earth,' (*Yeshiyah* 51:16) and 'Just as the new heavens and new earth which I make.' (*Yeshiyah* 66:22) The second passage does not state 'I made,' but instead 'I make,' [to specify that Hashem makes these new worlds all the time, from the ongoing *chiddushim* of Israel]. However, if, *chas-v-shalom* one would propose *chiddushim* based on grounds of 'tohu vavohu,' 'void and nothingness,' then the new heavens and earth which Hashem would build from them would also be void and worthless and this would only increase the influence of the forces of evil in the world, G-d forbid." (*Petuchei Chotem, Shemini*)

The Chayey Adam writes, "It is well-known that *Torah* study is [undertaken] primarily to know the commandments in detail." Elsewhere he testifies about his departed son: "His learning was perfect, for I can attest that his study was for the purpose of practicing." (*Chayey Adam* Intro)

Rav said, "The goal of [*Torah*] wisdom is repentance and virtuous deeds." (*Berachos* 17a)

Rabbeinu Bachyay tells, "The purpose of knowledge and toil in

*Torah* is not that one study hard, but that one should come to practice...
for the aim of learning is only that he should practice. Thus, have our sages
interpreted the verse, "Good understanding comes to all who practice
them" – not "to all who study them" but "to all who practice them."

One should learn in order to teach, observe, and practice – that is
*Torah lishmah*. Rashi says, "One who acts with an ulterior motive is one who
"does not learn in order to practice."

R' Aharon Lichtenstein, not one to be accused of mysticism:
"One's ultimate aspiration should be to focus on *Torah*, not *kemach*.
Practically, it means that he should try to maximize his *Torah* study and his
direct *avodas* Hashem...*Talmud Torah* is not just a daily obligation, but a
general direction in a person's life. 'You shall meditate upon it day and
night.' (*Yehoshua* 1:8) Through Hashem's revealed word, we can come to
know Him, approach Him, relate to Him. This is a value, a goal to be
maximized as far as one can." (*By His Light*, p. 41)

The Ran explains, "It is well-known that the intent of *Torah* [study]
is to instill reverence for G-d, not to acquire wisdom..."

"...Establish many students..." (*Avos* 1:1) The sages should
attempt to have as many students as possible. They should not emulate
Rabban Gamliel in this matter, who when head of the academy,
proclaimed, "Any student whose mouth and heart are not equally sincere,
shall not be given access to the academy." (He argued that if a person's
motives in studying *Torah* were not entirely pure, then it was better for him
not to study at all.) Instead the sages should emulate what Rabbi Elazar
did when he became head of the academy. He permitted all students to
enroll in the academy, arguing that even if a student had ulterior motives,
the study of *Torah* would improve him. When a student has the
opportunity to learn, he will come to recognize the excellence of *Torah* and
will keep its commandments. (*Berachos* 28a)

Rava posed a contradiction: In *Psalm* 57 it says, "Your Grace
extends to Heaven", but in *Psalm* 108 it says, "Your Grace extends above
Heaven"! How can we resolve this?

Here (108) we are discussing those who do *lishmah*, there (57) those
who do *shelo lishmah*. This resolution follows the statement of R. Yehudah
in the name of Rav, for R. Yehudah said in the name of Rav "A person
should always be deeply involved in *Torah* and *mitzvos* even *shelo lishmah*,
because *shelo lishmah* will lead to *lishmah*." (*Pesachim* 50b)

I think some people misinterpret learning *lishmah* to be learning
without enjoyment. They conclude that if your enjoying your study then
you're doing it for you and not totally for Hashem. This is not correct, as

*Torah* study with joy is more everlasting and easier to recall later. Actually, if your study isn't joyous, maybe then you should evaluate if it's really *lishmah* because if you love Hashem, how can you not enjoy every moment of truthful service?

Rabbi Avraham Borenstein writes, "I thought I'd mention the opinion of some people who, straying from the path of the intellect, say that one who is creative and derives pleasure from the intellectual aspects of *Torah* study is not learning *lishmah* as much as if they were learning straightforwardly, deriving no pleasure, but rather learning only for the sake of the commandment. They suggest that one who enjoys learning is mixing his own pleasure into the learning. Actually, this is a blatant error, for the essence of the commandment to learn *Torah* is that one be delighted by it, for then it is absorbed into the blood, and one who derives pleasure from *Torah* becomes attached to it." (Introduction to the *Eglei Tal*)

Too many times people get caught up in the *kollel* or community scene. People learn because everyone else is doing it and it can actually become "cool" to study. Wives brag about the late nights their husbands spend in the *bais midrash*. Little do they realize that the *Torah* is more external for them and if nobody was around, they wouldn't be so involved in their study. You can see this when *bain hazmanim* comes around and suddenly all the *Torah* books become covered with dust. Venturing around the countryside, happily visiting park after park while not carrying even a single *Torah* book along. It is impossible for a true scholar to take a vacation from the *Torah*. If he must leave the *bais midrash*, he takes the *Torah* with him. A man is required to fix a schedule for the study of *Torah* at least once by day and once by night, as it is said: "And you shall study it by day and by night." (*Yehoshua* 1:8) The commandment never rests. Our time in this world is limited, before we know it, years will pass by.

The *Rosh HaYeshivah*, Rabbi Yehudah Zev Segal was rarely seen without a *sefer* in his hand. His learning was not measured in minutes, but in seconds. His face glowed as he sang out the *Gemarah*. (*Torah Luminaries* p.193)

Rabbi Yehoshua Cohen recommends, "During *bain hazmanim*, it is very worthwhile to study and prepare at least a few pages of the upcoming *Gemarah*. This is very useful, as it will allow you to start off the new *zman* with some knowledge of the topics dealt with in the tractate. This will help you to know and understand the tractate, motivating you to complete it.

"When, right from the start, you know something about the topics being studied in the *yeshivah*, you get the feeling that you can easily reach the level of having 'your studies in the palm of your hand.' (*Bava Basra* 10b)

This in turn increases your desire to learn and encourages you to study throughout the entire *zeman* with great diligence. Thus, you will be able to complete and know the whole tractate." (*Kerem Yehoshua* p. 129)

I personally feel an obligation to increase my studies during this time to compensate for all the confusion around me of people not learning. The very air of *bain hazmanim*, with the children home and people off schedule seems to confuse me, so I have to exert even more effort and time for the learning of *Torah*.

## Set Times for Learning Torah

It is so important to keep set times for study. The Piaseczner Rebbe recommends:

"Set a time limit for all your actions. If you are about to eat, set a time limit beforehand. 'I will spend half an hour' or 'fifteen minutes eating'. If you are going to your friend's home to engage in conversation for a little while (if you cannot then study *Torah*), set a time limit beforehand. 'I will spend this amount of time there and no more.' This is excepting the case where you are going to have a discussion about religious things and *chassidus*.

"In general, you should feel yourself to be like a soldier in the army, whose time is not his own – where each set time is followed by another, and where each activity is followed by another." (*B'nai Machshavah Tovah, Seder Hadracha v'Klalim*, #13)

"Every man of Israel, whether poor or rich, healthy or sick, should have a fixed time in the day and another at night when he will learn *Torah*, each person according to his own ability and understanding. Whether much or little, it is all one thing as long as his heart is directed to *Shamayim*. Moreover, he should fix the time so that it is not omitted for any reason in the world, even if he has an opportunity to earn a great deal of money. Let him relinquish all the money but not give up his set time for *Torah*.

"This is the whole point of fixing a time. That it is actually fixed and an obligation, not something haphazard that can be forgotten or neglected if something else comes up. In that case its being fixed has no significance; it seems that he is just learning *Torah* because he has not anything else to do. So, when something comes up, he leaves the *Torah* and does that instead. This is nothing other than belittling the *Torah*, *chas-v-shalom*. So, when you study *Torah*, fixing the time, you should not interrupt you're learning for the sake of anything else… but learn for the set amount of time uninterruptedly, finish, and only afterwards attend to your other concerns." (*Seder ha-Yom*, p. 22b)

"In his youth, Rabbi Tzvi Hirsh of Ziditchov, divided up the twenty-four hours of the day and wrote on a piece of paper a schedule when he would do each thing. For example, he set aside a specific amount of time for learning each *Torah* subject; similarly, he specified when he would not chat with others, and so too for other *hanhagos* for each and every part of the day. When he came to the Seer of Lublin [who became his rebbe] he highly praised this practice of his." (*Ha-Chozeh mi-Lublin*, p. 138)

A *talmud chacham* should be like the *'Aron'* (Ark) which was plated with gold within and without. Rabbah said, "A *Torah* student who is not inwardly what he is outwardly, is no *Torah* student." (*Yoma* 72b)

Rabbi Pinchus said, "*Torah* study should be done out of love for *HaKadosh Baruch Hu* rather than as a struggle arising from obligation."

I was standing next to a *Torah* scholar watching the bon fire for a while during *Lag B'Omer*. He told me he wanted to go back to my house to study *Torah*. I told him, "in the fire is *Torah*." He didn't seem to agree with so much and he still wanted to return home but instead, he began telling me a *d'var Torah*. When he completed it, I turned to him and said, like I said, "in the flames is *Torah*." Then he got it. You know the bon fire on *Lag B'Omer* isn't just a normal bon fire, it is a fire that can ignite your soul for the entire year. Look deep into the flames and think how to mold yourself into a *ben Torah*.

Speaking of returning home. The *pasuk* says, "Return to your tents." (*Devarim* 5:27)

The Kotzker Rebbe began to explain:

Having delivered his admonishments to the nation, Moshe reviews the giving of the *Torah* on Mt. Sinai. He relates that after that great event, Hashem told him to instruct the people of Israel to return to their tents.

The Kotzker Rebbe interpreted this verse as meaning that Hashem was saying to Moshe: I want to see how they will behave in their homes. It is true that here, at the mountain, which is ablaze with fire, their hearts are all directed towards heaven. But go tell them, Return – bring this burning enthusiasm back with you into your tents. Only then will the *Torah* achieve permanent existence.

Only if we enthusiastically live according to *Torah* in our homes, as well as in public holy places, will the *Torah* be forever. (*And Nothing but the Truth*, p. 14)

## *Arrogance vs Lishmah*

A scholar has to be very careful not to become arrogant from his *Torah* wisdom. This is usually one of the first obstacles a person faces as they begin to take their *Torah* study more seriously. But *Torah lishmah* is, "For the sake of Heaven and not to become great and arrogant." (*Riv'van* to *Pesachim* 50b)

The Kotzker Rebbe explained, "It is not in Heaven." (*Devarim* 30:12) The *Torah* is not found among those who think they have reached the heavens.

R. Eliezer son of R. Tzadok said: "Do things for the sake of their Maker and speak in them *lishmah*. Do not make them a crown to be exalted through them, nor a shovel to dig with. A fortiori: If Belshazzar, who only used for his own benefit sacred utensils which had lost their sanctity, was uprooted from the world, all the more so one who uses the crown of *Torah* for his own benefit!" (*Nedarim* 62b)

A *beraisa* teaches that R. Benaah would often say: "Anyone who is deeply involved in *Torah lishmah*, his *Torah* becomes an elixir of life for him, as Scripture says, 'She is a tree of life for those who grasp her.' (*Proverbs* 3:18) But 'anyone who is deeply involved in *Torah shelo lishmah*, it becomes an elixir of death for him.'" (*Tannis* 7a) It also says, "Anyone who does *shelo lishmah* would have been better off had he not been created…"(*Berachos* 17a)

"There are two kinds of *shelo lishmah* - if he acts out of love or fear, or to know the wisdom of *Torah*, then "out of *shelo lishmah* comes *lishmah*". But if he involves himself to become great or to attack, he would have been better off had he not been created." (*Maharam Chalava* to *Pesachim* 50b)

"Once *shelo lishmah* has come up, I'll say something else about it. Rabbienu Tam said there are two types of *shelo lishmah*, one forbidden and one permitted. But I, insignificantly small, say that all *shelo lishmah* is the same, and all are transgressive. But that transgression is permitted if it will lead in the end to a *mitzvah*, like when a man saves a woman in a river or digs someone out of a pile on *Shabbos*. This is also implied by the comparison (of a *mitzvah shelo lishmah*) to Yael (whose seduction of Sisera is called a '*sin lishmah*'). But one who stiffens his neck, who will never do the *mitzvah*, better for him not to have been created." (Responsa of R. *Chayim Ohr Zarua*)

The *Talmud* in *Nedarim* (45a) says, "What is the meaning of 'And from the desert [they went to] *Matanah* and from *Matanah* [to] *Nachaliel* and from *Nachaliel* [to] *Bamos*? (*Bamidbar* 21:18-19) If a person equates himself to a desert, which is accessible to everyone, the *Torah* is given to him as a gift, as is written, 'And from the desert *Matanah*.' Once it is given to him, he is Hashem's portion, as is written, 'and from *Matanah, Nachaliel*.' Once he is Hashem's portion, he rises to greatness, as is written, 'and from *Nachaliel, Bamos*.' If he glorifies himself, the Holy One, blessed is He, lowers him, as is written, 'And from *Bamos* [to the] *Gai* (valley)'. (ibid. 21:20) Further, he is beaten to the ground, as it is written, '… and is discerned on the face of the wilderness.' (ibid.) If he repents, the Holy One, blessed is He, raises him, as is written, 'Every valley shall be elevated.'" (*Yeshayahu* 40:4)

The Maharal explains that the message of the [*Gemarah*] is that the *Torah* is suitable only to a person without vanity; a person to whom all are equal – he is the one who deserves the *Torah*.

Another dimension [of the *Gemarah's* intent]: The *Torah*, too, is available to all. As *Devarim* (4:44) states, "This is the *Torah* that Moshe placed before *B'nai Yisrael*." Thus, only a person who is himself universally available, like the *Torah* is, can relate to the *Torah*.

Why is the *Torah* available to all [and why is that only a person who is himself universally available can relate to the *Torah*]? The *Torah* is not of this world but the elevated world. Because of its [resultant] quality of basic simplicity, it belongs to everyone equally, with no person having a great portion [in it] than his fellow. Therefore, when a person makes himself available to all, exhibiting the quality of basic simplicity in himself, the universally available *Torah* suits him. This concept is spelled out in the *Midrash Bamidbar Rabbah* (1:7), which states that the *Torah* was given in the midst of desert, fire and water; just as these are available to all, so is the *Torah* available to all.

The *Gemarah* continues: When a person accepts the *Torah*, he is the portion of Hashem Yisborach. This is because he has departed the realm of the material to acquire the level of the intellective; he is at that point the portion of Hashem – and as such, he rises to greater heights.

If he glorifies himself, the Holy One, blessed be He, lowers him. He was raised to his level by Hashem Yisborach, the very One who humbles the haughty, so he, especially, is humbled. This is the meaning of, "he is beaten to the ground": He is forcefully propelled away from Hashem Yisborach because he did not achieve his level on his own merit but was raised to it by Hashem Yisborach. He now gives himself airs, so he is rejected with force. A man who is vain about self-achieved merit is not beaten down with force; he [at least] is intrinsically worthy of the merit. This person, on the other hand, who is not worthy of greatness on his

110

own score but was raised by Hashem Yisborach, deserves a forceful downfall from Hashem Yisborach.

It has been demonstrated that preparation is required in order to acquire the intellective *Torah*. The key is humility, as we have explained; the trait which above all others is preparation for the *Torah*. (*Nesivos Olam, Nesiv HaTorah*, p.75)

The Klausenburger Rebbe told how the Beis Yisrael had taken him to visit Reb Simcha Bunim at his room in Galei Zanz Hotel. Before knocking on the door, the Beis Yisrael told the Klausenburger to peer through the keyhole, where he saw Reb Simcha Bunim engrossed in *Torah* learning. By the time he opened the door for them, the *sefarim* were gone, a copy of *Hamodia* religious newspaper in their place.

Rabbi Moshe Feinstein said, "In our generation we must do everything we can to enable others to learn from us, to study *Torah* and perform *mitzvos*. In previous generations, when there were numerous righteous people, an individual could choose to hide himself. However, in our day and age, we need to study *Torah* and do charitable deeds openly in a manner that will serve as a positive model for others." (*Dorash Moshe*, ch. 8, p.24)

I think all too often the excuse given to us by the *yetzer hara* is to not publicly show our *avodas* Hashem. Therefore, he convinces us that it's better not to learn now or to *daven* with *kavanah*, rather do it later. However, "later never coming" was his plan all along. When there are so many ways today to have arrogance through *gashmious*, I wonder if being arrogant in *Torah* really applies as much. I guess it all depends on the person and the situation. However, be careful not to be fooled by your *yetzer hara* convincing you not to give all your effort in *Torah* and *tefillah*. "The righteous are as bold as a lion [in their service of Hashem]." (*Proverbs* 28:1)

## D'vekus in Learning

The purpose of learning is to come to know Hashem. Not spoken enough about is, *d'vekus* in learning *Torah*. That you're learning *Torah lishmah* should bring you joy, *d'vekus* and an increase in love of Hashem.

"[Someone who truly loves the *Torah* and appreciates how precious it is] will not rest or relax from meditating on it whenever he has a chance, even for one minute. Instead of wasting that minute in worthless things or talk, Hashem save us, he will grab whatever holy book is near at hand, whatever it is, and look in it to learn, even a few lines or words, for that minute – because of his deep love for the *Torah*." (*Tzva'a Yekara* of Rabbi

Alexander Ziskind, #35)

The Baal Shem Tov taught, "You should continually remind yourself before Whom you are learning, because it happens that even while you are learning *Torah* you could easily lose your awareness of Hashem. So, you should bring yourself back to that awareness again and again, every minute." (*Tzavaas ha-Rivash*, p.19)

He also said, "As you learn you should think... [and] say to yourself, 'Has not Hashem contracted Himself, so to speak, and descended into his *Torah* that I am studying?' Realizing this [that you are now with Him and close to Him], you should learn with joy, and with fear and love of Hashem." (ibid.)

When the Seer of Lublin was a young man and a disciple of Rabbi Shmelke of Nikolsburg, Rabbi Shmelke asked him to sit near to him when he was learning *halacha* and *Tosafos* – for these subjects require such intense mental concentration that he might be distracted from his *d'vekus*. So, Rabbi Shmelke told him that if it appeared to him that this was happening, he should pull his sleeve a little to remind him.

The Lubliner recalled that it never did happen that Rabbi Shmelke needed his reminder, for he saw that he was never without *d'vekus*, even while learning the most complicated *Torahs*. Once, however, the Lubliner had noticed that Rabbi Shmelke was very deep in his concentration, and he was concerned that perhaps he had become separated from his *d'vekus*, and he wanted to tug gently on his sleeve, as he had been told to do. However, before he could do so, Rabbi Shmelke turned to him and said, "My son, my son, I remembered on my own." (*Mazkeret Shem ha-Gedolim*, p.60)

Rabbi Mordechai of Tchernobil writes, "When you are learning *Torah* and praying from the *siddur*, appreciate that the holy letters are like chambers of a palace in which the King dwells. Should you intend wholeheartedly to attach your soul to the King who is there, you will be able to say the words with great fear and love of Hashem." (*Hanhagos Tzaddikim*, p. 63, #3)

It is very easy to learn *Torah* robotically. We must not fall into this trap because true *Torah lishmah* is done in order to bring gladness to Hashem. So, what can a person do? "[He is] to imagine the light of the *Shechinah*... above his head and as if the light is flowing down around him. He is in the midst of the light, sitting in the pure air, and he trembles with joy... Through this he can come to the state of the separation of the soul from the body and senses, taking off materiality as one removes a garment... So, he should sanctify his little space of prayer and his little space of *Torah* study and imagine that the light is glowing around him." (*Or ha-Ganuz l'Tzaddikim*, p. 10; cf. pp. 11 & 22)

Don't underestimate the importance of connecting yourself to Hashem during your *Torah* learning. Then you can fulfill the verse in the *Torah*, "Today you are standing before G-d." (*Devarim* 29:9)

The Baal Shem Tov said, "The purpose of *Torah* study for its own sake is to cleave in *d'vekus* to the One who is hidden within it, and to become a chariot for Him." (*Avodah u'Moreh Derech*, chap. 8, p. 16)

Rabbi Avraham of Slonim writes, "When you are learning *Torah*, you should picture yourself standing in the midst of a great fire and surrounded by fire." (*Toras Avos*, p. 166)

Rabbi Yosef Kahanaman, the Rav of Ponevez said that, "The Chofetz Chaim would go to the *bais midrash* and learn eight hours straight without a break. This is what it means to feel a love for *Torah* study." (*Beair Mechokaik* ch. 7, p. 149)

The more you increase your love for the *Torah*, the more devoted you will be to its study. "When you open a book to learn and when you close it, kiss the book." (*Derech Chayim*, 5-61) Any small gesture that will increase your joy and appreciation in *Torah* learning will help grow your passion for her. You have to be excited about what you're learning and how your performing it. You must appreciate the greatness of what you're doing, as "*Talmud Torah kneged kulam*, Torah study is equivalent to all the *mitzvos* in the *Torah*." (*Peah* 1:1) The Vilna Gaon comments: "When someone learns just one page of *Gemarah*, he covers hundreds of words, each of which gives him more *kedusha* than a lifetime of doing *mitzvos*."

"Just as water nourishes plant life, so *Torah* – studied with proper intensity – nourishes whoever toils in it." (*Shir HaShirim Rabbah* 1)

Rabbi Chaim Volozhiner related, "When a person toils over any word [of *Torah*], that word – literally – cleaves itself into a shaft of fire [as it issues] from the mouth of the Blessed One, as it were, and it is considered as if he has now received it at *Sinai*." (*Nefesh HaChaim* 4:14)

One of the *gabbaim* recollects how Rav Yidele Horowitz would learn every day without interruption for at least eight hours straight. Often, he learned the entire day from dawn to dusk. When he didn't want to be disturbed, he would not open the door to those who came to see him, including his *gabbaim*. Once he locked himself in his study for three consecutive weeks and did not interrupt his learning for anything. His meals were brought to the study door. He would take the food and immediately shut the door again.

Mesilas HaShas - מסילת הש"ס
# Torah by Heart

It was very common for scholars to memorize pages and passages of *Mishniyos* and *Talmud*. This was because the *Torah* was everything to them. Just like a musician will memorize hundreds of notes, because he is so eager to play his craft, so too did the scholar become one with his instrument, that of the *Talmud*.

The "pin test" was done to see how proficient a scholar was in all of *Shas*. Here's how it worked: Pick a word on a page, pierce it with a pin from first page to last. In order to pass the test, the scholar will recite precisely which word the pin pierces on both sides of each page first to last.

It wasn't that these scholars simply memorized each page, they were so devoted to the *Talmud* that it was a natural as breathing for them.

According to Simon Holloway PhD., he stated, "It was likely a magic trick of some description. How the trick was done, I do not know. But I do know that while a lot of people have acquired a most profound familiarity with the *Babylonian Talmud*, that degree of [the pin test] memorization is probably impossible." (Quora Dec. 7, 2007)

That is what is so amazing about knowledge of the *Torah*. Even if someone were to have a photographic memory, the "pin test" would still be virtually impossible. However, the *Torah* is beyond logic. For those who toil in her, amazing things happen. When I was younger, I met a few scholars of this caliber. For instance, Rav Ruderman, the *Rosh HaYeshivah* of Ner Yisrael. He was known to have completed the "pin test." Today, well, not so many.

A lot of this talent comes from a person's youth, learning in *cheder*. When I was in *cheder*, the schools used to have contests to see who could memorize the most *Mishniyos* and we would ALL receive prizes. Once our minds were accustomed to memorizing passages, it would become much easier. It was so exciting; it was something that all of us would talk about. I can tell you that out of an entire class of thirty boys, nobody from my class failed to memorize a few *prakim* of *Mishniyos*, no matter what level of learning we were all on. When the desire is there, the mind adjusts and can-do amazing things.

My special friend, a holocaust survivor, Rabbi Patoki, told me how when World War II first started, and they were rounding up families, his rebbe in *cheder* closed their *Gemarahs* and told them that 'when there is a knife to your neck, a person needs to recite the Psalms.' He then went on to teach them all of *Tehillim* by heart. There was no boy in the *yeshivah* that

114

didn't learn the entire book and all of them were able to recite *Tehillim* by heart. He went on to tell me that till this day, he never missed saying the entire book of *Tehillim* twice daily by heart.

Since I am already speaking of this wonderful *tzaddik*, let me tell you what else he taught me. When I used to walk him home each week from *shul* Friday night, he would teach me how to recite the *Kaddish* and answer *Yehey Shemay Rabbah*. He taught me to see and feel the six million. "Tonight," he would say, "I want you to listen to me reciting the *Kaddish* with all my heart because when I do so, I feel the pain of the six million." Then as I walked him home, he would ask me, "Did you understand. Did you feel my *Kaddish*?" This happened dozens of times until, I too could feel it. If only people understood the greatness of answering *Yehey Shemay Rabbah* with all their heart.

So, how did Rabbi Patoki become so special? The last minute as he was reciting *Shema* for the last time, they opened the door of the gas chamber, needing a few young lads for labor, so this holy soul could live on to teach me and others this lesson. In order that he could recite the *Kaddish* every day of his life and elevate these holy souls. But not only him, his holy *rebbetzin* too, she would recite *Tehillim* and *Shir HaShirim* by heart, every day. I am so blessed that they became regulars at my *Shabbos* home to inspire me.

So, do we really need a knife to our necks in order to memorize *Torah* by heart? Well back then, not only did they not have technology, but they went to sleep early and arose at the crack of dawn. People were masters in *mussar* and devoting themselves to their study. We are all capable of the same. Nothing has changed except our will power and that is entirely in our control.

Rabbi Simcha Wasserman would emphasize that the human brain has much superior capacity than we are accustomed to utilizing. He said that we had only to look at the generation before the war to see how remarkable a mind can become through immersion in *Torah*. He would insist that strengthening our grasp of *Torah* by remembering each word, understanding the meaning of each word and applying each principle derived through such careful study were within our mind's reach. When he heard that neurologists believe that people only have access to a fraction of their brain's potential, he would declare, "They never knew Reb Aharon Kotler! They never watched my uncle Reb Chaim Ozer!" Often, he would refer to the anecdote about a secular thinker who met the Rogatchover Goan, Rabbi Yosef Rosen, and commented that one man like this could make ten Einstein's. (*Torah Luminaries* p. 60)

115

"It is important for any *Torah* scholar to know some *mesecheta* of the *Torah* by heart and at least some chapters of the *Mishnah* — for often you are in a situation where you cannot learn from a book, especially when you are traveling." (*Darka Shel Torah*, #2, in YHvT, p. 101)

A *rosh hayeshivah* mentioned to me that this was very hard for him to do. He forced himself to memorize some *Mishnayos* by heart, but it wasn't easy to review them while mobile and traveling. I mentioned to him, that it is much easier to do this if you also know some basic *kavanos* Arizal. Because when it comes to *kavanos*, you can picture them in your mind and meditate. Simple ones don't have to tax your mind. Then you can fulfil the holy teaching of Rav Yochanan ben Zakkai, to not walk more than four *amos* without learning *Torah*. (*Succah* 28a) The Arizal says that *Yechudim*, are even higher than *Torah* study. You can learn some basic *Yechudim* from my book, *Chassidus Kabbalah and Meditation*. Even picturing YKVK in your mind along with the passage, "שויתי ה' לנגדי תמיד", *Shivisi Hashem L'negdi Tamid*," (*Tehillim* 16:8) is a small *Yichud* that you can meditate upon that is considered *Torah* study.

Rabbi Arele Roth writes, "Happy is he who knows words of *Torah* by heart, which he can continually go over [when walking outside, etc.], for they will certainly save him from undesirable and low thoughts." (*Noam ha-Levavos*, p. 40)

"Before the Grace after Meals, recite a chapter of *Avos* each day until you know the whole thing by heart." (*Tzavaas Rabbi Yehudah ben Asher*) I think if you were to choose a *Mishniyos* to memorize, *Mesechta Avos* would be the best to start with.

I really like what Rabbi Yehoshua Cohen teaches about memorization. When it comes to the *Talmud*, he recommends not to memorize in the beginning word for word but rather the contents and discussions of the *daf*. Afterall, that is the main thing to review, not the actual wording itself. That can come with time.

If a person is motivated, they really are capable of a lot, but you have to really have a goal in mind and a positive attitude that nothing will get in your way. Becoming a *talmud chacham* takes a lot of planning and it requires a positive attitude.

Rabbi Chaim of Volozhin told, "When someone runs away from something of which he is afraid, his speed will depend on the extent of fear he is experiencing. The larger the fear, the faster he will run. Similarly, when a person runs to receive something positive, his speed will be in proportion to its value to him. Should a powerful king issue a command, a loyal subject will run as fast as he can, regardless of the specific nature

116

of the request. This same concept pertains to *Torah* ideas. The greater
awareness one has of the immensity of the reward for the fulfillment of
positive deeds and the punishment for transgressions, the quicker he will
run. One who is strongly motivated to fulfill the Will of the Almighty will
run with the greatest speed to fulfill every aspect of His Will." (*Ruach
Chaim*, Ch. 4, 4:2)

Rabbi Chayim Mordechai Katz said, "In order to attain high
spiritual levels, it is absolutely essential to be ambitious. You must have an
inner passion and perfect will to strive to reach exalted levels. You must be
determined to raise yourself above all situations. Only then, will you
develop into greatness. Along with a stout passion for greatness, you must
also be willing to work to reach the lofty levels you are striving for. These
two factors are prerequisites for greatness: ambition and hard work." (*Beair
Mechokaik* Ch. 7, p. 47-9)

An *apikoris* once challenged the Chofetz Chayim when he was a
youngster. He said, "The sages state that those who toil in *Torah*, 'You are
praiseworthy, and all is well with you.' (*Tehillim* 128:2) 'You are praiseworthy
in this world and all is well with you in the next world.' (*Avos* 6:4) Now, can
you honestly tell me that this is true? So many *Torah* scholars live in abject
poverty and deprivation. Where is the happiness? Where is the fortune?"

"Show me true toil in *Torah*," the boy retorted with conviction,
"and I will show you true happiness and fortune."

Toil in *Torah* must be accompanied by the joy of observing the
commandment of *talmud Torah*. A person can have a desire to toil in any
matter or thing but only when they do so with joy, will they completely
succeed. That is why it is so important not to remove the joy of learning.
Sometimes we can toil so persistently in *Torah* that every day of study is
literally impossible to complete. This makes us constantly go up and down
on an emotional rollercoaster. Remember that Hashem is with you through
all your trials. "It is the Eternal your G-d who will battle for you." (*Devarim*
3:22) Make sure that your learning is for Him, to bring glory to your
Creator. If the *Shechinah* is with you, then you will be able to accomplish
far more than your capabilities.

A happy person has a good memory to recall what he learned and
to apply it. If your sad, all will be forgotten and sooner or later you will
burn out. If you serve Hashem *lishmah*, then even if you do not complete
the task at hand, you will accomplish wonderful things for your soul and
the world around you. Ultimately, it isn't what you complete in your
learning of *Torah* but your sincerity in its study. "He [Rabbi Tarfon] used
to say: It is not upon you to complete the task, but you are not free to idle

from it. If you have learned much *Torah*, you will be given much reward. And faithful is your Employer that He will reward you for your labor. And know that the reward of the righteous will be in the World to Come."(*Avos* 2:21)

# *Building yourself up*

You have to make sure you create for yourself solid landing gear... You know landing gear isn't just used for the plane to land, it is also needed in order for the plane to take off. So too, build for yourself a solid foundation of Judaism and its study. Find balance in your life and plant your feet firmly on the ground by keeping a consistent daily schedule of *Torah* and *mitzvos*. Stop trying to fly the plane only by the instruments or only through looking out the window. Rather, be both technical and have spiritual awareness. Build a solid foundation for yourself because through this, you can soar...

Rabbi Yosef Hurwitz, the Alter of Nevardok, told, "Remember the principle: *'Ain dovor sheomaid bifnai harotzon.'* That is, there is nothing that can stand in your way when you have a powerful desire to accomplish something." (*Madraigos Haadam, Bakashas Hashlaimus*)

Rabbi Yisrael Salanter explains the inspirational story of Rabbi Akiva who had not yet learned any *Torah* by the age of forty. Once, while standing near a well, he observed a hollowed-out stone, pondering how it happened. He was told that the constant dripping of water on the stone every day had finally bored a hole throughout the rock. Hearing this, Rabbi Akiva learned a *Kal Vochomer* for himself and eagerly began learning *Torah*, eventually emerging as the famed Rabbi Akiva, *Rabbon Shel Kol Yisrael*. Why was Rabbi Akiva affected so much by the "secret" of that hollowed stone?

Rabbi Yisrael Salanter explains (*Ohr Yisrael*, section 10) that when Rabbi Akiva began learning he was very depressed when he could not detect the results from his efforts in learning. But then he understood that the hollowing out of a stone didn't happen at once, but rather only after the constant dripping of water over a prolonged period of time. Surely, every drop had its effect, only it was not recognizable until many years had passed. This gave Rabbi Akiva new strength when he realized that the effect of his *limud haTorah* was already underway and would surface at a future time and be outwardly discernible. From this, every person should learn that the success of a *ben Torah* comes slowly. Even if at first the feeling of real accomplishment is lacking, he should still know that if he carries out his *avodah* of *Torah* and *yirah* as a faithful worker, day in and day out with a constant *seder*, he is guaranteed that over the period of many days he will sense in himself a great change. Then he will see the fruit of his labor and patience. "We have to be *mechazek* ourselves in the learning of *Torah* with a belief in the power of the *Torah* and the light within it, and Hashem will not hold back good from those who follow Him sincerely." (Rabbi Chaim Ben Alil)

A person who is very attached to *Torah* must not be separated from it, because should he separate from it, there would be no greater sin. This is in line with what Rabbi Shimon bar Yochai, of blessed memory, has written (*Chagigah* 9a), "The only person called incorrigibly corrupt is a person who was originally perfect and became corrupt." Who is this? A *Torah* scholar who has abandoned the study of *Torah*. According to this, one only calls another a traitor if he used to study *Torah* and deserted its study.

Rabbi Yaakov Abuhatzeira explains, "One who looks into the matter will understanding that it is not only one who leaves *Torah* study altogether who is called a traitor, but also a person who used to study *Mishnah* and *Gemarah* and who reverts to studying only *Chumash*. This is also true of one who used to study *Chumash*, *Mishnah*, *Gemarah* and *Kabbalah* and who gives up studying *Kabbalah* – he is also a 'traitor.'" (*Alef Binah* 175)

I think it's clear that a person who used to study in *yeshivah*, who knew the importance of making *Torah* first in their life, cannot simply ignore the calling. They might have other things in life that need attending too but *Torah* learning must coincide with this. Not only this, should a person have skipped ahead of their level, even though they must go back and build a proper foundation, they shouldn't completely abandon the studies they have begun, even if it was before the proper time.

Rav said: "As soon as man goes forth from the study of *halacha* to the study of Scripture, he no longer has peace. Shmuel explained: "It means one who leaves *Talmud* for *Mishnah*." And Rav Yochanan said: "Even from *Talmud* to *Talmud*." Rashi explains: "from *Talmud* to *Talmud*: from *Talmud Yerushalmi* to *Talmud Bavli*, since the former one is deeper." (*Talmud Bavli*, *Chagigah* 10a, Rashi *Chagigah* 10a, d.h from *Talmud* to *Talmud*)

Everyone has their own personal interpretation on how this applies but let me give you a different angle entirely. This *Gemarah* is teaching us the importance of learning properly. If you right away skip to studying the *Talmud*, it will be much harder to go back and study the required prerequisite, the *Mishnah*.

People are all the time jumping ahead of their level and they don't understand how important it is to build up a solid foundation before falling into daily, intense *Talmud* study. A wise person understands that before you walk, you have to crawl.

120

## The Path to Finishing Shas

I believe that most people never finish *Shas* or that it takes them literally forever to complete it, simply because they haven't previously finished all of *Tanach* and *Mishniyos*.

It's like telling a child once they have tasted ice cream to go eat a dish of vegetables. They can only think of the ice cream. People are so devoted to their *yeshivos* and trying to keep up with everyone else that they can't seem to humble themselves and learn the basics.

I was speaking with a *bachur* who studied in renown Brisk and the Mir Yeshivos. I told him how important it is that he make a *seder* to study *Mishniyos*. He responded, "why?"

Once I spoke to a *rosh hayeshiva* of a *yeshiva ketana* for teenage boys. I asked him, why don't you teach them *Mishnayos*. He responded, "That's not the way today."

My friends, this is why we have several mediocre *rabbanim* and *Torah* scholars today. This is why so many people in *yeshivos* never become big *talmedei chachamim*. Nobody understands how important core *Torah* study is anymore. If you question them on this, they just brush you off as if you don't have any idea what you're talking about.

So, what the *rabbanim* are telling us in *Gemarah Chagigah* is quite fundamental. If you go forth and study too far ahead, it will be very difficult to go backwards, and your study won't give you peace of mind. So, please stop what you're doing straightaway and prioritize learning in the proper order unless you have a good reason to continue to push this off further.

A friend who is a *talmud chacham* said to me the other day... "I wish I could do it all over; I would learn *Tanach*, *Mishnah*, then *Talmud*... the system messed me up." This is coming from a scholar with over 40 years in *yeshivos*, teaching and learning. He was ecstatic when I told him I was going to write this important work. Every few days he inquires if the book is completed yet.

I can't emphasize enough how important it is to learn the *Torah* in order. It builds structure to your learning. When I was around twenty-three, I finished the *Kabbalistic* work of the Zohar and my *rabbi* at the time (the Hornosteipel Rebbe of Betar, Israel) told me with a deep stare of his eyes, "You're doing it all wrong. First comes *Tanach*, then *Mishnah*, afterwards *Talmud* and then *Kabbalah*." He saved me by telling me this... When I returned back to my home in America, I put aside all my other books and studied all of *Tanach* finishing it in a half a year. Then I went on to complete the entire *Mishnah* as he instructed thereafter. I then repeated studying it again slower with more detail. Once I completed the work the first time, it became easier to complete each time thereafter. My only regret is that I didn't learn all of *Mishniyos* a dozen times before returning to the *Gemarah* back then.

Today, if you attend a *kollel*, they don't let you just learn whatever you want or what is best for your individual soul, so you can't start over and fix what you missed because you simply don't have enough time... but for us not stuck in the system... we can do it the right way! So, if you can, study in the proper order and build yourself a solid foundation in *Torah*, you won't regret it! (From my book, *The True Intentions of the Baal Shem Tov*)

I recently asked Rabbi Nosson Maimon how many times his father-in-law, Rabbi Rosenfeld finished *Shas*. He said, "Well over twenty times." Wow, *tzaddikim* who devote their lives to *Torah* are so special and they accomplish the unthinkable.

So, how does a person finish *Shas*? He starts by finishing the *Tanach* and *Mishnah*! It just takes just one year to finish *Mishnayos* if you study for approximately two hours a day, completing one and a half *prakim* a day. *Mishnah* has the same letters as *neshamah*... finishing *Mishnayos* is a turning point in a scholar's life and it is a must for every soul. If you finish all of the *Mishnah*, you're bound to one day do the same with the *Talmud*. Learn to finish many smaller works in order to get in the habit of not skipping around, completing what you start, no matter what. This is the main problem people have, finishing *sefarim* from beginning to end. They are so used to skipping around and going out of order. Once you commit to a *sefer*, stick with it, no matter what, from start to finish. You will see that as you complete the first quarter of the *sefer*, the book starts to open up to you. You're then able to double the number of pages in the same period of time. It always takes me a little while to adapt to the fresh style of writing and mindset of a *sefer*. What I always do is start slow, knowing that every week or two, I will increase the pages I complete every day. In this way, with a steady increase in quantity, I can train myself to study the book faster. Comprehending the same amount of information in a shorter period of time is completely possible, it is just a matter of training one's mind to think faster.

About Reb Meir Chodosh they would say, "His every action was weighed in advance on the most delicate scale. So too, was his every minute precious beyond description. Anyone who had ever entered into his room would tell you the same story:

"He would be sitting in his chair, his eyes glued to the *sefer* before him, his head moved slightly from left to right and back again, line after line, totally unaware of people surrounding him on all sides. Then, as his finger would draw near to the conclusion of the page he was learning, he would quickly turn the page in a manner clearly perfected so as not to waste a split second. Then his eyes would instantly glue themselves to the next page; and his head would begin swaying again, ever so slightly: following the words of the *sefer*, still totally unaware of those near him.

This could go on for ten, fifteen, or twenty minutes up until he would become conscious of his guests (or until someone finally would grow impatient and interrupt him). Surprised, he would glance up, greet his guests warmly, and then lavishly give of his time for whatever their needs would be.

People don't realize how much time they waist by learning with laziness. They don't understand how much more they could accomplish with better focus, when they push themselves to get used to thinking faster. The exact same learning and thoughts could take the same person one minute that usually could take five, should they train themselves to study more quickly. Don't misunderstand, we are not talking about learning less material or trying to comprehend less here, we are simply talking about processing material more efficiently. People get in the habit of being lazy when they read and learn, they underestimate the brilliance of their mind to take in data. Our minds are the greatest computers in the world. It is like using a supercomputer, one of the fastest processors and underclocking it to run slower. Rather, respect the technological advancement and its ability to compute and use it efficiently. Just like a person has to be trained to use a computer, so too we must train ourselves to use our minds, memory productively for the utmost Torah comprehension.

So, here is how I would start a new round of *Mishniyos* to complete it in one year? I'd begin learning a half a *perek* a day for a week. Then at the end of the week, I would increase it slowly to one *perek*. This would take place in the same allotment of time. Then after two weeks, I would raise the amount to one and a half *prakim*. While I continue on this pace, usually I am surprised that automatically after a month's time, I will naturally be able to accomplish even two *prakim* or more. You would be surprised how subtle things can help you to improve your study habits. For instance, I might use a paper divider that allows me only to see the line I am studying, so that my eyes don't wander. I also might stand up while I study as I find that sometimes as this helps me to learn quicker with a clearer mind.

"Do not look away in the middle of *Torah* study so that your *kavanah* is disturbed; just look at what you are learning." (*Marganita Taba*,

#26, in YHvT, p.92)

Rabbi Elimelech of Lizensk would say, "You should concentrate fully and see that you make no interruption at all, not even by thinking a thought that has nothing to do with the learning." (*Tzetl Kaban*, #10)

These small enhancements can make a dramatic difference in making sure you don't fall into unhealthy habits and that you stay focused. It really is amazing what more you can accomplish when you give your studies your full attention. Surprisingly, for some, some relaxing music in the background might even help, classical music or the like. HaRav Chaim Belsky zt"l would often listen to classical music during his private studies. For me, some calm acoustic guitar or piano solos work best as too many instruments are distracting for me.

After completing the preliminary works using these methods, you can move on to studying *Talmud* in the same way. Start with one *amud* a day. Then go to *blat* a day, move to two *blats* after some weeks, then to three *blats* in the same allotted period. I know it might seem a lot but eventually you can reach seven *blat* a day in order to finish the *Talmud* yearly. It is simply a matter of training. You just have to teach yourself to not waist time, training yourself to get to *p'shat* quickly without going on tangents and loosing focus. During your first few rounds of *Shas* or any *sefer* for that matter, the main goal should be to cover ground and to understand the simple meaning and *p'shat*. Then on further review of these *sefarim*, you can delve more deeply. Surprisingly, after you will have finished the entire *sefer*, during your next round studying it, naturally you will understand far more. While you will be on your second or third round of *Shas*, your friend will still be struggling to complete one or two *blats* a day. Constantly he will be looking up the *meforshim*, the Rambam, Tosefos and others. Sometimes taking twenty minutes to an hour to look up a simple question which the *Gemarah* will soon answer on the next *daf*. He already understood *p'shat*, yet he seeks more, does he really seek the *emes* or did he want to take a break from the *Gemarah* and his studies to look around the library to answer a question that has nothing to do with the simple *p'shat* of the *Gemarah*? This would be fine during his *beiyun* learning *z'man*, but this is how he learns all the time, never completing *sefarim* and with a relaxed mindset in the *bais midrash*, never really under any pressure to accomplish more than what is required of him. One who masters and completes many *dafs* of *Talmud*, he is able to seek reasons from one *daf* by deducing it from another. Therefore, for him, it only takes seconds to understand *p'shat* because he and the *Talmud* think alike. This is why it's so important to complete ones first round of *Shas* even in the simplest way with just the *p'shat*. I really wanted to call this *sefer*, *Seven Blat of Talmud Daily*, but I thought you would think I was crazy. Know that this truly is the way, seven *blat* a day *bekiyus*, along with a separate daily *b'inyun zeman*. However, this is only possible if one goes back to the basics and completes *Tanach* and *Mishniyos*.

It is a miracle that a man can survive spiritually even one day without learning a *daf* of *Talmud*. The entire world wishes to swallow up our souls, our only pure oxygen is the *Torah*. Without *Torah*, what will become of our souls? How could we make it through one day in this world without allowing our souls to breath and take in pure oxygen?

Shimon asked me: "Why am I still confused in my *Torah* learning?" I responded, "Because you skipped around, didn't finish *Tanach* and all of *Mishniyos* first. You skipped ahead to *Chassidus*, *Talmud* and *Kabbalah*. You didn't even finish learning how to walk, and you decided to run. Of course, you're going to trip and fall." I then went on to advise him a new schedule of learning.

It is a bit of a myth that *Chassidim* learn *Chassidus* all day. If you walk into *Chassidic yeshivos*, you will see they indeed learn similarly to the *Litvish* style of learning, but maybe they will add a half-hour or more for *Chassidus*. Also, they might spend more time on praying since that was the way of the Baal Shem Tov who believed true *avodas* Hashem required emphasis on prayer besides *Torah* study. Even the holy Rav Meir Shapiro who is responsible for hundreds of thousands of people learning *Gemarah*, was himself really a *chassidishe rebbe*. His grandfather introduced him to the Chortkover Rebbe, and thus began his passion for *Chassidus*, and the beginning of his relationship with the Chortkover Rebbe whom he considered his main *rav*.

Maybe it was his *chassidish* mindset that allowed him to innovate his glorious program of *daf yomi*. To think out of the box and really look to make a major change in *Klal Yisrael*. If he was alive today, I think his focus would be on fixing the *cheder* system as everything starts from a person's youth.

"At age five [one is ready] for Scripture; at ten, for *Mishnah*; at thirteen for *mitzvos*; at fifteen, for *Talmud*..." (M *Avos* 5:21)

"One who toils in the *Talmud* will progress. But one should not pass over Scripture and *Mishnah* to concentrate on the *Talmud*; rather, he should study Scripture and *Mishnah* in order to reach *Talmud*." (MK *Sofrim* 16:9) "Rather than jumping from Scripture to *Midrash* to *Talmud*, one should learn Scripture [completely], then *Mishnah*, then *Talmud*." (*Rosh, Bava Metzia*, 2, end)

R. Yomtov Lipman Heller taught, "One should learn all of

Scripture, then the entire *Mishnah*, then *Talmud*." (Intro to *Ma'adaney Yom Tov, Bava Kama*)

Prepare your work outside and make it fit in the field for yourself; afterwards you shall build your house. (*Proverbs* 24:27) "Prepare your work outside" – this is Scripture. "And get it ready in the field" – that is the *Mishnah*. "Thereafter: build your house" – that is the *Talmud*. (*Nachalas Avos* 5:21)

Shlomo HaMelech taught, "For you shall wage war for yourself with strategies, and the victory results from the superiority of the counselor." (*Proverbs* 24:6)

Who [is victorious in the battle of *Torah*? (*Sanhedrin* 42a) He who masters many *Mishnayos*. (Rashi: "The battle of *Torah*" – Its teaching, and reduction to essentials and principles; [this battle can] not [be waged] by a sharp-witted person who analyzes and dissects, nor by one who is a master of theory, but never learned many *Mishnayos*...; for whence would he discover the truth? Rather this alludes to one who masters many *Mishnayos*, so that, if he seeks a reason for one [*Mishnah*], he can deduce it from another.) (An allusion to *Proverbs* 24:6)

Even though many teachings about the correct order of learning are directed towards children because of our generation's unhealthy habits in teaching and learning, we must all in some way return to the learning of the youths.

Rabbi Yehudah HaChassid writes, "Educate the youth according to his way; even when he grows old, he will not deviate from it." (*Proverbs* 22:6) If he excels in Scripture but not in *Talmud*, don't pressure him to study *Talmud*. [Primarily] – educate him in what he knows. If a person sees that his son in incapable of *Talmud*, he should teach him *halachos, gedolos, midrashim*, and *keriah* reading the *Torah* [Scripture]. (*Sefer Chassidim* 308)

The Maharal emphasizes, "The *Rishonim, Tannaim, Amoraim, Geonim*, and *Acharonim* all learned in a set order – first Scripture, then *Mishnah*, then *Talmud*. But in this generation, they begin with the *Talmud*: they educate youngsters in the *Talmud* at age six or seven and only at the end do they advance them to *Mishnah* – not to study it, but only to seek out specific *halachos*... Now, one has nothing left – no *Talmud*, no rule, and no decisions, unless he searches for them." (*Derech Chayim* 6 (fol. 117b)

Therefore, let's turn back the clock if we have to and start learning the right way. Let us seek out what is truly best for our souls and the level we are indeed on? Let us demand of ourselves to review and build ourselves up with foundational study. Let us not get lost in the incorrect habits of the generation, when for hundreds of years, this (as taught here) was the correct way of study and the scholars of those generations easily surpassed us in wisdom. Let us admit our laziness to do things appropriately and begin a program to fix ourselves. A curriculum unique to our own personal souls and not one geared to the average of the vast majority.

Often, the *Rosh HaYeshivah*, Rabbi Simcha Wasserman would emphasize that *Klal Yisrael* is compared to the stars, wherein each star is a world unique unto itself, but that it is still part of a much broader cosmic system.

He once gave a lecture in which he emphasized the Chofetz Chayim's view that regardless of our subjective or relative sense of importance, we can all view ourselves as having a vital role in the service of *Klal Yisrael*. Some of us are officers, a small number achieve the role of generals, most of us are infantrymen, but we are all nonetheless functioning in our respective roles in the "army of Hashem."

The Gaon of Vilna wrote, "He who walks in uprightness, fears Hashem. Each person has to walk in his own distinct way, for people's characteristics are not all the same." (*HaGra*, commentary on *Proverbs* 14:2)

Similarly, the Or Sameach wrote, "All *mitzvos* are applicable to all persons, from the least to Moshe, our teacher... Each person is to act according to his own nature and his own spiritual capacity; for the obligation of *Torah* study is not the same for the person who has a fine intellect and is eager to study and the one who is intellectually more lethargic. It is evidently impossible to establish an absolute measure." (*Or Sameach, Talmud Torah* 1:2)

For example, Rabbi Shimon bar Yochai and his comrades were exclusively occupied with the *Torah* to such an extent that they were exempt from the obligation of daily prayer. (*Shabbos* 11a) On the other hand, "The Early Pious Ones spent nine hours each day in prayer – but because of their piety, their *Torah* knowledge remained intact, even though they did not spend much time studying it." (*Berachos* 32b)

The Nativ told, "The form of service of Hashem is not the same for all persons – one occupies himself with *Talmud Torah*... and another... with divine service, and another with doing acts of kindness, but all for the sake of Heaven. And even in *Torah* study itself, not all methods of study are the same. Also in fulfilling the *mitzvos*... and performing acts of kindness; not all those who perform them have the same way of life, and if someone were to ask which is the proper way... [the answer is:] 'that which graces [i.e. suits] the person' – the person who chooses will do so according to his own nature, depending on whether he is talented in *Torah*, divine service, or performing acts of kindness." (*Ha'amek Davar*, *Bamidbar* 15:41, referring to *M Avos* 2:1)

"Earlier generations set time limits on educating the youth according to his way: at age five, Scripture; at age ten *Mishnah*; at fifteen, *Talmud* – adjusting the burden to what he can handle; for the youth will accept that which he can bear... And when he concludes his study of the *Mishnah*, the great foundation and pillar of the entire *Torah*, and approaches the sacred study of the *Talmud*, he will be competent to build a tower reaching heaven, and not a pebble of it will fall. All this is possible because of the existing firm basis, i.e., the *Mishnah*... And afterwards, if he must fight the battle of *Torah*, then his hands will be well-prepared, laden with the armaments of *Torah*, which serve him as arrows in the hand of a warrior, striking their mark without fail; and these will forsake him neither when he lies down nor when he rises.

"It is incumbent on the shepherds who lead the flock not to pressure or exhaust them with deceptive shortcuts – which are really the long route – because they will die before they reach the realm of *Torah*." (*Guy Aryeh*, *Deuteronomy* 6:7)

It is so heartbreaking that it is engrained in us from our youth, from *cheder* to *yeshivah* to just take shortcuts in learning. So much so, that even when we hear the sages' wise words here, our minds are fighting to internalize them. We think of every excuse to continue in the same path, instead of humbling ourselves to start over.

"First, one should obtain [knowledge of] Scripture, which is the root and the beginning. Afterwards, the *Mishnah*, for the Written *Torah*, alone, is like the root of a tree and cannot reach the goal which is to convey the quality and substance of the *mitzvos*. That is why they arranged for the *Mishnah* to follow, for it will help one grasp this quality and substance... But in the current generation, this arrangement has been disturbed to the greatest possible extent... Surely no one can retain what is beyond his intellectual capacity." (*Maharal*, *Tiferes Yisrael* 56)

"One must also follow the learning schedule we have outlined – first, *Mishnah*; afterwards, *Talmud*; and he must constantly review everything. This is the path trodden by the *Rishonim* and *Acharonim*." (*Derush Al HaTorah*, s.v. *velachein banay shim'u*, fol. 27a)

"He should start by filling himself with [knowledge of] Scripture, *Mishnah*, the *Bavli* and *Yerushalmi Talmud's*, etc... But one who changes the order of learning... will lose even the little Torah he heard from his youth." (*Even Shelemah* 8:2)

The Shelah writes, "Even though the obligation to learn *Torah* is fulfilled by studying the *Babylonian Talmud*... it is essential to study [Scripture] as well as *Mishnah* and *Talmud*; and he should learn *Torah*, Prophets and *Kesuvim* in sequence, one after the other. Thereafter, the oral *Torah*, in the order of the *Mishnah*... And he should study [the *Mishnayos*] enough times to become fluent in them and learn them by heart. And [one should learn] *halacha* from the *Talmud* each day, fulfilling the requirement to divide one's day into three, etc..." (*Shelah*, *Shavuos*, beginning)

Rabbi Pinchas of Polotzk, a disciple of the Goan of Vilna told over: "This is the proper sequence. Scripture must precede *Mishnah* and *Mishnah* must proceed *Talmud* – whoever reverses them is a boar." (*Rosh Hagiv'ah*, fol. 11a)

Speaking of the proper order of study, "Study the Wisdom of the *Torah* in depth. Why did they abandon this path? Why did they pervert it? By misunderstanding one dictum of the sages, they have caused much straying." (*Horeb* 551)

The *Torah* is so much more beautiful when a person doesn't skip around going from place to place. When he learns in order, the entire *Torah* feels open to him. Rabbi YomTov Lipman Heller tells, "When they say that one should not skip from Scripture to [*Mishnah*], this means that he should not advance to the corresponding *Mishnah* before finishing all of Scripture. He should not learn one section of Scripture, then leave the rest and skip to the corresponding [*Mishnah*] and thence to *Talmud*. Instead, he should finish studying Scripture in its entirety, then the entire *Mishnah* and then the *Talmud*." (Introduction to *Ma'adaney Yom Tov, Bava Kama*)

"*Mikra* (*Torah*) is compared to water, *Mishnah* to wine, and *Shas* to *konditon* (a very sweet wine mixed with pepper and honey). As the world requires (cannot live without) water, wine and *konditon*, and a wealthy man is nourished by all three, so the world cannot exist without *mikra, Mishnah* and *Shas*." (*Sofrim* 15:7)

"The Chakham Tzevi took up the task of righting the widespread wrong: the disruption of the learning schedule. The masses generally did not study Scripture at all, to such an extent that there were ordained rabbis who had never read Scripture and knew no *Mishnah*!" (Rabbi Yaakov Emden, *Megilah Sefer*)

Rabbi Yaakov Emden insists, "He should learn all of Scripture, that is, the complete *Tanach*... What sense does it make to enter the *Torah's* inner sanctum, where the Oral *Torah* is revealed, if one has not been given the outer keys, the requisite simple explanations of Scripture?

"[By learning] in this manner, he will build a solid foundation on which the edifice of the desired learning can stand firm and straight.

*Talmud* study will be easy for him; he will reach his goals faster, and whatever time was expended learning Scripture will be more than compensated for by the time saved when studying *Talmud*, the Tosafos, and all the other great works. But those who disrupt the order lose [the time spent on] both. It is not necessary to expand on this, as any intelligent person knows it; but it is difficult for someone to change his habits and to swim against the tide of his environment. Even the sages said that the 'teachers knew this but ignored it.' What more can I say?" (*Migdal Oz*, beginning)

I hope I haven't gathered these holy words of our sages in vain. Maybe before you read all of these wise words, you could excuse your actions as being naive. But now that you have read this, what could possibly be your excuse for delaying the inevitable? It is time for you and me to begin our studies anew, refining how we study and to take the opportunity to grow from *Torah* learned in the proper order. Should you have already completed these important works, then these words should also remind you to review the fundamental works again and again in order that they should be a pillar on which your *Talmud* study should stand. No matter how wise of a scholar you are, there is no reason why you shouldn't make every effort to review the *Tanach* and *Mishniyos*. Even if a large building has been built, the contractor can still secure the foundation to be even stronger so that the building can withstand more aging and weather. So too, must a scholar constantly review the fundamental works of *Torah*. Raish Lakish knew all of *Shas* yet still he reviewed the *Mishnayos* forty times before learning the *blat* with Rav Yochanan. (*Tannis* 8a)

# *Teaching our Children*

This method of the old school learning was proven over and over to be successful, yet we continue to ignore it. Those few schools that I know of that have tried to return to this method usually fail only because the teachers taught without heart and without seeking to teach the children understanding. The idea is for the child to first complete all of the *Tanach* and *Mishniyos* but with a basic understanding of the material, not just to complete the work for the sake of completion. It isn't about rushing and memorizing the material, as if it is some textbook.

Rabbi Sheftel, son of the Shelah told, "I passed through the Amsterdam Jewish community. There I found distinguished men, many of them scholars, and I visited their study halls; each of them has his own domain. I saw that the young children learn Scripture from the beginning of *Bereshis* to the end of *Devarim*, and after that the [rest of] Scripture, and then all the *Mishnayos*. And when they come of age, they start to study *Talmud* with the Tosafos. They grow and thrive and produce fruit. And I wept – why cannot this system be followed in this country? Would that this custom spread throughout the Jewish world. What harm can there be in filling one with Scripture and *Mishnah* until thirteen, and [only] afterwards starting the study of the *Talmud*? For certainly, in one year he will reach the goal and, with Hashem's help, [gain] a deeper understanding of the *Talmud* than our style of learning grants him in several years..."

The Maharsha writes: "The *Bais* [in the word *Bavel* (Babylon), as the second letter of the Hebrew alphabet] infers that there are two *Torahs* – the Written and the Oral... which in their arrogance, the [Bablyonian Jews] studied out of order: at age five they should have learned Scripture, but instead they learned *Mishnah*. At the age they should have studied *Mishnah*, they studied *Talmud*. When in their youth they learned *Mishnah* and *Talmud* together because of their arrogance. This is the situation about which Rabbi Yirmiyah invoked the verse: 'He made me dwell in gloom.'" (Maharsha on *Sanhedrin* 24a, end, referring to *Lamentations* 3:6)

Rav Kahane said, "Jerusalem was destroyed only because the education of *yeshivah* children was neglected, as is written, 'pour it out, because of the children in the street.' Why, 'Pour it out'? Because of the children in the street." (*Shabbos* 119b)

Timing is so important when it comes to our growth. It says is the
131

*Psalms*, "'[That] which bears its fruit at the proper time and its leaves do not wither.' (*Psalms* 1:3-5) If one teaches with his student's age in mind, his leaves will not wither; otherwise, the verse articulates of both student and teacher: 'but not so the evil-doers, who are as chaff blown about the wind.'" (Maharsha on *Avodah Zara* 9b)

Rabbi Shelomoh Efrayim Luntschitz writes, "The proper sequence is to first teach him the translation of the entire *Tanach*... After he has studied all of Scripture and is familiar with Hashem's commandments, one should teach him *Mishniyos* – first those that are applicable nowadays and afterwards even those that are not... After he has taught him all this, he can also teach him *Talmud*.

"*Avos* instructs that 'at age five, [one is ready] for Scripture; at age ten, for the *Mishnah*; at age fifteen, for the *Talmud*.' It would seem that even a bright student should not start learning *Talmud* before completing [memorizing] the six orders of the *Mishnah*... but this is not necessarily so. In their day, the words of the *Mishnah* were not written down and it was forbidden to record them... Therefore, they needed much time to learn [memorize] *Mishnah*. Nevertheless, people certainly did not delve into the minutiae – which can be derived through critical examination – until they had learned all, or at least most, of the *Mishnayos*." (*Amudey Sheish* 24, end)

Rabbi Yosef Yosfa Hahn tells, "He should learn all of Scripture, not as they do in our generation, when many rabbis have never seen the [whole of] Scripture. He should immerse himself in Scripture until he is entirely familiar with it, before he begins *Mishnah* and *Talmud*... and when he turns ten, he should be taught *Mishnah* even if he lacks understanding." (*Yosif Ometz*, p. 270 and p. 284)

We are doing a disservice to the children by not teaching them core material while they are young. "When a youngster reaches age eight or nine, he begins with the *Talmud*. Does he really have the mental capacity for it? Surely no one can retain what is beyond his intellectual capacity." (Maharal, *Tiferes Yisrael* 56)

Rabbi Yoel Sirkes the Bach writes, "A person is obliged to [teach his son] the Written *Torah*, including the *Naviim* and *Kesuvim*... Therefore, the public is mistaken not to pay money to teach their sons these subjects." (Bach on *Tur Yoreh De'ah* 245, s.v. *hayah minhag*)

The current status quo seems to be to rush through less than a quarter of the material allowing only the bright students to grow in *Torah*. Those students that need more work and attention are usually ignored and forgotten about. Most teachers don't interact enough with the students, rather they just stand at the podium and tell over the *Torah* and whoever grasps it, grasps it. There is no real heartfelt devotion in their attitude. Many are teachers not because they have teaching skills or desire the wellbeing of children, but only to supplement their income. They can't seem to make it in the *kollel* environment, so they go into *chinuch* in order to still involve themselves in *Torah*. However, by nature, they are horrible with children and lack the patience to teach.

Schools seem to take a lot of interest in their student's family life. Sometimes principles placing excess stress on families to abide in the home by their so-called *Torah* rules, fences for the *Torah* as they may perceive them, all the while, these same teachers don't live up to the standards of proper *rabbeim* to our children. Treating the children with anger, hostility, lack of respect, hitting them and emotionally scaring them for life. They take little responsibility for the students *neshamah* but rather pretend they care, taking their own life's stresses out on students. We already spoke before about my son who was slapped for not being capable at the time of committing a *Mishnah* to memory. Are these teachers leading our children to *Torah* or into the abyss?

When applying to one *yeshivah*, I was given a two-page rule list to sign and commit to in order to attend the *yeshivah*. Some of the rules made no sense and as a boy of thirteen, I didn't understand it all. I thought I was going to *yeshivah* not jail. *Payos* behind the ear, only so long, clean shaven at all times, black pants only made out of a certain material, stripped shirts but only certain colors, black socks and shoes.

My rebbe in *cheder* decided he didn't like my *payos*, so he decided to try to cut them off. For years afterwards I was in trauma. Other teachers used to hit us with a stick if they felt we weren't behaving or listening during class. Some yelled loudly and even threw chairs at us or around the room. They accuse students of having learning problems when the teachers themselves need to be the ones on medication for hyperactivity and attention issues (ADHD). Children grow up bullied in schools and not only do teachers look the other way, it could be that even the teacher themselves are bullies, they just do it in a more roundabout way.

If a child doesn't understand a passage, instead of repeating it, the teacher moves on to a new topic. Most children grow up disliking to learn *Torah* and it's for obvious reasons. The love of learning *Torah* was never taught to them. They were taught the *Torah* in a cold way, some even scolded or embarrassed for their lack of comprehension. The Chazon Ish said, "Every student is a possible *gadol hador*." Most of the *roshei yeshivos* of today were not the same people thought to become great in their youth. Those same delinquent children that were ignored, many on their own accord became great *roshei yeshivos*. Can you imagine if each child were nurtured and taught as if they were the future leaders of the generation? So, each student should be looked at in such a way, with enormous potential ready to be unleashed if we as parents and teachers do our job correctly.

How many teachers lash out at students instead of finding a calm way to reach deep into their souls? The Rambam says, "One should teach his students calmly and softly without shouting." (*Rambam* 2:15)

In the old days, a teacher remained with the same students year after year, following their progress. Today, you can have a teacher for one year and then he will ignore the student in the halls as if they are a stranger the next year. Where is the love of raising our next generation?

Chazal say, "Teach them thoroughly to your children." (*Devarim* 6:7) "Your children", refers to your students. (*Sifrei*) This means that you should view your students as your own children and truly care about them. It says in the *Talmud*, "Whoever teaches another man's son *Torah* is considered as if he had borne him." (*Sanhedrin* 19b)

Rabbi Shalom Schwadron often relates the following incident to illustrate how different a person will react when feeling their own suffering or someone else's suffering.

A little lad was playing opposite Rabbi Schwadron's house in Jerusalem. The child fell and obtained a nasty cut. Hearing the child crying, Rabbi Schwadron ran outside, put a towel over the cut, and hurried over with the lad to the home of a doctor who lived nearby. As he was running, an elderly lady observed his concern and distress and, thinking it was one of Rabbi Schwadron's own children, she called out, "Don't worry, don't worry, Hashem will help."

It so happened that the boy was actually the woman's grandson. Rabbi Schwadron was curious to perceive her reaction when she would comprehend the child's identity. Sure enough, the moment she realized that it was her own grandson, she stopped saying, "Don't worry," and started blaring at the top of her lungs, "My Meir! My Meir!" while neighbors attempted to calm her down.

When someone else's child is involved, you might detachedly say, "Don't worry"; but when your own child is involved, you'll shout. (*Love Your Neighbor* p. 129)

We need a new generation of teachers that will care about students as if they were their own children. Principles and parents should expect nothing less from the schools as they are helping to raise the next generation of *tzaddikim*.

"And those that bring righteousness to the many shall be like the stars forever and ever." (*Daniel* 12:3) This refers to the *Torah* teachers of school children. Such as who? Rav said, "Such that are as devoted as Rabbi Shmuel bar Shailas." Rav once met Rabbi Shmuel bar Shailas standing in his garden. He asked him, "Have you abandoned the children who have been entrusted to you?" Rabbi Shmuel bar Shailas replied, "Twelve years have already passed since I last saw this garden, and even now my thoughts are with the children." (*Bava Basra* 8b)

A father brought his only son to the Volozhin Yeshivah. The father spoke to Rabbi Naftoli Tzvi Berlin, the *Rosh HaYeshivah*, and asked him to take particular care of his son, since he was an only child.

"You have but one only son," said Rabbi Berlin, "I have four hundred only children." (*Yechidai Segulah*, p. 61)

Rabbi Yisrael Yaakov Lubchanski once tried to influence a certain student for many mouths. Although he spent much time with the *bachur*, his efforts were of no avail. The boy just would not yield. As Rav Yisrael Yaakov put it, "It came to the point where I discovered an indifference within me toward that boy. I simply rejected him."

Then one day a thought dawned upon him: "Hashem did not bless me with any children. But supposed that boy were my son. I would not ignore him. Then why do I reject him now? Because he belongs to someone else?"

As Rabbi Lubchanski later related the incident, he told how he became overwhelmed with a love for the boy at that moment. His previous indifference changed to love. He began to work with him anew, and eventually the boy grew up to be an outstanding leader. (Rabbi Chayim Shapiro in *The Jewish Observer*, Jan. 1971)

Rabbi Avraham Pam taught, "What are we to learn from the fact that Hashem rejoiced when He presented us with the *Torah*? This teaches that joy is a primary factor in the proper transmission of *Torah*. Hashem, Who, 'teaches *Torah* to His people Israel,' does so with joy. In the same way, every teacher of *Torah* must impart the *Torah's* teachings with joy and enthusiasm, for only in this method will his words leave their desired impression upon his students."

Rabbi Yechezkel Feivel of Vilna was a frequent visitor with the Goan of Vilna. He told, "If Israel's youngsters were well-versed in the Written *Torah* from the beginning of their studies, it would undoubtedly be much easier for them to follow the reasoning of the *Mishnah* and *Talmud*. Not so in our time – when the children come to school, virtually the entire Written *Torah* remains a hidden treasure, and when they learn *Mishnah* and

*Talmud* it is extremely difficult for them because all the subject matter is foreign to them." (*Toldos Adam* 3)

The Zera Emes writes, "We cannot close our eyes to the order of learning. The *chachamim...* their words are divinely inspired... It is fairly clear that we should not encourage the unfortunate modern custom of teaching small boys *Talmud*, for which they seek support from the mighty oak, Rabbeinu Tam... based on the derivation of the word *Bavli* [=Babylonian – from the word *balul* = mixed], because the Babylonian *Talmud* is a mixture of Scripture, *Mishnah* and *Talmud*... for this refers not to the proper education of children but of adults, after they have become *Torah* scholars." (Responsa Zera Emeth, *Yoreh De'ah* 107)

Rabbi Sheneor Zalman of Liadi said, "Nowadays, it is no longer customary to teach children the whole of Scripture – merely the *Pentateuch*, for they rely on the child to learn [the rest] on his own, when he grows up." (SA HaRav, *Hilchos Talmud Torah* 1:1)

However, we see that this idea doesn't work, when the children are older, they don't go back and fill in the gaps. Rather a scholar could spend dozens of years in learning without any proper basic foundation. You could ask him simple questions from the *Tanach*, and he could be clueless. What has happened to us?

# *Teaching the Masses*

The Kotzker Rebbe once referred to someone with the reputation of a righteous man as a, "*tzaddik* in pelz.*" In its literal translation, it means a *tzaddik* in a fur coat. When queried what he meant by that, he responded:

"Once upon a time there were two people. One bought himself a fur coat for the winter, while the other purchased firewood.

"What is the difference between the two?

One wanted to keep himself warm, while the other one was concerned with keeping others warm.

"The same," resolved the Rebbe, "is with our faith. Some people keep faith for themselves. They wear it like a fur coat to keep themselves warm. They do not benefit anybody else with it. But some light a fire with their faith in order to warm others as well."

The *Talmud* says, "He who gathers flocks (students) to the study of *Torah*, shall dwell in the partition of Hashem." (*Gittin* 7a)

When you hear of a person deeply involved in *kiruv* today, people bare them little respect. It's almost as if they look at someone doing *kiruv* as a guy who can't make it with the rest of the learners in *yeshivah*, quite the contrary.

The Kotzker Rebbe once remarked that he believed he could bring the dead back to life, but he much preferred to try to bring the living back to life!

"*Adam L'Amal Yulad* – Man was born to toil." (*Iyov* 2:7) The acrostic of the word *L'Amal* is "*Lilmod A Means Lelamed* – To learn in order to teach." (*Maharsha Sanhedrin* 99b)

Rabbi Eliezer ben Rebbe said in the name of Rabbi Acha: "If he learned but failed to teach, there is no greater vanity and futility than that." (*Vayikra Rabbah* 22:1)

Rav Sheishes said, "Whoever teaches the *Torah* in this world is deemed worthy of teaching it in the World to Come as well, as it is written, 'And as to the quencher, he too shall continue to quench.'" (*Proverbs* 11:25) (*Sanhedrin* 91b)

This is really an amazing concept that should not be overlooked. Whichever students you helped prosper in *Torah* in this world, students of any age, those same people will have access to your *bais midrash* to learn from you in the World to Come. Amazing! Those same people teaching *Torah* here below, will continue educating and spreading the *Torah* up above! Not only this but if we learn from someone in this world or study their *sefarim*, we will also have access to that *tzaddik's bais medresh* up above.

"The *Torah* must be studied as a whole, since one ambiguous passage may be clarified by another. One must be careful to take an overall view, and not interpret any scripture out of context." (*Bamidbar Rabbah* 19:17; *Berachos* 10a)

HaRav Noah Weinberg, founder of Aish HaTorah and a leader in outreach for nearly half a century, cites a passage in the *Chovos Halevavos* (*Duties of the Heart*) calling it, "the single most remarkable statement I have ever seen regarding *kiruv*."

The *Chovos Halevavos* says: "You should know, my brother, that even if a believer were to attain the utmost limit in the improvement of his own soul in his devotion to Hashem; and even if he were to approach the level of the prophets as far as their personal virtues, their praiseworthy conduct, their effort in serving Hashem, and their pure love for Him are concerned, his merits would not equal those of one who guides others to the right path and directs the wicked to the service of the Creator." (*Sha'ar Ahavas Hashem, perek* 6)

Rabbi Weinberg explains, "A person can raise himself to the level of the angels. He can be an angel in his spiritual understanding, an angel in his business dealings, an angel in his relationships with other people, completely *l'shem Shamayim*, serving Hashem with all his heart, yet the *Chovos Halevavos* states clearly: 'He cannot compare to someone who teaches other people about Hashem. Rather, someone who has the privilege to teach other people that there is a Hashem has achieved more than those who have scaled the heights of self-perfection.'"

"The root of this understanding takes us all the way back to Avraham Avinu," tells Rav Weinberg. "The Rambam, in *Hilchos Avodas Kochavim* (1:1-3), teaches us that the world spiraled downward from Enosh, until Avraham found *Hakadosh Baruch Hu*. The Ra'avad on this Rambam asks: "What about Shem and Ever, who taught *Torah* long before Avraham's birth? They also lived during Avraham's time and had a great *yeshivah* where both Yitzchak and Yaakov studied. Why aren't they credited with having saved the world?

"The answer given by the Kesef Mishneh (Rabi Yosef Caro) is that though Shem and Ever were loyal and lofty servants of Hashem, and taught *Torah* to those who came to their *yeshivah* (including Yitzchak and Yaakov), Avraham was the first to be '*korei shem Hashem*'. The difference between their conduct and that of Avraham is that the latter called out in the name of Hashem, traveling and reaching out to teach people about the one G-d, giving *tochachah* to idol worshippers, showing them the falsehood of their beliefs, and drawing them near to Hashem.

"What does it mean that Avraham was *korei shem Hashem*? Avraham was impassioned for the *kavod* of *HaKadosh baruch Hu*. It was not enough that he recognized Hashem and conducted his life in accordance with this recognition, when he was surrounded by a world that did not. He felt compelled to go forth and bring others to the recognition and service of their Creator, and this distinguished him. The path to recognizing and promoting *kavod Shamayim* in our time is not to reject and ignore those Jews who have no concept of *HaKadosh Baruch Hu*, which perpetuates a *chillul Hashem* of catastrophic proportions. If 90% of Jewry is not keeping *mitzvos*, then each of us has a share of the accountability, for we are all responsible for one another. For the *kavod* of *HaKadosh Baruch Hu*, we must do something about it!"

*Pirkei Avos* (1:12) quotes Hillel as saying that one should be among the disciples of Aharon, "…*oheiv es habrios u'mekarvan la'Torah* – loving your fellow men and drawing them near to the *Torah*." On this *Mishnah*, Rav Chaim Volozhin says, "the highest act of *v'ahavta l'rei'acha kamocha* is to give another Jew *Torah*. When we help him draw near to the *Torah*, we are tending to his deepest need and giving him the greatest gift."

In *Chomas Hadas*, the Chofetz Chaim examines the *mitzvah* of *hashavas aveidah*, the obligation to return a lost item to its owner. If this *mitzvah* applies to objects, then *kal v'chomer* (all the more so) to lost souls. When we reach out and "touch" an assimilated Jew, we are helping him repossess his *neshamah*, which has become lost to him through lack of proper education and exposure to Jewish life. Furthermore, when we help a fellow Jew return to *Torah*, we are giving back to *Hakadosh Baruch Hu* one who has gone far away from Him.

The *Torah* instructs us not to stand idly by while someone's blood is being spilled. The Chofetz Chaim provides the example of people drowning. Would we say we don't have time to help, that we are not cut out for trying to save someone? Or would we do everything in our capacity to rescue those whose lives are in danger, either directly or with the help of others?

The Chofetz Chaim goes on to explain that if this is true physically, it is all the more so spiritually. When we see a Jew who is spiritually drowning, it is our obligation to extend him a lifeline.

Rabbi Simcha Wasserman remarked, "The *Torah* does not need

salesmen; the *Torah* is its own best salesman." While this may be true, I personally have seen that the best *kiruv rabbis* are usually very good marketers and salesmen. We are just marketers, working for Hashem so remind others of the *Torah's* greatness. I have told business owners many times that if they want to hire a good marketer, find someone in *kiruv* and hire them. I think today, to spread the *Torah* and be *mekariv* people takes the greatest of social and marketing skillsets. That is how far our generation has fallen. At the same time, Rabbi Wasserman is correct, in that once you open someone's heart to listen, the *Torah* itself will teach them.

The *Gemarah* in *Shevous* (39) brings the idea from a *pasuk* of *areivus* (responsible for a community) that not only does a person have to help individuals but also bring a community closer. This is because all Jews are guarantors for one another and hence responsible for the others wellbeing.

When speaking about *ahavas* Hashem, loving G-d, The Rambam explains that part of the mitzvah is the desire to spread the knowledge of Hashem in the world. This should obligate us to educate those ignorant of the *Torah* and inspire them to fulfill it. (Sefer HaMitzvos #3)

People have to understand how connected we are as Jews. They must realize that as long as others haven't fulfilled their mitzvah, there's a lacking in my fulfillment of my own mitzvah. Sometimes it's even better to lessen my own mitzvah in order to facilitate others fulfilling theirs (see Magen Avraham to Orach Chaim 658, 12, 671.1). This shows how important it is to ensure all the Jews are doing what they are supposed to be doing. Reb Yisrael Salanter said, "When a *Yid* in Vilna closes his *Gemarah*, a *Yid* in Paris is *mechalel* shabbos."

Reb Meir Shapiro would not allow anyone to interrupt him while he was learning *Torah* with his students. One time, the *rosh hakahal*, a wealthy and prestigious leader of the community, arrived the *beis midrash* while Reb Meir was in the midst of delivering a *shiur*. Apologizing profusely, he asserted that Reb Meir come to his house immediately to discuss an important matter.

Reb Meir refused to leave his *talmidim*. The *rosh hakahal*, for his part, would not take no for an answer. Reb Meir lastly turned to him with a big smile and invited him to join him for a meal.

"What?" questioned the bewildered gentleman. "Why would I come to eat with you now?"

Reb Meir could not help but smile as he explained, "The *Talmud* says that 'if someone stops learning *Torah* to get involved in a conversation, he is fed the burning embers of a broom fire.' (*Chagigah* 12b) Why should

140

I eat alone? Come and join me."

There's a curse against those who do not uphold the *Torah*. (*Devarim* 27:26) The Yerushalmi (see Ramban ad. loc.) explains that this incorporates making sure those that are ignoring the *Torah* to fulfill it. The Chofetz Chaim maintains that anyone who can influence others to fulfill the *Torah* and decides not to should be very afraid that this curse not affect him. Those who do inspire others are therefore included in the corresponding blessing for those who uphold the *Torah*.

Let us not forget that *kiruv* is not just about bringing back lost Jews, it is about inspiring any person on any level to come closer to Hashem. It is our responsibility from the *mitzvah* of loving our neighbor that we should not ignore this mandatory responsibility.

Rabbi Yaakov Abuchatzeira taught, "An honest and *yiras Shamayim* person must be generous with his money and even generous with his *Torah*. Because of his love for Hashem *Yisbarach*, he must not be stingy with anything. Being generous with *Torah* denotes teaching it to others happily and freely, and then understanding will be given to him generously from Heaven, even in those matters which have been difficult for him; they will teach him the true way, and truth will not be withheld from him by Heaven."

This might be what is meant by the verse, "Do not withhold good from its owners, when you have it in your power to do good." (*Proverbs* 3:27) The good meant by "Do not withhold good" is *Torah*, and the meaning of not withholding it is to teach it to Israel, who are "its owners," for all of Israel are considered the owners of the *Torah*. Thereby, when you teach *Torah* to others, it becomes "in your power to do so" because from Heaven you are helped to teach it. Should there even be a subject in *Torah* which you have been unable to understand, you will be helped to attain and understand it.

This is also what is intended by "Hashem, please desire my mouth's offerings." (*Tehillim* 119:108) The offering of my lips is my teaching others. The verse requests of Hashem to desire this study, and in exchange, "teach me your statutes," teach me the laws of the *Torah* correctly so that I should make no mistakes, *chas-v-shalom.* (*Alef Binah* 124)

Resh Lakish said, "He who teaches *Torah* to his neighbor's son is regarded by Scripture as though he had fashioned him, as it is written, 'and the souls which they had made in Haran.'" R. Eleazar said, "As though he himself had created the words of the *Torah*, as it is written, 'keep therefore the words of this covenant, and make them.'" Raba said, "As though he had made himself, for it is written, 'and make them': render not them but

yourselves." (*Sanhedrin* 99b)

The Maharal explains, "Rava said it is as if he created himself. This means that he himself is rendered more complete when he brings his *Torah* to fruition by imparting it to others [than he is by his own study]. [The teaching to others] affects him personally; it is man's most exacted form of completeness, in that man is actualized to the fullest extent when he imparts *Torah* to another, as we explained earlier. The true purpose of the intellective *Torah* is served when it imparts to another, thereby creating something new. [One who accomplishes this] is thus considered as if he has created himself. He has fully realized the level of the intellective by imparting [*Torah*] to and actualizing another; the result is that he is himself a complete and fully actualized man." (*Nesivos Olam, Nesiv HaTorah*, p.175)

# Yeshivas Chachmei Lublin and Daf Yomi

Rabbi Meir Shapiro conceived of a *yeshivah* for *Chassidic* Poland, modeled after Lithuanian *yeshivas* such as Volozhin, Slabodka and Novardok, but which would train *Chassidic* rabbis of the next generation to lead Polish Jewry. The Yeshivah Chachmei Lublin as it was called, housed in a massive building, housed hundreds of students, and had a vast library of over 100,000 *sefarim*.

Rabbi Shapiro explained why he made this prodigious *yeshivah*: "Now a word to my brethren," he exclaimed. "What was it that moved me to build this *yeshivah*? If you have ever seen how the *yeshivah bachurim* are

142

forced to sleep in the stores and shops while working as night watchmen, or if you have ever observed their poverty, then you will understand why I built a *yeshivah* like this one."

The *yeshivah* only accepted accomplished *talmidei chachamim*; in order to be admitted, a *bachur* had to have mastered by heart over 200 *blats* of *Gemarah*. The *yeshivah* soon became a bastion of *limud haTorah*. Even though many were not excepted, it became the talk and inspiration of every *bachur* to increase their learning throughout Europe. One student, Rabbi Yechiel Benzion Fishoff said, back then, "everyone wanted to go to Yeshivas Chachmei Lublin."

During its inauguration, tens of thousands of Jews took part in the celebration. The students in the *yeshivah* were of the highest caliber, many of them were of genius quality and the *yeshivah* produced many prodigious *Torah* leaders until its tragic end at the hands of the Germans and Poles in World War II.

Rabbi Yechiel Meir (Henri) was a staff assistant in the *yeshivah*. He describes the *Simchas Torah* holiday in the *yeshivah*: "We didn't have enough *sifrei* Torah to give everybody for *hakafos*. We had 5 or 10 *sifrei Torah*, so we gave out *Gemarahs*... so we had *Shas*. So, we called out, 'Mr. So, and So is honored with *Mesechtos Kesubos*... Mr. So, and So is honored with *Mesechta* [*Tannis*...What a joyous *Simchas Torah* we had that year celebrating it in honorable simplicity]."

He continued, "I heard one *Gemarah* class from the *rav*. He began *Mesechtos Yoma*. He began like this... We all sat down, and he stood at the *bima* in the middle. He then opened the *Gemarah*, "So says the holy *Mishnah*! 'Seven days before *Yom Kippur*, we separate the *Kohen Gadol* from his house into the *Palhedrin* chamber.' When he said the words, *'zucht der haliga Mishnah*, So, says the holy *Mishnah*,' everybody shivered. You just got electrified from it. You could see the flames in the air. The way he said it. He had such an oratory power."

"I realized last *siyum daf yomi*, we didn't realize it then, but we can see it now. Hashem needed somebody to give an injection. Hashem needed somebody to give a lift up to Jewry. He brought up a man to 46 years old and he turned everything upside down. Yeshivas Chachmei Lublin which was for honor and beauty. To honor the Torah which was then at a depressed state. Before then, the worst thing was a *yeshivah* student. A *yeshivah bachur* was considered a *'shnoror'*. Nobody wanted to talk with him. But when I came home from *yeshivah* for the holidays, people looked at me and pushed and said, 'Let me look at him!' That's how much honor for the Torah the *yeshivah* inspired. And then he made the *daf yomi* (learning one page of *Gemarah* daily to complete the cycle in 7 years). It's unbelievable what Rav Meir Shapiro did but that's what Hashem wanted."

One Jewish newspaper ran a report detailing the phenomenon of *daf yomi* that was sweeping through the Jewish community:

"It is amazing. On the first day of *Rosh Hashanah*, they began with the study of the first *daf* in *Berachos*... Even people, who until now, felt that their jobs did not allow time for Torah study, have joined daily *shiurim* to study the *daf*...The degree to which the study of *daf yomi* has spread is evident from the fact that one cannot find a single volume of *Mesechtos Berachos* in any *sefarim* store! In fact, they have even begun buying up volumes of *Mesechtos* Shabbos out of concern that none will be available when the *daf yomi* begins that *mesechta* [next]. Multitudes of *yiras Shamayim* Jews have joined the *geonim* and *tzaddikim* of the generation in accepting with great love the study of *daf yomi*. It is to be hoped that the study of *daf yomi* will, with time, spread more and more..."

By the time of the second *Siyum Hashas* in 1938, the number of participants in the *daf yomi* program had grown to hundreds of thousands. Now the number is so vast, who can count how many are involved? All this because one *rabbi* had a dream to spread *Torah* and uplift the masses.

But it wasn't just him alone that had to believe in the vision. Without the Chofetz Chaim's support by standing up for Rav Shapiro when he entered the room at the *Agudah* Convention, it may be that others would not have given him the respect on this important platform which would then launch *daf yomi*. Then there were all the thousands of contributors that gave money to the most expensive *yeshivah* of its time. Rav Meir traveled tiredly for years raising the necessary funds in order to pull off this tremendous feat. But most importantly, there were his closest followers who were willing to give up their life for their rebbe.

At the end of the First World War, a typhus epidemic spread like wildfire across Galicia. Made worse by deprivation and poor sanitation, the epidemic claimed many lives. One of those who stumbled upon this grievous illness was Rav Meir Shapiro. His condition deteriorated rapidly until a hairsbreadth separated him from death. *Talmidim* and followers gathered to his bedside to be with him in his last moments. Suddenly an elderly *Yid* by the name of Reb Alter Phemrener called out, "I give away five years of my life to the *Rav*."

Some of the others present followed this *Yid's* self-sacrifice and also announced that they were willing to give away some of their years to their *rebbe*. The total amount of years accumulated to sixteen. The day this incident took place was 7 *Cheshvan*, 5689 (1918). Reb Meir Shapiro was *niftar* sixteen years later to the day, on 7 *Cheshvan* 5705 (1934).

A few hours before his *petira*, he motioned to his *rebbetzin* to draw close to his bed. Unable to talk, Reb Meir wrote a note with shaking hands. "Why are you crying?" he wrote. "Now there will be the real joy."

Reb Meir then gestured to his *talmidim* to dress him in a new white shirt and to arrange his *peyos*. Signaling again for a pencil, he wrote, "All of you should drink a *lechaim*."

Whiskey and cake were brought in and distributed among those present. *Brachos* were made and then each *talmid*, in turn, stood before Reb Meir and shook his hand. Reb Meir warmly held onto each of his *talmidim* for a few moments while looking deeply into his eyes.

After each one had bid his *rebbe* farewell, it became obvious that Reb Meir was struggling to talk. Finally, he formed the words, "*Becha botchu avoseinu*, our fathers trusted in You." The *talmidim* recognized that Reb Meir wanted them to sing the melody he had composed to accompany these words.

As the *talmidim* sang, they commenced to dance. They danced as they had never danced before. Tears rolled down their cheeks as their hearts were breaking, but they continued to dance around their *rebbe's* bed. While they were dancing, hundreds of other *bachurim* stood in the next room tearfully reciting *Tehillim*, hoping for a miracle.

With every passing moment, Reb Meir's condition worsened. The *talmidim* realized that within a few moments their *rebbe* would leave them for the eternal world.

Reb Meir detected the *bachurim's* muffled sobs and motioned for one of them to come near. "*Nor mit simcha*, only with joy," he whispered.

I think his last message is really an important one for *Torah* students around the world. The way to acquire *Torah* must be through joy. Otherwise, it will be impossible because there is no end to the learning of *Torah*. One has to be happy each step of the way as he accomplishes each small goal, leading to the greatest goal of learning, to study purely *lishmah* and to really know *Shas*.

At the *levaya* of Rav Shapiro, the Imrei Chaim of Vizhnitz, spoke of the thousands of *blat Gemarah* that greeted the Lubliner Rav in Heaven. Can you imagine all the *talmidim* he has accumulated as well? I saw a *chazal* that said, "Anyone who has *talmidim* in this world, he will continue to teach them in the next world."

Every *bachur* who learns in *yeshivah* today and has accommodations owes *hakaros hatov* to Rav Shapiro. He really understood how someone who is learning *Torah* also needs physical comfort because the learning of *Torah* weakens a person due to its intensity.

# *Study Tanach*

The key to finishing the *Talmud* is to first finish all of *Tanach* and *Mishnah* and to always study in the proper order.

The Goan of Vilna cautioned, as quoted by his sons, "first become well-versed in the twenty-four books [of Scripture], with their vocalization and cantillation... including the study of grammar." (*HaGra*, Intro to commentary on *SA Aruch Chayim*)

"The *Tanach* (*Torah*, Prophets and Scriptures), is a collection of all inspired writings that Hashem meant to be read and studied for all times." (*Midrash Tehillim* 1:8)

Similarly, "The *Tanach* contains all prophecies that have a message for future generations. Its historical events were recorded, so that they would teach a lesson for all time." (*Abrabanel*, *hakdamah* to *Yehoshua*)

It isn't that a person should just learn the Scriptures, but they should actually be diligent in them.

"Just as a bride is adorned with twenty-four ornaments, the scholar must be diligent in the twenty-four books [of Scripture]." (*Midrash Rabbah Shemos* 31:5; MRT *Ki-Siso* 16; quoted by Rashi on *Shemos* 31:18)

Rarely will you see a scholar learning a full *zeman* of *Chumash* with Rashi. It is almost as if he doesn't want others to know that he is studying such a simple work, that he isn't scholarly enough for the *Talmud*.

The Chida, Rabbi Chaim Yosef David Azulai, complained of those who only study *Talmud* and *poskim* and do not sufficiently appreciate the study of *Tanach*, *Mishnah* and *mussar*.

Rabbi Yosef Te-omim the author of *Peri Magadim* writes, "As for those students who are ashamed to learn a section of the *Tanach* with Rashi or a chapter of *Prophets* or *Kesuvim* – if they were at all wise, they would learn this first of all..."

"[Be not] like those who learn *Talmud* with the Tosfaos and, if they can ask an appropriate question or resolve a difficulty, are immediately called "wise" and "rabbi," although they have no knowledge of Scripture." (*Peri Magadim* on *SA Arach Chayim*, beginning)

Rabbi Avraham Horowitz, brother of the Shelah says:

"Certainly, study of the *Tanach* is a principal and basic requirement for any aspiring scholar. Furthermore, how can we possibly justify

147

ourselves before Hashem if we reject His pride, the holy *Torah*, which issued foremost from His mouth?

"In my opinion, this obligation [to learn *Tanach*] is also contained within in the verse 'and you shall heed his voice,' which our Sages interpreted as the voice of the Prophets... It makes no difference whether the Prophets are alive, and we heed their voice or whether it is [only] their words that are alive and present... If you do not study them, know them, and become well-versed in them, how can you heed the voice and fulfill them? And even for a person whose only occupation is *Torah* study – no study in the world is entirely comparable to that of the Bible, that is, to *Torah, Prophets*, and *Kesuvim*, from beginning to end, and one should become well-versed in them. Therefore, there is no valid objection or excuse by which a person can free himself from this obligation...

"They say that one should divide his time into three equal parts: one-third of the day for Scripture, one-third for *Mishnah* and one-third for *Talmud*. Rabbeinu Tam comments that one who has sated himself with Scripture and is thoroughly versed in the twenty-four sacred books... need not devote one-third of the day to them, for the *Babylonian Talmud* is permeated with them. However, to neglect Scripture to the point where one is not completely familiar with the twenty-four bridal adornments [books of *Tanach*] – *chas-v-shalom*... [is] to cast off the yoke of the *Torah*!" (R. A. Horowitz, glosses on *Yesh Nochlin*, appended to Shelah, based on *Devarim* 4:30)

Rabbi Yaakov of Lissa, author of *Nesivos HaMishpat* writes: "Maintain a daily study period of Scripture and *Mishnah*. For the Talmudic declaration, that the *Babylonian Talmud* contains all, applies to those who have already sated themselves with Scripture and *Mishnah*. Furthermore, the evil urge to study for ulterior motives is absent when learning Scripture and *Mishnah*." (*R.Y. of Lissa, Testament*)

This letter was written by R' Pinchas Altshul (1747-1823), a student of the Vilna Gaon and *maggid* / preacher of Polotosk, to his children as a *tzava'ah* / final instruction before his death regarding their service of Hashem. This excerpt is part of his instructions regarding *Torah* study.

"Our Sages say (*Kiddushin* 30a), One should always divide his years— i.e., each day—in thirds: one-third for *Tanach* / scripture, one-third for *Mishnah* and one-third for *Gemarah*. *Tanach* precedes *Mishnah*, and *Mishnah* precedes *Gemarah*; one who reverses them is a *golem* / a body with no mind. The order of learning *Tanach* is to learn the book of one prophet with the commentary of Rashi and then to review it numerous times without Rashi until it is fluent in your mouth [i.e., memorized].

"Even if you study it additional times with Rashi, don't try to memorize all of the *midrashim* that Rashi quotes. The main thing is to be sure to understand the *pshuto shel mikra* / plain meaning of the verse. That is what you should remember. Remember that your goal is to learn *Tanach*, not *Midrash*. If you want to learn *Midrash*, do that separately, for what does *Midrash* have to do with the meaning of the verse?

"In this aspect, our nation has gone astray. Because of the *Midrash*, they don't know *Tanach*. In all probability, if you ask someone about a verse, he can tell you a *Midrash* about it but doesn't know the verse's meaning. He won't know which Prophet said it, to whom, why, when, or about which exile or consolation - all because of the *midrashim* that confuse him and his mind. You, my son, pay attention to know the verse's meaning, to whom it was said, why, and about what, and don't confuse yourself with *midrashim*—then you will succeed..." (*Rosh Ha'giv'ah*)

Rabbi Yehudah HaChasid taught that if a person needs to sell some of his *sefarim*, he should sell his books of the Oral *Torah*, which is to say his volumes of *Mishnah* and *Talmud* and their commentaries, rather than books of the Written *Torah*. The Written *Torah* may be compared [to raw material] like wool or linen, whereas the Oral *Torah* corresponds to the process of weaving the wool or linen into cloth. The word *mesechta*, meaning Talmudic tractate, is indicative of this. The term *mesechta* is etymologically related to the biblical word *maseches*, "web," as in the verse, "Samson said, 'If you weave seven locks of my head into the *maseches* [web]'" (*Judges* 16:13) Indeed, a Talmudic *mesechta* "weaves" the various *halachos* into chapters, which is to say that in a *mesechta*, all laws pertaining to the same subject as assembled and categorized.

The Written *Torah* takes precedence over the Oral *Torah*, because if you have no wool or linen, how are you going to weave? (*Sefer Chassidim* 17 (928)

"We are satisfied and satiated with five joys: the *Torah* (*Tanach*), *Mishnah*, *Gemarah*, *Toseftas*, and *Aggados*." (*Vayikra Rabbah* 30)

It really is another world, that is, a scholar who has properly prepared himself. The preparation gives him a balance prospective, fear of Heaven and an understanding of *Torah* unequal to the scholars who took shortcuts.

Rabbi Yaakov Abuchatzeira taught, "The key which causes man to cleave to the fear of Hashem is constant engagement in *Torah* study." (*Alef Binah* 175)

The concept of studying *Torah* in the proper way not only is uncommon but seems misunderstood today. People really think that they

149

can skip around all their life, learning whatever they feel like without any consequences. I've heard so many excuses as to why a person can't be bothered learning *Tanach*.

Some of which are, "that is not the way today", "the *Tanach* is full of mistakes", "I don't have time", "my *Kollel* and *rabbi* won't allow me to", "the *rabbis* say you don't have to." The list goes on and on. The only one that loses with this perspective, is you. So, what if many *rabbis* today emphasize going straight to the *Talmud* for whatever reason. That isn't going to help you to become a *talmud chacham*. So, what if it's embarrassing to learn *Chumash* with Rashi in your *kollel* while everyone is learning *Talmud* and the Tur. Maybe not in two months or six months, nor a year, but in a few years, you will be holding on an entirely different *madrega* than them. With patience and perseverance, you will give yourself a wonderous foundation for *Torah* and Hashem will bless your study, you will create tremendous *chiddushei Torah*, all because you filled your vessel with strength. All because you decided to make yourself into a *kli* for the *Torah*.

# *Study Mishnah*

The *Mishnah* was initially brought into order and arranged into the six principal divisions by Hillel (*Nasi* of the *Sanhedrin*) in the time of Herod. This system was further advanced upon by Rabbi Akiva and subsequently by Rabbi Meir. Lastly, Rabbi Yehudah Hanasi (*Nasi* of the *Sanhedrin* who flourished towards the end of the century) completed the work.

The authorities quoted inside the *Mishnah* belong to three different periods: *Sofrim* (scribes), *Zugos* (pairs), and *Tannaim* (teachers). The *Sofrim*, also termed *Anshei Kneses Hagedolah*, succeeded Ezra for about two hundred years; the *Zugos*, from Yose b. Yoeser till Hillel, stood in pairs at the head of the *Sanhedrin*, one as *Nasi* (president) and the other as the *Av Beis Din* (vice-president) and flourished till the time of Herod; the *Tannaim* commenced with the disciples of Hillel and Shammai. (10 BCE to 220 CE).

Rabbi Yehudah Hanasi, Rabbeinu Hakadosh, compiled the *Mishnah*. From the time of Moshe till that of Rabbeinu Hakadosh, no work had been composed from which the Oral Law was publicly taught. He collected together all the traditions, enactments, interpretations and expositions of every person of the *Torah*, that either had come down from Moshe Rabbeinu, or had been deduced by the court's successive generations. Compiling this material, he redacted in the *Mishnah*, which was diligently taught in pubic. Copies of it were made and widely dispersed so that the Oral Law might not be forgotten in Israel. Why did he act so and not leave things as they were? He had observed that the numbers of disciples were diminishing, renewed calamities were continuously happening, the wicked government was extending its domain and increasing in power, and Israelites were wandering and emigrating to distant countries. He hence composed a work to serve as a handbook for all, and the contents of which could be rapidly studied and would not be forgotten. (Rambam, *Hakdamah L'Mishnah Torah*)

The *Anshei K'neses HaGedolah* codified the Oral *Torah*. This codification was identified as the *Mishnah* from the word *'shanah'* which means to review over and over until memorized. *'Mishnah'* also denotes its secondary (*sheni*) position to the Written *Torah*. (*Aruch, Mishnah*)

"The body of law known as *Mishnah* is divided into six סדרים orders: זרעים מועד נשים נזיקין קדשים טהרות. The initial letters of these titles for the acronym זמן נקט hold on to the time – an exhortation of the student of

*Torah* to make the most of every precious moment that can be utilized for *Torah* study. Hold on to the time! Don't let the moments slip by." (*For Love of Torah* p. 37)

The Oral *Torah* was originally meant to be transmitted through word of mouth. It was spread from master to student, in such a manner that if the student had any question, he would be able to ask, and thus avoid being ambiguous. A written text, however, no matter how perfect, is always subject to misinterpretation. Furthermore, the Oral *Torah* was intended to cover the infinitude of cases which would arise in the course of time. It could never have been written in its entirety. It is thus written, "Of making books there is no end." (*Koheles* 12:12) Hashem therefore afforded Moshe a set of rules though which the *Torah* could be applied to every possible case. If the entire *Torah* would have been given in writing, everyone would interpret it as he desired. This would lead to division and discord among people who would follow the *Torah* in diverse ways. The Oral *Torah*, on the other hand, would require a central authority (The *Sanhedrin*, rabbis of each generation) to preserve it, thus assuring the unity of Israel. (*Gittin* 60b; *Chagigah* 11b; *Moreh Nevuchim* 1:71)

The *rabbis* teach us about the greatness of the Oral *Torah*:

"The Oral *Torah* is even more dear to Hashem than the written *Torah*." (*Y. Megillah 4:1; Bamidbar Rabbah* 14:12)

"The Oral *Torah* is the means through which we devote our lives to Hashem and His teachings." (*Tanna d'bei Eliyahu Zutta* 2:4a)

"The Oral *Torah* is the basis of Hashem's covenant with Israel." (*Gittin* 60b)

"A person learns only that which his heart desires." (*Avodah Zara* 19a) It is important to make your *Torah* study fun and exciting. That is what is nice about having the goal of finishing *sefarim*, it gives vitality to your learning. You no longer are just learning a *seder* inside the *Talmud* or other *Torah* works, but you have a goal of actually completing something important.

All too often the *Torah* is taught in a dry and unfulfilling way. While some new scholars will be drawn to the *Talmud*, others will find it dull and tedious. That is because nobody has taught them how sweet the *Talmud* and *Mishnah* really is. They are taught to break their neck over one *daf* of *Talmud* while missing out on the entire *sugya* as a whole. You have your entire lifetime to go back and learn the *daf* in detail, knowing something as a whole has boundless benefits.

You might have someone who has traveled Europe in great detail, visiting the most important sights but he can't compare in broad knowledge to the person who has also visited and experienced all the continents. This person has so much exposure that he really understands the world as a whole.

Then after completing his vast travels, he can go back again to his favorite places and visit them in detail. In the end, he will have accomplished far more than the person who is tearing apart just this one *sugya*. However, this is not how the *yeshivas* of today teach people. They figure, if they want to make *talmidei chachamim*, they have to teach them how to learn in depth and perfect their skills.

The *Torah* thereby ends up feeling a bit dry and they may never in their lifetime finish *Shas* or for that matter, even basic works. After a few years in *yeshivah*, they will have to work to support their families and will probably fall back on learning only during night *seder*. They might be experts in tearing a *daf* of *Gemarah* apart but the sweetness of *kol haTorah kulah* isn't with them to inspire their life.

The only thing left to save them will probably Rabbi Shapiro's *daf yomi*, so valuable is it for *baalei batim*, to learn one *blat* of *Talmud* together with others. However, should they have spent the time earlier in life completing the *Tanach* and all of *Mishniyos* while they had the time, it would have changed their life forever. Maybe they would have even finished all of the *Talmud* while still in their youth, should the system have encouraged them to lay down a foundation for study.

I can tell you, once you have completed the *Talmud*, your life is changed forever. There is no such thing as learning *Torah* part-time anymore. Even if you have to work, it will only be in order to finish another *blat* of *Gemarah*.

But all this can't take place if one doesn't humble themselves and first relearn the basics of study. When Rabbi Akiva became a *ba'alei teshuvah*, he wasn't embarrassed to start at the beginning and learn the basics at the age of forty.

One of the reasons that *yeshivos* might push *Talmud* study is because they feel it's more interesting to the new scholar. I am all for this, but it shouldn't comprise the majority of their entire day. The main thing is to fill yourself with core study that is primary. After this, then the *Talmud* can become the core and basis of your daily study.

Rabbi Eliyahu, The Goan of Vilna, wrote similarly: "'He who walks in his uprightness, fears G-d' – Each person has to walk in his own unique way, for people's characteristics are not all the same.'"

Reish Lakish said, "If you see a student whose studies are as hard to him as iron, it is because his knowledge of the *Mishnaic* text is not arranged [in an organized fashion]." As it is explained by Rashi: "One does not understand his studies because he has distorted what comes first [i.e. *Mishnah*, which comes before *Gemarah*]." What is his remedy? He should spend more time [studying] in a *yeshivah*, where the other students review the *Mishnaic* text, as it is said [in the continuation of that verse]: "He should be fortified by the legions of students." However, as the verse concludes: "but the advantage of wisdom is greater, i.e. all the more so would his studies have progressed if his knowledge of the *Mishnaic* text had been arranged properly in the first place." As exemplified by the case of Reish Lakish, who would review his *Mishnaic* text forty times, corresponding to the forty days during which the *Torah* was transmitted to Moses at Sinai, and only then appear before Rabbi Yochanan to study *Gemarah*. Also, "Rav Adda bar Ahavah would review his Mishnaic text twenty-four times, corresponding to the twenty-four books of the *Torah*, *Prophets*, and *Writings*, and then appear before Rava to study *Gemarah*." (*Tannis* 8a)

A parallel interpretation: Rava said: "If you see a student whose studies are as hard to him as iron, it is because his teacher does not show him a cheerful countenance, as it is said: 'And he does not understand his studies because [his teacher] distorted his face.' What is his remedy? He should send numerous friends to [his teacher] to intercede on his behalf, as it is said, in the continuation of that verse: 'he should overwhelm his teacher with legions of friends.' However, as the verse concludes: 'but the advantage of wisdom is great, i.e. all the more so would his studies have progressed if his behavior had been pleasing to his teacher in the first place.'" (ibid.)

Once, when R' Yaakov Yisrael of Cherkassy became seriously ill and the physicians did not know what to do to revive him. He slipped into a coma for several days, and R' Motele of Hornosteipel could not be persuaded to depart from the bedside. Finally, one morning, just as abruptly as he had fallen ill, he arose from the coma. He turned to R' Motele and said, "I know the source of my illness."

"The 365 *Torah* prohibitions and the 248 positive *mitzvos* correspond to the 365 tendons and the 248 organs in the body. The organs and the tendons receive their spiritual nutrients when one observes the *mitzvos* of the *Torah*. If I neglected any of the *mitzvos*, the corresponding physical part lacks its nutrition and is affected.

"During the days that I seemed to be unconscious, in fact I was soul-searching, and that is when I discovered the cause of my illness. It is my studies in the esoteric aspects of *Torah*. They caused me to become derelict in *Talmud* study. Understanding the source, I accepted upon myself to learn eighteen chapters of the *Mishnah* between *Minchah* and *Marriv* each day. As soon as I corrected my dereliction, resolving to improve my studies, I became well." And with that, he rose from his bed, completely healed. (My Book, *A Journey into Holiness*, p.165)

The Tolna Rebbe, Rav Yochanan Twersky, would often bemoan the reality that people do not learn *Mishniyos*. They usually learn it only as a preface to understanding the *Gemarah*. The Rebbe decided to change this *derech*, and in 1986, he established *Mifal HaMishnayos*. Every person who joined the organization were required to learn twelve chapters of *Mishnayos* a month and then take a written examination. Those who excelled in the monthly tests were paid a substantial amount. Today, over two thousand people take the test each month.

"It is very important for a Talmudic scholar to continually review *Mishnayos*. By doing so, he is creating a solid foundation for his *Talmud* study to endure. So, every morning, after prayers, Reb Dovid'l Biderman would study eighteen chapters of *Mishnayos*, thereby finishing the entire *Mishnah* once a month." (My Book, *A Journey into Holiness*, p.77)

Maharal cites the words of R. Nathan, who states that whoever neglects the *Mishnah* "has treated G-d's word with contempt." (*M. Avos* 2:8) Maharal explains that the *Talmud's* current popularity is rooted in natural curiosity and not in a desire to become acquainted with the commandments themselves, as taught by the *Mishnah*, which is G-d's word in a more original form.

The Shelah writes: "Regarding the question of which should be given priority in apportioning one's time – *Mishnah* – *Talmud* – the *Talmud* says: 'In general, run towards the *Mishnah* more than the *Talmud*'... especially nowadays, when we have the benefit of the commentaries of Rambam and R. 'Ovadiah of Bartinoro, who explain the *Mishnah* according to the outcome of the [discussion in the] *Talmud*, and state the *halachos*, making the [study of] *Mishnah* of great value... Therefore, most of one's effort should go into *Mishnah*, studying and repeating it count-less times, without interruption."

"Additionally, R. Chaim of Volozhin considers the study of *Mishnah* especially suited for encouraging continual learning and the understanding of the basic meaning of *Torah* text. He suggests that everyone learn eighteen chapters each day, reviewing them two or three times until he knows them by heart. He adds that it is better to be thoroughly familiar with one tractate than superficially acquainted with many." (*M. Avos* 3:15)

"I wish to admonish and charge you that, besides the rest of the

*Talmud*, you should learn *Mishnayos* every day, until completing the six orders in all their glory. And every day of your life, review Scripture and *Mishnah* so you will not forget any of it." (Glosses on *Sefer Yesh Nochalin*, appended to Shelah)

Rabbi Samson Raphael Hirsch tells, "After five years of studying *Mishnah*, no subject discussed by the *Talmud* will be strange to him and he will comprehend its discussions and conclusions in depth… When will our people return to the study program our forefathers have taught us?" (*R.S.R. Hirsch, Sidur, Avos* 5:25)

Learn *Mishnayos* Project: Accept upon yourself *bli neder*, to finish all of *Mishnayos*. You can even learn it the first time in another language, English, Spanish, French… just in order to complete it. The main thing is to finish this important *Torah* work at your own level of understanding and comprehension without delay. It will then open up new spiritual doors for you and allow you a greater understanding of the *Talmud*. Don't skip around from *sefer* to *sefer* anymore, go from start to finish and complete this major work of *Mishnayos*, then move on to others.

## Other Works

Besides the *Mishnah*, the sages of the *Mishnah* also composed other works to expound the words of the *Torah*. Rabbi Hoshiah, a disciple of Rabbeinu Hakadosh, wrote an exposition of the book of *Bereshis*; and Rabbi Yishmael, a commentary of the *Torah*, from the beginning of the book of *Shemos* to the end of *Devarim*. This work is called *mechilta*. Rabbi Akiva also wrote a *mechilta*. Other sages, who lived subsequently, compiled *midrashim*. All these works were composed before the *Talmud Bavli*. Ravia, Rav Ashi and other colleagues were the last of the great sages who firmly established the Oral Law, made decrees, and ordinances and introduced customs. Their decrees, ordinances and customs obtained universal acceptance among Israelites wherever they settled. (Rambam, *Hakdamah L'Mishneh Torah*)

# *The Benefits of Ein Yaakov*

Ein Yaakov is a compilation of the *aggadah* (*Midrash*-style) teachings and stories from the *Talmud*. It was collected by Rabbi Yaakov Ibn Habib (1460–1516) of Spain, shortly after the expulsion.

Rabbi Ibn Ḥabib collected all the *aggadic* passages from the *Bavli Talmud*, and many from the *Yerushalmi Talmud*. The publication of this work commenced in 1516 and was completed by his son, Rav Levi. The *aggadah* focuses on the ethical and inspirational aspects of the *Torah*. Through a wealth of homilies, anecdotes, allegories, pithy sayings, and interpretations of biblical verses.

Rabbi Schneur Zalman of Liadi encouraged its study every evening, stating that, "most of the secrets of the *Torah* are concealed in it, and it atones for man's sins, as explained in the writings of the Arizal." (*Tanya, Iggeres HaKodesh* 23)

From all walks of *Torah* Judaism, its study was appreciated. Baba Sali would learn *Ayin Yaakov* and also encouraged its study profusely to his disciples along with studying *Chok Yisrael* daily.

The Besht would often take his disciples with him in his coach during journeys. Always valuing his time, during the trip some of those with him would recite the *Tehillim* out loud or read out loud from *Ein Yaakov* [the *aggadah* of the *Talmud*]. (*Emunas Tzaddikim*, p. 6, #3) The *Ein Yaakov* is really the perfect *sefer* for this; I too used to carry it with me for years during my travels. It is rather a light version of the *Talmud*, stories to be specific, that are perfect to think about while you journey. (My book, *Pathways of the Righteous* p. 124)

Rabbi Moshe Chaim Luzzatto explains that *aggadah* are multi-layered commentaries on the *Torah*. Each narrative has literal meanings (חלק המצות) and allegorical (חלק הסודות) or "secret" meanings. The "secret" components contain deeper aspects of the *Talmud* so powerful that the rabbis of the *Mishnaic* era "encoded" their messages as "stories" to prevent their power from being misused.

R' Pinchas Altshul writes: "This is the proper way to learn *aggados* [the non-*halachic* parts of the *Gemarah*; similar to *Midrash*]: Your goal should be to understand how the *aggadah* is interpreting the verse . . . Also, your intention should be to understand in each case what ethical lesson or guidance can be derived from each *aggadah*, for all good character traits and true piety can be found in the words. Nevertheless, you must be aware that our Sages intention in the *aggadah* was to conceal matters of *Kabbalah*. Thus, the *aggados* spoke in hints, parables and riddles, for it is an honor to Hashem to conceal these matters." (*Rosh Ha'givah*)

The Netziv writes that through studying the *Gemarah* and *aggadah*, "one can soar, attain fine character traits... and accomplish remarkable things for Israel. But the grand foundation of it all is the *Gemarah*, which is like rain. Afterwards, the *aggadah* – which is like dew – is also beneficial. And after all this, let him gain further strength by studying other wisdoms – which are like the sun." (*Harchev Davar* on *Devarim* 32:2)

"The Oral *Torah*, in its entirety, was handed down from Mount Sinai, but in unfinished form." (*Sanhedrin* 4:2) This leaves room for new interpretations and applications in its *halachic* and *aggadic* parts alike.

Innovation in *aggadah*, says the Rashbam, is an ongoing process. Regarding his grandfather Rashi, he wrote: "He admitted to me that had he had the time, he would have composed other commentaries according to the new interpretations that arise daily." (Rashbam on *Bereshis* 37:2)

R. Samson Raphael Hirsch describes *aggadah* as emanating from "the spiritual light within each individual. [*Halacha*] was sealed with the completion of the *Gemarah*. The domain of *aggadah*, however, is free and accessible to enlargement by all generations." (Intro to *Horeb*)

Even though *halacha* also allows for *chiddush*, innovation, in several ways, these must be carefully defined and limited to scholars of the highest levels having a full grasp of the Oral *Torah*. However, the *aggadah* are "Words which attract the heart of man," (*Shabbos* 87a) thereby opening up his mind and leading him to paths of *teshuvah*.

"If you wish to know Him at whose word the world came into being, then study the *'hagadata'* (homiletic literature), for through it, you shall surely come to know the Holy One, praised be He, and follow in His ways." (*Sifrei Devarim* 11:22)

There is a certain sweetness that comes from its study. "The homiletic (*aggadah*) interpretations taste like that of the pomegranate." (*Shir HaShirim Rabbah* 8:2)

"The *aggados* whose flavor and taste are like those of apples." (*Shir HaShirim Rabbah* 2:5)

Sometimes, when we learn *aggadah* in the *Gemarah*, we don't appreciate it enough because soon after we move on to the next *halachic* comment. *Ayin Yaakov*, since it comprises only the stories of the *Gemarah*, helps emphasis each and every story in parts, appreciating its hidden meaning. The *hagadata* seeks to inspire us and talk directly to our souls. It is always good to accompany a *halacha* with a story that emphasizes its purpose. That is why the sages put so much *hagadata* inside the *Gemarah*, knowing that a story would help us remember the proper way to act.

"Also helpful is the reading of those works which deal with incidents in the lives of the saints, for these incidents stimulate the intelligence to take counsel and to imitate the saint's worthy deeds." (*Mesilas Yesharim* ch. 21)

When I was younger, I wanted to always be familiar with the *Talmud* passages spoken by *rabbanim* during their *shirim* or general conversations. Therefore, I studied the *Ayin Yaakov* many times over in order to be familiar with it. It worked, without having completed the *Talmud*, I was able to "cheat" as I used to call it and know most of the conversations that would be quoted and talked about in *Talmudic* discussions. Not only that but the stories in *Ayin Yaakov* inspired me tremendously. It, therefore, became one of my favorite *sefarim* of all time.

My father, Rabbi Shlomo Zavel ben Yaakov *olav hashalom*, spoke about *Ayin Yaakov* very highly. He always wanted the English set which was out of print and a rare find. Once, I had mentioned to "Manny's" before he created his chain of bookstores, of my desire of the rare set of *Ayin Yaakov* to follow in my father's footsteps in learning. A few days later, to my surprise was sitting, in the electric box outside my brother-in-law's apartment in Jerusalem, the entire *Ayin Yaakov* set. It was truly a dream come true for me. In all excitement, I went immediately down to Ohr Somayach Yeshivah where he set up shop in those days, paying him its cost and these set of books are cherished by me always. The pages of my *Ayin Yaakov* set are worn to the brim from all the extended use I have made of them over the years. It truly is a classic in Jewish literature.

# Founding of the Talmuds

The combined *gematria* of תלמוד ירושלמי, the *Jerusalem Talmud* (1076), and תלמוד בבלי, the *Talmud Bavli* (524), is 1600. The square root of 1600 is 40, the number represented by the letter מ. The *Mishnah* begins (מאימתי) and ends (בשלום) with a מ. This indicates that the body of the Talmudic law is rooted in the *Mishnah* and conversely, a comprehensive understanding of the *Mishnah* requires the study of the *Talmud*. (*Metzareif Dahava*)

The Prophet states, "ציון במשפט תפדה ושביה בצדקה"-Zion shall be redeemed with justice, and they that return to her, with righteousness." (*Yeshayahu* 1:27) The words ציון במשפט תפדה, which refer to Jerusalem, have the same *gematria* as תלמוד ירושלמי (1076) The words ושביה בצדקה which speak of the returnees from Bavel, have the same *gematria* as תלמוד בבלי (524). This teaches that the Jewish people will merit redemption because of their observance of Hashem's laws as expressed in the Oral Law. (Vilna Goan)

Furthermore, it is in the merit of the Jewish people's collective fulfilment of the greatest *mitzvah* of all, *Torah* study, that the redemption will occur. So, let us now explore how we came to such a wonderful work of Oral *Torah*.

Rav Ashi and Ravina closed the list of the sages of the *Talmud*. Rav Ashi compiled the Talmud Bavli in the land of Shinar (Bavel), about a century later than Rabbi Yochanan compiled the *Talmud Yerushalmi*. These two *Talmud's* comprise an exposition of the text of the *Mishnah* and an elucidation of its abstruse points. Also, the new subject matter that had been added by the various courts from the days of Rabbeinu Hakadosh, till the compilation of the *Talmud*. The two *Talmuds*, the Tosefta, the Sifra and the Sifre, all the Tosefos are the sources from all of which is elucidated in the traditions received by the sages from their predecessors in unbroken succession up to the teachings of Moshe, as he received them on Sinai. (Rambam, *Hakdamah L'Mishneh Torah*)

After the court of Rav Ashi, who compiled the *Gemarah* which was finally finalized in the days of his son, an extraordinarily great dispersion of Israel throughout the world happened. Jews emigrated to remote parts and distant isles. The prevalence of wars and the march of armies rendered travel insecure. The study of the *Torah* weakened. The Jewish people did not flock to the colleges in their thousands and tens of thousands as they used to; but in each city and country, individuals who felt the divine call gathered together and occupied themselves with the *Torah*. They studied all the works of the sages; and from these, learnt the method of legal interpretation. (Rambam, *Hakdamah L'Mishneh Torah*)

The *chachamim* who arose after the compilation of the *Talmud*, were called *Geonim*. The *Geonim* who flourished in the land of Israel, Shinar, Spain, and France, instructed the method of the *Talmud*, elucidated its obscurities, and expounded the assorted topics with which it deals. For its method is exceedingly profound. Furthermore, the *Talmud* is composed in *Aramaic* mixed with other languages-this having been the vernacular of the Bavli Jews at the period when it was compiled. In other territories however, as also in Bavel, in the days of the *Geonim*, no one, unless particularly taught, understood that dialect. Many applications were made to the *goan* of the times by residents of different cities, asking for explanations of difficulties on the *Talmud*. These, the *Geonim* resolved the issues according to their ability. Those who had put the questions, collected the responses which they made into *sefarim* to study. The *Geonim* also, at various periods, composed commentaries on the *Talmud*. Some of which explained specific laws; others, particular chapters that represented difficulties to their contemporaries; others again expounded complete treatises and entire orders of the *Talmud*. They also made compilations of settled rules. (Rambam, *Hakdamah L'Mishneh Torah*)

The redaction of the *Talmud* didn't quite end with the death of Rav Ashi. His *talmidim* added several short sections. After Rav Ashi passed, his students subsequently led the *yeshivah*, one after the other, during the subsequent forty-seven years. Maremar, the student of Ravina commanded the *yeshivah* for five years, followed by Rav Idi bar Avin, who was among the older sages and had even merited to learn by Rav Papa (a scholar from the preceding generation); he led the *yeshivah* for twenty years. Rav Nachman bar Rav Huna ran the *yeshivah* for three years, Rav Tuvyami, or his more popular name, Mar bar Rav Ashi, who substituted his father's position, for fifteen years. After him was Raba Tosfoa, who was *Rosh Yeshivah* for six years. The last *Amora* was Ravina (not the same Ravina who was an associate of Rav Ashi). He was the *Rosh Yeshivah* in Sura for twenty-six years, during which time he concluded most of the *Talmud*. Ravina died in 4260/500 and that ended the Talmudic scribal era. The *roshei yeshivos* of the next generation were referred to and are known today as the *Sabora'im*.

The First Generation of the *Amoraim* lasted between 250 to 300 years. The first *Amora*, conceivably, was Rav Aba bar Ayvu, known throughout the *Talmud* simply as Rav. He was known by this name because he was the leader and rabbi of all the Jews in the Diaspora. Rav initiated the *yeshivah* in Sura, that continued to endure thru the days of all the *Amoraim* and even stretched into the days of the *Geonim*. The succession of *Torah* learning in this *yeshivah* sustained for 800 years.

Rav was from Bavel but traveled to *Eretz Yisrael* to study *Torah* from Rabbi Yehudah HaNasi. Upon returning to Bavel in 3979/219, Rava took with him the *Mishnah* that Rabbi Yehudah HaNasi had redacted, to teach it to the Jews of Bavel.

Rav was so very noble in *Torah* that, although he was an *Amora*, even the sages of his time considered him to be on the level of the *Tannaim*. The *Gemarah* teaches, "Rav is a *Tanna* and has the right to argue with the *Mishnayos*." (*Eruvin 50*)

His colleague Shmuel, who also traveled to *Eretz Yisrael*, learned under Rabbi Yehudah HaNasi, and returned to Bavel with the newly composed *Mishnayos*, to teach it to the Jews of Bavel, as did his associate Rav. He particularly desired to educate the Jews of Nehardea, where he opened his own *yeshivah*.

Rav was deemed the expert in *halachic* issues, and the *halacha* follows his rulings. In monetary issues, however, the *halacha* follows the rulings of Shmuel. Shmuel was a scholar of medicine and astronomy besides for his expertise in *Torah*. He testified about himself: "The roads of Heaven are as familiar to me as the roads of Nehardea." (*Brachos 58*)

The leaders of *Torah* in *Eretz Yisrael* during this period were the great *Amoraim*, Rabbi Yochanan, *Rosh Yeshivah* in Tiberias, and his student / *chavrusa* Reish Lakish. Collectively they continued the chain of *Torah* and taught the Oral *Torah* to the Jews in *Eretz Yisrael*. So great were they in *Torah* that their traditions stretched to all the way to Bavel. There were *Amoraim* who would journey back and forth between *Eretz Yisrael* and Bavel. They transported the new *chiddushie Torah* that were studied in each *yeshivah*. This is also what helped the Bavli to become more of the complete *Talmud* as they collected everything, they could from the scholars who would visit Eretz Yisrael. Ulla was one such *Amora*. There were also *Amoraim* who initially dwelled in *Eretz Yisrael* and moved to Bavel and they echoed the *Torah* of Rabbi Yochanan and Reish Lakish. Two Examples of this are the scholars Rav Dimi and Rav Avin (usually referred to as Ravin).

You can find many instances in *Shas* where the *Talmud* says, "When Rav Dimi came, he said in the name of Rabbi Yochanan" or "When Ravin came, he said in the name of Rabbi Yochanan." The intent was that when

162

they arrived in Bavel they repeated the *Torah* which they had heard.

There were also sages who emigrated from Bavel to *Eretz Yisrael* and they transmitted the Babylonian *Torah* to the Jews of Israel. Some of these sages were the *Amora*, Rav Kahana, who emigrated to Israel to learn *Torah* from Rabbi Yochanan, and Rabbi Eleazar (ben Pedas) who also relocated to Israel and was appointed as Rabbi Yochanan's replacement after his death. Rav Zeira, as well, emigrated to *Eretz Yisrael*.

Now let us speak about the Second Generation. As revealed before, the *Rosh HaYeshivah* of Nehardea was Shmuel. Following his death, Rav Nachman (bar Yaakov) was appointed to oversee his place as *Rosh Yeshivah*. The *yeshivah* didn't endure in Nehardea for long though. King Papa bar Netzer wholly destroyed the city of Nehardea. The students of the *yeshivah* were forced to flee to Mechuza, where they re-established the *yeshivah*.

Rav Yehuda was a dedicated student of both Rav and Shmuel. There are several instances in *Shas* where he quotes the words of his teachers. Ultimately, Rav Yehuda opened his own *yeshivah*, the renowned Pumbidisa Yeshivah. This *yeshivah* also persevered for a long time—800 years.

After Rav's death, the *yeshivah* of Rav which was in Sura, was taken over by Rav Huna.

Rav Chisda and Rav Sheishes were among the finest of *Amoraim* of that generation. They imparted *Torah* in the *yeshivah* in the city of Shilchi on the banks of the river Euphrates.

During that period, there were three big, central *yeshivos* that were inhabited by fine scholars, they were in Sura, Pumbidisa, and Mechuza. From these main Babylonia *yeshivos*, together with the many smaller *yeshivos*, the Oral *Torah* was assured for future generations.

The Third Generation began following the death of Rav Yehuda. Rabba (Rabbi Abba bar Nachmani) then was appointed the new *Rosh Yeshivah* of Pumpidisa. Along with him in the *yeshivah* was Rav Yoseif, who felt uncomfortable assuming the role of *rosh hayeshivah*, as long as Rabba was still alive. Following Rabba's death, Rav Yoseif administered for two-and-a-half years, until he passed away. During their times, the *Yarchei Kallah,* teacher's convention, the gathering *Torah* scholars, reached record breaking numbers: 12,000 students. (See *Bava Metzia* 86)

The Fourth Generation began after Rabba's death. Rav Zeira, Rabba bar Masna, Abaye, and Rava gathered to decide who should take over to lead. They determined that the scholar who could ask a question that no one could resolve should be the new *rosh hayeshivah*. Abaye triumphed above the challenge and took over. (see *Horiyos* 14). Subsequently, after the death of Abaye, Rava took the mantle. The numerous Talmudic discussions between Abaye and Rava became almost synonymous with the *Gemarah* itself, as the *Gemarah* is referenced many times as the discussions of Abaye and Rava.

The Fifth Generation began Following Rava's death. It was then that many small *yeshivos* opened their doors all over Babylonia. Rav Papa and Rav Huna held down the fort, teaching in Narash. Rav Nachman bar Yitzchok undertook the leadership of the Pumbidisa Yeshivah for four years. Rav Kahana became the *rosh hayeshivah* of Pum Nehara, and Rav Z'vid became the *rosh hayeshivah* of Nehardea.

The Sixth Generation, as mentioned earlier, began with Rav Ashi as the *rosh hayeshivah* in Mechasya (which was nearby Sura). Rav Ashi was special as he was a disciple of many scholars from the previous generation. These would include, Rav Papa, Rav Huna, Ulla, Rav Papi, and others. His main teacher, however, was Rav Kahana.

Here are some worthy *rabbanim* worth mentioning as their works are fundamental:

Rabbi Yitzchak Ben Yaakov Alfasi, otherwise known as the Rif, was born in Kila Chamad, Algeria, 1013. He died in Lucena, Spain in 1103. He was a Talmudist and *Halachic* codifier. He was a Student of Rabbi Chananel in Kairouan, who was active in Fez, North Africa until age 75, when he fled to Spain. He was instrumental in spreading Jewish knowledge into Spain as he was the first major *rabbi* in the vicinity. He authored hundreds of responsa in Arabic. He was primarily known as the author of *Hilchos HaRif,* a Talmudic code representing the initial rulings on the discussions of the *Talmud.* This was a primary source for the Rambam and the focus of great rabbinic studies in the following centuries. These were composed on *Seder Moed, Nashim, Nezikin* and tractates *Brachos* and *Niddah.*

Rabbi Shlomo Yitzchaki of Troyes, known as Rashi was born in Troyes, France in 1040. He died in Troyes, France in 1105.

He was able to trace his ancestry all the way to Dovid HaMelech through Hillel the Elder and other *Tannaim.* He Studied in Worms, Germany and settled in Troyes as a respected scholar when he was twenty-five years old. Wanting to make a difference, he began his commentary on the *Tanach,* centering on the plain and exact meaning of the text. His lucid and concise commentaries on the *Talmud* are instrumental in understanding the *Talmud* and made him arguably, the greatest Biblical commentator of all times. He wrote his commentaries and taught while earning his livelihood as a wine merchant. Rabbeinu Tam, his grandson stated, that his commentaries on *Chumash* were nothing short of *ruach hakodesh*.

Rabbi Moshe Ben Maimon, known as the Rambam or Maimonides, was born in Cordova, Spain in 1135. He died in Cairo, Egypt in 1204.

He became well known as a prodigious Talmudic commentator, *Halachic* codifier and philosopher. Born in Spain, he lived most of life in Egypt. He was a renowned physician and doctor for the Caliph. He authored a *Peirush HaMishnayos*, commentary on the *Mishnah, Sefer HaMitzvos*, an enumeration of the 613 commandments and an introduction to *Mishneh Torah*, a monumental and original code of Jewish Law. It was also known as *Yad Chazakah, Yad* having the numerical value of 14 the number of parts in this work, and *Moreh Nevuchim*, a philosophical treaty. Perhaps the most important *halachic* authority among *Rishonim*. His epithet reads "From Moses to Moses there is no one like Moses", the first Moses referring to Moses Rabbeinu.

Rabbi Asher Ben Yechiel was known as the Rosh. He was born in Germany, in c. 1250. He Died in Toledo, Spain in 1327. He was best known as a Talmudist and *Halachist*, a descendent of the Meor HaGolah. He was the leading student of the Maharam of Rotenburg and was regarded as the leader of Germany after his death.

Trying to leave, he was captured in the mountains of Lombardy having been recognized by a baptized Jew named Kneppe. He was then imprisoned in a fortress near Ensisheim in Alsace. Tradition has it that a large ransom of 23,000 marks silver was raised for him (by the Rosh), but Rabbi Meir refused it, for fear of encouraging the imprisonment of other rabbis.

He departed Germany in 1303 and was welcomed by the Rashba in Barcelona. He became the Rav of Toledo in 1305 where he introduced the methods of the *Tosefists* and *Ashkenazic minhagim*. He opposed any attempts to give precedence to secular learning, prohibiting such studies for anyone under the age of 25. He was the author of *Peirush HaRosh*, a commentary on the *Talmud* patterned after the *Rif, Hilchos HaRosh*. This was a compilation of *halachos* which is the basis for subsequent compilation including the *Tur, Tosefos HaRosh*, where he clarifies the *Tosefos*, and *Orchos Chaim*, on Ethics.

Another great *halachic* authority was Rabbi Yossef Karo known as the Beis Yosef. He was born in Toledo, Spain in 1488. He later died in Tzfat, Israel in 1575. His shul is Tzfat is visited by tens of thousands yearly. He was also known as the Mechaber (the Author).

He was one of the most authoritative Talmudists and codifiers of *halacha,* whose decisions have been accepted as binding in Jewish Law. He was the author of *Kesef Mishneh,* a commentary on the Rambam's *Mishneh Torah,* Beis Yosef, a commentary on the *Tur, Bedek HaBeis* and *Kelalei ha_Talmud.* Rabbi Yosef Karo's own proofreading of Beis Yosef, *Shulchan Aruch,* was first published around 1555, which contains the *halachic* decisions which are fundamental today.

Here is a wonderful *Torah* from the Maharal:

אַף תלמידי חכמים שֶׁבבבל, And there are those who say, also scholars in Babylonia." (*Pesachim* 113b):

As is known, a center point [of a circle] is single. Now, *Eretz Yisrael* is at the center of the world, as a single point is at the center of a circle. As such – as the center point of a circle, which is the point of connection for all the lines that radiate from the circle – *Eretz Yisrael* causes her scholars to be unified and bound together. This [unifying power] is all the more potent, since Hashem, Who is blessed, Who is one, is Ruler of *Eretz Yisrael.* Thus, [*Torah* scholars in *Eretz Yisrael* are united] even though there are perfectly valid grounds for there to be animosity among them – and there certainly are such grounds, since a scholar is the most individualistic of individuals, and we stated earlier that an individualistic being [-*gever-*] is someone who desires to assert his domination until it is all-encompassing and he is one and only; he would be thus [intrinsically] not connected with anything else.

As it says in *Baba Metzia* (85a), "When Rabbi Zeira emigrated to *Eretz Yisrael,* he fasted one hundred fasts in order to forget his Babylonian studies, so that they should not distract him."

Rashi of blessed memory explains that "his Babylonian studies" is a reference to our [Babylonian] *Talmud;* [Rashi comments that] "so that they should not distract him" means, "[They should not distract him] when he emigrated to *Eretz Yisrael* to be taught by Rabbi Yochanan." The *Amoraim* of *Eretz Yisrael* were not men of contention; they were deferential to one another like olive oil, as the *Gemarah* in *Sanhedrin* states, and they arrived at explanations [of *halachic* issues] without challenging [each other].

The Maharal continues by quoting the *Gemarah,* "R. Oshaia said: What is the meaning of the verse, And I took unto me the two staves; the one I called *No'am* [graciousness] and the other I called '*hoblim*' [binders]? — '*No'am*' refers to the scholars of Palestine, who treat each other graciously [*man'imim*] when engaged in *halachic* debates; '*hoblim*', to the scholars of Babylon, who injure each other's feelings [*mehablim*] when discussing *halachah.*

166

"[It is written]: 'Then said he, these are the two anointed ones etc.' [This is preceded by:] 'And two olive trees by it.' R. Isaac said: *'yizhar (oil)'* designates the scholars of Israel, who are affable to each other when engaged in *halachic* debates, like olive oil [which is soothing]; [whilst] and two olive trees stand by it, symbolize the scholars of Babylon, who are as bitter to each other in *halachic* discussions as olive trees." (*Sanhedrin* 24a)

The Maharal explains:

"It is important to realize that these two characteristics [of differences and sharpness] are the indigenous characteristics, respectively, of *Eretz Yisrael* and Babylonia. The *Torah* of the sacred *Eretz Yisrael* does not stray from the proper equilibrium and symmetry, as is true of men themselves [in *Eretz Yisrael*], as we explained earlier, since this sacred land lies at the center of the world and therefore tends to align everything within it into the proper equilibrium and symmetry. Babylonia, on the other hand, is so named because '[there] did [Hashem] confuse [the language of all the earth] (*Bereshis* 11:9),' which implies a jumble and a lack of unity. Dialectic is thus more common there since dielectric consists of one party attempting to refute the other – a relationship of opposition.

"Do not be misled, however, into believing that this [characteristic of *Babylonian Torah* study] implies a lesser status for the *Babylonian Talmud*; on the contrary, it is the greatest of boons, since dialectic is intellect and it is on the highest of levels. [The apparently negative references to the Babylonian technique in the *Gemarah*] mean only that before the *halacha* – that is, [true] intellect – is clarified, [the protagonists of the discussion] are aggressive, not deferential, in line with the prevalent tendency in Babylonia to diverge from equilibrium. It is this characteristic that the *Gemarah* alludes to when it says that even among scholars in Babylonia there is internal animosity.

"It is [because the scholars of Babylonia employ the dialectic process] also that the scholars of *Eretz Yisrael* referred to their Babylonian counterparts as 'dull witted' (*Pesachim* 34b) – because, for certain, when a thing is out of symmetry in even the slightest degree, it cannot possess wisdom. Via the dialectic process of challenge and response, the wisdom of the scholars of Babylonia did crash through [the natural barrier of Babylonia's divergence from equilibrium] and they did arrive at the correct understanding. However, employing the dialectic process to arrive at the truth requires extremely demanding and diligent analysis, and not everyone can successfully accomplish this. Thus, [the scholars of *Eretz Yisrael*] referred to their Babylonian counterparts as 'dull witted'.

When one of the Babylonian scholars emigrates to *Eretz Yisrael* he is the equivalent of two native scholars. (see *Kesubos* 75a) This is because of the Babylonian dialectic that he absorbed, and because once in *Eretz Yisrael* he acquires wisdom – accuracy in *halacha* – with composure. Thus, the wisdom [of the scholars who emigrated] is magnified exponentially.

Therefore, our *Babylonian Talmud* has greater primacy – the dialectic is perfectly explained. This is the intent of the *Gemarah* (Pesachim 113b) which states that "there are those who say, also scholars in Babylonia is now clear." (*Nesivos Olam, Nesiv HaTorah*, p.273-276)

So, what was the intention of the *Gemarah*? Wouldn't it have been far easier if we were just given a list of *halachos* to follow?

"The *Gemarah's* purpose is to clarify the *Mishnah*." (Rambam, *Hakdamah L'Mishnah*) There is no greater work of Oral *Torah*, covering all topics of Judaism such as the *Talmud*. It is now the main work of study in *yeshivos* across the world. If we just went straight to studying *halachos*, our performance of the *mitzvos* would lack meaning and understanding.

"For the purpose of studying, were you created." (*Avos* 2:8) "As to the studying of the *Talmud*, there is no more meritorious occupation than this." (*Bava Metzia* 33a)

For years you can study *Torah,* but one day it will just hit you... *Talmud* study is the main thing.... but how can this be? It is just a bunch of *rabbis* arguing about things you don't relate too... It is like telling Israelis that chocolate tastes good, but they are stuck on vanilla. But once you understand the beauty, once you experience it and really put your entire mind into the *Talmud*, you realize that everything is about making and eating chocolate. You become part of the *Talmud*... You can't sleep at night before you eat your chocolate. Then you need more chocolate in the morning, then again in the evening, but to appreciate chocolate, you have to become a factory and invite others to taste of your chocolate, because, how can you eat and truly enjoy anything alone... so join me in the *Talmud* chocolate factory and let's make some chocolate milk shakes.

It is the dream of every student to complete the *Talmud* in their lifetime. "The word *Gemarah* comes from the root *'gamar'* meaning both to study and to finish." (*Targum* on *Iyov* 22:22) Now that we have given you an introduction to its study, it's time to now embark on completing the platform, leading to the completion of this magnificent work.

# Talmud Yerushalmi

The Gerer Rebbe, Rabbi Simcha Bunim Alter, expressed his love of *Torah* in a variety of ways. At the sixth *Knessia Gedolah*, he instituted a *daf hayomi* for the *Yerushalmi Talmud*. Before this, the magnificent *Talmud* was only pursued by great *talmiei chachamim*, having already mastered the *Bavli*. The Chofetz Chayim had praised Reb Meir Shapiro for removing the dust from many *mesechtos* in *Shas* that had been ignored by all but a few individuals. Now the Rebbe hoped to open up the gates of the *Yerushalmi*, with the added intention that this would provide students with a link to *Eretz Yisrael*. Since then, there has slowly been a new interest in this holy work with new commentaries being published. Like the Gerer Rebbe, I figure, *Ohlom Habah* is a big place, there must be room for more people than just Rabbi Meir Shapiro who has seemed to capture room after room of glory with his fixing of the system of learning *Talmud Bavli*. There are other great works also forgotten that need much attention.

The Vilna Goan said, "In the initial stages of the Messsianic redemption, there will be a renewed interest in the study of *Kabbalah* and the *Talmud Yerushalmi*." (*Kol Ha Tor*)

Learning *Talmud Yerushalmi* is like drinking old aged wine. You can't really describe it to someone else, unless they have to taste it themselves to believe it...

When I personally learn a *mesechta* of *Talmud Yerushalmi* first before *bavli*, for me it makes the *Bavli* much easier... *Yerushalmi* is like the soul of the *Talmud* and the *Bavli* is like the body. The *Bavli* is how we live our life and *paskin halachos*... it is how we live our life today but the *Yerushalmi* is something more. It speaks directly to our souls. Some people say you can't understand it, it's not complete like the *Bavli,* but I don't agree. The *Yerushalmi* is perfect in its simplicity (my opinion, others will say the opposite) That to me is its beauty.

I was once listening to an audio *shir* explaining the difference between *Bavli* and *Yerushalmi*. The speaker was discussing why *Bavli* was the preferred *Talmud* for learning. He brought down different resources and opinions to prove his point. Towards the end of the *shir*, he just happened to mention that he never personally completed an entire *mesechta* of

*Yerushalmi.* I immediately turned off the *shir.*

I hear from so many *Kollel* guys how *Yerushalmi* is somewhat obsolete, irreverent and unimportant. They say it's not important to study and how everything you could possibly need is in the *Bavli*. They too have barely learned the *Yerushalmi,* also claiming that anything important in it would simply have been brought up by Tosefos. They obviously should not open their mouth on something they have no experience in. Anyone who properly learned *Yerushalmi* would cherish it as fine old wine. Everything they have said is to the contrary to the truth. *Yerushalmi* is one of the greatest works. When *Moshiach* comes, it will rise far above other Jewish literature and its treasures will be revealed. Due to Roman/Christian persecution, the *Yerushalmi* could be said to not be completely finished but then again, that is part of its beauty. The beauty of the Oral *Torah* is that it continues to develop with the times, yet remarkably, all was told on *Har Sinai.*

It could be said that maybe Rabbi Yochanan and his students wrote the Oral *Torah* in a difficult and foreign language – in order that it would not be too easy to learn, and people would not become habituated to it. That is because they believed that the Oral *Torah* really shouldn't be written down (*Gittin* 60b) and that hopefully one day, after the Roman persecution, it will return to only being taught orally. Therefore, they thought, it was best for people not to get used to an easy written text, so they chose a more difficult Aramaic language, rather than the easier mix of Hebrew and Aramaic of the Bavli. However, in Bavel, they seemed to have already understood that they would be in this for the long hall. Therefore, they sought to keep the text as easiest as possible to read.

It is my personal thought that maybe the language of *Talmud* is difficult in order to force a person to work harder grasping it and thereby receive a greater *mitzvah,* reward. It also protected its holiness in a way, by making it harder for those unworthy to learn it. Its difficult terminology forces people to return to finishing foundational, preliminary works that they rushed through like the *Tanach* and *Mishniyos.*

According to the opinion of Rabbi Yehoshua Cohen, he says, "there really was no difficulty in the first place. For we find in *Bava Kama* (82b): Rebbe said: 'Why do they speak Sursic in the land of Israel?' – meaning: Why do they speak such a difficult dialect of Aramaic? Let them speak either Hebrew or some other clear language!' From this we see that in those generations a difficult form of Aramaic ('Sursic') was the common language in the land of Israel. This is why the *Jerusalem Talmud* is composed in that language, and not for the reason proposed above. My point is clearly supported by Rashi to *Sota* 49b, s.v. (See also the end of Tosafos to *Berachos* 3a, s.v.)." (*Keren Yehoshua* p. 165)

For me personally, I enjoy the *Yerushalmi* far more than *Bavli*. I like when discussions are straight to the point and how all the *rabbanim* of Jerusalem always sought to find peace between their differences. I find the *sefer* warm and quenching my every thirst for *Torah*.

The only reason I regret learning it is because I find it too difficult to balance two *Gemarahs* at the same time. Being far more drawn to the *Yerushalmi*, I am always fighting what to study, as the *Bavli* is more practical for building myself up as a scholar, showing the way of debating in order to come to the ultimate truth and to then find the *halacha lemisa* of today.

If you put me on a desert island with a choice of *Bavli* or *Yerushalmi*, I will always take the *Yerushalmi*. Sometimes I leave *Yerushalmi* as my *Shabbos* learning. I refer to it as my "gift" for *Shabbos*, that is how much I appreciate it. So, when someone arguably bemoans the *Yerushalmi*, I won't even open my mouth to defend her. That is because I consider her my cherished secret. When a scholar is ready for it, he too will understand this on his own.

Every time I complete the entire *Yerushalmi*, I tell myself that I won't do it again, I can't. I must work on my practical studies using the *Bavli*, leading more towards *halacha lemisa*. However, soon after, maybe a few days, weeks, months and guess what? I find myself learning *Yerushalmi* again. Then I remind myself what Rav said and I feel comfort.

Rav said: "As soon as mangoes forth from the study of *halacha* to the study of Scripture he no longer has peace. And Shmuel said: "It means one who leaves *Talmud* for *Mishnah*." And Rav Yochanan said: "Even from *Talmud* to *Talmud*." Rashi explains: "from *Talmud* to *Talmud*: from *Talmud Yerushalmi* to *Talmud Bavli*, since the former one is deeper." (*Talmud Bavli*, *Chagigah* 10a Rashi *Chagigah* 10a, d.h from *Talmud* to *Talmud*)

As you know from reading this book, I am a huge fan for learning things in the proper order. Therefore, I don't recommend *Yerushalmi* until one completes all of *Bavli* a few times. However, a few *mesechtos* to experience her beauty is certainly recommended.

Once a *ba'al teshuvah* asked me for advice as he felt his mind couldn't handle learning *Gemarah*. Of course, I advised him to learn more *Mishniyos* but besides this, I told him he should buy a volume of *Yerushalmi* and try it out. Contemporary publishers such as Artscroll have done such a wonderous job at translating and explaining the text, that I find *Yerushalmi* to actually be easier to study for some people then *Bavli*. Instead of this person being discouraged, finding it difficult to comprehend the back and forth of *Bavli* discussions, the *Yerushalmi* will take him easily to the *p'shat*. That is, using the contemporary versions of *Yerushalmi* that clarify the text so that it is no longer difficult. However, with all *Talmud* study, remember that its point is to understand how the *halacha* was established, the final *halacha* should be looked up further in more contemporary works.

When Rabbi Ze'ira made *aliyah* to *Eretz Yisrael*, he davened and tried to forget the *Torah* knowledge he acquired in Babylon. He went to great lengths, taking upon himself many fasts in order to forget *Talmud Bavli* so that it should not distract him when he would learn the *Torah* of *Eretz Yisrael*. (*Bava Metzia* 85a)

The Maharsha tries to shed some light on this, he says, "Perhaps the *Babylonian Torah* scholars engaged in *pilpul* much like our generation; anyone who can outdo the other in spurious *pilpul* is considered praiseworthy. And each one tires to refute the arguments of the other.... Thus, they never reach any conclusion regarding the proper *halachah*... Such *pilpul* only leads a person away from the truth.

"In Bavel during that time period, they were accustomed to joust with each other and attempt to disprove each other's theories. While in *Eretz Yisrael*, the methodology was one of cooperative analysis and an unargumentative search for the truth, which flowed as smoothly as oil." (Maharsha on *Bava Metzi'a* 85 s.v. *de-lishtakach*, Ben Yehoyada; see *Sanhedrin* 24a; cf Ritva to *Yoma* 57a)

I think you can feel this in the very text of the *Yerushalmi*, the search for truth through complete Torah study *lishmah*. The *Yerushalmi* is one of the most precious of pearls in all of Jewish literature. It is a taste of the World to Come.

The great peace and unity between the scholars of Israel in those times, reminds me of this precious teaching:

The *Gemarah* says in the end of *Masseches Ta'anis*, that in the future, Hashem will have all the *tzaddikim* dance in a circle, with Himself sitting in the center of the circle in *Gan Eden*. Each one of the *tzaddikim* will then point to Hashem and say, "This is our G-d; this is Hashem, Whom we have so longed to behold!"

What is the symbolism behind a dance that is specifically in a circle around Hashem? Rav Akiva Eiger explains the lesson of this dance of the *tzaddikim* as follows:

"In this world every *tzaddik* has a unique, individual approach to serving Hashem. On the surface, every one of them appears to be heading in a completely different direction. The truth is, however, that this is not the case. All of the different *tzaddikim* are united by a common goal -- to

172

draw closer to Hashem and fulfill His Will in the best possible manner. In the World to Come this will become apparent to all. The *tzaddikim* will dance around Hashem 'arranged in a circle'. In a circle, every individual is facing a different direction -- yet they all revolve around the same central point. The *tzaddikim*, although each has a unique approach, are all trying to accomplish the same goal. Their lives revolve around the same central point, the point where 'Hashem is sitting'. In the World to Come, each of them will point to Him and announce to all that this is their G-d, Whom they had strived to come close to and serve throughout their lives!" (Rabbi Akiva Eiger, quoted in *Chut Ha'Mshulash* and *Toras Emes*)

# The Great Talmud

"If one studies Scripture [primarily], it is of limited value; if he studies *Mishnah*, it is of some value and he is rewarded but if he studies *Talmud*, there is nothing more valuable." (*Magen Avraham* 308, note 17)

If one is unfamiliar with the *Talmud*, he cannot apply the words of the *poskim* in rendering his own decisions. As Rosh declared: "Those who base their decisions on Rambam and are not conversant with the *Talmud*, so that they do not know how the Rambam reached his conclusions – are likely to err... They think they understand, but they do not; for if one is not well-versed in the *Talmud*, he cannot grasp a subject correctly." (*Rosh, Responsa*, 31:9) The Meiri bewails this phenomenon at length (*Bava Kama* 130b) and Rivash classifies those who decide *halachos* in this manner among "those who render decisions frivolously." (*Rivash, Responsa* 44)

The Maharal goes even further, branding them "destroyers of the world." He explains that if one has not plumbed the reasons behind a *Mishnah*, his study cannot be considered *Torah*. Since the world is based on Torah, such a person has crippled the basis of the world.

He continues: "[Even worse are] those who base themselves on the codifiers alone, who only wrote their works for practical application in specific instances... It is much more appropriate to base one's decisions on the *Talmud*. For even though he may then miss the wrong true path, failing to clarify the law properly... [this is not so bad] because a scholar can only follow the dictates of his own intelligence in interpreting the *Talmud*. If he is misled by his understanding and scholarship, he is nevertheless more beloved by G-d... than one who bases his conclusions on another's work without understanding the background." (*Netivos Olam, Nesiv HaTorah* 15, based on *Sotah* 22a)

You often hear people say, "don't come to the final *halacha* just from your *Talmud* study. That you have to study *halacha* to actually know what to do." While this may be true, its coming often from the mouths of those very same people who completed just a few *mesechtos* of *Talmud*, never having completed it in its entirety, who think they are experts in *halacha*. Who are they to give any advice at all about the *Torah* when they studied with shortcuts themselves? How many *rabbis* today are *paskening shilos* when they have never completed the basic mandatory works? It is true, from the *Talmud* we learn the source and reasoning behind the *halachos*; Then we have to study closely the *sefarim* that helped establish the final *halachos* and conclude with the latest *meforshim* on what is the *halachah lemisa* today. However, we can't come to the absolute *emes* of *halacha* without an understanding of its source. Learning a few *mesechtos* of *Mishniyos* and *Talmud* in a span of a dozen years, doesn't give you this.

Early *Achronim* (most Notably R' Chaim Soloveitchik, *Av Beis Din* Brisk) felt that nowadays, due to *yeridas hadoros* we need that of *iyun*. Bear in mind that R' Chaim also said that one cannot have any opinion in any *sugya* in learning until they have gone through all of *Shas*.

Apparently though, every Jew loves to have his opinion on any topic. He will fight you with *pilpul* in learning even having no authentic basis for anything he says. This is his way because he has spent a lifetime learning *Torah*, and nobody has every encouraged him to study the basics.

The Maharsha writes similarly: "People (other authorities) say that reading decisions without the necessary *Talmudic* background is like eating fish without spices; I, however, say that it is like eating spices without fish." (Maharsha, *Sotah* 22a, s.v. *yerei*)

The commentary of Rashi is foremost in the study of the *Talmud*. A remarkable job has been done by the latest *Talmud* publishers to include the summary of Rashi's explanation inside their translation of *Aramaic* to English or Hebrew. The main thing is to come to the *p'shat* of the *Talmud*, to understand and appreciate the basic meaning of the text and Rashi does exactly this.

A *daf* of *Babylonian Talmud*, includes the commentary of Rashi (Rabbi Shlomo ben Yitzchak), an eleventh-century rabbi and the pre-eminent *Talmudic* commentator, and of his grandchildren, collectively known as the Ba'alei Tosefos, or colloquially, Tosefos ("Additions"). While Rashi is primarily interested in explaining the text at hand, the Tosefos attempt to reconcile disparate sections of *Talmud*. In the course of their discussions, they often expand on and/or challenge Rashi's explanations. Later commentators, in turn, expand on and challenge the Tosefos.

The Goan of Vilna recommended that students pay close attention to the words of Rashi. (HaGra, Intro. To commentary on *SA Orach Chayim*.)

The Chasam Sofer advised his son to learn much *Talmud* with the commentary of Rashi. (Cited by R. Avraham Sofer in his Intro to Meiri's commentary on *Kesubos*)

The Chasam Sofer instructed his son, the author of *Kesav Sofer* to, "Learn much *Talmud* with Rashi, and wherever Rashi cites a second version, skip it." (Rabbi Avraham Sofer, Meiri on *Kesubos*, preface)

Rabbi Simcha Wasserman said, "Rashi is not *batul* to the *daf* (peripheral to the pages of the *Talmud*). Rashi was a *Rishon* and we must appreciate that every word he uses opens up the *sugya*. I once struggled for hours on a difficult *Gemarah* until I noticed a single word in Rashi that I had overlooked. That word provided me with the meaning of the entire passage!"

Rabbi Yehoshua Cohen recommends, "This is the way to study Rashi and Tosafos. You should make an effort to understand the reasons behind their overall approach and the specific differences between them. It is no disgrace if you do not understand them after trying. "The *Torah* is as difficult to acquire as the finest gold jewelry," (*Chaggigah* 15a) and, "no one understands the words of *Torah* unless he has first failed in them." (*Gittin* 43a, also see *Chaggigah* 14a, *Shabbos* 119b) (*Keren Yehoshua* p. 43)

He continues on his recommendation of Tosafos, "After learning one Tosafos, go over the flow of its arguments in your own words before proceeding to the next. When the Tosafos presents two different approaches, try to understand what the problem in the first approach that forced Tosafos to look for another [explanation]. Think about how and why the second approach disagrees with the first. Does the second one differ with the reasoning or legal conclusion of the first one, or does Tosafos simply feel that the wording of the *Gemarah* does not fit well with the first approach?" (*Kerem Yehoshua* p. 43)

However, most *rabbis* recommend that a person go through the *Talmud* first using the commentary of Rashi alone and only when repeating the *Talmud*, then to add Tosafos the following time. The Maharal has a lot to say on this subject.

The Maharal warns, "'Woe to us; in our day we are ensnared in this trap — we learn *halacha* in order to forget it...' If even one in a thousand [would show concern], we would find consolation in these few, but in that even one in a thousand cannot be found — on this I weep, my eyes overflow with tears on this breakdown of the honor and grandeur of *Torah*; I am despondent, I am dumbfounded.

"To my mind the situation verges on the one described by our sages of one who actively purges *Torah* from his consciousness. Even if the problem is not so drastic, still — the *Torah* requires safeguarding, as we have noted; we stand, *chas-v-shalom*, at the threshold of this punishment, for today's generation has deviated from the path of its predecessors; they do not walk in their footsteps. The essence of *Torah* was in their forebears' mouths and on their tongues, but today this circumstance is totally non-existent, and the effect on the generation is devastating in every respect. As the verse says, 'The thing is very near to you; in your mouth and in your heart, to do it,' (*Devarim* 30:14) and as we explained earlier.

"Let the reader not think that the absence of the *Torah* from the mouths of this generation, and the fact that the *Torah* is not near to them, is alone the full extent of its degeneration. [Though it is sufficient reason] to lament the depth of our downfall, as our sages additionally say, 'He who learns *Torah* and forgets it is comparable to a woman who buries her children.' (*Sanhedrin* 99a)

"The reason today's generation forgets their *Torah*, transgressing their obligation to retain it, is not due to the immense value of *Torah* they amass. Not at all! Whether a lot or little, they set out to learn *Torah* in such a way as not a shred of *Torah* can remain with them. This is a situation that perforce makes a man mourn. The honor of *Torah*, its grandeur and glory are exiled from us; we stand unclothed, without *Torah*. Woe to the scandal, the shame and the disgrace of our deviation from the ways of every previous generation!

"And all this for the sake of gaining repute as one who sharpens his [mind] with *pilpul*. Even if this goal is accomplished [it is misdirected effort, for] our sages stated in chapter *HaRo'eh* (*Brachos* 63b), 'Attend and hear, be silent and afterwards analyze.' Rashi of blessed memory explains, 'Quietly attend to the subject matter under review until it is familiar to you, then analyze it; ask the questions that occur to you and seek answers until you are satisfied.' [The *Gemarah* continues, 'This is] as stated by Rava, for Rava said, A man should always first learn *Torah* and then scrutinize it.' It is thus an established fact that even if one expounds a valid pilpul it must be preceded by a comprehensive understanding of the text. How much more so then [does the injunction of this *Gemarah* apply] when, rather than sharpening [their wits], they prattle utter foolishness?

"Indeed, we have the evidence of our own eyes to testify to this 'sharpening' and its effect on its practitioners. If young men were able to retain the study of their youth, there is no doubt that they would be familiar with and have mastered many, many tractates prior to their march under the *chupah* for marriage. As matters stand, they are left with nothing – entirely as a result of their study of extra-curricular matter, which is supplemental to the text. Would it not have been better to have beforehand mastered the substance of the *Talmud* itself? This [pitfall] is entirely a consequence of the publication of the Tosafos commentary alongside the

*Gemarah*; if the *Piskei HaRosh* or the novellas of later commentators, may they repose in honor, where there, everyone, even young men and children, would study with an eye to the process of *halacha*. Of what use are these things to the young? They cause the young student to remain unclear regarding the process of *halacha*. It is to be expected that adults and children should study in the same manner? Notwithstanding, telling a youngster's father to content himself with teaching his son the approach of *halacha* and to postpone the study of Tosafos is tantamount to telling him not to teach at all; the father is concerned solely with reputation." (*Nesivos Olam, Nesiv HaTorah*, p.129-131)

Rabbi Yechezkel Himmelstein told me in the name of Rabbi Berger, "Many of the great commentaries of the *Gemarah* were lost and Tosafos was saved and preserved by being inserted on the *daf* itself." Rabbi Yechezkel Himmelstein continued, "Tosafos is one of the most difficult *Rishonim,* therefore we need to have an appreciation of the great level that the *Rishonim* where on. We learn it in order to inspire ourselves to be on such a great level. As well, there are Tosofim that deal specifically with just *p'shat*, which covers points not discussed by Rashi and the *p'shat* that you might have missed had you not had the Tosafos. Not everyone learning the *Gemarah* is a genius and many people still need the Tosafos to still clarify the *Gemarah*. But you should learn the *Gemarah* and the *Mishnah* very well before going to Tosafos. Tosafos also addresses *halacha lemisa* issues, and we follow many of them. But we need to understand the Maharal, that we shouldn't jump the gun and really try to understand the basic concepts of the *Gemarah*, the clear *p'shat* with Rashi before going on to more intricate and sophisticated *Torah* ideas on the *Gemarah* that *Rishonim* and *Achronim* will discuss."

Both the Chofetz Chaim and Rav Shapiro would encourage people to learn *daf yomi* according to the *Midrash* that states that in the ultimate future, Hashem will reveal the deep secrets of the *sugyos* of *Shas* but one who has never even learned through a *mesechta* will not merit to enter the *shiur*. Even one who read through the *Gemarah* but did not understand it will be allowed entry into the *shiur*.

Rebbe Nachman of Breslov says something similar, that by finishing important works, it allows you to enter those *sefarim's* academy in *Ohlom Habah* and to study that work with the finest of *tzaddikim*.

Which do you prefer, to have a limited number of keys cards to enter rooms in *Shamayim* or to have access to study within hundreds of the *batei midrashim* on high? It's time to get working while there is still time in our life and don't procrastinate! There is work to be done, and only you can decide to do it! How much time do you waist each day with *bittle Torah*? How much time do you waist by learning the wrong material that is too high for you or not what your *neshamah* needs at this time? Is this coming from pride or arrogance?

Rav Ben Tzion Abbah Shaul, pointed out that the word *Gemarah* has the same root as the Aramaic word *"gumrah"* which means coals, to teach that the back and forth of *Gemarah* burns out all evil like burning coals.

The Gra would also say that one who learns *Gemarah* has an easier time changing the flaws within himself since he sees how little he knows. How often he is mistaken or that there is a side that he would not have thought of.

Also important is to be humble in your knowledge of *Torah*. Don't advertise your accomplishments unless you are doing so in order to encourage others. A *tzaddik* once said humbly, "In my house there is no bread and no garment; that is, I have in my hand neither knowledge of Scripture nor of *Mishnah* nor of *Talmud*." (*Shabbos* 120a)

Rav Yehudah said in the name of Rav: During the first three hours of each day, the Holy One, blessed is He, sits and involves Himself with *Torah* study. (*Avodah Zara* 3b) The *Gemarah* goes on to mention the other things Hashem is involved in throughout the day. However, *Torah* study even for Hashem comes first.

The *Gemarah* continues, during the second three hours, - He sits and judges the entire world... During the third three-hour period of every day, - He sits and provides nourishment for the entire world... During the fourth three-hour period of every day, - He sits and amuses Himself with the Leviathan.

Certainly, the world cannot exist without Hashem maintaining it in numerous ways, yet even for Hashem, *Torah* study comes first. In the same way, one must put their core learning first in the day.

The Skolye Rebbe would go to bed at two A.M. and would awake some three hours later. He never went to retire without meeting his minimum study requirements. They said of the Rebbe that he was as fluent in any topic of *Shas* as if he had learned it today.

After Reb Shlomke of Zvehil finished reciting *Tikkun Chatzos*, he would learn his nightly quota of eight *blat* of *Gemarah*.

Rav Chaim Kanievsky once advised a *rosh hayeshivah* that he should first study seven *blats* of *Talmud* at the beginning of the new day (at night) and then he could study whatever subjects he wanted thereafter. Reb Chaim explained, that this is what he does every day.

Following suit, I always try to immediately begin my *Talmud* study at *shkiya* and complete as many *blats* as I can in order to complete my committed daily learning as soon as possible. Without this practice, it would be too overwhelming to cover so much material each day. You therefore have to grab it right away, allowing nothing to interfere. I try to position any meetings or appointments in such a way as not to interfere with this. I can tell you that I feel relieved once I have completed the first *blat* or two, of my daily schedule, right away. It feels as if I have set a foundation for the rest of the day. So, always put your *Torah* study first and it will change your life. Everything you do thereafter, after you have already accomplished some learning first, just seems to work out better as if it has special blessing. Often, I say to others, "I will talk to you soon, let me finish my first *blat* of *Talmud* for the day first." Really this attitude is life changing, yet it is very simple, "*Torah* comes first!"

HaRav Matisyahu Solomon told a story of a *bachur* he met. "After the war, some young *bachurim* were brought to Gateshead Yeshivah to be rehabilitated. One boy, just sixteen years of age, was tested by the *rosh hayeshivah* for two hundred *blat, Gemarah bal peh*, that he had learned from his father in the concentration camp. His father was a *maggid shiur daf yomi*, from Lutsk, Poland, and as long as they were together in the camps, he taught him every moment he could, the *Torah* by heart."

Rabbi Yaakov Yosef of Polnoye, a principal disciple of the Baal Shem Tov, would study seven pages of *Talmud* before eating. Even during his meal, between dishes, he did not stop reciting his studies. (My Book, *Pathways of the Righteous* p. 48)

Today, when you have portable audio players and when you have amazing *maggid shiurs* in *Talmud* that do one *blat* in fifteen minutes (or up to two hours), it is amazing how much easier it is to study *Torah*. You can even mimic the ways of study as if you are a true *masmid*. I know someone that has finished *Shas* a half-dozen times just from reviewing the *Talmud* on audio. As I have said before, once you get used to thinking faster, even fifteen minutes to review a *blat*, becomes fairly easy. Wherever you go, when traveling or sitting down at a *simcha*, there is no reason you shouldn't be learning most of the time. Don't care what others think of you, the *Torah* is yours for the taking. I once asked the Biala Rebbe of New York, "Should I wear my *tefillin* in public while studying in the *bais midrash*?" He confirmed that I should. Don't use the excuse of humility to not open a *Gemarah* at a *simcha* or to wear your *tefillin*. Sit more in the corner if needed, but you don't have time to waste your life away, to just sit in place stagnant for hours at social gatherings. Even your socializing must have limitations placed upon it, in order to not take away time from *Torah*. I don't understand it, some people study all day long in *kollel*, yet when they travel to and from *kollel* they don't study. I can understand this from a regular person who hasn't devoted their life to *Torah* yet, but a future scholar. Someone who is supposed to be all day learning *Torah*…

If you see *rosh hayeshivos* without a *sefer*, it is because they have already memorized so much *Torah* study and *kavanos*, that in all likelihood, they are preparing a *d'var Torah* in their mind and meditating on what they learned that day. But for us, who are we to go anywhere without a *sefer* in hand or a *Torah shiur* ready do listen too?

"It is told that the Kotzker Rebbe, in his younger days, was so assiduous in continual *Torah* study that he learned while standing up the entire day, holding in his hands a large, heavy copy of the Amsterdam edition of the *Talmud*, with its wooden covers and heavy clasps of burnished brass." (My Book, *Pathways of the Righteous* p. 62)

"It is told of Rabbi Zusha of Hanipoli: It was his holy way, that after praying the evening service, he would study *Torah* all night, while standing. Not only this, but he also slept only two hours." (ibid.)

"According to the Chidushei Harim, when Reb Dovid of Lelov was only twenty-five years old; he had already learned the entire *Talmud* twenty-four times. Yet his close friend and *mechutan*, the Yehudi Hakodesh, knew nothing about his brilliance. One day when he found out of Reb Dovid's brilliance in *Torah*, he jumped onto the table and started dancing for joy." (My Book, *A Journey into Holiness*, p. 69)

"In Grudno, it was not uncommon for a *bachur* to finish all of *Bavli* and *Yerushalmi Talmud* by age sixteen, maybe even three times by the age of eighteen. Every five months Rabbi Zelig Reuven Bengis, Rav in Yerushalayim, would make another *siyum* after completing *Shas*." (Excerpt from my book, *Kavanos Halev, Torah* study)

The sages of the *Talmud* remarked, "It says in *Yeshiyahu* 3:5, כל משען לחם, every support of bread." The *Talmud* explains, "This refers to *Torah* scholars who support the world with *Torah* like ones eating of bread." (*Chagigah* 14a)

Reb Moshe Feinstein was one such scholar. His son told over that he never saw his father learn less than thirteen hours a day.

When I was a *bachur*, I struggled at first to study the entire day. It felt as if my mind was going to burst. I learned over time that if you build it up slowly, every person is capable of learning all day. Your study habits do not need to emulate someone else. You have to search out your own path for what works for you best. Your goal should be to be the best person that you can be, not the best your friend can be. Don't compare yourself to others. Be you because Hashem loves His creation, that is why he made you. Hashem didn't create any person completely identical to another. We each have our own struggles. That is because He wants us to all be different.

The Chofetz Chayim told, "The *manna* which the Jews ate throughout their forty-year sojourn in the wilderness had the taste of whatever food the person was thinking of at the time. However, what if they weren't thinking anything at all? The Chofetz Chayim answered by coining an adage: '*Az men tracht nisht, hot es kein ta'am nisht.* If you don't think, it has no taste.'" He clarified that the *manna* was a spiritual food which fell from Heaven. "A person who performs spiritual deeds without thought derives little pleasure from his deeds."

The Chofetz Chayim continued, "What can be tastier than a piece of *Gemarah?*" He then kissed the tips of his fingers, saying, "It is so sweet, but only if you think. If you don't think, you sit by the *Gemarah* and it has no flavor at all."

Rabbi Boruch had a son enrolled in a *yeshivah*. Upon turning eighteen, the son purchased for himself a small *Shas* costing thirty dollars. This was a lot of money back then. Rabbi Boruch's wife became so emotional when she saw the *Shas* and insisted on having a share in it. She presented her son ten dollars, but given their financial situation, she cautioned him not to reveal her deed to father, lest he become upset at the both of them.

When Rabbi Baruch returned home that evening, he noticed the *Shas* sitting on a shelf in his bookcase. He wept tears of joy for having finally merited to have a *Shas* in his home. With a happy heart, he insisted on paying for it in its entirety.

Some years later, this episode repeated itself. Rabbi Boruch's son came home with a large *Vilna Shas* which he had obtained for one-hundred dollars. His mother gave him twenty-five dollars and directed him not to say anything to his father. Then, Rabbi Baruch returned home, wept tears of joy for having merited to have a large-size *Shas* in his house and insisted on paying the full one-hundred dollars.

The Imrei Emes of Ger, once remarked in jest, "Every person needs a trade. I am a librarian!" He once said, I do not place a *sefer* into my bookcase without first studying it and gaining knowledge of its contents." Have in mind that he had one of the largest personal libraries of *sefarim* in the entire region! Rabbi Yisrael Alter remarked about his father the Imrei Emes, "My father loved *sefarim*, but the *sefer* he loved the most was his

*Gemarah*!"

One *chassid* came to the Imrei Emes complaining. He said that with the stress of earning a living, he lacked the concentration necessary for *Gemarah* study. "Open your *Gemarah* and sit there," came the Rebbe's reply. "Something is bound to come from it."

# Talmud For Halacha

According to R. Sheneor Zalman of Liadi, the purpose of *Mishnaic* study is to learn concluding decisions. Nevertheless, as he explains in his *Shulchan Aruch*, "one-third [of one's time should be devoted] to *Talmud*, which presents the reasons for the *halachos* in the *Mishnayos*, *Beraisos* and pronouncements of the *Amoraim*. In our day, this includes the works of the early *poskim*, which outline the reasons for the final outcomes... For if one does not know the reasons for the *halachos*, he cannot understand the *halachos* themselves." (Chapter 3, section 1. See also chap.7, section 4 and in part 2, chap. 4, section 2) Thus even the *Talmud* is learned to clarify the *halachos*.

Even though it is my way to push the learning of *bekiyus* in *Talmud*, when learning *halacha,* I am extra careful to be sure I have a clear understanding of the *halacha*, so as not to drill into my mind the wrong method of action.

The Goan of Vilna says: "Better to learn a little, review it constantly, and know it clearly, than to amass much [information] without knowing the law." (*Magen Avraham* on *SA Aruch Chayim* 290) Furthermore, "This is what it means to toil in the *Torah*: to extract the clear *halacha*." (*Hagera* on *Proverbs* 13:25, *Even Shelemah* 8:7, ibid. 8:11) His disciple, Rabbi Chaim of Volozhin, identifies this extraction "the entire fruit of study," implying that learning without reaching a conclusion is like working the soil and planting trees without reaping the fruits. (Intro. To the Goan of Vilna's commentary on SA)

On this same idea, Rabbi Samson Raphael Hirsch writes: "Guide him toward the sources of *Torah* wisdom — *Mishnah* and *Talmud*. But his ultimate goal should always be life and the knowledge of the obligations and life of Israel. Only then will his *Torah* life become strong and shining." (R.S.R. Hirsch, *Horeb* 551)

In other words, the learning of *Torah* is in order to come to action and to apply what you study. Therefore, *halacha* study should be daily and study should be done with the purpose of further serving our Creator according to the proper path.

In the introduction to *Mikeves HaMishneh*, the author describes

184

three kinds of students: The first studies only to gain knowledge of the text, without any analysis, while the second concentrates only on analysis, finding imaginary differences and neglecting the truth. Such studies "do not know the ins and outs of the *Talmud* or the scholars... as they lack a historical perspective." He reserves his praise for the third type of student, who "deals with the subject matter to arrive at the *halacha*... Cling to this [method] and do not be diverted from it."

Rabbi Yisrael Salanter says: "The highest level of *Torah* study is the ability to render true, proper decisions in Israel, based on the *Talmud* and the *poskim*, without having to search through the decisions of the later *Acharonim*." (*Ma-amar Be'Inyan Chizuk Lomdey Torah* 20. Reprinted in *Or Yisrael HaShalem*, p. 148)

In fact, the "Chofetz Chaim" authored books specifically to help people draw conclusions from their *Talmud* studies, "to know the essence of the *halacha* that derives from the discussion – which is the goal of *Torah* study." (Intros to *Likutey Halachos* and *Mishnah Berurah*)

As you know, the Rambam did likewise. The *Mishneh Torah*, was compiled in the 11th century. The sixteenth-century Sephardic Rabbi Yosef Caro developed a handbook of *halacha*, the *Shulchan Aruch*. Supplemented by the comments of Rabbi Moses Isserles, the leading Polish *rabbi* of the time, the *Shulchan Aruch* became the worldwide standard of *halacha*, authoritative (even if not the final authority) even now in the eyes of observant Jews everywhere.

These *rabbis* thought it was too much for the scholar to go through dozens of *sefarim* in order to find the final *halacha*. There needed to be simple works that the average person could follow. As it says, "there shall be one *Torah* and one law for you." (*Bamidbar* 15:16)

The word *'halacha'* literally means 'going.' It is the way in which the Jewish people should go, as it is written, "You shall teach them the way in which they shall go." (*Shemos* 18:20) (*Aruch, Halach*)

Rabbi Avraham Bornstein of Sochaczov writes, "It has come to my attention that nowadays young students are preoccupied with *sevara* and not with the simple explanation and clarification of the issues – which are also essential in *halacha*." (*Egley Tal*, Intro.)

Similarly, the Chozon Ish counsels: "One must be cautious not to spend too much time expanding on *sevara*; rather, spend this time on the *Talmud*, investigating the simple explanation and clarifying its conclusions." (*Igros Chazon Ish* I 2.)

The *Shiyarey Keneses HaGedolah* concludes that, "a scholar who resolves *halachic* questions is called to the *Torah* before one who learns dialectically but does not decide such questions." (*Shiyarey Keneseth Gedolah* on *SA Aruch Chayim* 135, note 9) This view is shared by *Eliyahu Rabbah* and *Peri Megadim*, the later explicitly basing his conclusion on the Talmudic decision that the master of *Sinai* is preferred. (*Eliyahu Rabbah* 136; *Peri Megadim, Aruch Chayim, Eshel Avraham* 136, end)

Concerning *halachic* decision-making, broad knowledge is clearly essential. The Ish Chay emphasizes the importance of familiarity with the writings of even the very latest *Acharonim*. (Intro to *Rav Pe'alim*)

A considerable number of *Acharonim* protested the learning of the final *halacha*, such as *Mishnah Torah* or *Shulchan Aruch*, without first learning the relevant Talmudic passages. (see *Responsa Rosh* 31:9; *Responsa Rivash*, 44 end; *Kesef Mishneh* on *M'adaney Yom Tov, Berachos*, Intro. S.v. *ume-az*; Maharsha on *Sota* 22a; *Ma'adney Yom Tov* loc. Cit. s.v. *we-omer ani*, also quoted by *Peri Megadim*, "*Kelalim behoras...*," end; *Sema', Choshen Mishpat*, intro; *Mishkenoth HaRo'im*, "Cheth," 59)

"*Halacha* does not represent mere legal decisions, but the Will of Hashem. Therefore, through the study of *halacha*, one can gain a unique closeness to Hashem." (*Likutei Amarim, Iggeros Hakodesh* 26)

"Through *halacha* study, all things become part of Hashem's ultimate purpose." (*Darkei Hora'ah, Hakdamah*)

"He who studies *halacha* every day, is guaranteed a portion in the World to Come." (*Megillah* 28b)

Therefore, let us not allow a day to pass without learning *halachos*. The *Gemarah* in *Brachos* (8a) states that, "since the day the *Bais HaMikdash* was destroyed, Hashem has nothing in this world but the four *amos* of *halacha*." Thus, the Divine Presence only rests in the domain of *halacha*, and any deviance from the *halacha* and the tradition causes a breach in that sanctity.

"Indeed, there is no one on earth who is righteous, no one who does what is right and never sins." (*Koheles* 7:20) Without the *Torah's* constant study and review, it would be impossible for us not to sin. I am surprised how many religious Jews don't know basic *halachos*, yet they take upon themselves loads of *hanhagos*. Maybe they are hiding behind all these *hanhagos*, thinking themselves to be righteous, yet they fail at the basic laws. Have they simply never learned them or chosen only to be stringent only on the *halachos* they desire? I honestly think they don't know better.

Many people complete major *halachic* works like the *Mishnah Berurah*, receive *smicha* from their *yeshivah* and never review the material. When I completed learning *soferous* from my *rebbe*, Rabbi Shmuel Rosenberg, I asked him for a *tudah*, *smicha* in *soferous*. You know what he told me? He said, "So many people have *tudahs*, but they don't review the *halachos* of *soferous*. I'm teaching you to constantly review the *halachos*. To know the questions that a person should ask. The *tudahs* don't have expiration dates so what are they worth if someone doesn't make an effort to constantly review the *halachos*."

You have to understand how much time and effort went into these *halachic* works. The Shach, Rabbi Shabsi Kohen writes about this, "With truth and wholesomeness, I expended effort upon effort and toil upon toil. I did not become occupied with any other matter nor did I not grant sleep to my eyes or slumber to my eyelids. I did this for many years until I had made my goal a reality. I sifted and weighed [every point] upon a scale, reviewing every angle and every point of every angle. Not only once or twice, but one-hundred and one times. I did this for the distinguished and beloved colleagues, who gave their attention to my words.

"Anyone who was not with me would not believe it, my exhaustive efforts to search through the sea of *Talmud* and the codes until I had clarified everything." (From the preface to his commentary on *Shulchan Aruch*)

Rabbi Yaakov Abuchatzeira taught, "Through clarifying the *halacha* truthfully, our Almighty's *Shechinah* is beautified and renewed like a fresh rose with all of the thorns and thistles surrounding it destroyed. Every person who delves into the study of *halacha* and invests additional time toiling over it in order to understand its true interpretation has boundless reward, for he breaks the power of the *klipos* [the forces of impurity] and beautifies the *Shechinah*. (*Alef Binah* 20, 36, 66)

Rabbi Yaakov Abuchatzeira taught, "A person must toil in order to know the laws of the *Torah* clearly, for this brings about an elevation of the *Shechinah*. As the *Zohar Hakodesh* writes in the name of the "loyal shepherd" [Moshe Rabbeinu]: Every *halacha* which is in doubt and is not clarified properly makes the wings of the *Shechinah* heavy so that she does not have the strength to rise and ascend on high. But when the *halacha* is clarified truthfully and properly, then the *Shechinah* does have the strength to rise and ascend on high." (*Alef Binah* 12)

The Maharal explains, "The school of Eliyahu taught, all who review *halachos* are assured of the world-to-come, as is stated (*Chabakuk* 3:6), '*halichos olam lo*.' Read this not '*halichos olam*'... but rather '*hilchos olam*'"...

"The *Gemarah* conveys the exalted character of the *Torah* and, particularly, the advantage obtained by one who reviews *halachos*. The notion that the primary objective of a man's learning is to gain wisdom in the nature of reality, or of heavenly bodies, or of the angels – and that the *Torah* that pertains to civil damages, or to questions of pure or impure, is not on the same level – is a gravely dangerous misconception. We elaborated on this in our discussion of '...the laws of bird-offerings and those regarding the beginnings of menstrual periods [are the essential laws],' (*Maharal, Derech Chaim* on *Avos* 3:23) where we also cited this *Gemarah*.

"The *Gemarah's* lesson is that fundamental success in learning is dependent on the study of *halacha*, that, to elaborate, *halacha* is the *Torah's* unswerving truth, veering neither to the left nor to the right. This is the actual meaning of the word *halacha* as our scholars use it when they say, 'The *halacha* is so and so': The just course of action that does not deviate to the right or to the left is as follows: The study of *halacha* ushers one into life in the world-to-come, for the path to the world-to-come is the path that does not bend rightwards or leftwards.

"As we have explained previously in the context of 'the crossroads is a reference to a scholar's culminating his study of a topic of law with a definitive knowledge of the law's application,' to pass a crossroads is to disengage from paths that diverge from the straight and true and to walk the rightful path. Thus, all who review *halachos* are assured of the world-to-come, as is stated, '*halichos olam lo*' – the direction and path to the world-to-come are provided them by the *halachos* of the *Torah*."

"And thus, 'The laws of bird-offerings and those regarding the beginnings of menstrual periods [are the essential laws],' as we have said elsewhere (in *Derech Chaim*), and not other aspects of wisdom.

"May He, Who is blessed, grant that our lot be with those who review *halachos*, and with those who study for the sake of explaining other things may we not be associated." (*Nesivos Olam, Nesiv HaTorah*, p.57)

The Maharsham always tried to rule according to the lenient opinion if possible. In the introduction to his *sefer, Da'as Torah* he explains: "I have tried to always rule according to the lenient opinion. This is because the *Torah* is careful not to waste the money of *Yidden*. I have another motive for this, which I received from the giants of *Torah*, but I am unable to reveal it due to the those who might misuse it."

The Maggid of Kolomai, Rav Yitzchok once shared that he was present when a certain *rav* told the Maharsham that his *sefarim* were very popular because he was lenient in *halachos*. That he was clever enough to even "purify an insect with a hundred and fifty different reasons." The Maharsham whispered in the *rav's* ear, "It is true that I am very lenient, but one day, when I will be laid to rest, the insects will leave me in peace. Woe is to those *rabbanim* who will have to answer to all those poor people that were caused so much suffering through needless *chumros*."

Despite the opposition to his lenient rulings, the Maharsham was acclaimed as possessing faithful and true *da'as Torah* on whom one could rely in any situation. It is unbelievable how many *chumros* haunt the orthodox community. So much so that people don't know the difference between an *halacha* or a *chumrah* and will actually embarrass or make an effort to correct innocent people who are following the basic *halachos* just fine. This provides added stress to the entire community of *Yidden*, when *chumros* become the norm while basic *halachos* are forgotten. Not just this but people have the audacity to judge another *Yid* for not following their *chumrah*. What a mess that things have become, that *chumros* are followed more than basic *halachos*.

Reb Shlomo Mordechai, the Maharsham moved back to Zlotchov, where he opened a wine store. Although generally his wife managed the shop, the Maharsham would spend a few hours a day in the store serving customers. Years after he told one of his sons that during the three years that he owned the store, he managed to complete the whole of *Shulchan Aruch* with all the commentaries four times in those hours he spent working in the shop.

The Maharsham asked Rav Meir Shapiro to bring him a *Tur* to show him where the *Darkei Moshe* was written that he overheard them discussing. When the Maharsham noticed signs of amazement on Reb Meir's face, that even during his weak condition he was able to recall the exact page of the answer to his *shila*, the Maharsham asked, "Why are you so amazed?"

He then turned to the end of the volume and showed Reb Meir Shapiro what he had written, "With the help of Hashem... I have completed *Tur* and *Shulchan Aruch* one-hundred and one times."

As far as the Maharsham's *Gemarah* accomplishments, well, his program was intense. He learned sixteen hours a day. The material he covered included four *blats* of *Gemarah,* in depth, and sixteen *blats* in *bekiyus.*

The Chofetz Chaim once said about him, "There is only one person who is familiar with absolutely every aspect of *Shas*, and that is Rav Schwadron. Only he is capable of answering such a complex question on the spot."

When the Pshevorsker Rebbe was asked how many times he completed *Shulchon Aruch, Yoreh Deah,* he humbly responded when pressed, "Forty times for sure and after that, I stopped keeping count."

In our day and age, a scholar will finish these fundamental works just once or twice and think themselves to be a great *talmud chacham*. Bragging to our *chaverim* of our learning accomplishments and *smicha* declarations, yet we haven't even touched the surface. All I can say is, review, review and review some more. There is nothing wrong with having some self-confidence but to be a great *posek*, you have to have humility and be ready to look-up, ask those greater and never stop reviewing the fundamental materials.

# *Types of Seder*

Every day one should learn *Talmud* both in the style of *bekiyus* (learning quickly on a more superficial level to cover ground) and *beiyun* (slower, more in-depth study). For someone who is already a *talmud chacham*, *daf yomi* may not fit into either of these methods. That is because it's not particularly slow and in depth as a true *beiyun seder* and it's not particularly fast for someone who truly is comfortable learning *bekiyus*. However, every person is different in their speed of comprehension and prior *Torah* knowledge, so you really can't make a blank statement like this. *Daf yomi* could be *bekiyus* for one person while *beiyun* for another. It also depends on how good the *maggid shiur* is or how fast your mind comprehends material based on prior wisdom and understanding. It could also be that the *maggid shiur* is able to cover more in the same allotted time, even making the *shiur* very in depth.

That is what is so wonderful about the *daf yomi,* you have so many *shiurim* now available to you on replay or live, that you just have to choose which one fits your style of learning. However, let's just assume for a moment that everyone here is the same in their level of comprehension. That would make *daf yomi* fall right in the middle of *beiyun* and *bekiyus* and not necessarily swing one way or the other. *Daf yomi* was truly meant for the regular person who wasn't in the *bais midrash* all day and didn't have time to study in depth or very quickly but rather to fulfil his daily requirement of *Talmud* study. In other words, Rabbi Shapiro saved the *Talmud* and gave it to everyone. It is so wonderful that working people and normal students can now imagine themselves completing the entire *Shas* in their lifetime.

The Bluzhever Rebbe writes, "I had the privilege of attending the first *Knessia Gedolah* in [1923] of Agudath Israel when the world-renowned *goan*, the Lubliner Rav, Rabbi Meir Shapiro, presented his plan for the study of *daf yomi*... The tumultuous excitement with which the *geonim* and *tzaddikim* of that time reacted to his wonderous proposal still rings in my ears... It was an awesome sight."

The *Knessia Gedolah* was beyond excitement as they accepted the new plan of learning. On *Rosh HaShananah* of that year, the study of *daf yomi* commenced. Two weeks after, Rabbi Shapiro received a letter from his sister. She was completely unaware of his grand plan for all of *Klal Yisrael*, after the first *daf yomi* cycle began. In the letter his sister wrote, "On the night of *Rosh Hashanah*, I had a dream: I saw you in Heaven, dear brother, surrounded by a great mass of angels with striking figures, all radiant as the light of the firmament; and you, my brother, were standing in their midst, your face alight like the sun in its full strength; and they were all smiling to you, as they thanked you and rejoiced with you very, very greatly...Please dearest brother: let me know what the dream means..."

Kever of Rav Meir Shapiro in Har Hamenuchos

As we know, the *mitzvos* that we do in this world elevate the souls of our relatives up above and those who inspired the original *mitzvah* observance. Can you imagine Rabbi Shapiro's reward in the next world, having inspired hundreds of thousands?

In Rabbi Shapiro's great *yeshivah*, Chachmei Lublin, it was not uncommon for *yeshiva bachurim* to have already finished *Shas* two or three times before they were nineteen years of age. They didn't do this through the *rosh hayeshivos* method of *daf yomi* however, or it would have taken seven years to have completed it. Seven years is plenty of time for the average learner but for someone who wishes to become a leader in our generation, they have to know all of *Shas*, yesterday. To do this, you need study devotedly in both methods, *beiyun* and *bekiyus*, in both extremes. In other words, *daf yomi* isn't the best way to finish *Shas* for a scholar, even though its ingenious. However, in Chachmei Lublin, most everyone still made time for the daily *daf yomi* because of the discipline it instilled and the unity it provides, which would later change the world.

Orchos Tzaddikim writes: "In France, they labored hard and long, sitting in one place learning the entire *Talmud* and going over it time after time. The words of *Torah* were constantly on their lips, and they emulated the *Rishonim*. One should learn even if the material he learns is not clear to him, for we say that a person should first learn and then theorize. But all this is not what we do today." (*Orchos Tzaddikim, Sha'ar HaTorah*)

That is what is so special about *daf yomi*, no matter what, a person completes the daily *daf* at their current level. If they don't understand something, they accept that they did their best and move on further covering ground and slowly building up their wisdom. Then in the future, as their mind expands and matures, the passages on the next repetition of *Talmud* will by themselves become clear.

The *Talmud* in *Horayos* 14a, records a disagreement between Rabban Shimon ben Gamliel and the *rabbis*. One party says a "*Sinai*" is preferable. This refers to a scholar whose greatness lies in his broad knowledge of *Mishnahs* and *Beraisos*. That he is preferable to a scholar who excels in powers of analysis. Rashi explains that he is called a "*Sinai*" because of his familiarity with the *Mishnayos* and *Beraisos* is so profound that their rulings are as clearly organized in his mind as on the day they were given at *Sinai*. The Meiri explains that the *Talmud* is not referring to someone who can merely recite the *Tannaic* texts by rote. Rather, he is also well versed in their explanations and the laws that emerge from them, that he also possesses the ingenuity to draw analogies between cases and to derive one law from another. Someone who lacks this, even if he can recite the texts fluently, can't really be referred to as a "*Sinai*".

The other party disagrees and says that an "uprooter of mountains" is more preferable than someone who is a "*Sinai*". His sharp powers of analysis are preferable. Rashi explains that a scholar is superior to a "*Sinai*" in powers of analysis, but his knowledge of *Mishnah's* and *Beraisos* is not as extensive. The Ramah says, he is called an "up-rooter of mountains" because even a problem that seems as insurmountable as a mountain falls away in the face of his logic.

The Ramah explains, Not knowing which *rabbi* to choose as their next leader, the rabbinical students sent this message to *Eretz Yisrael* asking, "Which one of them takes precedence?"

They replied back to him; A "*Sinai*" takes precedence because everyone needs the owner of wheat. Rashi explains, "A scholar who has amassed knowledge is likened to a merchant who has gathered grain to sell." (Rashi to *Berachos* 64a)

193

"Man cannot live without bread." (Rabbeinu Gershom to *Bava Basra* 145b) Thus, even a person of great wealth is helpless unless he can find someone from whom to buy bread. Likewise, the brilliant scholar needs encyclopedic knowledge because without broad based knowledge, his brilliance is to no avail. (Ramah, cited by *HaKoseiv* in *Ein Yaakov*)

As you see from this *Gemarah*, one could say that having a broad range of *Torah* knowledge which can only be attained through learning vast amounts of material, through *bekiyus*, this is fundamental towards becoming a *talmud chacham*. If you have never seen the material and you apply yourself only to study in the style of *beiyun*, you won't accumulate enough broad knowledge to understand the *Torah*. Your mind is small; you haven't seen enough of the vast world of *Torah* in order to infer one idea from another. While you might have more in-depth knowledge of certain subjects, your lacking in other subjects and a true scholar examines the *Torah* as a whole. When a sage has to guide someone in their life, or to answer a *halachic* question, he needs to have the entire *Torah* before him in order to clarify its meaning. Therefore, if you're going to have to choose a leader, you would certainly want the *rabbi* who is more broadminded. He therefore can decipher what the proper pathway for each person and understand the question full circle.

The Maharal teaches, "When one becomes distant from the *Torah* and the *Torah* is not with him, *mitzvah* performance is lacking, as is evident in today's generation. Similarly, when the *Torah* is not with a person, fear of Heaven is lacking, as our sages stated, 'If there is no wisdom there is no fear.' (*Avos* 3:21) The reason for this [relationship between *Torah* and fear of Heaven] is that fear can only be present when man is near to Hashem *Yisborach*; only then can fear grip him, in a manner similar to a human king, where a person is not enveloped in fear until he comes near to him. A person can only come near to Hashem *Yisborach* through the *Torah*, because on the basis of man's flesh-and-blood nature [alone], there can be no proximity. The intellective *Torah* is the only avenue of approach man has to his Creator; once he travels that avenue, he sustains fear.

"Do not let it enter your mind to believe that a person is considered a master of *Torah* when, a *Mishnah* or *Gemarah* in front of him, he is able to engage in dialectic, to debate, to query and to 'uproot mountains'[with it]. Do not say that such a person is a master of *Torah*, because the *Torah* is not with him; he is merely clever, and talented in debate – in what sense is it appropriate to say to him that he possesses *Torah*? Only when the *Torah* is with him first, and he can analyze and discuss in *Torah*, is he indeed a scholar, with respect to the *Torah* that he possesses. It is absurd to take the position that a person is worthy of being called a master of *Torah* on the basis of being able to question and retort when presented with a *halachic* opinion. In what way is such a person deserving of the title, master of *Torah*? That, he is not. He is simply canny, a gifted debater.

"Therefore, you students of *Torah* who engage in long-term study: Be strong and strengthen others for the sake of the *Torah* of our G-d; repair this breach, follow in the footsteps of our *Rishonim*; stand with them as pillars of *Torah* and receive the reward [of everyone you strengthen], as is written, 'They have nullified Your *Torah*; it is time to act [for Hashem].' (*Tehillim* 119:126) It will be as if they made the entire generation, since it is [otherwise] without *Torah*." (*Nesivos Olam, Nesiv HaTorah*, p. 133)

R. Kahana said, "By the time I was eighteen years old, I had studied the whole *Shas*, yet I did not know that a verse cannot depart from its plain meaning until to-day. What does he inform us? — That a man should study and subsequently understand." (*Shabbos* 63a)

Rabbi Yisrael Gustan would say, "The *bachur* from Grodno would strive for total perfection in *Torah*. One who does not know the entirety of *Torah* is not fit to answer the simplest question in the laws of *netillas yadayim*. In Grodno, whatever one had achieved in *Torah* was never enough. Had one finished *Bavli* and *Yerushalmi* at sixteen, *Bavli* with *Rishonim* three times by eighteen – so what. The *Torah* demanded nothing less."

That is how common it was for a *bachur* to finish *Shas*. He certainly didn't attain this from learning with shortcuts and skipping over the basics. When it came to *paskining*, Rabbi Gustan would say, "You have to first *paskin* the person before you can *paskin* the *She'eila*."

There are too many *poskim* out there that only see the situation in black and white. They might *paskin* a matter in business when they never worked in their life. With a broader knowledge of the *Talmud*, they would able to compensate for their lack of worldly understanding to better decipher the correct *halacha* for the particular situation, even though they might lack worldly inexperience. Since everything is in the *Torah*, a broad-minded scholar could still come to the truth of the situation. However, there are too many situations where the wrong *halacha* is given, due to not fully understanding the situation. It is important that *rabbanim* take the time to fully understand the question given to them and to understand the person's difficulty and lifestyle. We are not all images of black and white.

For the person that always learns *beiyun*, he is missing out on so much. He will always argue that it's more important to learn material the right way than to rush through study. You will ask him, how many important works of the Ramchal, Rambam, *halachic sefarim* he has completed, and it will be few. Many times, he will get caught up in the same page of study for many days at a time, trying to decipher its hidden meaning, while the answer is simply written on the following page, should he have simply moved forward.

If a person trains themselves to come to *p'shat* as quickly and as simply as possible, it would help them profusely. So much time is waisted in learning, going in circles, opening stacks of books instead of sticking to the current topic. Do not allow yourself to go on tangents but stay focused.

On the other side of this, the person who is studying always *bekiyus*, has rushed through so many important concepts, maybe even so fast that he might make a mistake. There is a *machlokis* between Rava and Rav Dimi from Nehardia. The *Talmud* discusses which type of teacher you should hire for your son. The teacher who rushes to the point and might make a mistake or the one who goes slowly, barely covering ground, making sure to never err on a matter. (*Bava Basra* 21a) The Ritva says on this *Gemarah* that Rava isn't referring to a teacher who actually makes mistakes because for sure the other teacher is preferred, but to someone who doesn't check whether his students are reading accurately and rushes them through even the basics. Therefore, the point of learning quickly isn't to err and allow mistakes. One should teach and learn the simple *p'shat*, not getting lost in the extra meanings of the teaching, that is, during *bekiyus zeman*.

During *beiyun*, I remember a great sage comparing our generation to theirs in learning:

"The amount of learning one can accomplish when he has an ardent desire to come close to *HaShem Yisborach* is remarkable. Rabbi Gustman told his students, "The difference between us is that, when you have a difficulty, you just look around a little to see if the *Acharonim* talk about a solution. If you can't find an answer quickly, you go off to eat, to sleep. When I have a difficulty, then there is no eating, there's no sleeping until I have found a clarification." (My Book, *Kavanos Halev* p. 71)

"I heard that Rabbi Nachman once mentioned that he had learned all four sections of the *Shulchan Aruch* three times. The first time he learned it simply. The second time, he learned it in depth. He knew the source of each law in the *Talmud*, Rashi and Tosefos. The third time, he understood the mystic reason behind every law.

"He accomplished this while a youngster, for he afterwards reviewed the *Shulchan Aruch* a number of times more… He always learned exceptionally quickly. He would learn a few pages of *Shulchan Aruch* in one hour, together with all the commentaries on the page of the large edition: the *Turei Zahav*, the *Magen Avraham*, the *B'er Hagolah*, the *Pri Chadash*, the

*Ateres Zekeinim,* and so on.

"He said that when everyone else is getting ready to go to prayers in the morning, he learns four pages of *Shulchan Aruch.* He learned everything—*Talmud, Shulchan Aruch* and so on—very quickly.

"He spoke to us at length about this, saying that it is good to learn quickly without being pedantic. One should learn simply and fast. One shouldn't confuse oneself by comparing what one is learning in one place with what one recalls from another place. One should simply see that one understands the topic that one is presently learning.

"At times, a person may not understand something. But he shouldn't spend too much time worrying about it. He should let it go and continue learning further. Usually, as a result of his steady learning, he will later come to understand what was puzzling him.

"Rabbi Nachman said that in learning, one needs to do no more than simply say the words. Then, in the process itself, one will come to understand. One shouldn't confuse oneself when one first starts learning by trying to understand immediately. With such an attitude, a person will immediately run into problems, and he won't understand anything. Instead, he should put himself in the mind-set of learning. He should say the words quickly. Then he will eventually come to understand. If he doesn't understand now, he will understand later.

"If there remain a number of matters that he still doesn't understand, what of it? He will have more than made up for that imperfection with the vast amount of learning that he has accomplished, for that is of supreme value. As our sages said, 'A person should first learn and only then seek to understand, even if he doesn't know what he is saying' (*Shabbos* 63a).

"As a result of his speed, he will learn a great deal and he will come to review the texts several times. As a result, he will understand the second or third time whatever he didn't grasp at first. Rabbi Nachman spoke of this a great deal. It is impossible to clarify these matters fully in writing.

"This is a truly wonderful approach to learning. Using this technique, one can learn an extraordinary amount, reading a vast amount of material and ultimately coming to understand them much better than if one had learned pedantically, for a stress on understanding every detail confuses a person very much. Many people stopped learning *Torah* entirely because they had been so concerned with details. In the end, they were left with nothing.

"But when a person accustoms himself to learn quickly and without being over-precise, he will acquire the *Torah.* He will be able to learn a great deal: *Talmud, halachah, Tanach, Midrash, Zohar* and other books of *Kabbalah,* and all the other literature.

"Rabbi Nachman said that, every year, a person should learn the entire *Talmud* together with the commentaries of the Rif and the Rosh; the four sections of the *Shulchan Aruch* with its commentaries; all the collections of *midrash;* the *Zohar,* the *Tikkunei Zohar* and the *Zohar Chadash;* and all the Kabbalistic teachings of the Ari. In addition, a part of one's daily learning should be given over to learning with some degree of in-depth study.

"Then he added a number of other things: a person should say *Psalms* every day, as well a very great amount of prayers. In the course of this talk, Rabbi Nachman began to discuss the idea that a person should learn very quickly without worrying about learning in-depth and comparing texts. These techniques have been tested and found to work." (*Rebbe Nachman's Wisdom* 76)

"[As Aryeh Kaplan has pointed out in his translation of Rabbi Nachman's Wisdom], Rabbi Nachman's schedule here is immense: 30,000 pages of material per year. It would be a full-time task for most people just to rush through and say the words, much less to have the most basic idea of what one is saying.

"Nevertheless, there are many *Torah* leaders who have demonstrated remarkable abilities to learn *Torah,* extraordinarily quickly and with great comprehension. For instance, Rabbi Kook learned more than seven *dafs* of *Talmud* per hour. Rabbi Nachman is giving a person a vote of confidence and expanding his horizons. This is similar to the breaking of the four-minute mile. Originally, such a feat was considered impossible. But as soon as it was broken, many other runners followed suit. Their own mental constraints had been expanded, and they now allowed themselves to accomplish what they had previously told themselves could not be done." (Yaakov Dovid Shulman)

Similarly, the Maharshal encourages one to cover a lot of ground in their *Talmud* study. "The Maharshal bemoans the fact that the scholars of his day covered too little of the *Talmud,* spending day and night on one page, and the day after it is forgotten... They are guilty of diminishing the *Torah* and its students." (*Yam Shel Shelomoh, Chullin,* Intro)

So, should one focus more on *bekiyus,* trying to learn and remember what it says, or is he better off with *beiyun,* learning slowly but with much more depth? Let's conclude with the sages who preferred both methods as their daily practice.

The Shelah tells, "Many consummate *Torah* scholars customarily study two tractates each day. From one they learn much quickly, without analysis. From the other they learn a little, but with close analysis, pilpul, and dialectics." (*Shelah*, *Shavuos*, fol. 30)

The Chidah says, "The *Rishonim* had the custom of learning *Talmud* for a set period, merely to amass knowledge, while at other times they would devote themselves to pilpul and deep analysis of the *halacha*." (Chida, *B'ris Olam* on *Sefer Chassidim* 288)

Rabbi Yaakov of Lissa said, "If you are privileged to learn [*Torah*], set aside a period each day for simple study, to cover not less than a folio of the *Talmud*, sequentially, besides a study period for intensive learning; this should be a hard and fast rule for you." (Rabbi Lissa in his ethical testament, possibly the source for Rabbi Meir Shapiro establishing the *daf yomi*)

I once wrote to my followers. "I see it with my own eyes, the difference between how a man talks before or after he learned a *blat* (a page of *Talmud)* that day... So, I beg of you for the sake of the holiness of your souls, please men, accept upon yourself one *blat* of *Talmud* per day, preferably at the start of the evening... you will feel the difference yourself. You will have so much more clarity when you think, talk, or even do business thereafter. It doesn't have to take one hour, a *blat* with simple understanding could also take twenty minutes. Please... try."

Rabbi Mordechai told, "As soon as one can learn *Talmud* with the Tosefos on his own, he should set aside two study periods: one for intensive study of *Talmud* and the Tosefos and another, lasting half the day, for reviewing *Talmud* without the Tosefos, to acquire broad knowledge." (Levushey Mordechai on *Bava Kama*, Intro)

One *rosh hayeshivah* took a step back and looked at the conclusive results of both methods of study. Through this, he concluded an amazing feat which is a lesson for all of us, as to how we should study.

Rav Isser Zalman Melzer, Rav Shach's *rebbe* and uncle and the famed *rosh hayeshivah* of Etz Chaim, said that this was an unresolved question even in Yeshivas Volozhin. Some worked solely on *bekiyus* while others focused on *iyun*. Still others spent some time trying to attain depth in learning while also spending part of their time working on learning through the breadth of *Torah*.

Rav Melzer recounted, "Of those who learned only *iyun*, very few people attained greatness in *Torah*. Of those who learned only *bekiyus*, no one attained greatness in *Torah*. Most of those who attained *Torah* greatness, used their time to gain mastery in both areas of *Torah*."

Therefore, there really is no debate. Both methods should be applied to perfection and tuned to each individual's learning abilities. When you learn *bekiyus* or *binyun*, make sure that you do so as its "meant to be", thereby becoming both a "uprooter of mountains" and a "*Sinai*". However, if you have to choose only one, "*Sinai*" seems to be the preferred method according to my humble opinion and the majority of the masters of *Talmud* that I have quoted here.

Reb Meir Shapiro formed many *chaburos* of *limud* in Yeshivas Chachmei Lublin. One such program was divided into three stages. Each stage would take two years to finish. The first two years would be spent learning the *Gemarahs* of *Brachos, Shabbos, Pesachim, and Beitzah* with the relevant *halachos* in *Shulchan Aruch*. The *bachurim* would also have to know all the various *midrashim* connected to the topics they were learning, as well as the classic commentaries on the *Torah*. Besides these *mesechtos*, the *talmidim* also had to study *Yoma, Tomid, and Middos*, with all the relevant *halachos* of the Rambam.

In the second stage of the learning program, the *bachurim* would learn for *semicha*. They had to acquire a deep knowledge of all the necessary parts of *Yoreh De'ah*, which was to be studied along with *Chullin* and *Bechoros*. In addition, they had to be fluent in the laws of *challah* and *mikva'os* and the *halachos* pertaining to the *kashrus* of *sifrei Torah, tefillin*, and *mezuzos*.

The concluding stage in the *yeshivah* was intended only for those who would take up positions as *rabbanim*. During these last two years, the *bachurim* learned *hilchos gitten, chalizah,* and *takonos agunos*, followed by *choshen mishpat*, which deals with the various complicated monetary laws. The *talmud* also had to review the entire *Seder Nashim* and *Nezikin* with the commentary of the Rosh. At the termination of the six-year course, the *talmid* was ready to assume position as a *rav* or *rosh hayeshivah*.

With such a program, it is clear why the *yeshivah* was intended only for the most brilliant. Such a heavy and exhausting program could only be tackled by the elite. This was one of many *chaburas* in the *yeshivah*.

Reb Meir's *talmidim* did not let him down; many of them completed the program without a problem. The *bachurim* of Chachmei Lublin became known as true *geonim*, despite their youth. Many were fluent in all of *Shas*. Unfortunately, a lot of these great *b'nei Torah* were lost during the war. However, the dozens that remained became outstanding leaders of the next generation.

# *Chazarah (Review)*

When "G-d's *Torah* is perfect" then, "it restores the soul."

When people have this great love for the *Torah* and can sense its true sweetness, then "it restores the soul."

When people find the *Torah* without fault, then their love makes them worthy of continuous perseverance in its study. (*Rebbe Nachman's Wisdom* 91)

Rabbi Chayim Mordechai Katz says, "Only with a true love of *Torah* would you be willing to review it over and over again."

The sages teach that if one learns much at one time without going over it repeatedly, his learning will decrease; but if he studies with deliberation, it will increase. (*Avodah Zarah* 19a & Rashi ad loc.)

"If you forsake me [the *Torah*] for a day, I will forsake you for two days." (*Yerushalmi Brachos* 9:5) What does this mean? It means that every day you should give 100% effort to learn *Torah*. If you are devoted to her, she will be there for you to protect you and open up her gems. If you skip days, not reviewing and learning *Torah*, it will be more difficult to study *Torah* the next time.

"Perfume yourself with the words of *Torah*, and do it, a second, and a third, and a fourth time." (*Sifrei Devarim* 306)

The Torah says: "Review me Steadily." (*Tosefta, Oholos* 16:8)

Rabbi Yehoshua ben Karchah compares one who learns *Torah* without reviewing it to one who sows but does not reap. Such a person is very foolish, for he not only forgoes all profit from his work, but also loses whatever he expended in sowing. (*Sanhedrin* 99a, based on *Numbers* 1:31)

Rabbi Sheneor Zalman of Liadi takes a strong position on this and says, "Anyone who forgets a single [*Torah*] matter for lack of adequate review is as if he has forfeited his life. Furthermore, he transgresses a commandment of the *Torah*." (*SA HaRav, Hilchos Talmud Torah* 2:4)

However, if you do in fact forget, though not purposefully, understand that this too is from Hashem. Another words, the *Torah* is very difficult, it is not like other types of worldly study, it is very intricate and complex. It is hard to remember every detail and that is why *Torah* study should coincide with prayer to Hashem for success.

Were it not a fact that man forgets the *Torah*, if he does not study it constantly, man would learn all of the *Torah* and then become idle. This would lead him to boredom and sin. Therefore, it was decreed that the *Torah* is easily forgotten, so that man would occupy himself with *Torah* all of his days, and thus not come to sin. (*Koheles Rabbasi* 1:34)

Shlomo Hamelech, in *Proverbs* (24:30-31), wrote: "I went by the field of the slothful and the vineyard of the man void of understanding; and lo, it was grown with thistles, the face thereof was covered with nettles, and the stone thereof was broken down." He who does not constantly review his *Talmud* will first forget the chapter headings, then he will change the words of *chazal*, and finally he will say of unclean that it is clean and of clean that is unclean, and thus he destroys the world. (*Avos de R' Noson* 24)

I think people assume that the only way to review material is to learn it again immediately. While this is also good, by learning something *bekiyus*, completing the book as a whole, and returning to it again months down the line, this is also considered reviewing. The main thing is to do your best to remember what you can and to remember in order to practice.

Rabbi Yehoshua Cohen tells, "My grandfather completed the entire *Talmud* scores of times. He would rise at two in the night and learn thirty pages of *Gemarah* with Tosafos by eight in the morning. Although he had studied each page innumerable times, nevertheless he learned each time as if it were the first time, with attention and thought about each word. That is really review." (*Keren Yehoshua* p. 56)

Rabbi Cohn explains, "The advice of Ben Zoma – 'Who is the wise man? He who learns from everyone' – is likewise intended to teach the way to achieve the broadest and most accurate knowledge of *Torah*. Ben Zoma teaches that even if you have attained excellent knowledge of the *Torah*, you should not rely upon your own astuteness and learn without a partner or belittle your partner's opinion. If you do so, you are sure to make mistakes sometimes, as the *Gemarah* says (*Makos* 10a): '*Torah* can only be acquired in a group.' The *Talmud* adds that one who learns by himself will eventually become foolish.

"As the author of *Mesilas Yesharim* writes (Ch. 22, 'Humility'):

"'There is no scholar who never errs, and who does not need to learn from his colleagues, and many times even from his students.' Thus, if you learn by yourself you are sure to make mistakes." (ibid. p. 140-141)

Rabbi Yisrael Shklover writes of his master and teacher, the Vilna Goan, "He reviewed all of *Talmud Bavli* each month. His toil in study of the holy *Torah* was indescribable. He would review every chapter and *mesechta* hundreds or even thousands of times. Out of immense love for the holy *Torah*, he once devoted a long winter night reviewing [again and again] a single *Mishnah* in *Seder Taharos*." (Preface to *Pe'as Shulchan*)

Rabbi Leib, son of Rabbi Ber of Vilna, related to me: "Once upon a time, his father Rabbi Ber watched as the *tzaddik* Rabbi Zalman paced back and forth in his study. As was his way, studying and reviewing a Torah thought with a wonderous desire and powerful love, in a crisp, sweet voice that was music to one's ear. The soul of the listener was awakened to love of Hashem and a desire for wisdom and spiritual guidance.

"He reviewed the thought once, twice, three times... fifty times... one hundred times... until one lost count! He did this all with a gladness of heart and a boundless, powerful love, which mere words cannot describe.

"Rabbi Ber observed this in in complete silence and wonderment. In his heart, he thought, '*Torah, Torah*: How boundless is the love for you in Rabbi Zalman's heart! It is a fire which consumes fire!' He then grabbed hold of Rabbi Zalman and requested wholeheartedly, 'My brother, whose soul and flesh are a part of me: By the powerful love that exists between us, I demand that you tell me how many times you reviewed this matter.'

"When Rabbi Zalman saw the way in which Rabbi Ber was imploring him to reveal the absolute truth, he responded, 'In truth, I have reviewed the matter two-hundred-and-fifty times.'" (*Toldos HaAdam*)

## *How to Remember*

The Author of Beth Hillel speaks of his teacher and reports, "One semester, the *yeshivah* studied a tractate without the Tosefos, but with much repetition, until they were fluent in it; the following semester, they studied the same tractate very intensively with the Tosefos." (R. Hillel Ashkenazi, *Sefer Bet Hillel*, *Yoreh De'ah* fol. 86, in the name of his teacher R. Mosheh Lima)

Bruriyah saw a *talmud* learning quietly. She kicked him and said, "it says '*aruchah va'kol u'shmurah*.' If *Torah* is arranged in your 248 limbs, it will endure. If not, it will not!" (*Eruvin* 54a)

The numerical value of וּלַמְּדָהּ (and teach it), is equal to 85, the gematria of the word פֶּה mouth. This alludes to the teaching that when one studies *Torah*, he should verbalize the text, rather than simply ponder the subject matter in his mind.

Shmuel said to Rabbi Yehudah: "Sharp-minded one, open your mouth when you study the Written Law, open your mouth when you study the Oral Law, so that your learning will remain with you and your life will be lengthened. It is written, **כי חיים הם למוצאיהם** 'for they [words of *Torah*] are life to those who find them, and a cure for his entire flesh.' (*Proverbs* 4:22) Do not read it **למוצאיהם** to those who find them; rather, read it as if it were written **למוצאיהם** (like *'Motza'eihem'*) to those who express them **בפה**. With their mouths." (ibid.)

The *Gemarah* continues with Rav Yitzchak: "*Ki karov elecha ha'davar me'od b'ficha ubi'lvavecha la'asoso - Torah* is close to you when it is [audible] in your mouth and your heart. He intends to fulfill it." The Maharsha explains, "If it is audible in your mouth, you will remember it and be able to fulfill it."

Rava explains: We learn from "*Ta'avas libo nasatah lo va'areses sefasav bal manata selah.*" (*Ben yehoyada* - a *talmud* desires to be a *rebbe*. He will attain this if he merits to say the words nicely, for then he will remember them).

It says "*Ta'avas libo nasatah lo*" (Hashem answers prayer while it is still in the heart), but it also says "*va'areses sefasav bal manata*" (he must say it! *Ha'Ri*). Rava expounds the verse that it is referring both to *Torah* and prayer.

So, what does this mean? If one merits, Hashem grants his desire before he even requests it. If not, he is not answered until he requests. Rashi explains, *Maharatz Chayos* - if one merits, Hashem grants his desires according to his heart, i.e. only if it will be good for him; if one does not merit, his requests are granted, even if it will be bad for him. Shlomo prayed that Hashem answer Nochrim in this way. (ibid.)

"If a person makes himself [humble] like a [garden] patch on which everyone tramples, and like a fragrance with which everyone scents himself (he teaches *Torah*), his learning will endure. If not, it will not." (ibid.)

*Divrei Torah* are compared to a fig tree. (The figs ripen at different times.) Whenever one feels around, he finds figs; Likewise, whenever one ponders *divrei Torah*, he finds *ta'am* (taste, i.e. understanding).

R. Shmuel bar Nachmani asks, "What do we learn from "*Ayeles ahavim v'ya'alas chen*, *divrei Torah* are compared to a female deer?" It is always as dear to its mate as at the beginning. Likewise, *divrei Torah* are always as dear to one who learns, every time he reviews his learning, as at the beginning; "*v'ya'alas chen - Torah* gives grace [and honor] to those who learn it." The Maharsha explains, "even though they often neglect their food and appearance." (ibid. 54b)

"*Torah* knowledge can be obtained only by means of signs (rubricating by catchwords)." (ibid. 54b) Scholars who were better in languages had an advantage in this, as they were able to easily make signs for themselves inside their learning. Also, those who were masters at languages had an easier time remembering since many people get caught in the *targum* of the words.

Depending on how hard you work for it, so does the *Torah* return its wealth. As Rashi explains, "The words of *Torah* remain only with him who makes himself cunning about it (goes to work deliberately; studies systematically)." (Rashi, *Sotah* 21b)

What does it mean to study *Torah* systematically and by means of signs? Well for each person, they will have to find the right methods of remembering passages that works particularly for them. It could be that a certain *blat* number coincides with a *gematria* of the topic in question. Maybe through a play on words, you can better remember the passage and its location. Each chapter of *Talmud* has a title heading that usually relates to the material in question. It is good to memorize all of these. That is why I have tirelessly gathered them for you in a chart at the conclusion of this *sefer*.

For some people, if they don't tell over the *Gemarah* to someone else, they are unable to recall it later. Others actually have to prepare a *shir* in order for the lesson to really sink in. "Just as two knives become sharper when rubbed against each other, so when two clever people become close with one another, the wisdom of one will rub off on the other." (*Bereshis Rabbah* 69) Therefore, it is quite beneficial to study with a partner. It also forces you to learn out loud.

Then there are people who simply are blessed with a phenomenal memory, but don't be jealous of this, they probably also have trouble forgetting things in life they wish they could.

The Kotzker Rebbe understood the severity of Moshe's rebuke to the nation. He explicated: G-d did, after all, grant humans the faculty of forgetting. But this was given so that people might forget the trivialities and futilities of this world. Instead, we have forgotten the G-d that formed us! (...*And Nothing but the Truth*, p. 19)

One thing is for sure, that you must work diligently in your studies, taking it very seriously. "It would be unreasonable not to consider students like harvesters, for they work even harder." (*Y. Kesubos* 5:30b)

Do not get accustom to learn by rote and *chas-v-shalom* loose the realness of *Torah lishmah*. "As water does not taste well, if one is not thirsty, so it is with the *Torah*; unless a man wearies himself thirstily in studying it, he does not get the thirst-quenching taste of it." (*Shir HaShirim Rabbah* 1:2)

Rabbi Yehoshua Cohen writes, "The Vilna Goan said, 'it is possible for a person to spend his whole life studying *Torah* and to feel positive that when he dies and comes before the heavenly court, all the heavenly assembly will stand up and honor him because of the *Torah* he studied with such intense effort. Yet just the opposite happens to him. He comes before the court and he is spat upon; they accuse him, 'Disgusting creature, why did you despise Hashem's word?' (This follows *Sanhedrin* 99a, 'For he despised Hashem's word and broke His commandments' – *Bamidbar* 15:31; Rabbi Nehorai says: 'This refers to anyone who could have engaged in *Torah* study and did not.') The man will be astonished, 'I did not study? There are many millions of angels, created by my words of *Torah*, who will testify that I studied my whole life long! And with great diligence, as well. My lips never stopped repeating the holy words…'

"The Vilna Goan articulates that they will answer him, 'True you studied, but without method and without calculating how you could know and understand many parts of the *Torah*. Therefore, you are considered one who despised Hashem's word; moreover, you will be punished for *bitul Torah*, wasting time that could have been used in *Torah* study.'

"The Goan teaches us a great lesson: Neglecting *Torah* study (*bitul Torah*) in quality is no less a sin than neglecting it in quantity – Hashem save us! *Bitul Torah* can be said to equal all the other sins. (see *Mishnah Pe'ah* 1:1; *Pesichah* to *Midrash Eichah*, os 2) The first Temple was destroyed only for the sin of *bitul Torah* (Tractate *Kalah Rabasi*, ch.8) By the same token, even if a person studies with great diligence, but without a method and without calculating how best to use his time, and because of this he is missing many tractates he could have known, or does not really know and understand those that he has learned – this too is the grave sin of *bitul Torah*." (*Keren Yehoshua* p. 59-60)

## Total Dedication to learning

"If one does not labor to know Hashem's G-dliness, it would have been better for him had he never been created." (*Ma'aglei Tzedek* 8)

"The words of *Torah* remain only with him who kills himself (denies himself excessive enjoyments) for its sake." (*Berachos* 63b) I don't think people truly realize how much a true *talmud chacham* works and dedicates himself to his *Torah* study.

People think that the *Torah* was given to these scholars more easily. Maybe because they grew up in a family of scholars and *rabbanim*, they assume it comes effortless. However, this is far from the truth. Everyone has to work diligently in order to acquire the *Torah*. As it says in *Avos*, "*Torah* scholarship does not come to a person by inheritance (without toil)." (*Avos* 2:12; *Nedarim* 81a)

So, what do you do in order to acquire the *Torah*? "Exhaust yourself in the study of *Torah*." (*Toras Kohanim, Bechukosai*) However, you have to be willing to compromise on *gashmious*, to such an extent that your very limbs will feel tired. The *Talmud* says, "Why is the *Torah* called '*tushiyah*'? Because the study of it weakens the strength of man." (*Sanhedrin* 26b) "Through *Torah* study, the strength of man is broken, [because] it had been as hard as sapphires." (*Shir HaShirim Rabbah* 5:14)

However, the benefits for study return far more then what you lose by its dedication. Rabbi Yaakov Abuchatzeira taught, "Since the body weakens itself through *Torah* study, sickness does not come upon it." (*Petuchei Chotem – BeShalach*)

"Reish Lakish would go over a law (*Mishnah*) forty times before he came before Rabbi Yochanan." (*Taanis* 8a) Can you imagine how much time this must have taken? But it was worth the effort, "According to the pain (in studying) is the reward." (*Avos* 5:22)

R' Moshe Halberstam grandson told over the following during his grandfather's *hespid*:

"The *Gemarah* (*Eruvin* 54b) tells the famous story of Rav Preida, who, in a monumentally selfless act of dedication, would review each *Mishnah* with an especially weak student 400 times! Only after 400 times would this student fully grasp the material, and Rav Preida would not allow him to settle for anything less.

"Once, in the middle of their studies, there was a knock on the door. It seems Rav Preida's presence was requested at an urgent community gathering. He politely told them that he was presently in the middle of learning, and that he would come as soon as he finished reviewing the material with his student (little did they know what that meant!). Painstakingly, they continued to review the material 400 times, each time going over it as if it was the first. After the 400th time, Rav Preida, as he always would, asked his student to repeat it to him.

"This time, however, he couldn't. Try as he might, he stuttered and stumbled and just could not get things straightened out. 'My dear student,' said Rav Preida patiently, 'normally, after 400 times, you grasp the *Mishnah* with great clarity. Yet now, even after we have gone over it 400 times, you still stumble. What was different this time that you remain unclear?'

'Rebbe,' the student said, 'from the time that they came knocking on the door to call you, I could no longer concentrate. I kept thinking, soon Rav Preida will go... soon he will leave.'

"'Fine', said Rav Preida, 'I am here. I am not going anywhere until we are finished. Try and concentrate, and let's start again...' He proceeded to teach him the *Mishnah* another 400 times! The second time around, he got it straight.

"At that time, the *Gemarah* concludes, a heavenly voice rang out: 'Rav Preida, take your pick: Either to live 400 years, or that you and your entire generation will receive eternal bliss in the World to Come (in the merit of your great dedication)!'

"'I choose,' said Rav Preida, 'the World to Come for me and my entire generation.'

"Said Hashem to the angels, 'Give him both!!'

"An exceptional story, and an exceptional reward. But in another place, the *Gemarah* credits Rav Preida's longevity to something else entirely. Rav Preida's students once asked him: 'Rebbe, what did you do that you merited to live so long?' (Apparently, they never heard of this story.)

"His answer: 'I was always the first person to arrive in *beis ha-midrash* in the morning.' (*Megillah* 28a) Now even if they had never heard the story, he certainly hadn't forgotten it. So, why did he give them a different answer?

"Reb Moshe's grandson answered brilliantly: 'There are people who by nature are not particular about how they spend their time. For such a person, if he were to, say, spend three hours in the hospital visiting a lonely old man, it would be a great *mitzvah*, no doubt, but no great surprise. He may on other occasions spend three hours *shmuesing* with some friends about matters of no great significance. Perhaps, as a result, he'll sleep in, and catch a super-late *minyan*. This is not to diminish the *mitzvah* that he did. But for him, giving away even big chunks of time is something that comes naturally.

"But what if a person who is highly scheduled and never wastes even a minute were to spend the same three hours keeping the old man company—now that would be something to talk about!

"The fact that Rav Preida was willing to give vast amounts of his precious time to study with his student was in itself a remarkable feat. But taken in the context of Rav Preida's nature—this was the same Rav Preida who never wasted a moment, never slept in, and was always the first person to open the *beis ha-midrash* in the morning—it is truly astonishing!

"Reb Moshe, his grandfather, he said, was the same way. For eight hours a day, he would see people, answer their questions, offer them advice (*da'as Torah*), and help them work out their problems."

Rav Yaakov Yisrael Meisels said, "All over the world, old and young, *rabbanim* and laymen—whomever you asked would tell you, 'Reb Moshe—I'm very close with him!' And they all were. He gave endlessly of his time and energy to help others, always with a smile, and never asked for anything in return.

"Yet by nature, Reb Moshe was a very scheduled person. For many years, he would take a nap each afternoon—for exactly 13 minutes—no more, no less. In fact, after his death, when they were looking through some of his writings that he wrote when he was younger, it became apparent that his extreme generosity and ever-present smile didn't come naturally. Many times, he had written in his personal diary, 'Today I spoke to so-and-so impatiently—I have to work on that!'" *Ye'hi zichro baruch.* (Recorded by Rabbi Eliyahu Hoffmann)

So, how does a person become such a great *rabbi*? It all comes from their dedication to the *Torah*. Their love for the *Torah* is so great that it impacts their life to the core, making them desire to perform all the holy commandments.

"So, why is there so much emphasis on *talmud Torah* itself? It is because learning *Torah* is the doorway to everything else in a Jewish person's life. That is why the *Talmud* says, 'The study of *Torah* is equal to all the other commandments.' (*Shabbos* 127a) It is because through *Torah* study, you have the desire to perform all the other commandments. Without the continuous study of *Torah*, you would otherwise overlook much of the commandments. The *Torah* makes the *mitzvos* real and alive in the heart of a person. To perform them, to teach them and learn more about them." (*Chiddushei Torah* from my book, *Chassidus, Kabbalah and Meditation*, my book)

Tosafos says, "For a *talmud chacham*, *Torah* is his full-time occupation; he is involved in it and thinking about it all the time. He does not walk even four cubits without *Torah*." (*Sotah* 21a)

From a young age, Reb Meir Shapiro was not only an *illuy*, but a *masmid* as well. Due to the long hours behind *sefarim*, Reb Meir's health began to suffer. The doctors insisted that he spend less time at his studies.

At just eight years old, Reb Meir had memorized much of *Shas* with Tosafos. When his parents forbade him to learn for hours on end, he would take walks with a close friend and together they would review the *Gemarah* that he had memorized.

The two boys once disagreed over which *Amorah* said something in a particular *Gemarah*, so they decided to stop at the house of the local *shochet* to look up the source. They were so desperate to find the solution that although there was no one at home, they climbed in through an open window.

As it turned out, both *bachurim* were correct, the *Gemarah* quoted Rava, while in the margin it was corrected to Raba. The neighbors gathered around outside thinking they heard burglars entering the shochet's home. They were quite surprised to discover that the "thieves" were really two young scholars standing at the *shochet's* bookshelf.

By the time Reb Meir was nine years old, his fame had spread, and he was known far and wide as "the *Illuy* of [the town of] *Shatz*." *Rabbanim* came from throughout Poland and Galicia to test the young *talmud chacham* who knew the entire *Yoreh Deah, ba'al peh*.

Once, Reb Meir's grandfather, the Manestritcher Rav, came for a visit and took his grandson with him when he was called upon by the local *rav*. The two older men soon found themselves deep in a *sugya* and unable to resolve a puzzling question. Nine-year-old Reb Meir quickly explained away the difficulty with ease.

I think it's important to note, that a true scholar who is dedicated to the *Talmud*, also must be dedicated to the learning of *halacha* as we spoke of earlier. Total dedication to learning also means to be open minded and to learn through all important *Torah* books. To many new scholars limit themselves to study only one pathway, when a true scholar understands and learns all the paths of *avodas* Hashem in order to come to his own conclusions. When I sat down with Rav Malkiel Kotler to receive my first *haskamah*, on my book, *Kavanos Halev*, he proved this point to me quite clearly. One by one, as he glanced at the footnotes of my book, he began telling me about the *sefarim* I was quoting, who wrote them and what was inside them. It was obvious that every *Chassidic sefer* he was completely familiar with, even though he is a *Litvish rav*. His responses about each *sefer* was concise, as if he knew them all backwards and forwards. Rav Kotler then looked up at me with a smile and said, "You're probably wondering why I am looking through the footnotes and not the book itself. It is because you can tell everything about a book, its entire *derech* from the footnotes alone." But don't worry he told me, "I still plan to read the entire book," and surely, he did. Upon receiving his final approval after some months, he told me, "This is the first *sefer* on *hasgacha* that I have ever given a *haskamah* for."

210

# *The Chavrusa of your Dreams*

Learning with a *chavrusa* is certainly beneficial. Attending a *maggid shir*, will certainly clarify the passages of the *Talmud* for you. However, finding a *chavrusa* who also wants to tidy up his skills and foundation is not easy to come by. This is one project, *The Path to Finishing Talmud*, that you might have to go about alone.

Truly you have to be willing to do whatever it takes to complete the core study (*Tanach* and *Mishnah*) first, as we spoke about earlier.

You will be surprised how many people simply have no interest or don't appreciate its importance. But you can understand where they are coming from, because in all likelihood, you were also like this at one time, trying to know the entire *Torah* through shortcuts. At basketball camp, do they start out teaching campers to shoot from the three-point-line?

Don't give up on finding someone because at the very least, along the way, you will inspire others to study core material. The *Talmud* says that if you study the *Torah* without a partner, it's not a good thing as mentioned before. You can come to make many mistakes, but if there is no choice, it's still better to learn in the best way for you, even if that means alone sometimes. I know great scholars that till this day, struggle to find the right *chavrusas*.

For instance, you might find someone who is willing to learn the same material, yet he might have an overly aggressive attitude in how he studies. He always has to argue pointless things, just to win the conversation. Another may study way to slow, over evaluating meaninglessness things that have nothing to do with *p'shat*. Yet another may always come late or miss the *shiur* entirely. Too many people end up settling for the wrong *chavrusa* and wasting valuable time. Sadly, it might simply be better to learn yourself. However, in *yeshivos*, you might be forced to pair up with the only available guy, but for what purpose? You can't study *lishmah* while your suffering; *Torah* is meant to be enjoyable.

Is there a solution? Well I can tell you that you can't just settle and make the best of it. The right *chavrusa* is everything to a scholar and for his growth in *Yiddishkeit*. Pray to Hashem and go to your *rosh hayeshivah* for a solution. It may take a person years to find the right *chavrusa*, should you find him, you might decide to keep him for life. However, sometimes circumstances stand in your way. You both end up in different *yeshivos* in faraway cities. However, if you find the perfect *chavrusa*, do everything you can to stay with him, even if it's a financial burden, place your trust in Hashem as this person is truly a gift to your study. I think too often scholars allow the *kollel* paycheck to dictate their *Torah* learning. At some point, you might actually have to have some basic *emunah* in Hashem and realize that doing the right thing will carry with it the blessing of *parnasa* on its own.

In *Ethics of our Fathers* (1:6), it says, "procure yourself a teacher, a friend and judge all men favorably." Why doesn't it say, *chaverim*, friends in the plural instead of the singular? It is because you must choose your friends wisely. Better one or two friends then many who may confuse you, keep you away from learning *Torah* and even draw you away from Hashem. However, in the first *Mishnah* in *Avos*, it says, have for yourself many followers. If you're going to share *Torah*, then have many people around you, if not, keep your friendships in check because unfortunately, most people are selfish and, in their core, don't really value your time. I always liked the expression, "A person is the sum of the four people they spend the most time with." Time is your most valuable commodity, so value it and share it only with those deserving and appreciating it.

Should you find that special *chavrusa*, Hashem will listen to your studying of the *Torah* and it will be great appreciated.

The *Gemarah* says, "R. Abba said in the name of R. Simeon b. Lakish: When two scholars pay heed to each other in *halachah*, the Holy One, blessed be He, listens to their voice, as it is said, 'Thou that dwellest in the gardens, The companions hearken to thy voice: Cause me to hear it.' But if they do not do thus, they cause the *Shechinah* to depart from Israel, as it is said, 'Flee, my beloved, and be thou like, etc.'" (*Shir HaShirim* 2:17)

"R. Abba said in the name of R. Simeon b. Lakish: When two disciples form an assembly in *halachah*, the Holy One, blessed be He, loves them, as it is said, 'and his banner over me was love.' Said Raba: Providing they know the features of a subject; providing also that there is no greater [scholar] in the town from whom to learn." (*Shabbos* 63a)

The Maharal explains, "The *Shechinah* resides among *Yisrael* [only] because they possess a *Torah*, that, like Hashem Yisborach, is a unity. Similarly, the *Gemarah's* statement – that if scholars pay attention to one another the Holy One, blessed be He, listens to their voice – results from the fact that when they are joined through the *Torah*, which is a unity, the

Holy One, blessed is He, joins with them; for as we said, Hashem Yisborach resides with *Yisrael* by reason of their having been given the *Torah*, which is a unity." (*Nesivos Olam, Nesiv HaTorah*, p. 144)

# Kollel's and Yeshivah Curriculum

The *Yerushalmi Talmud* teaches, "Rav Chama and Rav Hoshea were strolling and viewing the synagogues of Lod. Said Rav Chama to Rav Hoshea, 'See how much money my forefathers invested in these beautiful synagogues!'

"Rav Hoshea retorted, 'See how many lives they destroyed in building these synagogues! Could they not have found people to sit and study instead for that money?'" (*Yerushalmi*, end of *Pe'ah*; There is another *Gemarah* that says the opposite because synagogues today represent a small version of the *bais Hamikdosh*, which is a house for the *Shechinah* and therefore should be made beautiful.)

I remember sitting in Kollel amongst *avrechim* who could barely manage to pay their bills. Bang, bang sounded the hammer as the *shul* was installing a $100,000 chandelier. We all looked at one another and wondered why. Obviously, a *shul* should be a beautiful palace for the *Shechinah* but at what cost?

I also remember making a *bris milah* for my first-born son in a caravan *shul*. Today it has been replaced by a multistory building. I'll tell you; nothing beats that small caravan. The davening, simplicity and holiness was not from this world. It was as if the simple atmosphere bonded us all together as one unit. When *kollels* or *shuls* grow in size, it seems to be missing something from its former charm, but I get it, expansion and growth is part of the way the world works. However, we have to try to hold onto that simplicity of a small group of guys coming together and making something *lishmah* for Hashem.

The *yeshivah* way of learning is not for everyone. I don't want to be a skeptic for the greatest institutions in the world, but all fine things can always look for improvement. Let's begin by speaking about *kollels*, the *yeshivos* for married men. These institutions are generally small and funded mostly by the *rosh hayeshivah* himself and a few philanthropists. These holy donors have their own opinion as to how they want their money spent. The subjects that interest them will most likely be those they wish learned in the *yeshivah*.

It makes sense, if you pay the bills then you should have some say in how your money is spent. Sometimes this might even override the *roshei hayeshivos* own desire for his *yeshivah*. The philanthropists may even decide

214

who stays and who leaves the *yeshivah*. Not being a *kollel* man himself, he may not have the experience or the wisdom to make these decisions, though that doesn't seem to stop him. Sadly, I have seen people segregated and not accepted due to their heritage of being *Sephardi* or *Ashkenazi*. Many being turned away due to a lack of wisdom or their status as a new *ba'al teshuvah*. Obviously, these situations aren't right and should be corrected.

In a better situation, the *rosh hayeshivah* has full control over everything. He chooses the desired subjects and how he wants the *yeshivah* to be run. In the same way though, he will push his personal pathway and hand pick the students he feels will follow his desired path of his *kollel*. Rav Aharon Kotler said in his *hesped* of the Chazon Ish, that the reason the Chazon Ish was bigger than him, was because the Chazon Ish had no *yeshivah* to run; he had nothing in his life except *Torah*. So, understand the huge sacrifice the *rosh hayeshivah* has made to get to this point and provide this holy service to you. Therefore, he might be a bit on your case at times. Usually the *rosh hayeshivah* is right there all the time watching you or he will have the *mashgiach* keep a close eye on everyone. Are you coming on time? Are you taking your learning seriously? Are you taking too many breaks or showing up late?

For some people, this becomes very annoying. They want to just learn in a relaxed environment. If they wanted a boss lurking over their head, they would get a full-time job. Some *mashgichim* take their job too seriously and drive everyone crazy. They start banning phones, breaks, food, water and who knows what else. I know one *rosh hayeshivah* that requested that people don't bring drinks, coffee or even water into the *bais midrash*. We are not in Grodno anymore! People don't have the emotional and physical stamina to be treated like workers. Then again, in the times of Grodno, I don't think people got paid a salary to study all day by the Rosh! On the other side of things, some *mashgichim* let too much go and there is a huge amount of slack in the *yeshivah* and *bittle Torah*.

The *kollels* are many times run like a business. They may even require time punch cards and deduct funds for tardiness. Maybe this would make sense to the student if he were actually being paid a decent salary. Some provide rewards and quizzes for extra money, though not everyone is good in taking tests, so why should they lose out when they are giving 100% effort and doing their best. However, you must appreciate that someone out there is dedicating their hard-earned money to help you learn *Torah*. So, just like you wish the *yeshivah* overlooks your flaws, so you should attempt to overlook some of theirs. That is, if it's not effecting the quality of your learning.

As far as learning core material, the *rosh hayeshivah* usually decides what you will study, as he wants everyone learning the same material, bringing unification to his *yeshivah*. That way people can ask questions to each other and have open conversations about the same material. It makes perfect sense in an ideal world. However, what if you need to study something different than everyone else? What about the core study you have been putting off for years?

I personally have yet to accept a *kollel* check for learning, even though I have studied in a few *kollels*. To me, I feel more the idea of *Torah lishmah* this way and I find it more enjoyable to not have anyone "in charge" of my studies. However, sometimes I still needed to follow the *kollels* rules of what to study and abide by their schedule non-the-less.

In one such *kollel*, my *chavrusa* and I used to hide the books we were really learning underneath the material the *kollel* preferred us to be studying. People used to come by and wonder why we were having so much fun and laughing as we studied. My friends, this is what happens when you study what you enjoy and not what is forced upon you. You enjoy it, you recall the information and you can't get enough of it.

As I started with a new *chavrusa* in a Jerusalem *kollel*, I told him, "Look, we are going to have fun and enjoy our *Torah* learning. Sometimes we are going to stand up and study the entire time, as I find it more enjoyable and proper. I don't care what people think." Surprised at my fun rules, he agreed to them and it reminded him of the fun times he used to have learning in *yeshivah* as a *bochor*.

Often there were glances across the room from others. People thought that because we were happy learning, maybe we were slacking off, to the contrary. I remember seeing the *rosh hayeshivah* peeking out of his *Gemarah* as to what we were doing. We were the only animated people studying, everyone else seemed to be robotically in a learning trans. If that works for them, then fine but I think they are missing out on the true enjoyment of the material by being so robotic. (Let's make *Torah* fun again!)

The *rosh hayeshivah* and fellow inmates, excuse the sarcasm, should be ecstatically happy when they are fulfilling Hashem's will. Unfortunately, I actually felt this *kollel* was too cold, and really needed a lifeline... I think we became that lifeline for the brief period we remained study partners there. Sadly, as he couldn't afford a car to visit Jerusalem daily, and the bus ride became to taxing, our study had to end abruptly, hopefully to be continued again one day.

If you see that your *yeshivah* is not a warm and happy place, find

216

somewhere else to study. The main thing is to enjoy the *Torah* and to feel G-dlines in your soul. If you're not feeling this, fix your environment, *yeshivah* and study partner. I think sometimes the *yeshivah* can become a crutch and people need to just move on to another *yeshivah* or get a job. I mean, what are you waiting for, a sign to drop out of the sky telling you that you need to search for a new place and change something in your life?

Let's not even address the issue of *kollels* promising to pay a salary and then failing to do so, due to mismanaging or being short on funds. Also, paying someone late when they rely upon this money to pay their bills and in order to keep *shalom bayis*. It is very important to pay teachers on time as well. If you're going to open a place, make sure you have sufficient funds many months ahead of time. Otherwise, instead of helping these people, you might be doing a disservice.

Don't forget the entire reason you're in *kollel* is to study *Torah lishmah*. If attending *kollel* makes your learning like a business and it loses its benefits for your soul, then maybe it's time to rethink. Your time is very valuable and a *kollel* check isn't worth compromising your study. I know this might sound difficult being that you may be studying in *kollel* for a substantial amount of years, but at some point you may have to realize that some *kollels* are just "adult babysitting" and you either have to study on our own or open your own "kindergarten" so you can do what is right for your soul. (Forgive the *lashon*.) If you're a philanthropist and want to change the world, you know where to find me. We will make the greatest *yeshivah* together. I really want to make a place that will have everyone finish all of *Tanach*, *Mishnah*, *Talmud* and *Mishnah B'rurah* every year. Also, we would study one *seder* a day of *beiyun*, *Tur Shulchan Oruch*, *mussar* and more. Maybe that sounds like a lot to accomplish but if you have the right people giving *shiur* and guiding you, everything is possible. We could even put a little gym with some treadmills to promote physical fitness along with *Torah*. My ideas are endless... "A *yeshivah* is a glorification of Hashem's name in the world," said the *Rosh HaYeshivah*, Rabbi Yehuda Zev Segal. One thing is for sure, anyone serious about learning *Torah* will not be turned away. The *Talmud* says, "The day Rabbi Elazar took office was remarkable also in many other ways. The doors of the Academy in Yavneh, were thrown open, and four hundred new benches were added for new students who hastened to be admitted into the Academy." (*Brachos* 28a) This was because nobody was turned away who was serious about their studies anymore. And on this day, hundreds of laws were clarified in *halacha*, so great of an event was it. But in our day, once again, many doors are closed like in the times of Rav Gamliel and only the elite or people with "*protectia*," connections can enter a *cheder* or *yeshivah*, what rubbish!

However, more important than anything else in the *yeshivah* is the connection between the *rosh hayeshivah* and his students. Reb Meir Shapiro's involvement in the progress of his *talmidim* was a 24-hour job. In a letter written in support of the *yeshivah*, the Boyaner Rebbe wrote, "The *Rosh HaYeshivah*, doesn't limit himself just to giving a *shiur*. He guides his *talmidim* and shows them how to improve their *midos*. He prays with them, eats with them and he knows how to instill into the heart of every *bachur* that he must one day be a *gadol b'Yisrael*."

Indeed, Reb Meir performed not just as a *rebbe* to his *talmidim* but also as a father. If a *bachur* became sick, Reb Meir would go immediately to visit him. One time, when Reb Meir went to visit an ill *bachur*, the boy was suddenly overcome with tremors at the sight of the *rosh hayeshivah*. Reb Meir was taken aback. Having managed to calm the *bachur*, he asked him what had caused the convulsions.

"In my previous *yeshivah*," the boy explained, "it was unheard of for the *rosh hayeshivah* to visit an ill *talmud*. Only if the *talmud* was desperately sick would he make a visit. Seeing the *rosh hayeshivah*, I suddenly became worried that I have a life-threatening illness and the doctor hadn't informed me."

The *rav* smiled and said, "To me every *talmud* is like a son. A father doesn't wait to visit his child until he is dangerously ill. He goes to see him on the first day."

In the spring of 1924, Reb Meir Shapiro accepted the prestigious position of *rav* and *av beis din* in Piotrkov, Poland. At the inauguration ceremony, one of the other *rabbanim* jokingly questioned him as to what he would do when all the former *rabbis* of Piotrkov return to life during *techiyas hameisim*.

"Their communities will return with them," responded Reb Meir with a smile. "Then each *rav* will have his own flock to take care of."

"But *rebbe*," continued the other *rav*, "what will you do if the *rabbanim* return, but their communities do not make it?"

Reb Meir's retorted, "Any *rav* who will not have the power in the Next World to bring his community back to life was not a proper *rav* in the first place. It is a *rav's* duty to elevate his community and make them into *ehrlicher Yidden*."

The *rosh hayeshivah* truly is a role model to his students. When a *chassid* asked the Shotzer Rebbe, how he was feeling (He had lost his wife and five children out of six and had a very difficult life), he answered, "Please don't ask me. You see the *Gemarah* on the table? This is my breakfast and my supper. I wake up with my *Gemarah*, and I go to sleep with it. In me has been fulfilled the *pasuk*, 'Were it not for the *Torah* that is my delight, I would have perished in my anguish.'" (*Tehillim* 119:92)

I don't know if people truly realize the suffering and dedication of *rabbanim*. Therefore, it is upon you to help them in any way that you can.

Rabbi Chayim Shmuelevitz remarked that the principle of *ahavas Yisrael* also applies to someone who comes to a *yeshivah*. Although a student might not be able to contribute in the physical betterment of the *yeshivah*, he is able to help in the spiritual betterment. How? By serving as a worthy example for others. He should come to *davening* and *seder* on time so that others will do likewise.

Sometimes scholars are tempted to learn in a way to show their *chavrusa* that they can create *pilpul*, veering from the spirit of the *Gemarah*. Rabbi Yaakov of Lissa comments, "The purpose of your learning should be to find the *halacha*, not the *pilpul*, which, to our disgrace, is so prevalent in this generation." (Author of *Netivos HaMishpat*, in his ethical testament, *hagadah Ma'aseh Nissim*)

One *kollel* I was attending used to have each person stand up and give a *d'var Torah* on the learning that week. When the time arrived for one particular fellow, he was in for a bit of a shock. He was the type of person that always used to correct other's mistakes in the *yeshivah*, and he looked at himself as above all the rest of us. When he got up that week to give his *d'var Torah*, he slowly unraveled his *pilpul* and one by one the rest of the *kollel* took it apart. He veered so far from the basic *p'shat* of the learning and *halacha lemisah*, that it was obvious that he understood nothing. Maybe in a another *kollel* he could get away with this but amongst this *kollel* of bright students, there wasn't a chance. I felt bad for him to stand up there and make mistake after mistake, only to be corrected by the entire assembly time after time. I guess he learned a big lesson that day, that *pilpul* without broad knowledge of *Torah*, goes nowhere.

Rabbi Samson Raphael Hirsch laments: "A new spirit is abroad, that of entirely abstract thought, without any association to the world. They do not study to fulfil their purpose in life, to understand the world and the commandments. Research is made into an end in itself, rather than a means to an end." He especially cautioned not to succumb to the temptation to compete with one's fellow students, which leads one into the trap of *pilpul*. (R.S.R. Hirsch, *The Nineteen Letters* 15)

Hence, he writes: "You should learn by the light of truth, in the warmth and loftiness of life. Do not concern yourself with what others say; do not fret if, in the straightforwardness of your spirit, you cannot shine in the *pilpulim* of the great analytic minds, whose purpose is neither truth nor practice. Also, do not despair if you cannot excel in the arts that, to you, are only auxiliary techniques." (ibid. 18)

The Chazon Ish also urges, "direct all your energy toward a proper understanding of the subject, using healthy logic and straightforward intellect to comprehend the true *Torah*." (*Igros Chazon Ish* I, 4 & 12)

I think it's all too easy to feel pressured while learning in *kollel*. A person doesn't want to feel as if their *Torah* study is lower than their fellow. They are working hard; they want to feel recognized for this. It is important to always give others *kavod* and encouragement. We are after-all, in this together. I have heard of so many stories where a person doesn't feel appreciated by his *rosh kollel* and peers. Sometimes, besides his *chavrusa*, nobody even recognizes his existence in the *yeshivah*. The same may also occur in the *bais hakeneses*. It isn't that this person wants *kavod*, he just wants people to ask him how he is doing, to know his name and who he is.

We have much to work on when it comes to making people feel welcome. Too many people are lonely and in need of decent quality friends, but nobody wants to be bothered putting in effort into a new relationship. Just a simple hearty "*shalom*" or "good *Shabbos*" can mean the world to someone who is quiet and more reserved, yet we overlook this common decency. It would be good if the *roshei hayeshivos* goal would also be to unite the students. Then again, his job makes him so busy, we really have to be thankful and appreciate him. Between collecting money, attending *simchas* and funerals, giving guidance to others, he really has to be commended for his efforts. I mean, how many students go to the *rosh hayeshivah* asking, "*Rebbe*, how can I help you out more around the *yeshivah*? Is there anything you need for yourself or your family?" Rather, the *rosh* just gives and gives of himself. At the very least, we must return the favor, and we must strive to accomplish wonderful things in our *Torah* study.

It was said of Reb Binyamin Beinush Finkel (Former Rosh HaYeshivah of the Mirrer Yeshiva), "He completed *Shas* dozens of times and *Mishniyos* hundreds of times. The sets of *Mishniyos* in his house were totally shredded."

He spoke about "the *daf*" (covering one *daf Gemarah* daily) that he had tried so hard to establish in *yeshivah*. He had sensed for many years that the pace of learning in the *yeshivah* could not possibly produce *talmidei chachamim*. Was it acceptable that a person who learned for decades in one of the finest *yeshivos* in the world, at a time of relative tranquility, would only know twenty *blats* in each of eight *mesechtos*? He had attempted every means at his disposable to direct the *yeshivah* into completing a *mesechta* each *zman* (semester), and then encouraging the *avreichim* to finish other *mesechtos*. He strained convincing the *talmidim*; he attempted monetary incentives, and finally he refused to accept any new members to the *kollel* who did not undertake to finish the *mesechta*. A brief time before his *petira*, he awoke and exclaimed, "The *kedusha* of a *mesechta*! If only people would realize the *kedusha* of a *mesechta* that is completed... from cover to cover!"

Rabbi Yehoshua Cohen writes, "Those who sit and learn day and night, who discipline themselves, expending strenuous efforts, twelve or more hours a day at their studies – when they do not know at least a good part of the *Torah*, it is a terrible shame. To sit year after year in *yeshivah* and *kollel* and not know many whole tractates is shocking! Without a doubt they could have learned the whole *Talmud*, or at least a great part of it. After all, 'It is not in the Heavens.' (*Devarim* 30:12)

"In my humble opinion the underlying reason for this is that many students are not studying with the right method, and even those who do study with the right method are not reviewing. To review has become an embarrassment, a sign of weakness; only the less capable students do it. And the truth is that even if one reviews his studies many times, nevertheless if he does not do so in the proper order, or if he did not initially study with the proper order and method, his review is almost useless.

"On the whole, the situation in our generation is terrible. There are many who study all day long and only manage twenty pages a *z'man*, including both *iyun* and *bekiyus*! Many of these men have the attitude that they do not need to learn many pages a *z'man*, and there is no need to know many parts of the *Torah*, and certainly not the entire *Torah*. Some specialize more in *iyun*, and during an entire *zman* they manage to complete five pages, or ten pages of *Gemarah*, can that be called learning? When men sit day and night in uninterrupted *Torah* study, if they do not take advantage of the time to master a substantial portion of the *Torah* but are content with only a few pages a *zeman* – about that type of learning it is appropriate to say: May Hashem save us!

"I am not the one who is fit to say this. I am dust and ashes at the feet of everyone, but I say it in the name of the great *Torah* scholars, who have studied the entire *Talmud* hundreds of times, and who say that this type of study is almost equivalent to *bitul Torah*, to wasting time instead of studying!

"It is truly a pity if, for whatever reason, someone is incapable of mastering most parts of the *Talmud*. But one who is capable of it and does not do so – that is something over which 'even the stones of the wall cry out.' (*Chabakuk* 2:11) For, as I said earlier, nearly everyone is capable of accomplishing this.

"Believe me, '[The *Torah*] is not in the heavens.' (*Devarim* 30:12) Each and every one of us can know and master the entire *Torah*. It will be hard for some and even harder for others, but in the end, everyone is capable of it, with Hashem's help." (*Kerem Yehoshua* p. 34-36)

The Chofetz Chaim once expressed his appreciation of *daf hayomi* to Reb Meir Shapiro. "I am especially fond of you," he said. "And do you know why?" asked the Chofetz Chaim. "Because of what you have achieved through the *daf hayomi* study program."

"In the World of Truth," continued the Chofetz Chaim, "a person receives more honor for his *limud haTorah* than for his *ma'asim tovim*, his honorable deeds. Each Jew is honored in accordance with how much *Torah* he has studied. He is given a chair engraved with the names of the *mesechtos* he has learned.

"Until now, many of these seats were empty as people studied only certain *mesechtos* while others were neglected. Thanks to you," concluded the Chofetz Chaim, "all the seats are now occupied, and there is incredible *simcha* in *Shamayim*."

# A Gift of Tears

Rav Gershon Edelstein said, "A person who succeeds in *Torah* despite not having prayed for Divine assistance in his *Torah* study, is certainly missing a certain amount of holiness that his *Torah* study could have provided him, had he prayed for success in *Torah* study.

"This is as the *Midrash Tanchuma* maintains (*Matos* Ch. 5), 'Hashem created three good gifts in the world: wisdom, strength, and wealth. If a person receives one of them, he can yield what is coveted by the entire world…This is true if they are given to him as a present from Heaven, and they come from the strength of Hashem. However, if it's from his own strength and wealth (that he takes by himself) it is nothing.' This teaches us that if a person learns *Torah* because he is very intelligent and he does not receive this as a gift through praying for Divine assistance in *Torah* study, his *Torah* does not come 'from the strength of Hashem' and is therefore incomplete.

"The *Nefesh HaChaim* (1:3) states in the name of the Zohar, that *Torah* study without prayer does not 'fly above'. This means that if a person studies *Torah* and he does not have *yiras Shamayim*, his *Torah* does not ascend to the Heavens. He is therefore missing the amount of holiness that he would have had, if had he prayed for success in *Torah* study. In order to be considered a person who is complete in *Torah*, a person must not only diligently study *Torah*, but must also have *yiras Shamayim*, and pray for success and Divine assistance in his *Torah* study.

"The *Gemarah* in *Shabbos* (31a) quotes the *pasuk*, '*V'hayah emunas itecha chosen yeshuos chachmas v'da'as yiras Hashem hee otzaro* - The stability of your time and the strength of salvation is wisdom and knowledge.' The *Gemarah* teaches us that '*emunah*' refers to *Seder Zeraim* (the first order of *Mishnayos*). '*Itecha*' refers to *Seder Moed* (the second order of *Mishnayos*). The *Gemarah* continues to explain that all six orders of *Mishnayos* are alluded to in this *pasuk*. However, the *pasuk* concludes, '*yiras Hashem hee otzaro*' – 'Fear of Heaven is his storehouse.' The *Gemarah* explains that the *pasuk* concludes this way in order to teach that even if a person learns all six orders of *Mishnayos*, he will only be successful in *Torah* learning if *yiras Hashem* is his storehouse. In other words, just as a person requires a silo in order to properly protect and store his grain, so too a person requires *yiras Shamayim* as a 'silo' to properly protect and store his *Torah*. Without this silo of *yiras Shamayim*, a person's *Torah* will not stay guarded within him. This is as the *Mishnah* in *Avos* (3:17) states, 'If there is no fear, there is no wisdom.' Through *yiras Shamayim*, one also has the ability to be protected from the *yetzer hara*." (Rav Gershon Edelstein, *Sichah* 5775, #132)

Therefore, you must understand that even if you were to work harder than any person in the world, that still will not be enough to receive the *Torah*. Rav Moshe Stern stated, "*Torah* is beyond human understanding. Only Hashem can give us the gift of understanding."

Rabbi Pinchus cites the blessing in *Shemonah Eesreh*, "*Atah chonen l'adam da'as*...You graciously endow man with wisdom." This is the only blessing in which we thank Hashem for a gracious gift rather than make a request. Therefore, says Rabbi Zaidel Epstein, "We must pray to Hashem to grant us knowledge of *Torah* as we study. Then Hashem responds commensurate with our effort," writes Rabbi Schorr.

Rabbi Wolbe writes, "Nevertheless, we must take the first step to merit Hashem's assistance. Only after *B'nei Yisrael* proclaimed their acceptance of *Torah* with *na'aseh venishma* did Hashem teach Moshe the *Torah* and allow him to bring it down to us. "Hashem was the teacher not only of Moshe Rabbenu," writes Rabbi Friefeld, "but of each of us who toil and struggle with *Torah* study. When we put in the effort, Hashem Himself enters our mind and helps us understand, for Hashem gave us our brains to perceive the great truths of the world so that we may come close to Him. Hashem is the *chavrusa*/study partner of all who toil in *Torah*. So next time you feel alone without a *chavrusa*, realize that Hashem is your greatest *chavrusa*. He is also your greatest friend, giving to you constantly without you even realizing all of the wonderous things He does each moment for your benefit.

We learn this from Moshe Rabbenu himself, that he tried and tried to understand the *Torah* on *Har Sinai*, but it wasn't till Hashem bestowed it upon him as a gift, that he comprehended it, but how did this all come about, through his humility? Because he was humble, Hashem himself taught him the *Torah*. You can have the highest IQ and it wouldn't matter, the only way you can fully comprehend the *Torah* is if Hashem opens your heart to understand it.

When Moshe descended from *Shamayim*, Satan asked Hashem where is [the secret part of] *Torah*; He said that He gave *Torah* to the land. Satan asked [the angel appointed over] the land - [it claimed ignorance,] "*Elokim hevin darkah*..." He then went and asked the sea and the depth -

they denied having it, *"Tehom omer lo vi v'yam amar ein imadi; avadon v'maves amru b'azneinu shomanu shim'ah* (destruction and death said that they heard that *Torah* was given, but they did not know where)." Satan returned and He told Hashem that he did not find it anywhere in the land; Hashem told him to go to Moshe. "Where is the *Torah* that Hashem gave to you?" He asked Moshe. Moshe responded, "Who am I that Hashem should give to me His *Torah*?!" Hashem then said to Moshe, "do you lie?!" Moshe responded, "Your hidden treasure, which You delight in every day, can I say that I have it?! (I was not worthy of its secrets, just You spread Your *Shechinah* over me!)" Hashem blessed Moshe, "Since you lowered yourself, it will be called by your name – '*Zichru Toras Moshe avdi.*'" (*Shabbos* 89)

As you know, the angels were very jealous at first about the Jews receiving the *Torah*. However, "The angels held no beef against Moshe for receiving the 'external' *Torah* with its practically oriented commandments. They were only worried about mortal man receiving the 'hidden aspects' of the *Torah*," explains the Chasam Sofer.

They thought, certainly, mortal man is incapable of appreciating the hidden aspect of the *Torah*. However, Moshe proved them wrong because through his humility, he was able to take hold of the Throne of Glory. "The angels could only relate to its purely spiritual facet; the Jews, however, could connect to both its inner and outer aspects." (*Toras Chaim* to *Sanhedrin* 71a cited by *Gilyon HaShas*; see Maharsha)

"When the angels saw Moshe's humility, they loved him all the more." (*Derashos Chasam Sofer* III) It was his humility that enabled him to receive all aspects of the *Torah*, but this took forty days of trial and error. Hashem kept teaching Moshe the *Torah* and Moshe did *chazara*, but even that wasn't enough. He just kept forgetting and struggling to understand everything. He prayed, he cried, he humbled himself and Hashem relented, and he finally received and comprehended its beauty. So, must we do the same as Moshe Rabbenu. We must work hard, pray and humble ourselves before Hashem and our fellows. Then we too can comprehend the entire *Torah* as a gift from Hashem. Even through the *Torah* belongs to every single Jew, each small part that we understand is a special gift from Hashem. Like it says in *Proverbs*, The *Torah* isn't like other wisdoms of the world, it is Hashem's treasure. (*Proverbs* 2:1)

"Rebbe Nachman told us that all his studies required significant effort. When he began learning the *Mishnah* as a young child, he found it impossible to understand. He wept and wept until he was able to understand the *Mishnah* by himself.

"Later, when he studied more advanced works, he again found himself unable to comprehend them. And again, he cried bitterly until he was worthy of understanding. This was even true of such esoteric studies as the Zohar and the writings of the Ari, where understanding only came after long and bitter weeping." (*Sichos Haran* 8)

The Steipler told, "Even one who has an exceedingly poor comprehension will merit *siyata diShmaya* if he will invest significant effort in the study of *Torah*. He can grow to become a *gadol b'Torah* though such accomplishment, far greater than that which his innate abilities would allow."

He then related a story to prove his point:

"My uncle, the holy *Goan*, Rabbi Shimon Sofer of Cracow, related to me:

"In Dresnitz, a teenager of about sixteen or seventeen years old, came before the Chasam Sofer and made known to him that he desired to study *Torah* and that his soul yearned for it. When the [*yeshivah*] *bochorim* heard this, they laughed, for they wondered how a boy of his age, who all his life never experienced the light of *Torah* could now want to immerse himself in the study of *Gemarah*. Their *rebbe* [i.e. the Chasam Sofer] reprimanded them, 'Why do you laugh? Whoever desires to learn may come and learn.'

"He then drew the boy close and instructed the *bachurim* [regarding the boy], arranging that each one would study with him at a specific time, taking turns to instruct their new peer. However, aside from the fact that the boy was seventeen [and unlearned], there was an additional difficulty they were faced with. His comprehension was poor, as was his retention. If they were to learn a given *Mishnah* one hundred times, he would nevertheless quickly forget it; the next day, it would be as if he had never studied it. Nevertheless, his craving for *Torah* did not wane and he studied diligently to everyone's surprise. 'One who seeks to purify himself is granted Heavenly assistance.' (*Shabbos* 104a) It wasn't overnight but over the course of time, he became a superior student of *Torah* whose fear of Hashem was pure. He continued to flourish, and his efforts bore spiritual fruit; he became an outstanding *lamdam* (proficient *Talmudic* scholar) and was chosen *dayan* of the city of Mattersdorf, in the domain of his *rebbe*. Afterwards he became *rav* in the city of Shleiming, and then *av bais din* of Neizotz. He was outstanding in his knowledge of *Torah* and righteousness and is cited several times in the works of the Chasam Sofer.

"In conclusion, it is despair and lack of diligence which confine a student from attaining a true understanding of *Torah*. It is not, as people assume, that a lack of achievement leads to despair and a lack of intelligence; to the contrary, it is despair and a lack of diligence which prevent achievement, for, as the sages have taught, 'one who seeks to purify himself is granted Heavenly assistance.'" (ibid.) (*Chayei Olam* p.84)

Rebbe Nachman teaches, "Thought can bring about many things. When thought is intensely concentrated, it can exert enormous influence. Every faculty of the mind, both conscious and unconscious, down to the innermost point, must be focused without distraction. When many people do this, their thoughts can actually force something to take place.

"To accomplish this, the concentrated thought must spell out every step of the desired result in detail... You can make use of this in your studies. You can concentrate on something so strongly that it comes true. This is besides the benefit that such concentration will have on your understanding.

"For example, you can concentrate on the fact that you want to complete the four sections of the *Shulchan Aruch*. You can calculate that if you study five pages each day, you will finish all four in a single year.

"Picture in your mind exactly how you will go about this course of study. Concentrate so strongly that you are literally obsessed with the thought. If your desire is strong and your concentration intense enough, your plan will be fulfilled.

"The same concept can also be applied to other studies, such as the *Tanach*, or the *Talmud* with its major commentaries, the *Rif* and the *Rosh*, as well as the four *Turim*.

"The *rebbe* said that this is alluded to when the *Talmud* states that 'thought helps even for the study of *Torah*.'" (*Sanhedrin* 26b) (*Rebbe Nachman's Wisdom* p. 170)

Rebbe Nachman also recommends, "Attempt to go through all our sacred books in the course of your lifetime. You will have then visited every place in the *Torah*.

"The very rich constantly travel from land to land. They spend vast amounts just so that they should be able to boast that they have been to some faraway place. They consider it a sign of high status if, for example, they can boast that they have been to Warsaw.

"You should likewise travel everywhere in the *Torah*. In the future life, you will then be able to boast that you have visited every place in our sacred literature. At the time, you will also remember everything you have ever learned." (*Rebbe Nachman's Wisdom* 130)

"It is not hidden from you. It is not far from you. It is not in Heaven [for you] to say, who can ascend to the Heaven for us and take it

227

for us? Nor is it across the sea. Rather the matter is very near to you – in your mouth and your heart – to perform it." (*Devarim* 30:11-14)

Rav Abuchatzeira said, "A person cannot merit to know the truth of *Torah* except through tremendous toil and great exertion." (*Alef Binah* 89)

Inside each of us is a little, maybe big, *talmud chacham* just waiting for the right moment to hatch. Some of us just need someone to crack our exterior shell. While others, will simply hatch in the right moment, but you know, if you incubate the eggs and shine heat upon them, the fire of *Torah*, then they will hatch earlier. A young scholar must be nurtured by their parents, teachers and allow himself to shine in his own way.

"If he knocks, they will open for him (if he studies, he will enter into the interior of learning)." (*Pesikta Acharei* 176a)

"When Rabbi Meir of Kretchnif learned *Gemarah*, tears flowed from his eyes without ceasing. So much so that, sometimes the book that he was learning from would be altogether wet and waterlogged from the tears that fell down from his holy eyes." (*Raza d'Uvda*, p. 4)

"The *Torah* is not hidden," as it is clearly stated. (*Devarim* 30:11) "Rather it is hidden from you only through your own fault, for you did not take pains to study it." (*Midrash Tehillim* 119:18)

It really doesn't matter your level of intelligence and comprehension is. The *Torah* was created for every person and it will open should you come knocking with a truthful heart.

"I heard about a simple man who studied the *Gemarah* without understanding what the words meant. His practice was just to recite the words. Yet, through this he reached the level where he had mystical revelations of Elijah." (*Derech Tzaddikim*, p. 49, #10)

Rabbi Yehudah HaChasid taught, "'Scripture places the three flightiest leaders in Jewish history on par with the three mightiest leaders.' (*Rosh HaShanah* 25b, 26a) This is to teach you that Gideon, Samson, and Jephtah are equivalent to Moshe, Aharon, and Samuel. Insignificant leaders who work for the sake of Heaven are comparable to *tzaddikim*. In Hashem's view, the less astute people of later generations carry the same weight as the prodigies of earlier generations. If this were not so, every person could justifiably claim, 'Why wasn't I born in an earlier generation when people were much smarter? Then I could have learned much more *Torah*.' You can answer them, 'What difference does it make how much you learn? After all, the *Gemarah* says, 'It is the same whether you offer much or little, so long as your heart is directed to Heaven [you have the intention to serve Hashem].' (*Menachos* 110a) The main thing is that you don't sit around idle but study whenever you can, even if you are not the brightest student."

"[Rabbi Chaim Yosef Dovid Azulai (the Chida) comments on this paragraph that the Arizal was asked: 'The goodness and saintliness of the *Tannaim* and *Amoraim*, as it is described in *Talmud* and *Midrash*, were so extraordinary, how can anyone in the present generation do even one-thousandth of their good deeds?' Replied the Arizal, 'At the present time, the forces of Satan have gained the upper hand. Therefore, the few virtuous deeds we do are considered as meaningful to Hashem as the myriad of *mitzvos* of the earlier generations.'" (*Sefer Chassidim* 217 (945)

The Mezritcher Maggid once called in Reb Mendel Horodoker, Reb Pinchas Ba'al Hahafla'ah, and the Alter Rebbe, in order to ask them a complicated question in *nigleh*. After hearing the question, they departed from the *rebbe's* room to discuss the matter among themselves. Reb Zusha came over to them, inquiring what the question was that the *maggid* had asked, but Reb Mendel Horodoker told him that this was not his domain. A few minutes later, when Reb Levi Yitzchak of Berditchev came in, the *chassidim* told him the question, and Reb Zusha listened in with a keen ear. Reb Zusha then went to another side of the room and began crying, "*Ribono Shel Olam*! Zusha does not have a part in the *Torah*, it does not belong to him."

A while later, Reb Zusha approached the Ba'al Hatanya, for he was ashamed to tell the entire group, and he elucidated a possible explanation. To his amazement, the Alter Rebbe declared that this was *Torah* from *shamayim*. The Ba'al Hatanya went right to the *Maggid* with the explanation, in the name of Reb Zusha, and the *Maggid* accepted it.

This was always Reb Zusha's way, if he didn't know something in *Torah*, which was quite often as his mind wasn't as deep as that of his comrades, he would simply pray and cry with bitter tears. Hashem in His mercy would answer, and Reb Zusha was able to hold his own in *Torah*. For some scholars, the *Torah* comes a bit easier, while others must not only work hard but also must pray each time to understand the *p'shat*. But either way, the *Talmud* says that if a scholar tells you that the *Torah* came to him easily, don't believe him. For the *Torah* is only acquired by one who is willing to give up his life for it. (My Book, *A Journey into Holiness*, p.139)

And He took him outside, and said, "Gaze, now, toward the Heavens and count the stars, if you able to count them." And He said to him, "So shall your offspring be!" (*Genesis* 15:5)

Rabbi Meir Shapiro offered a beautiful explanation for the comparison between Abraham's descendants, the Jewish people, and the counting of the stars. When Hashem took Abraham outside to count all the stars in the sky, Abraham actually commenced counting them. Though he knew at the outset that the task was impossible, it did not obstruct him from making the attempt. Why? Because he understood that the feasibility, or lack thereof, of any endeavor is not the determining factor in its successful completion.

A Jew must make the effort, even though the deed in front of him seems to be unsurmountable. So long as there is a fervent desire and determination to accomplish the task at hand, he will ultimately succeed in achieving the impossible, regardless of his ability or strength.

"So shall your offspring be!" Hashem was telling Abraham that his descendants will emulate him and will continue to serve G-d and do the correct thing, even under the most challenging circumstances. The Jewish people will never allow lack of ability to stand in their way, and they will achieve the impossible and indeed we have.

Many times, people tell me of their struggles in *Torah* learning. They said that they "can't" learn. It's just too hard for them and that there is no reason for them to even try. The *Torah* is not in Heaven. It is there for your taking, for everyone no matter how difficult it might be for them to concentrate and learn. There is always a road and pathway that will open for them, should they make a legitimate effort to study. I don't think *Torah* has ever been this easy to attain should one desire it. There are endless amounts of translated books, audio files, video files and ways to attain *Torah* knowledge. The harder the challenge, the greater the reward.

# *Feeling the Realness of the Talmud*

When learning, you can make yourself into a chariot for the
*Shechinah*. Rabbi Yaakov Abuchatzeira taught, "The essential purpose of
*Torah*, Devine worship and the *mitzvos* is to rectify the *Shechinah*." (*Ma'aglei
Tzedek* 90)

Rabbi Elimelech of Lizensk once said that while learning *Torah*
one should think again and again, "I am making myself a chariot for the
*Shechinah*"…even a thousand times a day. He said that the body is much
sanctified by this, and that when one becomes accustomed to it, the mind
is purified and thoughts of sin disappear, and one is able to pray with holy
thoughts." (*Darkei Tzedek*, p. 5, #26)

To a businessman who was having a challenging time earning a
profit, the Imrei Emes advised, "Learn *Gemarah* every morning, even for a
quarter of an hour. Just the mere mention of the names of the *Tannaim*
and *Amoraim* is a *zechus* that can help you."

Rabbi Kalonymus Kalman Shapira taught, "When you learn
*Tanach,* try to identify with all the happenings as if you yourself were there
at the time. Go with Avraham and Yitzchok to the binding of Yitzchok
on the altar; involve yourself in the anguish and fear of Yaakov when he
prayed to Hashem to save him from the wrath of his brother Esav. And,
so too, when you learn *Midrash*, for there are many *midrashim* on verses
from the *Tanach* that reveal many additional things about the events."
(*Hachsharat ha-Abrechim*, chap. 7, p.33)

Rabbi Yaakov Abuchatzeira taught, "When one who has studied
*Torah lishmah* passes on to the next world, his lips continue to form words
in the grave whenever somebody in this world repeats a saying or words
of *Torah* in his name, as is written, 'Who causes the lips of the sleepers to
move.' (*Shir Hashirim* 7:10) You should realize that even after the body has
disintegrated to dust, when such a moment arises, all of his bones re-
gather and form a whole body. Then his lips move, and this is a very great
miracle." (Petuchei Chotem – *Bereishis*)

When a *Chassidic* master learns a *blat* of *Gemarah*, he connects
himself to the *Tannaim* in the *daf* of the *Talmud* to such an extent that it is
as if they are standing there with him, teaching him the page. Even though

this teaching is actually brought down in the *Talmud* itself, (*Talmud Yevamos* 97a) it is somewhat ignored. People think it is just a spiritual analogy to show that the *Talmud* has life to it. However, to a *chassid*, this is not just a simple teaching. It is something he yearns to experience himself during his *Talmud* study. The holy *Chassidic* masters, as well as Baba Sali and others did indeed imagine that the *Talmud* was being taught to them by the Talmudists themselves. That is why they were given the special power to bless those who came to them and that sometimes miracles were wrought through them. As it says, "And the *tzaddik* decrees and G-d fulfills." (*Moed Katan* 16b) (My Book, *The True Intentions of the Baal Shem Tov*, p. 76)

Reb Dovid of Lelov once happened upon his son, Reb Moshe, in the *beis midrash* pondering a *blat* of *gemarah,* on a purely intellectual level. To make his point, he went over to him and closed the *gemarah.* "This is not how one learns," his father said.

How then does one learn?

Another tale might shed some more light to this. It was the habit of Reb Dovid to test his grandson, Reb Yosef Hirsh, every *Shabbos*. One time, Reb Dovid being dissatisfied with his grandson's learning asked him to try again. His grandson Reb Yosef reviewed the material a second time, but Reb Dovid was still not pleased.

Reb Yosef Hirsh began to shed tears. "If I don't know it by now, I will never know it!"

"You understand the material fine," explained Reb Dovid, "But you lack something else. When you learn the *Gemarah*, and mention the name of the sage, it's not enough to know what he said. You must see him standing in front of you as if he were still alive." (My Book, *A Journey into Holiness*, p. 69)

Rabbi Simcha Bunim of Peshischa once related this story to his *talmidim*: Once he came to his *rebbe* The Holy Jew, of blessed memory. His rebbe was surprised to see how terribly depressed he appeared. He asked him what had happened and the reason for his sadness. Rabbi Simcha Bunim told him that someone had just humiliated him in the worst way, so that he was deeply hurt inside. His *rebbe* was surprised, and asked who would dare to do this, but Rabbi Simcha Bunim wouldn't tell him. He urged him to tell because he wanted to punish whomever it was. When he continued in his refusal, the *rebbe* became angry. He inquired of Rabbi Simcha what he answered back after he was humiliated. He told him that he kissed the one who did it, on the mouth. At this the rebbe was astonished and finally ordered him, as his rebbe, to tell him who it was.

'So, having no choice, I was forced to tell him. I said to him that in

232

the *Jerusalem Talmud* (*Shabbos, perek* 1, *halacha* 32) it says that when you are learning you should consider the master of the tradition as if he were standing before you. That was my thought while I was studying the book of character development, *Shevas Mussar*. So, the holy author was shaming and humiliating me greatly, until I saw that I hadn't even begun to serve Hashem, and that I hadn't the slightest bit of the fear of Hashem or holy shame or any one of the many virtues that a son of Avraham, Yitzchak, or Yaakov should have. When I saw that what he said was all true I was overcome with shame and almost fainted. But afterwards, I took the holy book in my hands, kissed it with all my heart, and then placed it back on the bookcase along with all the other books."

When the Holy Jew heard his disciple "explain" what had happened to him he became very happy and joyful at his wisdom. [This truly is how a *chassid* should learn *Torah*.] (*Simchas Yisrael* p. 27, #65) (My Book, *Pathways of the Righteous* p. 64)

Rabbi Yaakov Abuchatzeira taught, "Truly, if *Torah* study is learned *lishmah* with no ulterior motive, Hashem helps those who study it and shows them the true way to understand it so that they should not fail. The righteous souls of the *Tannaim* and *Amoraim* come to aid those who study their words *lishmah*. As we have seen, the souls of the righteous used to come to Rabbi Shimon Bar Yochai and his companions of blessed memory. They would reveal the secrets of the *Torah* to them, as we have observed that the Arizal would accomplish things through *yichudim*. (See my book, *Chassidus Kabbalah and Meditation*) In their generations, they merited these things because of their holiness and piety. (*Petuchei Chotem – Vayeitze*)

I wrote to some followers for encouragement:

"A page of *Talmud* is alive, in it contains all elements, fire, water, air and earth. Inside it is debates, peace, holiness, the *Tanach*, the *Mishnah*, stories and all wisdom. If a person places their mind and heart into the *Talmud*, instead of experiencing many difficult trials in life, they instead pass these tests through the study of *Talmud* alone. Since I started learning at least four hours of *Talmud* a day, I feel much less suffering in my life, days and weeks feel more complete. I suffer in comprehending a *sugya* instead of being out and about on the streets of the world being tested. I found a home. A place to run too when all else is chaos. My holy friends, you too can return home and begin your *Talmud* study today."

I have to tell you; the quality of my life has improved vastly since I increased my learning to seven *blat* a day. I really feel like the target of seven *blat* daily is the key to unraveling the hidden parts of your *neshamah*.

Even though it sounds like a large feat, it is certainly attainable in time. As I mentioned, once you learn a significant amount of *Gemarah* daily, the problems in your life don't affect you as much anymore. The *Torah* is your vitality, your food, your bread, your wine, your oil and your best friend.

It is a great *mitzvah* to sharpen one's mind. (*Likutey Moharan* 1:62) There is no greater exercise for the mind and soul then to study the holy *Talmud*. There is nothing you can't accomplish with the help of Hashem. May Hashem bless you and open your personal path to finishing *Shas*. *Amen*.

I know what I want for my next birthday present, do you? I want *Shas*! "All of Rav Meir Shapiro's thoughts and deeds were dedicated to expanding *limud haTorah*. One year, one of the *bachurim* approached Reb Meir and asked him what present he would like to receive on his birthday, the 7th of Adar," shared Reb Shmuel HaLevi Wosner.

"'I would like the entire *Shas*,' said Reb Meir. 'On the seventh of Adar, I would like each of the *bachurim* to learn several pages of *Gemarah* so that, together, all 250 boys will complete the entire *Shas* in one day.'

"On that day," continued Rav Wosner, "the walls of the *yeshivah* reverberated with the sound of *Torah*, while the boys remained bent over their *shtenders* the entire day. Reb Meir sat in his usual place at the front of the *beis midrash*. His eyes shone and it was obvious that his heart was full of true *nachas*.

"We finished the entire *Shas* with the approach of nightfall. The intensity of our joy was beyond description.

"One of the *bachurim*," recalled Rav Wosner, "was an incredible *illuy*. On that day, he learned one-hundred-and-seventy-six pages of *Gemarah*. His eyes never left the open *Gemarah*.

"From the greatness of the Reb Meir's students," concluded Rav Wosner, "it is possible to gain an understanding of his greatness."

# *Ahavas Yisrael*

I was asked by a *rav* to write my next book about *ahavas Yisrael*. However, if I write too much about this concept, I start to cry, as I don't understand why such an important concept is overlooked in *yeshivos* and *cheders*. For now, instead of devoting an entire book to this idea, I will try *bli neder* to always write about the concept in every book, just a little. As it says, "water wears away stone." (*Iyov* 14:19) The more we talk about the importance of this *mitzvah*, the better chance it will enter our hearts to wrought change. Because ultimately, it is through loving our fellow that will bring the final redemption.

Rabbi Yosel Frumkin writes, "Whenever I came across anyone whom I had an inclination to dislike, I would utter many blessings for his welfare, so as to turn my heart to love him and to desire his good." (*Imrei Kodesh*, #9, p.23)

Rabbi Simcha Zissel Ziv said, "In order to experience the suffering of others you should create mental images. When someone experiences suffering and pain, imagine a picture in your mind as if that were happening to you. Whatever you would desire other people to do for you in such situations, you should do for others. This is how to internalize the trait of sharing the burden of others." (*Chachmah U'mussar*, Vol. 1, p.2)

"Honor every person, whether poor or rich, and let your thought be that you are honoring them because they are created in the image of Hashem, and when you honor them you are honoring the Craftsman Who made them." (*Derech Chayim*, 6-48)

"A person might refrain from giving charity because he feels that he is losing money. Instead of considering it as a loss, however, he should consider charity as a loan and Hashem will return to him what he has given away." (*Ohr HaChayim* to *Devarim* 15:8)

Should it be difficult for you to love your fellow, then you must work on this and pray to Hashem for help. "If your heart is hard as iron when it comes to the poor, arise and call out to the L-rd your G-d. Pray that the King of Mercy give you a soft heart, a Jewish heart that hears the cry of the lowly and yearns to do kindness to the poor." (*Yesod Yosef*, p.59)

Practice doing lovingkindness until it becomes second nature to you. People continuously came to the Chazon Ish for advice on all sorts of problems. Two days before he passed away, his relatives wanted to stop people from disturbing him because he was extremely weak. The Chazon Ish, however, refused, saying, "How is it possible not to allow them to come in? They come with broken hearts." (*Rabosainu*, p.122)

The Chazon Ish's gives us wonderful advice on how to acquire the attribute of feeling another's suffering:

"For someone to be able to feel the suffering of others he must first train himself to do all that he can to help them and to save them from suffering. These activities will affect the emotions. Also, he should pray for the welfare of others even if at first he does not actually feel their anguish." (*Kovetz Igros Chazon Ish*, vol. 1, 123)

We can learn a lot from our holy mother Rivka on how to do *chesed*. Women seem to be keener and more nurturing to the needs of others, where as a man might naturally refrain from troubling himself for others.

"And it came to pass, before he [Eliezer] had finished speaking [to Hashem, requesting help in finding a wife for Yitzchak], that Rivka appeared with her pitcher upon her shoulder." (*Bereshis* 24:15)

Rabbi Yonasan Eybescheutz clarifies that the *Torah* emphasizes the fact that Rivka indeed carried her water pitcher upon her shoulder. Most people hide their pitchers to avoid the bother of lending them out. Rivka, however, publicized the fact that she had a pitcher so that others might ask to borrow it. (Tiferes Yonasan, on this verse)

"And the servant [Eliezer] ran to meet her [Rivka], and said, 'Give me a little water from your pitcher to drink.'" (*Bereshis* 24:17)

The *Midrash* cited by Rashi states that Eliezer ran because he saw the water from the well miraculously rise to meet Rivkah. Although Eliezer beheld this event, he did not consider it sufficient evidence to prove that she was worthy to be Yitzchak's wife. An assessment of her eagerness to do *chesed* was still necessary. From here we understand that even if a person is worthy of having miracles performed on his behalf, he is not deemed truly worthy unless he performs acts of *chesed*. (Rabbi Yosef Dov Soloveitchik, *Rosh HaYeshivah* of Brisk)

Rabbi Simcha Zissel Ziv explained, "We are obligated to emulate the ways of Hashem. We must bestow kindness upon others, just as He bestows kindness upon the entire world. If a person lacks the desire to emulate Hashem, it shows an absence of appreciation of Hashem's Divine Providence. For if a person is sincerely aware of Hashem's goodness to him, he too will bestow kindness upon others. Therefore, the failure to perform acts of *chesed* is not merely one specific fault; it implies a denial of

Hashem." (*Chachmah U'mussar*, vol. 1, p.32)

A person who fulfills this commandment [of *ahavas Yisrael*] will do all he can to give others pleasure. As the Vilna Goan wrote: "A great part of the *Torah* is concerned with a person's bringing happiness to others." (*Igeres HaGra*)

The sons of Rabbi Avraham Grodzinski told that their father worked for two years on acquiring a pleasant facial expression. Having then accomplished this feat, it became so ingrained in his character that even during the darkest and gloomiest days of the Second World War, when he and his family were incarcerated in the ghetto of Slobodka and their lives were in constant danger, his outward expression was always cheerful. (*Toras Avraham*, p.11)

The Baal Shem Tov used to say, "'Love your fellow man as yourself.' You know that you have many faults, nevertheless, you still love yourself. That is how you should feel toward your friend. Despite his faults, love him." (*Likkutai Avraham*, p. 221)

Rabbi Moshe Leib of Sassov disclosed to his followers: "I learned what true love is from a conversation I overheard between two drunk peasants. One asked the other, 'Tell me, friend, do you love me or not?'

The other responded, 'I love you very much.'

'Then tell me what I am lacking,' countered the first.

'How can I know what you are lacking?' asked the second.

'If you can't feel what I am lacking, how can you say that you love me?' remonstrated the first.

"That," exclaimed the Sassover, "is true love; to realize what others are lacking and to feel their suffering." (*Eser Tzichtzachus*, p. 52)

You know what was so beautiful about Reb Moshe Feinstein? If he noticed someone missing from his congregation for a few days, he would personally call them on the phone to make sure they were okay. Oh, what I would do to find such a *rav* today.

I was handed the flame to light the bon fire in honor of Rebbe Shimon Bar Yochai. I instead took the hands of those around me, each were *roshei hayeshivos* of *mechinas* in *Yerushalayim*, and I told them, "Together each Jew lights the flame of one another," and we then all three lit the fire together holding onto the stick as one... Then afterwards, I went to them both and told them, "Do you realize how deep it was, what I told you?" So deep my friends, so deep!

I ask you, please make more effort to befriend other Jews and to give a hearty shalom to your fellow. You don't realize how many people are thirsting for compassion and friendship. It says in the *Talmud* relating to Iyov, "It's either a good friend, or death..." (*Tannis* 23a) The beauty of the human experience manifests itself finest within the framework of human relationships. As it says, "And G-d said it is not good for man to be alone...." (*Bereshis* 2:18)

It says in tractate *Bava Basra* (p.16b), "Iyov and his three friends had crowns upon which their faces were engraved. If any of them fell into trouble or sorrow the image of that person's face would sadden on all of their crowns. This was a signal that they should come to his help."

Rabbi A. Leib Scheinbaum writes, "The Ben Yehoyadah explains that there are two types of friends. One is present to share in the good times: when everything is going smooth; life is well; the sun is shining in one's face. When the wheel of fortune' appears to be turning to what seems not such good times, this friend's phone does not work. He disappears, because he is only a 'good times' friend. Such a friend is obviously not much of a friend. Indeed, with friends like that, one does not need enemies.

"The other type of friend is one who is present in both good times and bad. He never forsakes his friend. When the going gets rough, he is there. When trouble looms on the horizon, he is present. He is also there for the good times - because he is always present. This is a true friend.

"A higher level of friendship, however, was evinced by Iyov's friends - one which I feel defines true friendship. This is a friend who is always present for the good and also for the bad. As soon as he hears that his friend is in peril, that he is afflicted, that things are not as they should be, he immediately drops his personal plans and joins his friend. He is a 'reactor,' reacting to the news when he is informed. While his actions are certainly laudatory, there is yet a higher - more desirable - more definitive form of friendship. I refer to he who is constantly looking out for his friend, who asks and seeks, questions and contemplates, worries and cares, wondering, 'Does my friend need me? Is he doing well? Could I be doing something to help? Perhaps he is covering up a problem?' This is a loyal friend. He does not wait for that phone call in the middle of the night, 'Help!' He sits by the phone making calls, trying to find out whether everything is truly all right or whether something is brewing, something which he could circumvent."

One issue with having too many friends is that they become a distraction from learning *Torah*. The biggest disadvantage is trying to be "good" friends with all of them. That means communicating with them often and making sure that their "needs" are being met when it comes to your friendship. There is a saying, "A friend of everybody is a friend of none." I have found that friendships with people that are very popular just leaves me disappointed in the end. Everyone seems to chase them because they want something in return, the person doesn't even realize this, and he overlooks his real, loyal friends, pushing them aside for all those that just give him attention.

It's also very easy to get used by people when you give completely of yourself to others. They might even get you to spend money needlessly on yourself or on them due to peer pressure. The moment you stop doing what they please, they no longer wish to be your friend. When I started having less friends, I found that my monthly bills actually decreased significantly. I actually had more time to accomplish things as well. Remember, friendship is about helping another person come closer to Hashem and helping them through their troubles. It isn't about wasting valuable time together.

Thereby, sometimes we have to realize that Hashem is our best friend and our closest ally. Nobody will ever love us unconditionally as much as our Creator. So, what has he given us to keep us company in all situations? He has given us the *Torah*! A *Torah* which nourishes our every thirst and need. If you have the *Torah*, you really don't need anything else.

"Rabbi Elazar said, what is the meaning of the verse (*Proverbs* 1:9), 'And they are as a necklace (the *Torah*) for your throat?' If a man behaves like the necklace, which hangs loosely on the throat, observing but not observed, his learning will endure; if not, his learning will not endure." (*Eruvin* 54a)

The Maharal explains, "The apparent explanation [of this *Gemarah*] is that man should make himself like the necklace which hangs loosely around but does not adhere to the throat; he should not be entrenched among the populace but should be in a position of observing without being observed. He should, in other words, observe fellow beings and not separate himself from them totally, to the extent that he would pay them no heed. At the same time, though, he should not be observed – he should not be joined with or intermingle among fellow beings. If he acts thusly his learning will endure, for when he relates to and equates with the intellective, he can attain the intellective *Torah*.

"Man's intellect, while it does adhere to him, does not do so to the extent that it is completely intermingled with the body. The scholar's relationship with fellow beings should be precisely the same: separated from fellow beings, but not completely separated. He should cultivate some connection with people but not permit himself to be on an overly familiar basis with them. If he does [permit himself to be overly familiar with other people], he resembles intellect entrenched in the material. If he is entrenched in the material, he cannot acquire the intellective *Torah*.

"When the scholar behaves in the manner just described, his learning endures. As we have said, the scholar's connection to fellow beings must correspond to the relationship between the intellect and the body; the scholar is as the intellect when measured against other people, who are [inclined to the] material; when in such a state [the scholar] is worthy of the *Torah*." (*Nesivos Olam, Nesiv HaTorah*, p.114-115)

A *chassid's* profession demanded that he spend much of his time traveling abroad. The Imrei Emes advised him, "Wherever you go, make sure to have good friends."

The *chassid* did not understand. "How can one have good friends when he doesn't stay at any given place for more than a few days."

"A *sefer* is a good friend," came the reply.

Please take a moment to ponder this as it is of vital importance. "After you master the ability to feel the pain of other people as if it were your own pain, the next phase is to feel the Hashem's pain, since the Creator has empathy for the suffering of mortals." (*Sanhedrin* 46a) (*Chachmah U'mussar*, Vol. 1, p.3)

"Not feeling compassion is considered a failure to emulate the Almighty's way. The *Torah* requires us to emulate His compassion and mercy. Therefore, failure to be compassionate is a severe fault. A person needs to utilize all of his inner resources to master this trait." (*Chachmah U'mussar*, Vol. 1, pp.302-3)

Once when Rabbi Zundel Salanter was riding in a wagon, the driver passed by an apple tree and was overcome by the desire to remove a few apples. Not knowing the identity of his passenger, the driver stated him, "You keep watch and see if you see anyone looking."

A few seconds later, Rav Zundel cried out, "Someone's looking!"

Alarmed, the wagon driver jumped onto his wagon and rode off. As he was driving away, he glanced back and did not see anyone.

"What's the idea of fooling me?" shouted the driver.

"My dear friend," responded Rav Zundel, "I wouldn't lie to you. G-d sees every action." (*Hatzaddik Rav Zundel*, p.134)

People don't realize how if someone asks you to aid them in doing something wrong, you become responsible like them for the sin. It is all too often that having the wrong friendships steer a person off the tract of *emes*. Not only this, but even if they realize that the friendship is unhealthy, it seems impossible to break it. Breaking free from a bad relationship is difficult at first but exhilarating at the end.

It may be that your kindness goes unnoticed by the physical world, but Hashem sees and hears all. The more you give unconditionally, the more He personally will return His kindness. Remember, He is always watching.

People are always angry at others for not fulfilling their desires when in fact, it is them who isn't doing enough. If a person were to give and give unconditionally, it is rare that the other person wouldn't reciprocate. If they don't, then maybe there is something wrong with them emotionally and it's not their fault because naturally, a good-hearted person would return kindness.

Rabbi Yisrael Salanter said, "When I first began learning *mussar* I became angry at the entire world, but not at myself. Afterward, I became angry at myself too. Finally, I became angry only at myself, and I judged the world *l'chaf zchus*". (*Ohr Hamussar*, vol. 1, p.55)

"As the Chozon Ish was walking toward his house on *Simchas Torah*, he met a convert to Judaism. The proselyte complained to him that people weren't befriending him, although the *Torah* obliges them to love a convert. The Chazon Ish told him that he would honor him with a song. Immediately, the Chazon Ish burst into song and danced before him in the street, not stopping until he saw that the convert was appeased." (*P'air Hador*, vol. 4, p.22)

I think we should make a campaign to have every *yeshivah bachur* smile each and every day. There are too many sad faces out there and its unhealthy to see. Positivity breaths further positivity.

"The *Talmud Kesubos* (111b) teaches that the verse, 'his teeth white with milk' can be deciphered (in the Hebrew) as "When one shows his teeth (in a smile) to his fellow man, it is worthier than giving him milk to drink." How mighty we would consider a man who gave drinks of milk to passerby daily. What a benefactor of mankind! A drink of milk offers essential nourishment and it turns into part of all that the recipient does thereafter. Yet this person does less than one who smiles at his fellow man. The smile pierces the recipient's mind and body and stimulates all the glands to produce their secretions in the most beneficial proportions. Every one of the thousands of intricate processes of physical function is optimally motivated." (Rabbi Avigdor Miller in *Sing, You Righteous*, p. 294)

The *Talmud Brachos* (17a) relates, "No one ever greeted Rabbi Yochanan ben Zakai first, not even a non-Jew in the marketplace."

"This statute is especially important if you meet someone who bears you hostility or is simply not on the best terms with you. Through greeting such a person pleasantly, you may be able to break down the barriers of misunderstanding and bitterness which separate you. There is nothing as potent as a smile in melting icy walls of hate." (*Ethics from Sinai*, vol. 2, pp. 141-2)

I began attempting to greet people first during business meets and appointments as advised by Rav Yochanan. In most cases when I greeted the person first, things always turned out the way I had hoped. During the conversation, I felt far more confident having initiated the first words of the dialog. I can't explain it, just try it yourself and you will see that it really works.

"If someone greets you, you are obligated to return the greeting. Failure to do so is tantamount to stealing." (*Brachos* 6b) That is how important it is to greet others and show respect. In most large cities, greeting a stranger on the street is awkward and not in the norm. I miss walking through the friendly small towns in American and Tzfat where everyone wished one another a hearty "good *Shabbos*".

"And Yaakov came in peace to the city of Shechem, which is in the land of Cannan, when he came from Padan Aram; and encamped before the city." (*Bereshis* 33:18)

The *Gemarah* (*Shabbos* 33b) explains that when Yaakov encamped by Shechem, he established something for the welfare of the city. Rav said that he minted coins. Shmuel said that he established markets, and Rabbi Yochanan said that he set up bathhouses for the residents of the area. The *Midrash* (*Bereshis Rabbah* 9:6) tells us that whenever we benefit from a place, we must show our gratitude by doing something for its welfare.

Reb Elya Meir once said, "Dovid HaMelech was the gentlest of souls. When he studied *Torah* and when he dealt with people, he was as refined and gracious as a human being can be."

Rabbi Yechezkail Levenstein told, "If you do not feel joy for the good fortune of another person, it is a sign of envy and you are considered a *ra ayin*." (*Ohr Yechezkail*, Vol 4, p. 74)

Rabbi Eliyahu Lopian explained, "Love is a concept that is often distorted. For example, a person will say that he loves fish. However, when we observe his behavior with fish, which he supposedly loves, what do we see? He cuts them up, fries or cooks them, and then swallows them. He doesn't really love fish, he loves himself."

"The *Torah* definition of love is feeling positive about somebody because you appreciate their virtues and positive character traits. When your love for someone is based totally on love for him and not on self-love, you will have a great deal patience. You will find it easy to wait for that person even for a long time, just as Yaakov did for Rochel." (see

*Bereshis* 29:20) (*Lev Eliyahu*, vol. 1, p. 254-5)

As a *bachur* in Yeshivas Mir, Rabbi Yehudah Zev Segal, was renowned for never speaking in matters unrelated to learning during *seder*. Therefore, it wasn't a surprise that during the last decade of his life one of his *Yomim Noraim* resolutions was not to spend a moment devoid of thinking in *Torah* and *mussar*. Yet in the last fifteen years of his life, he regularly learned with a telephone on his *shtender* so that he could answer immediately the calls that came from around the world. (*Torah Luminaries* p. 190)

Rabbi Yosef Hurwitz, the Alter of Nevardok, stated, "The behavior of the people to whom you are close will pull you just as powerfully as a magnet attracts metal. When you hear your friends being praised or condemned for some behavior, this will inevitably have some influence on you." (*Madreaigos Haadam*, p. 244)

So, if you truly want to perfect this important trait of *ahavas Yisrael*, then be around good-hearted people who do *chesed*. Ponder and begin thanking Hashem for all the kindness he bestows upon you each day. Learn to emulate the ways of Hashem which are all kindness. Don't forget that kindness starts at home, so be especially good to your spouse and children.

## *Neglecting One's Partner*

As we spoke about earlier, a person's family and spouse should feel like they are a part of the *Torah* study and not that it is a burden forced upon them.

Rabbi Naftoli Amsterdam remembered that soon after he was married, he was questioned by Rabbi Yisrael Salanter, "Rav Naftoli, do you do *chesed*?"

"My teacher," responded Rav Naftoli, "I don't have money to lend to others."

"I was not referring to *chesed* through money," Rabbi Salanter expressed to his disciple. "I meant doing *chesed* by helping your wife around the house. You must know that you didn't take a maid to serve you, but a wife, about whom the Sages say, "A man's wife is as himself." (*B'tuv Yerushalayim*, p. 392)

Not only is she brilliant in her wisdom and *daas* but her knowledge is just as relevant as her husbands. "She opens her mouth with wisdom, and the teaching of kindness is upon her tongue." (*Proverbs* 30:26) This holds true especially today, when the *Bais Yaakov* girls school system is so top notch when it comes to teaching girls *halacha* and *Torah*. Therefore, we should truly appreciate the *Torah* wisdom of our spouses.

Until his health was weakened, the Bluzhever Rebbe out of respect, prepared a cup of coffee for his wife each and every morning.

The following tale I can relate to, and I too am thankful for my wife's desire to live simply and without *gashmius*.

The Chofetz Chayim told, "It is to my wife's credit that I have been able to study *Torah* all my life and write *sefarim*. She was always happy with her lot and never pursued the enticements of this world. Thanks to her, I was always able to study amid tranquility."

You can tell from the following story how the wives of the sages have led their family on the path of righteousness:

When Rabbi Yisrael Zev Gustman was a newlywed of twenty-two, it was then that he succeeded his deceased father-in-law as a member of the *beis din* headed by Vilna's famed Rav, Rabbi Chaim Ozer Grodzensky.

Throughout the Second World War, Rabbi Gustman endured indescribable suffering. The Nazis murdered his infant son in front of his eyes. For five years, he, his wife and their young daughter hid from the Nazis in and around Vilna in the forests. Often, they subsisted themselves just on grasses from the fields and their surrounding moisture. In excess of one hundred times, Rabbi Gustman recited the *viduy* confession that is said when death seems imminent.

At the conclusion of the war, the Gustman's were among the very few Jews to return to Vilna. As they wandered through the remaining structures in the Jewish segment of the city, they came upon a room lined with *sefarim* which, for reasons unknown, the Nazis had not destroyed or confiscated.

Rabbi Gustman glanced over at his wife and daughter. They had not eaten the entire day. He told his wife that he would try to procure some food and commenced his way to the door. However, his wife stopped him.

"Are you serious?" she stated in wonderment. "It has been years since you have even seen a *sefer*, let alone studied from one! First learn, then find us some food."

People tend to only do *chesed* when their kindness can be seen. While this kindness might still be helpful, it's not completely pure. Even when nobody is watching, like a woman who cares for her household, one must still continuously give and give. If only a man understood and appreciated the kindness his wife does for him regularly. Most of a women's work is hidden yet "Her worth is far beyond that of rubies". (*Proverbs* 31:10)

Rabbi Shlomo Freifeld said, "Women are *Malchus*, royalty. They have special *ko'ach.*" He said you should always be sure that they have the spiritual sustenance they require. He told, "They are so self-sacrificing in their efforts to promote the *Torah* values of their families. Make sure that their needs are met."

Teachers complain about the lack of respect given to them by students but are they sensitive to the feelings of their students? A spouse complains that they aren't given enough *kavod,* but are they giving proper *kavod* and praise to their partner?

Rabbi Eliyahu Dessler stated, "When each person tries to pull the other one towards his own direction, there will be conflict. Without focusing on common goals, they will constantly quarrel. However, when people focus on their common goals, the differences between them will not cause difficulties, and they will have a peaceful relationship." (*Michtav Maieliyahu* vol, 4, p. 16)

When Rabbi Eliyahu Dushnitzer would walk up or down the steps of his *yeshivah* at evening, near the rooms where the students slept, he would remove his shoes. He would say, "I might awaken one of the students with the noise of my steps, and that would be stealing sleep." (*Nachalas Eliyahu*, p.23)

Respecting your wife, children and students is of vital importance. As a scholar you must set the example for those who are around you. It may not happen at first but slowly, you will transform everyone around you for the good. Even if they don't appreciate you, keep giving as then you will emulate the Holy One blessed be He, Whom gives unconditionally and receives little in return, yet Hashem continues to give and provide, nevertheless.

# Mussar Seder

The *Mishnah Berurah* (1:12) quotes the *poskim* as saying, "A person must have a set time when he learns *Mussar sefarim* every day; even if he only learns for a small amount of time."

The *pasuk* says (*Devarim* 4:9), "Guard yourself, lest you forget Hashem your G-d." This is why one must have a permanent *mussar seder* every day. It is the only way a person will not forget Hashem, because they will always be thinking of how to improve themselves. The *sefer Maseh Rav* writes in the name of the Gra, "One must learn *mussar* multiple times a day." (*Hilchos Tefilah*, letter *Samech*)

Rav Gershon Edelstein writes, "It is an important thing to be a very truthful person. The *Gemarah* in *Sanhedrin* (97a) relates that because the people of Kushta were very truthful people, the Angel of Death was unable to kill them. I believe I have seen in a certain *sefer* that if a person is a very truthful person, he cannot be deceived by false statements. Since truth is ingrained in him, he can immediately tell when someone is telling him something that is foreign to his nature." (*Sichos* 5775, #132)

Rabbi Eliyahu Dessler said, "It is very important to seek advice on matters from a *Torah* teacher who knows you well. Also, pray to the Almighty to lead you along the path of truth." (*Michtav MaiEliyahu* vol. 4, p.11)

Each of us has our own personality qualities to improve and balance. "One man is wrathful and always angry, and another even-tempered and never angry. Or, if he is, it only very negligible over a period of many years. One man is exceedingly proud, and another exceedingly humble. One man is lustful, his lust never being sated, and another exceedingly pure hearted not desiring even the few things that the body needs... One man afflicts himself with hunger and goes begging..., and another is wantonly extravagant with his money. And, along the same lines, the other traits are found, such as cheerfulness and depression, stinginess and generosity, cruelty and mercy, cowardliness and courage, and the like." (*Orchos Tzaddikim*)

Much of our personality can be understood from the hidden secrets of the letters of our names and the four elements which a person is comprised of, water, air, earth and fire. Above, in their root, the elements correspond to the four letters of Hashem's name, *YKVK*. But below (in our world), they are a mixture of both good and bad. Rebbe Nachman explains the *pasuk*, "'*Mashpil resha'im ah'dey eretz* - He casts the wicked down to the ground.' (*Tehillim* 147:6) The initial letters correspond to the initial letters of the four elements: *Esh, Ruach, Mayim,* and *Afar* (fire, air, water, and earth). They encompass all qualities and traits. A person has to completely purify these traits, so that none of the bad found in any trait of the four elements has any hold on him." (*Likutey Maharan* 8) This is the basic *tikkun* of man, to understand his inborn nature and to be balanced. That which is most challenging for him is usually the most important aspect to fix. The more a person perfects his character, the greater vessel he becomes for light and holiness. Many people cast aside their biggest fears and difficulties, but we learn from a person's name that everyone has inborn challenges to overcome. Each element also has great blessings and powers that can be used for good. (My Book, *Chassidus Kabbalah & Meditation* p. 67)

However, the only way to fix the elements and one's nature is to learn *mussar* and to pray for Hashem to open your heart. There is a reason why the older generations would treat one another kindlier, *mussar* learning was mandatory. We need to study more *mussar* in our *yeshivos* and *chedarim* today.

"All virtues and duties are dependent on humility." (*Duties of the Heart*) If a person isn't humble, they can't clearly see their nature to fix their wrongs.

"One hour of diligent, inspired *Torah* is better than many hours of study amid laziness." (Chazon Ish)

Often you hear the excuse that someone doesn't have time for a *seder* in *mussar*. However, let me give you an example of how beneficial it is to study *mussar*. The more *mussar* you learn, the more *Torah* you will desire to study. If you are learning *Torah* two hours a day with thirty minutes of *mussar* and you increased the *mussar* learning to one hour, you would then force yourself to learn four hours a day of *Torah*. Two hours of *mussar* a day, then you would find time to learn eight hours a day, etc... Without regular *mussar* study, you rise from level to level in *madrega*, you might gain wisdom, but you won't go up and up like your *neshamah* could if you would study *mussar*.

Rav Avigdor Miller taught, "How much time should you allot in your spare time also depends on who you are. But this I can tell you. That if you invest time in *mussar*, you're investing in your future. You're not giving away time, you're gaining greatness!" (Tape 403)

You will find that most *yeshivos* don't study a lot of *mussar* each day, only a *bisala*, little bit. You will find that much of what we have spoken about in this book isn't practiced. *Today*, everything is about shortcuts to come as quickly as possible to the level of a "paper *rabbi*". "In a place where there are no men strive to be a man." (*Avos* 2:6)

As a young man, Rabbi Yehuda Zev Segal thought to himself, "The Chofetz Chayim was the *gadol* and *tzaddik* of the previous generation. If he devoted himself to the cause of *shemiras halashon*, I too must work on this *midah*." He spread across his *yeshivah* the importance of learning the Chofetz Chayim, handing out a daily *luach* to encourage the study of proper speech to *bachurim*. So strong did he feel about this that he requested to be buried with a *luach* for *shemiras halashon* in his hand. He said, "This is my passport for *Ohlom Habah*."

Rabbi Dovid Lifshitz had tremendous *hasmada* in learning as a *bachur* in Grodna and the Mir. Even as he aged, he would never lie down during the day. Once when he was sick and was forced to rest, he told the *rebbetzin* not to say that he was in bed should anyone come to ask for him... "*Es iz a bizayon*. It's something to be ashamed of."

The *rav* would tell over the old days in the Mir. After davening, the *bachurim* would eat a rather quick *seuda*, only to return rapidly to the *beis midrash*. There they would remain studying until the early hours of the morning. In the middle of the night, should they feel hungry, they would take a break and eat a piece of kugel. This was how the *bachurim* developed into the next *Gedolei Torah*.

Rabbi Dovid Lifshitz once spoke and told about the *pasuk*, "the four *amos* of *halacha*", "A *ben Torah* never leaves the *yeshivah*. If he does, it is a sign that he never was in the *yeshivah*. For wherever he goes, his four *amos* should take possession — should be *mekadesh* — that which surrounds him and transform it into a *yeshivah*."

The Skolye Rebbe once turned to his companion and asked, "What are you thinking about right now?"

"Nothing in particular," came the response. The *rebbe* responded, "A Jew's thoughts must always have meaning."

During a conversation with an American *Torah* student, Rabbi Yaakov Kamenetzky spoke of his daily schedule as a student in Yeshivah Knesses Yisrael of Slobodka:

His studies would begin at five o'clock in the morning and conclude at eleven-thirty in the evening. Except for *davening* and meals, the only break in the *yeshivah's* daily schedule was a two-hour rest period in the afternoon. Rabbi Yaakov and his study partner utilized this rest time to pursue their regular studies in greater depth.

Rabbi Yaakov concluded, "This was my schedule. However, Rabbi Aharon Kotler's schedule was different. In all our years together in Slobodka, Rav Aharon was always learning in *beis midrash* when I entered in the morning [he was there] and [he was] still by his *Gemarah* when I left at night."

The Chasam Sofer once remarked that he rose above his peers because he always utilized those minutes which others allowed to go to waste.

Late one night, Reb Yisroel Salanter passed by a shoemaker's home. The shoemaker was sitting and doing his work by the flickering light of a candle that was about to go out.

"Why are you still working?" Reb Yisroel questioned him "The hour is late. Besides, your candle will soon go out, and you won't be able to finish."

"That's no problem," answered the shoemaker. "As long as the candle is burning, it is still possible to work and to repair."

Reb Yisroel was deeply impressed by these words, for if someone has to work for their physical needs as long as the candle is lit, *kal vachomer*, how much more so should someone work to serve Hashem and work on their spiritual improvement. Because, as long as the *neshamah*, "Hashem's candle" is still inside them, i.e. they are still alive, there is much they can do.

Rabbi Mordechai Gifter voyaged in his youth from America to Lithuania to learn *Torah* at Telshe Yeshivah. One time, on the first day of *Shavuos*, he and some friends set off for a walk after the daytime meal. On their way, they encountered one of the local residents, a scholarly layman, walking briskly in the direction of the *beis midrash*. One of the *bachurim* called out jokingly, "What is your hurry, *reb*? Aren't you still satiated after an entire night of study?"

The man paused for a moment and responded, "Have you ever heard a drunk say that he has had enough to drink?" Then he continued briskly on this way.

Rabbi Chayim Mordechai Katz advised, "Being organized will help prevent you from forgetting to do important tasks. Your being organized will also save you time as well.

"There is yet another important reason though. When you are organized and your mind is open, you will be able to think clearer. Lack of organization causes confusion. If you are disorganized, you will lack inner peace, even in the midst of your studies. It is therefore crucial to have inner peace when studying *Torah*, for only then will the Torah that you study become part of your very being." (*Beair Mechokaik* Ch. 7, p.153)

The Chofetz Chaim gave a nice *mashal* to explain what life really is: He explains that life is like a man who gives this poor person a huge loan. The person can do so, so much with it! The possibilities are almost endless, so to speak!

However, if the person merely took the money and put it away in a drawer, would the rich man not be very upset? He gave the poor person so much money, and it could have been used for much good, but the poor person just put it away into a drawer and didn't use it.

This, the Chofetz Chaim explains, is what happens with us [sometimes]. Hashem gives us a *neshamah*, such a wonderful thing that can used for so much good! But if we, *chas-v-shalom* don't use it correctly, and "put it away in a drawer" so to speak, Hashem will surely not be happy with this. Not using or utilizing this precious, precious gift, *chas-v-shalom*?! So much can be done with it! Do we even realize and properly appreciate how much potential Hashem has given us all?

Rabbi Yosef Hurwitz, the Alter of Nevardok, recommended, "The *Torah* and a person's life should be one and the same. When someone studies *Torah* the way it is meant to be studied, all of his deeds and actions will be concurring to the principles and values of the *Torah*. His actual biography will be outlined in the *Torah*. When someone lives according to the *Torah*, he himself is a living *Torah*. He applies its values in his daily living, and he develops his personality traits in accordance with the requirements of the *Torah*. It is not sufficient for a person to study *Torah* just for intellectual stimulation. Upon reaching the proper level, there will be no contradiction between the way he lives his life and the elevated requirements of the *Torah*." (*Madraigos Haadam, Birur Hamidos*)

It says in the *Gemarah*, "*Ashrei mi sheba lekan v'talmudo beyado* — fortunate is he who comes here with his learning in his hand because by the time *beis din* is finished with him, he is lucky to have left... *talmudo beyado* — the bit he holds in his hand." (*Kesubos* 77b)

At sixteen, the Machnovka Rebbe knew the entire *Shulchan Aruch* by heart, but rarely would he divulge this to others except when absolutely necessary.

Throughout his entire life he kept the same precise schedule of *avodas* Hashem. This included about eighteen hours of *Torah* study each day. He even appeared at the *shul* at the same particular minute every single day. It was told that even when he was in Siberia he never changed from this schedule. In ten years while there, he didn't even miss one day of immersing in the freezing *mikvah* waters.

When he first moved to *Eretz Yisrael*, the *rebbe* went through *Shas* eight times in four years. Upon selling his apartment, he told the buyer not to convert the study into a bedroom, since *Shas* was learned there so many times.

Rav Jose one day went for a walk with Rav Aha bar Yaakov. Neither spoke, but whereas Rav Aha meditated on spiritual matters, Rav Jose's mind was occupied with worldly things. As they were thus proceeding, Rav Yose suddenly beheld a wild beast running after him. He said to Rav Aha: "Do you not see the beast that's running after me?"

"No," replied Rav Aha, "I see nothing." Rav Yose ran, pursued by the beast. He fell, and blood gushed from his nose. Then he heard a voice say: "You only have I known, etc." Musing on these words, he said: "If I have been punished because my mind was but for one moment separated from the *Torah*, what must await him who is forever apart from her! It is written, "Who led thee through that great and terrible wilderness, wherein were fiery serpents and scorpions." (*Devarim* 8:15) Why fiery serpents? To punish Israel should she separate herself from the Tree of Life, which is the *Torah*. Hashem punishes the students of the *Torah* in order that they may not be separated from the Tree of Life even for a single moment. (*Zohar* III, 17b)

The Kotzer Rebbe addressed the following verse:

"Fear not, for you shall not be ashamed..." (*Yeshayahu* 54:4)

The verse continues, "... and be not embarrassed, for you shall not be put to shame..." [lit. you shall not be made to dig into the ground].

Why do you have no fear? Asked the Kotzker Rebbe. Because you have no shame. And why do you have no shame? Because you don't devote time to introspection. (...*And Nothing but the Truth*, p. 21)

"Thou shalt not steal." (*Shemos* 20:13)

When Reb Yechiel Meir of Gostinin returned home from Kotzk after the *Shavuos* holiday, his father-in-law asked him, sarcastically, "Did they receive the *Torah* differently in Kotzk?"

"Most certainly," he answered. "Here's a case in point: How do you interpret 'Thou shalt not steal?'"

"One is forbidden to steal anything from someone else," answered his father-in-law.

"By us in Kotzk," and Reb Yechiel Meir, "it is interpreted to mean: 'You shall not steal from yourself; you shall not lie to yourself; you shall not be a thief.'" (...*And Nothing but the Truth*, p. 51)

You can learn all the books of *mussar* but if you still lie to yourself and don't actually practice what you learn, the *Torah* just goes in one ear and out the other, baring no inherent change. One way to fix this is to *daven* about the *mussar* that you learned, that you should actualize it, so that it's no longer just an intellectual exercise but something that you will put into practice.

In this book, we started the first chapter talking about the importance of *derech eretz* and we ended on the note of learning and practicing *mussar*. This is because all the learning of *Torah* must be put into action and self-improvement. The question now remains, are you willing to toil and work hard in order to acquire the *Torah*? We quoted the greatest of sages who emphasized the proper order of learning. We included heartfelt pleas from *tzaddikim* who were far loftier than us, to follow the guidance laid out by the sages of old. You now have all the tools and knowledge you need in order to complete all the important *Torah* works, including the *Talmud Shas*. You have been given a complete *derech* on how to serve Hashem *lishmah* and how to follow the *Ratzon* Hashem. Now that the proper pathway has been opened for you, now the ball is in your court… Let the hard work and toil begin!

# *Introduction to the Talmud*

Rabbi Shmuel Ha-Nagid records for the beginner's path to *Talmud* and for advanced students to brush up on their basic knowledge. I have added my own small commentary to this (which is italicized and written following Rabbi Ha-Nagid's writings):

1. The *Talmud* is divided into two parts: (a) the *Mishnah*; and (b) the commentary of the *Mishnah* (*Gemarah*).
2. The *Mishnah* is what is called the "Oral Law". It contains the essential *Torah* transmitted orally from Moshe Rabbeinu to the time of Rabbi Yehudah the Holy, also known as Rabbi Yehudah the Prince [ca. 120-220 C.E], who committed it to writing to ensure its long-term survival in face of the danger that it might be forgotten and lost. [The *Mishnah* also includes much rabbinic legislation promulgated by the *rabbis* to safeguard the *Torah*, in the form of סִייגִים גְזֵירוֹת וּתקָנוֹת "fences", decrees and ordinances.]

*Without both the Written and Oral Torah, it is impossible to fully understand traditional Jewish teaching or thought. The Written Torah mentions each of the commandments, or mitzvos, only in passing or by allusion. The Oral Law fills in the gaps.*

*Here is an example of a mitzvah: "And you shall tie them as a sign on your arm and for (Totafos) between your eyes." (Devarim 6:8) This is the source for the mitzvah of tefillin), but it doesn't disclose that much. From this alone, we would never know how to perform this mitzvah. What are we supposed to tie to the arm? With what do we tie it? What are "Totafos?" What exactly is it a sign of? Without the Oral Law, quite frankly, there's no mitzvah of tefillin. Also, there aren't too many other mitzvos that'll make much sense either. Not, that is, without some form of commentary. Not without an Oral Torah!*

3. This work can also be divided into two parts: (a) [insofar as it refers to legislation contained in the *Torah* itself — *min ha-Torah*] is that which was learned direct from Moshe Rabbenu, who received it direct from Hashem. It may appear in the

name of a single sage or in the name of many, as will be explained later.

4.  "Rejected law" is that side of a dispute which though recorded has not been accepted. This may also appear in the name of a single sage or of many. The question may be asked: Why did Rabbeinu Ha-Kodesh (Rabbi Yehudah the Holy) record those matters which are not accepted as law? Surely it would have been better to include only such laws as are binding. The answer is that during the early times each sage recorded for himself all that he had learned, whether accepted or not. When Rabbeinu Ha-Kodesh came to record the *Mishnah,* he felt compelled to include those views which were not accepted, so as to avoid the possibility of someone bringing forward these opinions, which he may have heard from one of the sages and endeavoring to contradict the accepted law. If he did so, he could easily be refuted by pointing out that they represent views that have not been accepted. This is pointed out by the Sages in the *Mishnah* [*Eduyos,* chap. 1], where they say: "Why were the words of the single sage recorded besides the words of the majority to no apparent purpose? Because if anyone were to come and say, 'I heard such-and-such', they will be able to tell him 'You heard this from so-and-so'; meaning 'and this is not the law.'"

*Some laws in the Torah required procedures for their observance that were not explicit. At times conditions under which Jews were living were so different from earlier periods that the ancient rabbis simply enacted new rules in keeping with the laws of the Torah. This process of developing, interpreting, modifying and enacting rules of conduct is the method halacha develops from. The rabbis of classical Talmudic Judaism developed a system of hermeneutic principles by which to interpret the words of the Written Torah. Yet by recording both sides of the argument, they enabled our later generations to continue to develop the halacha with the times.*

*This is also a good lesson for us. Whenever there is an argument or discussion about anything, it's good to understand both sides of the story and opinions. We are all too fast to jump to a conclusion, when even if we are correct, it would be good to understand one's fellows reasoning for his opinion.*

5.  Thus far we have been discussing the first part of the *Gemarah,* which is the *Mishnah.* The second part, which is the commentary on the *Mishnah,* is called the *Gemarah* [i.e., tradition]. This comprises many components, twenty-one in all; such as *Tosefta, Beraisa,* explanations, questions, answers,

difficulties and their solutions, and many others, which will now be briefly explained.

The "give and take" or debate style which is characteristic of Talmud study is known by its Aramaic name – "shakla v'tariah". The basic unit of Talmudic argument is called a "sugya – סוגיא". There are certain basic terms in this debate style. For instance, there are two basic kinds of questions and two basic kinds of answers in Talmudic debate. The first kind of question represents a challenge to a previous position. Such a challenge is called a "kushia קושיא". A Kushiyah is usually answered by a "teirutz – תירוץ" which is a resolution of the challenge. An informational question is known as a "she'aalah – שאלה" and an answer to such a question is known as a "teshuvah – תשובה".

The first Mishnah in Brachos asks "FROM WHAT TIME MAY ONE RECITE THE SHEMA' IN THE EVENING?"

The entire Mishniyos starts out with a question, rather than a concept or a thought.

From when מאימתי,? the Mishnah asks.

It is the student who is bold enough to ask the question, that brings about a clearer insight into the Torah. If someone were learning by themselves, then they would not be able to grow from pondering and answering the question a fellow chavrusa or student would ask. If you are not willing to ask questions which might be embarrassing, difficult or if it's just hard for you to find the boldness to even ask, then you miss out on the point of Torah discussion.

Maharsha explains, "that there are two sides to the coin of boldness. 'A bashful person,' says Hillel, (Avos 2:6) cannot succeed in Torah study.' Only if one is bold enough to ask, to challenge and to debate can he truly learn Torah. On the other hand, however, if boldness is not tempered, it can prevent one from having a true respect for Divine authority."

מאימתי

Is the same gematria (501) as the word, Rosh (head). At first people are drawn away from a person that asks many questions. They may find it annoying that the person is challenging their thoughts and authority. However, in Torah we see that a person whose head is constantly thinking of questions, is he who is truly seeking to return and come closer to Hashem.

It is extremely rare that an Atbash gematria comes out exactly the same as the Mispar Gadal total. This is because the method of Atbash completely flips the letters of the alphabet. However, in this rare case, the Atbash gematria of מאימתי also totals 501. This can teach us an important lesson since nothing is by coincidence. Inside every question, when you ask something like מאימתי, is usually the answer itself. Just by asking the question, you already are closer to the p'shat. Without She'ela, Teshuvah, Difficulty, Resolution and other dialog terms of the Gemarah, there would be no

*Gemarah. The Gemarah is all about asking the right questions.*

[1] *Tosefta* ("Addition") is a form of *Beraisa* — *Mishnaic* material not included in the *Mishnah* — [and is appended to every tractate of the *Mishnah*.] In the *Talmud* it is usually introduced by the word תניה.

When it follows the rulings of the *Mishnah* it is accepted as law. [It contains much valuable information, throwing light on many *Mishnah's*.]

*The Tosefta closely corresponds to the Mishnah, with the same divisions for sedarim ("orders") and mesechtos ("tractates"). It is mainly written in Mishnaic Hebrew, with some Aramaic.*

*Sometimes the text of the Tosefta agrees nearly verbatim with the Mishnah. Other times, there are significant differences. The Tosefta often attributes laws that are anonymous in the Mishnah to named Tannaim. It also augments the Mishnah with additional glosses and discussions, offering additional aggadic and midrashic material. It sometimes contradicts the Mishnah in the ruling of Jewish law, or in attributing in whose name a law was stated.*

[2] *Beraisa* ("outside material") includes all the other *Mishnaic* material compiled and transmitted by sages after the *Mishnah*, such as the *Mishnaic* material compiled and recorded by Rabbi Chiya [favorite discipled of Rabbi Yehudah the Prince] and Rabbi Oshaya; the *Mishnah* of Rabbi Eliezer b. Yaakov, the *Mechilta* of Rabbi Yishmael, the Letters of Rabbi Akiva; as well as the legal *midrashim* which follow verses of the *Torah*, such as *Mechilta* on *Shemos*, *Toras Kohanim* (or *Sifra*) on *Yayikra* and *Sifre* on *Bamidbar* and *Devarim*. These are generally introduced by the words תנו רבנן

And conflicting statements by the words תניא אידך

תני חדא ...

All *Beraisa* material which is not contested in the *Gemarah* is accepted by law; where there is a dispute the law is decided according to the rulings given [see paragraphs [6], [7], [8] below].

*Rabbi Shmuel HaNaggid writes in his sefer Mevo HaTalmud: "Our rabbis the Amoraim, greatly needed the Beraisos, because from them were derived, based on the rules of the Gemarah, all of the deep knowledge to which the Mishnah alludes. Because Rebbe wrote only the main laws and didn't include all the many possible similar cases and their rulings." Those can be found in the Beraisa. (R. Yaakov Rich)*

*Several Amoraim gave special attention to the study of the Beraisa. The foremost of these in Babylonia were Rav Sheshes and Rav Joseph b. Ḥiyyah, of the third generation of Amoraim, who prided themselves on their knowledge of the Beraisa.*

*The era of the first Amoraim was a period of conflict between the Mishnah and the Beraisa; but at so early a period as that of the most prominent Palestinian Amoraim of the second generation. The regulation had been established that the*

*teachings not officially delivered in the academies could not lay claim to authority. (Yer. Eruvin. 19b) In the same spirit, the Babylonian Talmud ruled that no reliance should be placed on Beraisos not embodied in the collections of Rav Hiyyah and Rav Hoshaya (Chullin 141a); for these were the only Beraisa collections taught in the academies. (Sherira, First Letter, ed. Neubauer, p. 15) However, even these favored Beraisos, possessed authority only in so far as they did not clash with the Mishnah (for numerous instances see Sherira, ib.).*

[3] *Peyrush* (explanation) is the elucidation by the *Gemarah* on matters contained in the *Mishnah* and is marked by the words "What is so-and-so?" followed by the explanation.

*Peyrush is usually referring not to chazal but to the written commentaries of the Rishonim (1000-1500 CE) and Achronim (1500-today). Rashi's peyrush or elucidation on the Tanach and Talmud is the most celebrated peyrush of all. Pesher, which has the same letters but with the r and the sh reversed, appears in Koheleth and Daniel, meaning explanation or solution — almost the same as peyrush. Shlomo Hamelech asks in Koheleth (8:1): "Who is the wise one, and who knows the meaning (pesher) of these words?" A peyrush, pesher, makes something clearer and understandable. Today, these terms are not always used precisely. Someone might refer to a more contemporary work as a peyrush.*

[4] *She'ela* (Aramaic: בעיא) is a request for a ruling and may be addressed by one group to another (אבעיא להו), or by a group to an individual (בעו מיניה).

Or by one individual to another (בעא מיניה). The law is determined by the replies given.

[5] *Teshuvah* is the answer given to the enquiries mentioned above, and it is established as law in accordance with the rulings given.

[6] *Difficulty* (Aramaic: קושיא) refers to an objection raised against the opinion of an *Amora* by citation of an [apparently] conflicting source… If raised by more than one sage it is introduced by מיתיבי if by one: איתיביה.

[7] *Resolution* (Aramaic: פירוקא) is the answer given resolving the difficulty and if not disputed is [often] accepted as law. [See also [18] below.]

[8] *Refutation* (תיובתא) occurs where a ruling is refuted by clear proofs; the law is then decided according to the strength of the proofs. [If the statement of an *Amora* – a sage of the *Gemarah* – is found to be contradicted by a *Tanna* – a sage of the *Mishnah* – he is thereby refuted, unless he can find another *Tanna* to support him.]

[9] *Support* (Aramaic: סייעתא) is a source cited to strengthen a given

ruling and to support its acceptance; introduced by the words לֵימָא מְסַיֵּיע לֵיהּ.

[10] *Contraction* (רוּמְיָא) occurs when an apparent contraction between two [equivalent] sources is pointed out. Introduced by רָבִּי רָמֵי ורמינהי ורמינהו.

[11] *Necessity* (צְרִיכוּתָא): a demonstration that each of two or more apparently similar statements in a source is needed, [because each contains some information not provided by the other(s)]. Introduced by וצריכא.

[12] *Attack* (אִתְּקַפְתָּא) is an objection raised [on the basis of reasoning rather than the citation of conflicting sources]. It is found only in connection with *Amoraim* (the sages of the later, *Gemarah*, period) and is introduced by מַתְקִיף לַהּ רַבִּי. The decision is as in [8] above.

[13] *Case* (Heb. מַעֲשֶׂה; Aramaic: עוּבְדָה) is the citation of an actual happening on which a decision is reported.

[14] *Tradition* (Aramaic: שְׁמַעְתְּתָא) is a saying containing information on a *halachic* subject. Opposite: *Aggada* [see [19] below.]

[15] *Sugya* (סוּגְיָא) is a connected passage of *Gemarah* containing a series of questions and answers.

[16] *Hilcheta* (הִילְכְתָא): a decision rendered in a case of dispute, where the *Gemarah* concludes "The *halacha* is according to so-and-so."

[17] *Teyku* (תֵּיקוּ) [literally: "let it stand"] occurs where there is a doubt in the *Gemarah* on a point of *halacha* and the matter is left without decision. If it relates to a money matter the practice is to follow the lenient ruling [i.e., the defendant is exempted from payment]; and in the case of prohibitions, the practice is to follow the more stringent ruling [except in the case of some rabbinic prohibitions] ...

*Rav Matisyahu Solomon explains, "When there are difficult problems that can't be answered, nobody looks for an easy way out. We have a wonderful answer to every problem that we can't resolve, Taku. That is the answer to all our problems; we can wait for Mashiach or Eliyahu to explain but we are not going to look for makeshift answers. In our current society, every problem must have an immediate solution. Every question has to have an immediate answer. Makeshift now takes prevalence over reliable authentic later, we can wait. We can remain with a question. Taku, that is the answer."*

*Rabbi Yaakov Abuchatzeira taught, "We read in the Torah, 'If a matter should be too challenging for you to decide, between pure blood and impure blood and between one sort of blemish and another sort of blemish, [and there are] disputes in your courts, you should arise and travel up to the place,... and come to the kohanim, the leviim and to the judge who will be in those days...' (Devarim 17:18) This might be hinting that matters which the Amoraim would be unable to resolve, they would leave undecided and label "taku," an acronym meaning "Tishbi Yitaretz Kushios Ub'ayos, Eliyahu will settle difficulties and problems." The purpose of the term is that when Eliyahu comes with Mashiach Tzidkeinu, speedily in our days, he will resolve everything. Likewise, several differences between the Tannaim and the Amoraim were left for Eliyahu who will explain everything when he comes.*

*"However, even though the expression is that Eliyahu will elucidate things, it cannot be him alone, for Eliyahu was a student of Moshe and if Moshe doesn't come, why should Eliyahu? It is apparent that the expression must mean that everything will be clarified through Moshe, Eliyahu and Mashiach. It can also be that Moshe was essentially alluding to [taku] when he said, 'If a matter should be too difficult for you to judge,' meaning that there are opinions in both directions. Then know what to do: arise and go up, 'vekamta ve'alita'. The term 've'alita' has the same gematria as 'taku,' so the meaning of 'arise and go up' is 'settle the matter that you had differences about and that you declared 'teiku.' Also, the word 'vekamta' has the identical letters as 'takum' and takum can be read 'taku,' as 'teiku' is the Aramaic translation of takum. The meaning then is that when you attempt to understand [difficult issues], you will find all of the difficulties clarified, but when is that? When you go up to the location which Hashem has chosen, that is, when Mashiach Tzidkeinu, who should come quickly in our time, amen, collects all of the lost ones to the Holy Temple in its glory. Then at that period, you will come to the kohanim who are leviim, who are Moshe Rabbeinu and Eliyahu Hanavi, and 'to the judge who will be in those days,' who is Mashiach Tzidkeinu, 'and you will investigate and ask and they will tell you the ruling.' (Petuchei Chotem – Shoftim)*

[18] *Interpretation* (Aramaic: שינויא): where a sage is faced with a contradiction from an accepted source and he endeavors to re-interpret the source so that it no longer conflicts with his view...

[19] *Aggada* (Aramaic: אגדתא): everything mentioned in the *Gemarah* which is not directly connected with the *halachic* aspect of a commandment. One should learn from such statements only those things which our minds can grasp. It is important to know that all matters which our Sages established as law, in connection with a commandment transmitted by Moshe Rabbenu who received it from the Almighty, cannot be augmented or diminished in any way. However, the [*aggadic*] explanations they rendered of biblical verses were in accordance with their individual views and the ideas which occurred to them. We should learn from them insofar as our minds can grasp them; but otherwise we should not build upon them. [Since we have not succeeded in understanding the deeper meaning of their words, we should not attempt to use them as the

basis of our thinking.]

*We are told to use our common sense to decide whether an aggadah is to be taken literally or not. This is because some aggadah in the Talmud contained hidden messages and metaphors, while others are completely factual. One thing is for sure, there is always something to learn from an aggadah.*

*Rabbi Moshe Chaim Luzzatto, the Ramchal, discusses this two-tiered, literal-allegorical mode of transmission of the aggadah. He explains that the Oral Law, in fact, comprises two components: the legal component (חלק המצוות), discussing the mitzvos and halacha; and "the secret" component (חלק הסודות), conferring the deeper doctrines. (Discourse on the Haggados). The aggadah, alongside with the Kabbalah, falls under the latter. The rabbis of the Mishnahic era believed that it would be dangerous to record the deeper teachings in the obvious Mishnah-like, medium. Instead, they would be conveyed in a "concealed mode" and via "paradoxes". Due to their importance, these teachings should not become accessible to those with wrongful intentions and of bad character. Also, due to their depth they should not be made available to those "not schooled in the ways of analysis". This mode of the transmission was nevertheless founded on consistent rules and principles. This was so that only such that those "equipped with the keys" would be able to unlock their meaning; to others they would simply appear as non-rational or fantastic.*

*(See more above in Chapter. Ayin Yaakov)*

[20] *Teaching* (הוראה) is a tradition regarding a commandment issuing from the sages in assemblies or academies.

[21] *Shitta* (Heb. שיטה) refers to a number of individual sages each reported as holding a similar opinion and cited together as such in the *Gemarah*; in which case we are told that the decision is not like any of them. {You should know that the *Gemarah* was completed in the time of Ravina and Rav Ashi [5ᵗʰ C.] and it is they who taught us the secrets of its compilation, including such rules as the above.}

*Extras*

[22] *Drasha is usually used as referring to a current rabbi's lecture (but could be used interchangeably with midrash, for they are from the same root).*

6. The rules for arriving at decisions in disputes between *Tannaim* [sages of the *Mishnah*] are as follows:
[1] One against many: the *halacha* (final decision) is like the many.
[2] A dispute in one *Mishnah* followed by an anonymous statement [representing one of the views] in another *Mishnah* means that the *halacha* is in accordance with the latter. [This applies only within one tractate].

[3] An anonymous *Mishnah* followed by a *Mishnah* containing a dispute on the same point means that the *halacha* is not like the anonymous *Mishnah*. [This also applies only within one tractate.]

[4] If there is a dispute in a *Mishnah* and an anonymous statement in a *Beraisa*, we do not say the *halacha* is like the *Beraisa*, because we say "If Rabbi [Yehudah the Prince] did not teach it, how could Rabbi Chiya [the editor of the *Beraisa*] know it?"

7. Further rules relating to *Mishnah* and *Beraisa*:

[1] An anonymous *Mishnah* is according to Rabbi Meir.

[2] An anonymous statement in *Sifra* is like Rabbi Yehudah;

[4] and in *Sifre*, like Rabbi Shimon; and all of them are in general agreement with Rabbi Akiva, whose disciples they were.

[5] Where Rabbi Meir is named in a source, and his decision is disputed, either by Rabbi Yehudah, Rabbi Yose, Rabbi Shimon or Rabbi Eliezer ben Yaakov, the *halacha* is like his opponent.

[6] Rabbi Yehudah against Rabbi Shimon: the *halacha* is like his opponent.

[7] The *halacha* is always like Rabbi Yose, even against more than one (named) *Tanna*.

[8] The *Mishnah* of Rabbi Eliezer ben Yaakov is "small but pure" [i.e., he is not mentioned often, but when he is the *halacha* is always like him].

[9] "Some say" (יש אומרים) means Rabbi Nathan.

[10] "Others say" (אחרים אומרים) means Rabbi Meir.

[11] Wherever Rabban Shimon Ben Gamliel appears in our *Mishnah* the *halacha* is like him, except in there (named) cases...

[12] The *halacha* is always like Rabbi [Yehudah the Prince] where he disputes with one other sage...

[13] However, wherever Rabbi [Yehudah the Prince] disputes with his father [Rabban Shimon Ben Gamliel] the *halacha* is like his father.

[14] Wherever a *Mishnah* is cited in the name of Rabbi Shimon ben Elazar and there is no dispute mentioned, the *halacha* is like him.

[15] Rabbi Eliezer against Rabban Gamliel: the *halacha* is like Rabban Gamliel...

[16] The *halacha* is always like Rabbi Akiva when in dispute with one other sage.

[17] Bais Shammai against Beth Hillel – the *halacha* is like Beth Hillel, except in six cases, where the Sages said the decision is like neither of them and in three cases where the *halacha* is like Bais Shammai.

[18] Whenever a *Tanna* qualifies his remarks by stating "in which case does this apply, במה דברים אמורים or when does this apply?" In such-and-such circumstances, the *halacha* is like him. Similarly, a *Mishnah* introduced by the words, "In truth they said "באמת אמרו represents the undisputed *halacha*.

[19] We do not learn the *halacha* from a *Mishnah* alone, but only from the decision given in the *Gemarah*.

8. These are the rules relating to disputes between Amoraim (the sages of the *Gemarah*):

[1] Rav against Shmuel – the *halacha* is like Rav in prohibitions and like Shmuel in civil laws. [Rav is Rav Abba Aricha (the Tall), 3rd C. The title 'Rav' is given to *Amoraim* of Babylon. *Amoraim* of *Eretz Yisrael*, like *Tannaim*, are all called 'Rabbi'.]

[2] Rav Chisda against Rav Huna: the *halacha* is like Rav Huna.

[3] Rav Sheshes against Rav Nahman – the *halacha* is like Rav Sheshes in prohibitions and like Rav Nahman in civil laws.

[4] The *halacha* is never like the disciple when in dispute with his teacher.

[5] If a later sage is in dispute with an earlier sage, the *halacha* is like the later sage. [Since both are within one era – the era of the *Amoraim* – and therefore of equal status, the opinion of the later one prevails, since he has had the opportunity of considering all the developments of the argument that have taken place in the interim period.]

[6] Rav Yehudah against Rabbah: the *halacha* is like Rav Yehudah.

[7] Rabbah against Rav Yosef: the *halacha* is like Rabbah, except in three (named) cases.

[8] Rav Aha against Ravina: the *halacha* is like Ravina, except in three (named) cases.

[9] The compilers of the *Talmud* were Rav Ashi and Ravina and their colleagues [5th C.]; and in their time the *Talmud* was completed.

[10] The *halacha* is like Mar the son of Rav Ashi except where he is in dispute with his teacher...

[11] Wherever the *Gemarah* says, "So-and-so is refuted" [see 5 [8], above] the *halacha* is not like that sage. [However, where the *Gemarah* concludes merely with the word *kashya* ("this is difficult") this indicates that the difficulty is merely textual and can be resolved.]

[12] Any dispute which is merely theoretical and has no practical relevance does not have the words "the *halacha* is like so-and-so" applied to it.

# Learning Mesechtos Charts

| זרעים SEEDS | מועד HOLIDAYS | נשים WOMEN | נזיקין DAMAGES | קדשים HOLY THINGS | טהרות PURITY |
|---|---|---|---|---|---|
| The laws relating to agriculture and Israeli crops; leaving offerings to the Priests and the Levites; giving gifts to the poor | The laws relevant to the Shabbos, the festivals, fast days, and other significant holidays | The laws pertaining to the husband/wife relationship, starting from the marriage ceremony, to adultery, incest, divorce, vows and property. | The laws regarding civil jurisprudence and penal law; Rabbinic courts; errors in judgement; vows; punishments etc. Also deals with some religious criminal law, like pagan worship. | The laws mainly pertaining to the Temple and its sacrifices. Also, laws on ritual slaughter, and kosher and non-kosher foods. | The laws of ritual purity and impurity. Also, laws of women's menstrual cycles and family purity. |
| Berachos- ברכות | Shabbos – שבת | Yevamos – יבמות | Bava Kama – בבא קמא | Zevachim – זבחים | Keilim – כלים |
| Peah – פאה | Eiruvin – עירובין | Kesubos – כתובות | Bava Metzia – בבא מציעא | Menachos - מנחות | Oholos – אהלות |
| Dmai – דמאי | Pesachim - פסחים | Nedarim – נדרים | Bava Basra – בבא בתרא | Chullin – חולין | Negoim – נגעים |
| Kilayim – כלאים | Shekalim – שקלים | Nazir – נזיר | Sanhedrin - סנהדרין | Bechoros - בכורות | Poroh - פרה |
| Shvi'is – שביעית | Yuma – יומא | Sotah – סוטה | Makkos – מכות | Eiruchin – ערכין | Taharos – טהרות |
| Trumos - תרומות | Sukkah – סוכה | Gitin – גיטין | Shevuos – שבועות | Tmurah - תמורה | Mikvaos – מקואות |
| Maasros - מעשרות | Beitzah – ביצה | Kiddushin – קידושין | Ediyos - עדיות | Krisus - כריתות | Niddah – נדה |
| Maasar Sheni – מעשר שני | Rosh Hashanah - ראש השנה | | Avodah Zarah - עבודה זרה | Meilah - מעילה | Machshirin - מכשירין |
| Challah - חלה | Taanis – תענית | | Avos - אבות | Tomid – תמיד | Zavim – זבים |
| Orlah - ערלה | Megillah – מגילה | | Horiyos - הוריות | Middos – מדות Kinim – קינים | Tvul Yom - טבול יום |
| Bikkurim - ביכורים | Moed Katan – מועד קטן | | | | Yodayim – ידים |
| | Chagigah – חגיגה | | | | Uktzin – עוקצין |

264

# *A Timeline of the Transmission of Torah*

| JEWISH YEAR | SECULAR YEAR | EVENT / ERA | PERSONALITIES | NOTES |
|---|---|---|---|---|
| 2448 | 1313 bce | Giving of the Torah | Moses | 10 / 613 Commandments. Moses begins teaching the Oral Law |
| 2488 | 1273 bce | Jews enter Israel | Joshua | |
| Until 3461 | Until 300 bce | Neviim – Prophets | Samuel, Elijah, Isaiah, Jeremiah, Ezekiel, Haggai, Zecharia | The era of prophecy ends in beginning of the 2nd Temple period |
| 2516 – 2871 | 1245 bce – 890 bce | Shoftim – Judges | Osniel ben Knaz, Deborah, Gideon, Samson, Eyli-High Priest | |
| 2882 – 3338 | 879 bce – 423 bce | Melochim – Kings | Saul, David, Solomon | Ultimately, Jewish Kingdom split: Judah and Israel |
| 2928 – 2935 | 833 bce – 827 bce | 1st Temple Built | King Solomon | |
| 3338 | 423 bce | Destruction of 1st Temple | Babylonians led by Nebuchadnezar | Jews exiled to Babylonia |
| 3408 – 3412 | 353 bce – 349 bce | 2nd Temple Rebuilt | Ezra, Nechemia | Few Jews return to Israel. 2nd Temple less grand than 1st. |
| 3412 – 3581 | 349 bce – 180 bce | The Great Assembly | Shimon Hatzaddik | Canonized the Bible. Formalized liturgy. |
| 3581 – 3801 | 180 bce – 40 ce | Zugot - Pairs | Shmaya and Avtalyon, Hillel and Shammai | President, and Head of Court |
| 3621 | 140 bce | Hasmonean Revolt | Matisyahu, Judah the Maccabite | Chanukah story |
| 3623 | 138 bce | Chanukah Miracle | Hasmoneans | |
| 3658 – 3685 | 103 bce – 76 bce | Alexander Yannai's reign | Shalomit, Shimon ben Shotach | Sadducee / Pharisee tension |
| 3801 – 3961 | 40 ce – 200 ce | Tannaitic Era | Yochanan ben Zakkai Akiva ben Yosef, Shimon bar Yochai, | New stage in teaching, interpreting, and collecting the vast |

| | | | | amounts of scholarly teachings |
|---|---|---|---|---|
| **3829** | 70 ce | 2nd Temple destroyed | Romans, led by Titus | |
| **3949** | 189 ce | The Mishnah | Judah the Prince | Closing the Tannaitic Era |
| **3960 – 4260** | 200 ce – 500 ce | Amoraic Period | **Babylonia**: Rav, Shmuel, Raba, R Yosef, Rava, Abaye, **Israel**: R Yochanan, R Kahana, R Ami, R Asi, R Zeira | Interpretation and elucidation of Mishnah |
| **4140** | 380 ce | Redaction of Jerusalem Talmud | | |
| **4261** | 500 ce | Redaction of Babylonian Talmud | R Ashi, Ravina | Closing of Amoraic Period |
| **4261 – 4461** | 500 ce – 700 ce | Svoraic Era | | Final editing of Babylonian Talmud |
| **4461 – 4791** | 700 ce – 1030 ce | Gaonic Era | R Saadia, R Shrira, R Hai | Served as Rabbinic advisory center for distant communities |
| **4798** | 1037 ce | End of Babylonian schools | | |
| **4791 – 5261** | 1030 ce – 1500 ce | Rishonim | Sephardi: R Chananel, R Nissim, Maimonides, Nachmanides, Rashba Ashkenazi: R Gershom, Rashi, Tosafot – Rashbam, Rabbeinu Tam, Riy, Maharam of Rothenburg, Tur | Emergence of 2 styles and geographical locations of schools – Sephardi and Ashkenazi. Comprehensive analysis and commentary on the Talmud. First halachic codes also authored. |
| **5261** | 1500 ce | Achronim | Maharsha, Maharam Lublin, Maharshal, | |
| **5323 / 5330** | 1563 ce / 1570 ce | Shulchan Aruch and Ramo | R Yosef Kairo, R Moshe Isserles | Most authoritative legal Code published, serving both Ashkenazic and Sephardic communities |
| **Present** | | | You and I | " תורה צוה לנו משה "מורשה קהילת יעקב |

# Talmud Chapters and Blats Guide

| | | | |
|---|---|---|---|
| **Zeraim Seeds** | **Mesechta Brachos** | | |
| | Chapter 1<br>Mei'Eimasai-2a-13a | Chapter 2<br>Hayah Korei<br>13a-17b | Chapter 3<br>Mi Shemeiso<br>17b-26a |
| | Chapter 4<br>Tefillas Hashachar<br>26a-30b | Chapter 5<br>Ein Omdin<br>30b-34b | Chapter 6<br>Keitzad Mevarchin<br>35a-45a |
| | Chapter 7<br>Sheloshah She'achlu<br>45a-51b | Chapter 8<br>Eilu Devarim<br>51b-53b | Chapter 9<br>Haro'eh<br>54a-64a |
| **Moed Festivals** | **Mesechta Shabbos** | | |
| | Chapter 1<br>Yetzios Hashabbos<br>2a-20b | Chapter 2<br>Bameh Madlikin<br>20b-36b | Chapter 3<br>Kirah<br>36b-47b |
| | Chapter 4<br>Bameh Tomnin<br>47b-51b | Chapter 5<br>Bameh Beheimah<br>51b-56b | Chapter 6<br>Bameh Ishah<br>57a-67b |
| | Chapter 7<br>Klal Gadol<br>67b-76b | Chapter 8<br>Hamotzi Yayin<br>76b-82a | Chapter 9<br>Amar Rabbi Akiva<br>82a-90b |
| | Chapter 10<br>Hamatznia<br>90b-96a | Chapter 11<br>Hazoreik<br>96a-102a | Chapter 12<br>Haboneh<br>102b-105a |
| | Chapter 13<br>Haoreig<br>105a-107a | Chapter 14<br>Shemonah<br>Sheratzim<br>107a-111b | Chapter 15<br>Eilu Kesharim<br>111b-115a |
| | Chapter 16<br>Kol Kisvei<br>115a-122b | Chapter 17<br>Kol Hakeilim<br>122b-126b | Chapter 18<br>Mefanin<br>126b-129b |
| | Chapter 19<br>R' Eliezer D'Milah<br>130a-137b | Chapter 20<br>Tolin<br>137b-141b | Chapter 21<br>Noteil<br>141b-143a |
| | Chapter 22<br>Chavis<br>143b-148a | Chapter 23<br>Sho-eil<br>148a-153a | Chapter 24<br>Mi SheheChshich<br>153a-157b |

| Mesechta Eruvin | | |
|---|---|---|
| Chapter 1<br>Mavoi Shehu Gavo'ah<br>2a-17b | Chapter 2<br>Osin Pasin<br>17b-26b | Chapter 3<br>Bakol Me'Arvin<br>26b-41b |
| Chapter 4<br>Me Shehotziuhu<br>41b-52b | Chapter 5<br>Keitzad Me'Abrin<br>52b-61b | Chapter 6<br>Hadar<br>61b-76a |
| Chapter 7<br>Chalon<br>76a-82a | Chapter 8<br>Keitzad Mishtatfin<br>82a-89a | Chapter 9<br>Kol Gagos<br>89a-95a |
| Chapter 10<br>Hamotzai Tefillin<br>95a-105a | | |
| **Mesechta Pesachim** | | |
| Chapter 1<br>Or L'arbaah Asar<br>2a-21a | Chapter 2<br>Kol Shaah<br>21a-42a | Chapter 3<br>Eilu Ovrin<br>42a-50a |
| Chapter 4<br>Makom Shenahagu<br>50a-57b | Chapter 5<br>Tamid Nishchas<br>58a-65b | Chapter 6<br>Eilu Devarim<br>65b-73b |
| Chapter 7<br>Keitzad Tzolin<br>80b-86b | Chapter 8<br>Ha'Ishah<br>87a-92b | Chapter 9<br>Mi Shehayah<br>92b-99a |
| Chapter 10<br>Arvei Pesachim<br>99b-121b · | | |
| **Mesechta Yoma** | | |
| Chapter 1<br>Shivas Yamim<br>2a-21b | Chapter 2<br>Barishonah<br>22a-28a | Chapter 3<br>Amar        Lahem<br>Hamemuneh<br>28a-39a |
| Chapter 4<br>Taraf Bakalpi<br>39a-46b | Chapter 5<br>Hotzi'u Lo<br>47a-62a | Chapter 6<br>Shnei Se'irei<br>62a-68b |
| Chapter 7<br>Ba Lo<br>68b-73b | Chapter 8<br>Yom Hakippurim<br>73b-88b | |
| **Mesechta Succah** | | |
| Chapter 1<br>Succah Sheihi<br>Gevohah<br>2a-20b | Chapter 2<br>Hayashein Tachas<br>Hamitah<br>20b-29b | Chapter 3<br>Lulav Hagazul<br>29b-42b |
| Chapter 4 | Chapter 5 | |

| | | |
|---|---|---|
| Lulav Va'aravah 42b-50a | Hechalil 50a-56b | |

### Mesechta Beitzah

| | | |
|---|---|---|
| Chapter 1 Beitzah 2a-15a | Chapter 2 Yom Tov 15b-23b | Chapter 3 Ein Tzadin 23b-29b |
| Chapter 4 Hameivi 29b-35b | Chapter 5 Mashilin 35b-40b | |

### Mesechta Rosh HaShanah

| | | |
|---|---|---|
| Chapter 1 Arbaah Roshei Shanim 2a-22a | Chapter 2 Im Einak Makirin 22a-25b | Chapter 3 Ra'uhu Beis Din 25b-29b |
| Chapter 4 Yom Tov 29b-35a | | |

### Mesechta Taanis

| | | |
|---|---|---|
| Chapter 1 Me'emasai 2a-15a | Chapter 2 Seder Taaiyos Kitzad 15a-18b | Chapter 3 Seder Taaniyos Eilu 18b-26a |
| Chapter 4 Bishloshah Perakim 26a-31a | | |

### Mesechta Megillah

| | | |
|---|---|---|
| Chapter 1 Megillah Nikreis 2a-17a | Chapter 2 Hakurei Lemafrei'a 17a-21a | Chapter 3 Hakorei Omeid 21a-25b |
| Chapter 4 B'nei Ha'ir 25b-32a | | |

### Mesectha Moed Katan

| | | |
|---|---|---|
| Chapter 1 Mashkin Beis Hashelachin 2a-11a | Chapter 2 Mi Shehafach 11b-13b | Chapter 3 Ve'eilu Megalchin 13b-29a |

### Mesectha Chagigah

| | | |
|---|---|---|
| Chapter 1 Hakol Chayavin 2a-11b | Chapter 2 Ein Dorshin 11b-20b | Chapter 3 Chomer Bakodesh 20b-27a |

| **Mesectha Yevamos** | | |
|---|---|---|
| Chapter 1<br>Chamesh Esrei<br>Nashim<br>2a-17a | Chapter 2<br>Keitzad<br>17a-26a | Chapter 3<br>Arbaah Achin<br>26a-41a |
| Chapter 4<br>Arbaah Achin<br>35b-50a | Chapter 5<br>Rabban Gemliel<br>50a-53b | Chapter 6<br>Haba Al Yevimso<br>53b-66a |
| Chapter 7<br>Almanah Lekohen<br>Gadol<br>66a-70a | Chapter 8<br>He'areil<br>70a-84a | Chapter 9<br>Yeish Mutaros<br>84a-87b |
| Chapter 10<br>Ha'ishah Rabbah<br>87b-97a | Chapter 11<br>Nosse'in Al<br>Haanusah<br>97a-101a | Chapter 12<br>Mitzvas Chalitzah<br>101a-106b |
| Chapter 13<br>Beis Shammai<br>107-112b | Chapter 14<br>Cheireish Shenasah<br>112b-114b | Chapter 15<br>Ha'ishah Shalom<br>114b-118b |
| Chapter 16<br>Ha'ishah Basra<br>119a-122b | | |
| **Mesechta Kesubos** | | |
| Chapter 1<br>Besulah Niseis<br>2a-15b | Chapter 2<br>Ha'ishah<br>Shenisarmelah<br>15b-28b | Chapter 3<br>Eilu Ne'aros<br>29a-41b |
| Chapter 4<br>Naarah Shenispatesah<br>41b-54b | Chapter 5<br>Af Al Pi<br>54b-65b | Chapter 6<br>Metzias Haishah<br>65b-70a |
| Chapter 7<br>Hamadir<br>70a-77b | Chapter 8<br>Ha'ishah Shenaflu<br>78a-82b | Chapter 9<br>Hakoseiv Le'ishto<br>83a-90a |
| Chapter 10<br>Mi Shehaya Nasui<br>90a-95b | Chapter 11<br>Almanah Nizoness<br>95b-101b | Chapter 12<br>Hanosei Es<br>Ha'ishah<br>101b-104b |
| Chapter 13<br>Shnei Dyanei | | |

**Nashem Women**

| | | |
|---|---|---|
| 104b-112b | | |
| **Mesechta Nedarim** | | |
| Chapter 1<br>Kol Kinuyei<br>2a-13b | Chapter 2<br>Ve'eilu Mutarin<br>13b-20b | Chapter 3<br>Arbaah Nedarim<br>20b-32b |
| Chapter 4<br>Ein Bein Hamudar<br>32b-45a | Chapter 5<br>Hashutafin<br>45b-48b | Chapter 6<br>Hanoder Min<br>Hamevushal<br>49a-53b |
| Chapter 7<br>Hanoder Min Hayarak<br>54a-60a | Chapter 8<br>Konam Yayin<br>60a-63b | Chapter 9<br>Rabbi Eliezer<br>64a-66b |
| Chapter 10<br>Naarah Hame'orasah<br>66b-79a | Chapter 11<br>Ve'eilu Nedarim<br>79a-91b | |
| **Mesechta Nazir** | | |
| Chapter 1<br>Kol Kinuyei Nezirus<br>2a-8b | Chapter 2<br>Hareini Nazir<br>9a-16a | Chapter 3<br>Mi Sh'amar<br>16a-20b |
| Chapter 4<br>Mi Sh'amar<br>20b-30b | Chapter 5<br>Beis Shammai<br>30b-34a | Chapter 6<br>Sheloshan Minin<br>34a-47a |
| Chapter 7<br>Kohen Gadol<br>47a-57a | Chapter 8<br>Shenei Nezrim<br>57a-61a | Chapter 9<br>Hakusim Ein<br>Lahem<br>61a-66b |
| **Mesechta Sota** | | |
| Chapter 1<br>Hamekanei<br>2a-14a | Chapter 2<br>Hayah Meivi<br>14a-19a | Chapter 3<br>Hayah Noteil<br>19a-23b |
| Chapter 4<br>Arusah<br>23b-27b | Chapter 5<br>Kesheim<br>Shehamayim<br>27b-31a | Chapter 6<br>Mi Shekinei<br>31a-32a |
| Chapter 7<br>Eilu Ne'emarin<br>32a-42a | Chapter 8<br>Meshuach<br>Milchamah<br>42a-44b | Chapter 9<br>Eglah Arufah<br>44b-49b |
| **Mesechta Gittin** | | |
| Chapter 1<br>Hamevi Get<br>2a-15a | Chapter 2<br>Hamevi Get<br>15a-24a | Chapter 3<br>Kol Haget<br>24a-32a |
| Chapter 4 | Chapter 5 | Chapter 6 |

| | | |
|---|---|---|
| Hasholeiach 32a-48b | Hanizakin 60b-62a | Haomer 62b-67b |
| Chapter 7 Mi Sheachazo 67b-77a | Chapter 8 Hazoreik 77a-82a | Chapter 9 Hamegaresh 82a-90b |

**Mesechta Kiddushin**

| | | |
|---|---|---|
| Chapter 1 Ha'ishah Nikneis 2a-41a | Chapter 2 Ha'ish Mekadeish 41a-58b | Chapter 3 Ha'omer 58b-69a |
| Chapter 4 Asarah Yochasin 69a-82b | | |

**Mesechta Bava Kamma**

| Nezikin Damages | | | |
|---|---|---|---|
| | Chapter 1 Arbaah Avos 2a-17a | Chapter 2 Keitzad Haregel 17a-27a | Chapter 3 Hamaniach 27a-36a |
| | Chapter 4 Shor Shenagach Dalet V'hei 36a-46a | Chapter 5 Shor Shenagach Es Haparah 46a-55a | Chapter 6 Hakoneis 55b-62b |
| | Chapter 7 Merubah 62b-83a | Chapter 8 Hachoveil 83b-93a | Chapter 9 Hagozeil Eitzim 93b-111a |
| | Chapter 10 Hagozeil U'Ma'achil 111b-119b | | |

**Mesechta Bava Metzia**

| | | | |
|---|---|---|---|
| | Chapter 1 Shenayim Ochazin 2a-21a | Chapter 2 Eilu Metzios 21a-33b | Chapter 3 Hamafkid 33b-44a |
| | Chapter 4 Hazahav 44a-60b | Chapter 5 Eizehu Neshech 60b-75b | Chapter 6 Hasocher Es Ha'Umanin 75b-83a |
| | Chapter 7 Hasocheir Es Hapoalim 83a-94a | Chapter 8 Hashoel Es Haparah 94a-103a | Chapter 9 Hamekabel 103a-116a |
| | Chapter 10 Habayis Veha'aliyah 116b-119a | | |

**Mesechta Bava Basra**

| | | |
|---|---|---|
| Chapter 1 | Chapter 2 | Chapter 3 |

| | | |
|---|---|---|
| Hashutafin 2a-17a | Lo Yachpor 17a-27b | Chezkas Habatim 28a-60b |
| Chapter 4 Hamocheir Es Habayis 61a-73a | Chapter 5 Hamocheir Es Hasefinah 73a-91b | Chapter 6 Hamocheir Peiros 92a-102b |
| Chapter 7 Beis Kor 102b-108a | Chapter 8 Yeish Nochalin 108a-139b | Chapter 9 Mi Shemeis 139b-159b |
| Chapter 10 Get Pashut 160a-176b | | |
| **Mesechta Sanhedrin** | | |
| Chapter 1 Dinei Mamonos Bishloshah 2a-18a | Chapter 2 Kohen Gadol 18a-22b | Chapter 3 Zeh Borer 23a-31b |
| Chapter 4 Echad Dinei Mamonos 32a-39b | Chapter 5 Hayu Bodkin 40a-42a | Chapter 6 Nigmar Hadin 42b-49a |
| Chapter 7 Arba Misos 49b-68a | Chapter 8 Ben Sorer Umoreh 68b-75a | Chapter 9 Hanisrafin 75a-84a |
| Chapter 10 Nanechnakin 84b-90a | Chapter 11 Chilek 90a-113b | |
| **Mesechta Makkos** | | |
| Chapter 1 Keitzad Ha'eidim 2a-7a | Chapter 2 Eilu Hein Hagolin 7a-13a | Chapter 3 Eilu Hein Halokin 13a-24b |
| **Mesechta Shevuos** | | |
| Chapter 1 Shevuos Shtayim 2a-14a | Chapter 2 Yedios Hatumah 14a-19b | Chapter 3 Shevuos Shtayim II 19b-29b |
| Chapter 4 Shevuas Ha'eidus 30a-36b | Chapter 5 Shevuas Hapikadon 36b-38b | Chapter 6 Shevuas Hadayanim 38b-44b |
| Chapter 7 Kol Hanishba'in 44b-49a | Chapter 8 Arbaah Shomerin 49a-49b | |
| **Mesechta Avodah Zara** | | |

| | | |
|---|---|---|
| Chapter 1<br>Lifnei Eideihen<br>2a-22a | Chapter 2<br>Ein Maamidin<br>22a-40b | Chapter 3<br>Kol Hatzelamim<br>40b-49b |
| Chapter 4<br>Rabbi Yishmael<br>49b-61b | Chapter 5<br>Hasocher Es<br>Hapo'el<br>62a-76b | |

**Mesechta Horayos**

| | | |
|---|---|---|
| Chapter 1<br>Horu Beis Din<br>2a-6b | Chapter 2<br>Hora Kohen<br>Mashiach<br>6b-9b | Chapter 3<br>Kohen Mashiach<br>9b-14a |

**Mesechta Eduyos**

| | | |
|---|---|---|
| Chapter 1<br>Shammai Omeir<br>2a-3a | Chapter 2<br>R' Chanina<br>3b-4b | Chapter 3<br>Kol Hametame'in<br>4b-6a |
| Chapter 4<br>Eilu Devarim<br>6a-7a | Chapter 5<br>R' Yehudah<br>7a-7b | Chapter 6<br>R' Yehudah Ben<br>Bava<br>8a-8b |
| Chapter 7<br>He'id R' Yehoshua<br>8b-9a | Chapter 8<br>He'id R' Yehoshua<br>Ben Beseira<br>9a-9b | |

**Mesechta Zevachim**

| | | |
|---|---|---|
| Chapter 1<br>Kol Hazevachim<br>2a-15b | Chapter 2<br>Kol Hazevachim<br>Shekiblu<br>15b-31b | Chapter 3<br>Kol Hapesulin<br>31b-36b |
| Chapter 4<br>Kol Hapesulin<br>36b-47a | Chapter 5<br>Eizehu Mekoman<br>47a-57b | Chapter 6<br>Kodshei Kodashim<br>58a-66a |
| Chapter 7<br>Chatas Ha'oph<br>66a-70b | Chapter 8<br>Kol Hazevachim<br>70b-83a | Chapter 9<br>Hamizbei'ach<br>Mekadeish<br>83a-88b |
| Chapter 10<br>Kol Hatadir<br>89a-92a | Chapter 11<br>Dam Chatas<br>92a-98b | Chapter 12<br>Tevul Yom<br>98b-106a |
| Chapter 13<br>Hashocheit<br>Vehamaaleh<br>106a-112a | Chapter 14<br>Paras Chatas<br>112a-120b | |

**Kedoshim Holy Things**

## Mesechta Menachos

| | | |
|---|---|---|
| Chapter 1<br>Kol Hamenachos<br>2a-13a | Chapter 2<br>Hakometz Es<br>Haminchah<br>13a-17a | Chapter 3<br>Hakometz Rabbah<br>17a-38a |
| Chapter 4<br>Hatecheiles<br>38a-52b | Chapter 5<br>Kol Hamenachos<br>Baos Matzah<br>52b-63b | Chapter 6<br>R' Yishmael<br>63b-72b |
| Chapter 7<br>Eilu Menachos<br>Nikmatzos<br>72b-76b | Chapter 8<br>Hatodah Hayesah<br>Ba'ah<br>76b-83b | Chapter 9<br>Kol Korbenos<br>Hatzibbur<br>83b-87a |
| Chapter 10<br>Shtei Middos<br>87a-94a | Chapter 11<br>Shtei Halechem<br>94a-100b | Chapter 12<br>Hamenachos<br>Vehanesachim<br>100b-104b |
| Chapter 13<br>Harei Alai Issaron<br>104b-110a | | |

## Mesechta Chullin

| | | |
|---|---|---|
| Chapter 1<br>HaKol Shochatin<br>2a-26b | Chapter 2<br>Hashochet<br>27a-42a | Chapter 3<br>Eilu Tereifos<br>42a-67b |
| Chapter 4<br>Beheimah<br>Hamekashah<br>68a-78a | Chapter 5<br>Oso 'es Beno<br>78a-83b | Chapter 6<br>Kisuy Hadam<br>83b-89b |
| Chapter 7<br>Gid Hanesheh<br>89b-103b | Chapter 8<br>Kol Habasar<br>103b-117b | Chapter 9<br>Ha'or Veharotev<br>117b-129b |
| Chapter 10<br>Hazero'a<br>Vehalechayayim<br>130a-134b | Chapter 11<br>Reishis Hageiz<br>135a-138b | Chapter 12<br>Shiluach Hakein<br>138b-142a |

## Mesechta Bechoros

| | | |
|---|---|---|
| Chapter 1<br>Halokei'ach Ach<br>Ubbar Chamoro<br>2a-13a | Chapter 2<br>Halokei'ach Ach<br>Ubbar Paraso<br>13a-19b | Chapter 3<br>Halokei'ach<br>Beheimah<br>19b-26b |
| Chapter 4<br>Ad Kammah<br>26b-31a | Chapter 5<br>Kol Pesulei<br>Hamukdashin | Chapter 6<br>Al Eilu Moomin<br>37a-43a |

| | | |
|---|---|---|
| | 31a-37a | |
| Chapter 7<br>Moomin Eilu<br>43a-46a | Chapter 8<br>Yesh Bechor<br>46a-52b | Chapter 9<br>Maasar Beheimah<br>53a-61a |
| **Mesechta Arachin** | | |
| Chapter 1<br>Hakol Ma'arichin<br>2a-7b | Chapter 2<br>Ein Ne'erachin<br>7b-13b | Chapter 3<br>Yeish Ba'arachin<br>13b-17a |
| Chapter 4<br>Heseig Yad<br>17a-19a | Chapter 5<br>Haomer Mishkali<br>Alai<br>19a-21b | Chapter 6<br>Shum Hayesomim<br>21b-24a |
| Chapter 7<br>Ein Makdishin<br>24a-27a | Chapter 8<br>Hamakdish Sadeihu<br>27a-29a | Chapter 9<br>Hamocheir Sadeihu<br>29b-34a |
| **Mesechta Temurah** | | |
| Chapter 1<br>Hakol Memirin<br>2a-13b | Chapter 2<br>Yeish B'Korbenos<br>14a-17b | Chapter 3<br>Eilu Kodashim<br>17b-21b |
| Chapter 4<br>Vlad Chatas<br>21b-24a | Chapter 5<br>Keitzad Ma'arimin<br>24b-27b | Chapter 6<br>Kol Ha'asurin<br>28a-31a |
| Chapter 7<br>Yeish B'Kodshei<br>Mizbe'ach<br>31a-34a | | |
| **Mesechta Kereisos** | | |
| Chapter 1<br>Sheloshim V'Sheish<br>2a-8b | Chapter 2<br>Arbaah Mechusrei<br>Kapparah<br>8b-11b | Chapter 3<br>Amru Lo<br>11b-17a |
| Chapter 4<br>Safeik Achal Cheilev<br>17a-20b | Chapter 5<br>Dam Shechitah<br>20b-23b | Chapter 6<br>Hameivi Asham<br>23b-28b |
| **Mesechta Meilah / Kinnim / Tamid / Middos** | | |
| Chapter 1<br>Kodshei Kodashim<br>2a-8a | Chapter 2<br>Chatas Ha'oph<br>8a-10b | Chapter 3<br>Vlad Chatas<br>10b-14b |
| Chapter 4<br>Kodshei Mizbei'ach<br>15a-18a | Chapter 5<br>Haneheneh Min<br>Hahekdesh<br>18a-22a | |
| **Kinnim** | | |

| | | |
|---|---|---|
| Chapter 1<br>Chatas Ha'oph<br>22a-22b | Chapter 2<br>Kein Susumah<br>23a-23b | Chapter 3<br>Ba'meh Devarim<br>Amurim<br>23b-25a |

**Tamid**

| | | |
|---|---|---|
| Chapter 1<br>Bishloshah Mekomos<br>25b-28b | Chapter 2<br>Ra'uhu Echav<br>28b-30a | Chapter 3<br>Amar La'hem<br>Hamemunneh<br>30a-30b |
| Chapter 4<br>Lo Hayu Kofesin<br>30b-32b | Chapter 5<br>Amar La'hem<br>Hamemunneh<br>32b-33a | Chapter 6<br>Heicheilu Olim<br>33a |
| Chapter 7<br>Bizman Shekohen<br>Gadol<br>33b | | |

**Middos**

| | | |
|---|---|---|
| Chapter 1<br>Bishloshah Mekomos<br>34a-34b | Chapter 2<br>Har Habayis<br>34b-35b | Chapter 3<br>Hamizbei'ach<br>35b-36a |
| Chapter 4<br>Pischo Shel Heichal<br>36b-37 | Chapter 5<br>Kol Ha'azarah<br>37b | |

**Mesechta Niddah**

| | | |
|---|---|---|
| Chapter 1<br>Shammai<br>2a-12b | Chapter 2<br>Kol Hayad<br>13a-21a | Chapter 3<br>Hamapeles<br>Chatichah<br>21a-31b |
| Chapter 4<br>Bnos Cusim<br>31b-39b | Chapter 5<br>Yotzei Dofen<br>40a-48a | Chapter 6<br>Ba Siman<br>48a-54b |
| Chapter 7<br>Dam Haniddah<br>54b-57a | Chapter 8<br>Haro'ah Kesem<br>57b-59a | Chapter 9<br>Ha'ishah Shehi<br>Osah<br>59b-64b |
| Chapter 10<br>Tinokess<br>64b-73a | | |

**Tehoros Purity**

# הַדְרָן

On the completion of an entire tractate, along with a festive
meal, the following is customarily recited.
The first paragraph is recited three times

**הַדְרָן** עֲלָךְ מַסֶּכֶת _____ וְהַדְרָךְ עֲלָן, דַּעְתָּן עֲלָךְ מַסֶּכֶת _____ וְדַעְתָּךְ עֲלָן. לָא
נִתְנְשֵׁי מִנָּךְ מַסֶּכֶת _____ וְלָא תִתְנְשֵׁי מִנָּן, לָא בְּעָלְמָא הָדֵין וְלָא בְּעָלְמָא דְאָתֵי.

**יְהִי רָצוֹן** מִלְּפָנֶיךָ אֱלֹקֵינוּ וֵאלֹקֵי אֲבוֹתֵינוּ שֶׁתְּהֵא תוֹרָתְךָ אֻמָּנוּתֵנוּ בָּעוֹלָם הַזֶּה וּתְהֵא עִמָּנוּ
לָעוֹלָם הַבָּא. חֲנִינָא בַּר פָּפָּא, רָמִי בַּר פָּפָּא, נַחְמָן בַּר פָּפָּא, אַחַאי בַּר פָּפָּא, אַבָּא מָרִי בַּר
פָּפָּא, רַפְרָם בַּר פָּפָּא, רָכִישׁ בַּר פָּפָּא, סוּרְחָב בַּר פָּפָּא, אַדָּא בַּר פָּפָּא, דָּרוּ בַּר פָּפָּא.

**הַעֲרֶב נָא** ה' אֱלֹקֵינוּ, אֶת דִּבְרֵי תוֹרָתְךָ בְּפִינוּ וּבְפִיפִיּוֹת עַמְּךָ בֵּית יִשְׂרָאֵל. וְנִהְיֶה [כֻּלָּנוּ,]
אֲנַחְנוּ וְצֶאֱצָאֵינוּ [וְצֶאֱצָאֵי צֶאֱצָאֵינוּ] וְצֶאֱצָאֵי עַמְּךָ בֵּית יִשְׂרָאֵל, כֻּלָּנוּ יוֹדְעֵי שְׁמֶךָ וְלוֹמְדֵי
תוֹרָתֶךָ [לִשְׁמָהּ]. מֵאֹיְבַי, תְּחַכְּמֵנִי מִצְוֹתֶךָ, כִּי לְעוֹלָם הִיא לִי. יְהִי לִבִּי תָמִים בְּחֻקֶּיךָ, לְמַעַן
לֹא אֵבוֹשׁ. לְעוֹלָם לֹא אֶשְׁכַּח פִּקּוּדֶיךָ, כִּי בָם חִיִּיתָנִי. בָּרוּךְ אַתָּה ה' לַמְּדֵנִי חֻקֶּיךָ. אָמֵן אָמֵן
אָמֵן, סֶלָה וָעֶד.

**מוֹדִים** אֲנַחְנוּ לְפָנֶיךָ ה' אֱלֹקֵינוּ וֵאלֹקֵי אֲבוֹתֵינוּ שֶׁשַּׂמְתָּ חֶלְקֵנוּ מִיּוֹשְׁבֵי בֵית הַמִּדְרָשׁ, וְלֹא
שַׂמְתָּ חֶלְקֵנוּ מִיּוֹשְׁבֵי קְרָנוֹת. שֶׁאָנוּ מַשְׁכִּימִים וְהֵם מַשְׁכִּימִים, אָנוּ מַשְׁכִּימִים לְדִבְרֵי תוֹרָה,
וְהֵם מַשְׁכִּימִים לִדְבָרִים בְּטֵלִים. אָנוּ עֲמֵלִים וְהֵם עֲמֵלִים, אָנוּ עֲמֵלִים וּמְקַבְּלִים שָׂכָר, וְהֵם
עֲמֵלִים וְאֵינָם מְקַבְּלִים שָׂכָר. אָנוּ רָצִים וְהֵם רָצִים, אָנוּ רָצִים לְחַיֵּי הָעוֹלָם הַבָּא, וְהֵם
רָצִים לִבְאֵר שַׁחַת, שֶׁנֶּאֱמַר: וְאַתָּה אֱלֹקִים, תּוֹרִדֵם לִבְאֵר שַׁחַת, אַנְשֵׁי דָמִים וּמִרְמָה לֹא
יֶחֱצוּ יְמֵיהֶם, וַאֲנִי אֶבְטַח בָּךְ.

**יְהִי רָצוֹן** מִלְּפָנֶיךָ ה' אֱלֹקַי, כְּשֵׁם שֶׁעֲזַרְתַּנִי לְסַיֵּים מַסֶּכֶת _____ כֵּן תְּעַזְרֵנִי לְהַתְחִיל
מַסֶּכְתּוֹת וּסְפָרִים אֲחֵרִים וּלְסַיְּמָם, לִלְמוֹד וּלְלַמֵּד, לִשְׁמוֹר וְלַעֲשׂוֹת וּלְקַיֵּים אֶת כָּל דִּבְרֵי
תַלְמוּד תּוֹרָתְךָ בְּאַהֲבָה. וּזְכוּת כָּל הַתַּנָּאִים וְאָמוֹרָאִים וְתַלְמִידֵי חֲכָמִים יַעֲמוֹד לִי וּלְזַרְעִי,
שֶׁלֹּא תָמוּשׁ הַתּוֹרָה מִפִּי וּמִפִּי זַרְעִי וְזֶרַע זַרְעִי עַד עוֹלָם. וְתִתְקַיֵּים בִּי: בְּהִתְהַלֶּכְךָ, תַּנְחֶה
אֹתָךְ, בְּשָׁכְבְּךָ תִּשְׁמֹר עָלֶיךָ, וַהֲקִיצוֹתָ הִיא תְשִׂיחֶךָ. כִּי בִי יִרְבּוּ יָמֶיךָ, וְיוֹסִיפוּ לְךָ, שְׁנוֹת
חַיִּים. אֹרֶךְ יָמִים, בִּימִינָהּ, בִּשְׂמֹאולָהּ עֹשֶׁר וְכָבוֹד. ה' עֹז לְעַמּוֹ יִתֵּן, ה' יְבָרֵךְ אֶת עַמּוֹ
בַשָּׁלוֹם.

(If you have 10 men present)

**יִתְגַּדַּל** וְיִתְקַדַּשׁ שְׁמֵהּ רַבָּא. (אָמֵן.) בְּעָלְמָא דִּי הוּא עָתִיד לְאִתְחַדָּתָא, וּלְאַחֲיָאָה מֵתַיָּא,
וּלְאַסָּקָא יַתְהוֹן לְחַיֵּי עָלְמָא, וּלְמִבְנֵא קַרְתָּא דִּי יְרוּשְׁלֵם, וּלְשַׁכְלְלָא הֵיכָלֵהּ בְּגַוַּהּ, וּלְמֶעֱקַר

פֻּלְחָנָא נֻכְרָאָה מִן אַרְעָא, וּלְאָתָבָא פֻּלְחָנָא דִּי שְׁמַיָּא לְאַתְרֵהּ, וְיַמְלִיךְ קֻדְשָׁא בְּרִיךְ הוּא בְּמַלְכוּתֵהּ וִיקָרֵהּ, [וְיַצְמַח פֻּרְקָנֵהּ וִיקָרֵב מְשִׁיחֵהּ (אָמֵן.)] בְּחַיֵּיכוֹן וּבְיוֹמֵיכוֹן וּבְחַיֵּי דְכָל בֵּית יִשְׂרָאֵל, בַּעֲגָלָא וּבִזְמַן קָרִיב. וְאִמְרוּ: אָמֵן. (אָמֵן. יְהֵא שְׁמֵהּ רַבָּא מְבָרַךְ לְעָלַם וּלְעָלְמֵי עָלְמַיָּא.) יְהֵא שְׁמֵהּ רַבָּא מְבָרַךְ לְעָלַם וּלְעָלְמֵי עָלְמַיָּא. יִתְבָּרַךְ וְיִשְׁתַּבַּח וְיִתְפָּאַר וְיִתְרוֹמַם וְיִתְנַשֵּׂא וְיִתְהַדָּר וְיִתְעַלֶּה וְיִתְהַלָּל שְׁמֵהּ דְּקֻדְשָׁא בְּרִיךְ הוּא. (בְּרִיךְ הוּא.) °לְעֵלָּא מִן כָּל (בעשי"ת: °לְעֵלָּא וּלְעֵלָּא מִכָּל) בִּרְכָתָא וְשִׁירָתָא תֻּשְׁבְּחָתָא וְנֶחֱמָתָא, דַּאֲמִירָן בְּעָלְמָא. וְאִמְרוּ: אָמֵן. (אָמֵן.)

עַל יִשְׂרָאֵל וְעַל רַבָּנָן, וְעַל תַּלְמִידֵיהוֹן וְעַל כָּל תַּלְמִידֵי תַלְמִידֵיהוֹן, וְעַל כָּל מָאן דְּעָסְקִין בְּאוֹרַיְתָא, דִּי בְאַתְרָא הָדֵין וְדִי בְכָל אֲתַר וַאֲתַר. יְהֵא לְהוֹן וּלְכוֹן שְׁלָמָא רַבָּא, חִנָּא וְחִסְדָּא וְרַחֲמִין, וְחַיִּין אֲרִיכִין, וּמְזוֹנֵי רְוִיחֵי, וּפֻרְקָנָא מִן קֳדָם אֲבוּהוֹן דִּי בִשְׁמַיָּא [וְאַרְעָא]. וְאִמְרוּ: אָמֵן. (אָמֵן.) יְהֵא שְׁלָמָא רַבָּא מִן שְׁמַיָּא וְחַיִּים [טוֹבִים] עָלֵינוּ וְעַל כָּל יִשְׂרָאֵל. וְאִמְרוּ: אָמֵן. (אָמֵן.) עֹשֶׂה שָׁלוֹם בִּמְרוֹמָיו, הוּא בְּרַחֲמָיו יַעֲשֶׂה שָׁלוֹם עָלֵינוּ, וְעַל כָּל יִשְׂרָאֵל. וְאִמְרוּ: אָמֵן. (אָמֵן.)

# Glossary

ACHARONIM – LEADING RABBIS LIVING ROUGHLY IN THE 16TH CENTURY TO THE PRESENT

AGGADIC – STORIES FROM THE TALMUD

AHRON – HOLY ARK

ALIYAH – GOING UP TO ISRAEL

AMORA, AMORAIM – CREATORS OF THE TALMUD, SUCCESSORS OF THE TANNAIM

AMOS – UNIT OF LENGTH OR DISTANCE

APIKORIS - HERETIC

AV BEIS DIN - THE HEAD OF THE JEWISH COURT

AVAIROS - SINS

AVODAS HASHEM - SERVICE TO G-D

AVRECHIM – MARRIED MEN WHO LEARN IN KOLLEL

BA'AL TESHUVAH, BA'ALEI TESHUVAH – A PERSON WHO REPENTS. USUALLY REFERRING TO SOMEONE WHO RETURNS TO ORTHODOX JUDAISM

BAALEI BATIM – WORKING PEOPLE

BACHUR, BACHURIM – SINGLE YESHIVA STUDENT / STUDENTS

BAIN HAZMANIM – THE VACATION PERIOD BETWEEN LEARNING SCHEDULE

BAIS HAKENESES - HOUSE OF STUDY, SYNAGOGUE

BAIS HAMIKDASH – HOLY TEMPLE

BAIS MIDRASH - HOUSE OF STUDY, SYNAGOGUE

BAL PEH – BY HEART

BARUCH HASHEM – THANK G-D

BATUL - NULLIFIED

BEIYUN - SLOWER, MORE IN-DEPTH STUDY

BEKIYUS - LEARNING QUICKLY ON A MORE SUPERFICIAL LEVEL TO COVER GROUND

BEN TORAH – STUDENT OF TORAH

BERAISA, BERAISOS – COLLECTION OF TANNAIC TRADITIONS

BIMA – ALTER PLATFORM IN A SYNAGOGUE

BITTLE TORAH – WASTING TIME THAT COULD HAVE BEEN USED TO STUDY TORAH

BITUL - NULLIFIED

B'KIYUS – LEARNING QUICKLY FOR P'SHAT

BLAT – FOLIO OF TALMUD

BLI AYAN HARA – WITHOUT AN EVIL EYE

BLI NEDER – WITHOUT AN OATH

B'NAI YISRAEL – CHILDREN OF ISRAEL

B'NEI - DESCENDANTS

B'NEI TORAH – SONS OF TORAH

B'NEI YISRAEL – SONS OF ISRAEL

BRACHOS - BLESSING

CHABUROS – GROUND OF

LEARNING PARTNERS STUDYING A
SPECIFIC SUBJECT OR BOOK
**CHACHAMIM** - SAGES
**CHALLAH LAWS** – LAWS
OF THE SEPARATION OF DOUGH
**CHAREDI** - RELIGIOUS
**CHAS-V-SHALOM** - IT
SHOULDN'T HAPPEN
**CHAVRUSA, CHAVRUSOS**
– STUDY PARTNER(S)
**CHAZAL** - SAGES
**CHEDARIM, CHEDER** -
RELIGIOUS SCHOOL FOR BOYS
**CHESED** - KINDNESS
**CHIDDUSHIE TORAH,**
**CHIDDUSHIM** – ORIGINAL
TORAH THOUGHTS
**CHILLUL HASHEM** –
DISGRACING HASHEM'S NAME
**CHINUCH** – UPBRINGING
OF CHILDREN
**CHUMROS** -
STRINGENCIES
**CHUPAH** – WEDDING
CANOPY
**DA'AS** - UNDERSTANDING
**DAF YOMI** – DAILY FOLIO
OF TALMUD
**DALED AMOS** – 4 STEPS
**DAVENED, DAVENING** –
PRAYED, PRAYING
**DAYAN** - JUDGE
**DERECH ERETZ** – WAY
OF LIFE
**DERECH HALIMUD** –
WAY OF LEARNING
**D'VAR TORAH** - WORDS
OF TORAH
**D'VEKUS** – SPIRITUAL
DEDICATION & EXCITEMENT
**EHRLICHER YIDDEN** –
HOLY JEW
**EMUNAH** - FAITH
**FRUM** - RELIGIOUS

**GABBAI, GABBAIM** -
(ARAMAIC) (A) THE PERSON
RESPONSIBLE FOR THE PROPER
FUNCTIONING OF A SYNAGOGUE
(B) AN OFFICIAL OF THE REBBE'S
COURT, WHO ADMITS PEOPLE FOR
PRIVATE MEETINGS
**GADOL** – GREAT RABBI
**GADOL B'TORAH** –
GREAT SAGE
**GADOL B'YISRAEL** –
GREAT JEWISH SAGE
**GADOL HADOR** – GREAT
RABBI OF THE GENERATION
**GAN-EDEN** – WORLD TO
COME
**GASHMIOUS** -
MATERIALISM
**GEONIM** – GREAT
RABBINICAL SCHOLARS
**GEONIM** – THE HEADS OF
THE RABBINIC ACADEMIES OF
BABYLONIA
**GUF NAKI** - CLEAN BODY
& MIND
**HAGADATA** - STORIES
HAKADOSH BARUCH HU –
G-D
**HAKAFOS** – CIRCLING
WITH THE TORAH ON SHAVUOS
**HAKARAS HATOV** -
APPRECIATION
**'HALACHA LEMISA** –
PRACTICAL JEWISH LAWS
**HALACHIC, HALACHOS** –
JEWISH LAWS
**HALEVEI** – IF ONLY
**HANHAGOS** -
STRINGENCIES
**HASHEM YISBORACH** –
G-D
**HASHGACHA** – DIVINE
WILL OF HASHEM
**HASKAMAH** – APPROVAL

# Mesilas HaShas - מסילת הש״ס

HASMADA – LEARNING & DOING MITZVOS WITHOUT A STOP

HESPID – EULOGY

ILLUY - PRODIGY

INYAN – MATTER OF POINT

IYUN – CLOSE EXAMINATION

KAL VOCHOMER – DERIVES ONE LAW FROM ANOTHER

KAVANOS – HOLY MEDITATIONS

KAVOD - RESPECT

KEDUSHA - HOLINESS

KENEGED KULAM - EQUAL TO ALL THE COMMANDMENTS

KESUVIM - WRITINGS (IS THE THIRD & FINAL SECTION OF THE BIBLE)

KIDDUSH HASHEM - SANCTIFICATION OF HASHEM'S NAME

KIRUV - OUTREACH

KLAL YISRAEL – THE CHILDREN OF ISRAEL

KLI - VESSEL

KO'ACH - STRENGTH

KOL HATORAH KULAH – ALL OF THE TORAH

KOLLEL – YESHIVAH FOR MARRIED MEN

KOSHERUS – KEEPING KOSHER

KRIYAS SHEMA – SEE SHEMA

LAG B'OMER -- A JEWISH HOLIDAY CELEBRATED ON THE 33RD DAY OF THE COUNTING OF THE OMER CELEBRATING THE END OF RABBI AKIVA'S STUDENTS DYING. IT IS ALSO THE MEMORIAL OF REBBE SHIMON BAR YOCHAI.

LASHON HARA - GOSSIP

L'CHAF ZCHUS – JUDGING SOMEONE FAVORABLY

LECHAIM – TO LIFE

LEVAYA - FUNERAL

LIMUD HATORAH – LEARNING TORAH

LISHMAH - PERFORMING A COMMANDMENT FOR THE MITZVAH ITSELF, WITH COMPLETE SINCERITY

L'SHEM SHAMAYIM – FOR THE SAKE OF HEAVEN

LUACH - CALENDAR

MACHALAH- SICKNESS

MACHLOKIS - DISAGREEMENT

MADREGA – SPIRITUAL LEVEL

MAGGID SHIURS – RABBI GIVING LECTURES

MALACHEI HA'SHARES - ANGELS

MALACHIM - ANGELS

MAMINIM - BELIEVERS

MARRIV – EVENING PRAYER

MASHAL – A SIMILE, PARABLE, PROVERB

MASHGIACH, MASHGICHIM – A JEW WHO SUPERVISES KASHEROUS

MASMID, MASMIDIM – COMPLETED DEVOTED TO LEARNING EVERY MINUTE

MECHALEL SHABBOS – BREAKING THE LAWS OF SHABBOS

MECHAZEK – TO INSPIRE

MECHINAS – YESHIVAH HIGH SCHOOL

MECHUTAN – SON-IN-LAW'S / DAUGHTER-IN-LAW'S

282

FATHER

**MEKADESH** - SANCTIFY

**MENSCH** – ALL AROUND
GOOD PERSON

**MESECHTOS** –
INDIVIDUAL BOOKS OF TALMUD

**MIDAH, MIDOS** – GOOD
CHARACTERISTICS

**MIKVAH, MIKVA'OS** –
HOLY IMMERSION WATERS

**MIN HASHAMAYIM** –
FOR THE SAKE OF HEAVEN

**MINCHAH** – AFTERNOON
PRAYER

**MINHAG, MINHAGIM** -
TRADITION

**MINYAN** – GATHERING
OF 10 MEN PRAYING

**MITZVOS** -
COMMANDMENTS

**MOSHIACH** - MESSIAH

**MUSSAR** – STUDY OF
CHARACTER CORRECTION

**NACHAS** – PRIDE AND JOY

**NAVIIM** - PROPHETS

**NESHAMAH, NESHAMOS**
– SOUL

**NETILLAS YADAYIM** –
WASHING OF THE HANDS

**NIDDAH** –
MENSTRUATION CYCLE

**NIGLEH** – THE
REVEALED TEACHINGS OF TORAH
LAW

**OHLOM HABAH** –
WORLD TO COME

**PARNASA** – SUSTENANCE

**PARSHAS** – WEEKLY
TORAH READING

**PASKENING** – RAV GIVING
AN ANSWER TO A QUESTION IN
HALACHA

**PASUK** - VERSE

**PAYOS** - SIDEBURNS

**PETIRA** - DEATH

**PILPUL** – SHARP ANALYSIS

**PRAKIM** - PARAGRAPHS

**P'SHAT** -LEARNING IN
ORDER TO ARRIVE AT THE TRUE
AND BASIC UNDERSTANDING

**RABBANIM, RABBEIM** -
RABBIS

**RATZON HASHEM** - THE
WILL OF HASHEM

**RAV** - RABBI

**REBBETZIN** – WIFE OF
THE RABBI

**RIBONO SHEL OLAM** –
G-D

**RISHONIM** – THE
LEADING RABBIS & POSKIM WHO
LIVED APPROX. DURING THE 11TH
TO 15TH CENTURIES, IN THE ERA
BEFORE THE SHULCHAN ARUCH.

**ROSH** - HEAD

**ROSH CHEDARIM** –
HEAD OF SCHOOL

**ROSH HAYESHIVAH,
ROSHEI YESHIVOS** – HEAD OF
YESHIVAH

**SECHEL** – MIND WITH
CLEAR UNDERSTANDING

**SEDER** – ORDER OF
STUDY OR TIME ALLOTTED FOR
STUDY

**SEFORIM** - BOOKS

**SEUDAS** – FESTIVE MEALS

**SHABBATONS** – SHABBOS
GATHERINGS

**SHALOM BAYIS** – PEACE
BETWEEN SPOUSES

**SHAMAYIM** - HEAVEN

**SHAS** -COMPLETION OF
THE TALMUD

**SHAVUOS** – JEWISH
HOLIDAY CELEBRATING THE
GIVING OF THE TORAH

**SHEBAL PEH** – BY HEART

Mesilas HaShas - מסילת הש"ס

SHECHINAH - THE DIVINE PRESENCE
SHELO LISHMAH – NOT FOR THE RIGHT REASONS
SHEMA - A PRAYER THAT SERVES AS A CENTERPIECE OF THE MORNING AND EVENING PRAYERS
SHEMIRAS HALASHON – THE STUDY OF SPEAKING PROPERLY
SHILOS – QUESTIONS
SHITOS - ASSOCIATIONS
SHIUR, SHIURIM – CLASS OF TORAH HEARD FROM A RABBI
SHMUESING - TALKING
SHNOROR – SOMEONE COLLECTING FUNDS
SHOCHET – SLAUGHTERER OF KOSHER ANIMALS
SHTENDERS - PODIUMS
SHULS - SYNAGOGUES
SIFREI TORAH – TORAH'S
SIMCHA - JOY
SIYATA DISHMAYA – AN UNDERSTANDING FROM G-D
SIYUM – PARTY FOR COMPLETING A TORAH BOOK
SIYUM HASHAS – PARTY FOR THE ENTIRE COMPLETION OF THE TALMUD
SOFEROUS – WRITING OF SCROLLS
SUCCOS – JEWISH HOLIDAY
SUGYA - TYPICALLY COMPRISE A DETAILED PROOF-BASED ELABORATION OF THE MISHNAH
TACHLIS – TO THE POINT
TALMIDIM, TALMID - STUDENT

TALMUD CHACHAM, TALMIDEI CHACHAMIM - SAGE
TALMUD TORAH – THE STUDY OF THE TORAH
TANACH - BIBLE
TANNAIM – THE RABBINIC SAGES WHOSE VIEWS ARE RECORDED IN THE MISHNAH
TARGUM - LANGUAGE
TECHIYAS HAMEISIM – REVIVAL OF THE DEAD
TIKKUN, TIKKUNIM – REPAIRING THE WORLD
TOCHACHAH - INSTRUCTION
TUDAH – LICENSE
TUMA - IMPURITY
TUSHIYAH – SOUND WISDOM
TZADDIK, TZADDIKIM - RIGHTEOUS PERSON
TZAROS - DIFFICULTIES
TZEDAKAH - CHARITY
YERIDAS HADOROS – DESCENDING GENERATIONS
YESHIVAH GEDOLA – YESHIVAH FOR OLDER BACHORIM
YESHIVAH, YESHIVOS – LEARNING TORAH CENTER
YETZER HARA – EVIL INCLINATION
YICHUDIM – SPIRITUAL UNIFICATIONS
YIDDEN - JEWS
YIDDISHKEIT – YIDDISH FOR JUDAISM
YIRAH - FEAR
YIRAS SHAMAYIM – FEAR OF HEAVEN
YISRAEL - ISRAEL
ZECHUS – MERIT
ZMAN – TIME PERIOD

284

RABBI MEIR SAID,

"WHOEVER OCCUPIES HIMSELF WITH THE STUDY OF
TORAH FOR ITS OWN SAKE MERITS MANY THINGS; AND
NOT ONLY THAT, BUT THE ENTIRE WORLD IS
WORTHWHILE BECAUSE OF HIM." (AVOS CH. 6)

Printed in Poland
by Amazon Fulfillment
Poland Sp. z o.o., Wrocław

53418083R00161